EUROPEAN COMMISSION

The Single Market Review

DISMANTLING OF BARRIERS

TECHNICAL BARRIERS
TO TRADE

The Single Market Review

SUBSERIES III: VOLUME 1

OFFICE FOR OFFICIAL PUBLICATIONS
OF THE EUROPEAN COMMUNITIES

KOGAN PAGE . EARTHSCAN

This report is part of a series of 39 studies commissioned from independent consultants in the context of a major review of the Single Market. The 1996 Single Market Review responds to a 1992 Council of Ministers Resolution calling on the European Commission to present an overall analysis of the effectiveness of measures taken in creating the Single Market. This review, which assesses the progress made in implementing the Single Market Programme, was coordinated by the Directorate-General 'Internal Market and Financial Services' (DG XV) and the Directorate-General 'Economic and Financial Affairs' (DG II) of the European Commission.

This document was prepared for the European Commission

by

W. S. Atkins

It does not, however, express the Commission's official views. Whilst every reasonable effort has been made to provide accurate information in regard to the subject matter covered, the Consultants are not responsible for any remaining errors. All recommendations are made by the Consultants for the purpose of discussion. Neither the Commission nor the Consultants accept liability for the consequences of actions taken on the basis of the information contained herein.

The European Commission would like to express thanks to the external experts and representatives of firms and industry bodies for their contribution to the 1996 Single Market Review, and to this report in particular.

UNIVERSITY OF PLYMOUTH

Item No. 900 3571113 4

Date 2 4 MAR 1998   B

Class No. 382.7094 TEC

Contl. No. 0749423242

LIBRARY SERVICES

© European Communities, 1998

No part of this book may be reproduced, stored in a retrieval system, or transmitted in any form or by any means, electronic, mechanical, photocopying, recording or otherwise without written permission from the copyright holder.

Office for Official Publications of the European Communities
2 rue Mercier, L-2985 Luxembourg
ISBN 92-827-8789-3   Catalogue number: C1-69-96-001-EN-C

Kogan Page . Earthscan
120 Pentonville Road, London N1 9JN
ISBN 0 7494 2324 2

WITHDRAWN
FROM
UNIVERSITY OF PLYMOUTH
LIBRARY SERVICES

90 0357113 4

The Single Market Review

DISMANTLING OF BARRIERS

TECHNICAL BARRIERS
TO TRADE

THREE DAY LOAN
This book is to be returned on
or before the date stamped below

2 6 NOV 1999	
1 6 DEC 1999	
2 1 MAR 2000	
3 1 MAR 2000	
1 4 MAR 2002	
2 1 MAR 2002	

UNIVERSITY OF PLYMOUTH

PLYMOUTH LIBRARY
Tel: (01752) 232323
This book is subject to recall if required by another reader
Books may be renewed by phone
CHARGES WILL BE MADE FOR OVERDUE BOOKS

WITHDRAWN
FROM
UNIVERSITY OF PLYMOUTH
LIBRARY

The Single Market Review series

Subseries	I —	**Impact on manufacturing**
Volume:	1	Food, drink and tobacco processing machinery
	2	Pharmaceutical products
	3	Textiles and clothing
	4	Construction site equipment
	5	Chemicals
	6	Motor vehicles
	7	Processed foodstuffs
	8	Telecommunications equipment

Subseries	II —	**Impact on services**
Volume:	1	Insurance
	2	Air transport
	3	Credit institutions and banking
	4	Distribution
	5	Road freight transport
	6	Telecommunications: liberalized services
	7	Advertising
	8	Audio-visual services and production
	9	Single information market
	10	Single energy market
	11	Transport networks

Subseries	III —	**Dismantling of barriers**
Volume:	1	Technical barriers to trade
	2	Public procurement
	3	Customs and fiscal formalities at frontiers
	4	Industrial property rights
	5	Capital market liberalization
	6	Currency management costs

Subseries	IV —	**Impact on trade and investment**
Volume:	1	Foreign direct investment
	2	Trade patterns inside the single market
	3	Trade creation and trade diversion
	4	External access to European markets

Subseries	V —	**Impact on competition and scale effects**
Volume:	1	Price competition and price convergence
	2	Intangible investments
	3	Competition issues
	4	Economies of scale

Subseries	VI —	**Aggregate and regional impact**
Volume:	1	Regional growth and convergence
	2	The cases of Greece, Spain, Ireland and Portugal
	3	Trade, labour and capital flows: the less developed regions
	4	Employment, trade and labour costs in manufacturing
	5	Aggregate results of the single market programme

Results of the business survey

Table of contents

List of tables

List of figures

List of abbreviations

Note: names of chemical compounds, companies, trade associations and ministries are not included if defined in the text of the report.

AENOR	Asociación Española de Normalisación
AFNOR	Association Française de Normalisation
AG	Agreement Group
AIMD	Active implantable medical devices
APETCE	Asociação Para o Estudo e Desenvolvimento Tecnológico de Cabos Eléctricos
APLAC	Asia Pacific Laboratory Accreditation Council
ASTM	American Society for Testing of Materials
BF	blast furnace
BOF	blast oxygen furnace
BS	British Standard
BSI	British Standards Institute
CCA	CENELEC Certification Agreement
CCS	cahiers des charges spéciales
CCT	cahiers des clauses techniques
CEC	Commission of the European Communities
CEN	Comité Européen de Normalisation
CENELEC	Comité Européen de Normalisation Electro-technique
CO	carbon monoxide
CPD	Construction Products Directive
CPSC	Consumer Product Safety Council
CR	CEN/Cenelec Report
CSTB	Centre Scientifique et Technique du Bâtiment
DEHP	Diethyl Hydrogen Phosphite
DGCCRF	Direction Générale de la Concurrence, de la Consommation et de la Répression des Fraudes (France)
DIN	Deutsche Industrie Norm
DIY	do-it-yourself
DTI	Department for Trade and Industry (UK)
DVGW	Deutscher Verein Gas und Wasser (Germany) (gas and water industry association)
EAC	European accreditation of certification bodies
EAL	European cooperation for accreditation of laboratories
EC	European Commission
ECISS	European Committee for Iron and Steel Standardization
ECJ	European Court of Justice
ECOSOC	Economic and Social Council
ECU	European Currency Unit
EEC	European Economic Community
EFTA	European Free Trade Agreement (Switzerland, Austria, Sweden, Finland, Iceland, Liechtenstein up to 1995)
EMC	electro-magnetic compatibility
EN	European standard
ENV	European Pre-Standard
EOTC	European Organization for Testing and Certification
ER	essential requirement
ESB	European Standards Body
ETSI	European Telecommunications Standards Institute
EU	European Union
FMCG	fast moving consumer goods
FSD	flame safety device
GAD	Gas Appliances Directive
GADAC	Gas Appliances Directive Advisory Committee
GATT	General Agreement on Tariffs and Trade
GDP	gross domestic product
GLP	Good Laboratory Practice Agreement (mutual recognition arrangement for chemicals testing)
GS	Geprüfte Sicherheit (German safety mark)
GVA	gross value added
HAR	Harmonized Cables Agreement Group
HD	harmonization document

ILAC	International Laboratory Accreditation Conference
IMAC	Internal Market Advisory Committee
ISO	International Standards Organization, Geneva
IT	Information technology
LSF	low smoke and fume
LUMAG	Luminaires Agreement Group
LVD	Low Voltage Directive
MD	Machinery Safety Directive
MR	mutual recognition
MRA	Mutual Recognition Arrangement
MRP	Mutual Recognition Principle
NA	New Approach
NACE	Nomenclature générale des activités économiques dans les Communautés européennes
NATO	North Atlantic Treaty Organization
NDT	non-destructive testing
NF	Norme Française
NoBo	Notified Body
NO_x	oxides of nitrogen
NSB	national standards body
OECD	Organization for Economic Co-operation and Development
OEM	original equipment manufacturer
OJ	Official Journal of the European Communities
OPC	ordinary Portland cement
prEN	Draft European Standard
PRODCOM	Common product nomenclature of the European Communities
QA	quality assurance
R&D	research and development
RDA	recommended daily allowance
RFI	radio frequency interference
SMEs	small and medium-sized enterprises
SMMT	Society of Motor Manufacturers and Traders
SMP	single market programme
SNC	special national condition
SPV	simple pressure vessel
TBT	technical barriers to trade
TC	Technical Committee (CEN)
TIPS	Tarif inter-ministériel des prestations sociales (France)
TÜV	Technischer Überwachungsverein (German technical control association)
UKAS	UK Accreditation System
VAT	value added tax
WECC	Western European Calibration Cooperation
WELAC	Western European Laboratory Accreditation Council
WG	Working Group (CEN)

Acknowledgements

The project was directed by Stuart Reynolds, and the country interviews and case studies were carried out by Jane Stonebanks, Dirk Frame, Virginie Vernin, Bérangère Mira-Smith, Patrick Stratton, Lionel Platteuw and Neal Hattersley, all of WS Atkins Management Consultants.

The collaboration and assistance of many representatives of national bodies and government departments, trade associations and enterprises is gratefully acknowledged, and these organizations are listed in the appendix. We also thank many officials of the Directorate-General for Industry (DG III), the Directorate-General for the Internal Market and Financial Services (DG XV), and the Directorate-General for Consumer Policy (DG XXIV) of the European Commission who provided information and advice. Naturally, the conclusions and analysis and any errors in interpreting the views of interviewees are the responsibility of the Consultant.

Notice to the reader

The information in this study reflects the position as at November 1996, the date of the submission of the report to the European Commission.

Throughout the report, anecdotal evidence from interviewees which has not been independently substantiated is presented in small type and indented. The Consultant's opinions and comments are presented in square brackets.

1. Summary

1.1. Introduction (Chapter 2)

As part of the 1997 Single Market Review, this report assesses the effectiveness of measures taken to remove technical barriers to trade (TBTs), by means of a literature review, interviews with national bodies in the 15 Member States and with EC officials, and detailed case studies of 13 sample product sectors.

1.2. Technical barriers to trade (Chapter 3)

TBTs are of two types: technical regulations imposed by national governments, mainly for health, safety and environmental protection of consumers; and non-regulatory barriers imposed by users' groups, trade associations, institutions, insurance bodies, or by non-mandatory government guidelines and advice to customers. The single market programme (SMP) measures can only deal with regulatory barriers. In either case, the barriers may impose requirements for either

(a) the use of technical specifications or standards defining some technical aspect of the products; or

(b) testing and certification of products or suppliers.

TBTs impose additional costs on importers of a product which are not faced by domestic suppliers. The magnitude of these costs vary. In some cases manufacturers customarily produce to a wide range of specifications and carry out routine, low-cost testing (e.g. steel, cables), and the barriers may not be significant in terms of their effect on trade (but manufacturers may still complain). In other cases, the cost of product adaptation and undergoing testing and certification in the target country, with attendant language problems, may make imported products uncompetitive (e.g. off-the-shelf machinery). TBTs in the form of a ban on ingredients or registration requirements (pesticides, fortified foods) may make some products unacceptable in the target market. Quite commonly it is the delays caused by conformity testing and the demand on limited management resources (e.g. specialist machinery, innovative electronic equipment) which create an effective barrier to entry to other markets.

Some non-regulatory barriers are *de facto* mandatory because of mandatory requirements on their use (especially insurance requirements, e.g. for pressure vessels, construction).

Some customer testing or product adaptation requirements may also be justifiable commercial requirements (e.g. on subcontract suppliers to retailers of own-branded goods) which are normal marketing costs, not TBTs.

1.3. EC policies (Section 4.1)

TBTs are prohibited under Art. 30 of the EEC Treaty, unless they are justified for reasons of consumer protection or protection of the environment, or under Art. 36 on the grounds of public morality, public policy or public security, protection of health and life of humans animals or plants, protection of national treasures, etc., or the protection of industrial and commercial property. Under normal circumstances, the Mutual Recognition Principle (MRP) is assumed to apply, by which goods lawfully manufactured and marketed in one Member State must be allowed free entry into other Member States. This requires each Member State to recognize the equivalence of the regulations in the others. Where the approach or objectives of regulations are so different that this is not feasible, the Commission proposes harmonization measures, which may follow the New Approach to harmonization of technical specifications and conformity procedures, with the development of harmonized standards mandated to European standards bodies.

1.4. The Mutual Recognition Principle

1.4.1. Basis and functioning (Section 4.2)

The MRP works without problem for many non-contentious products (e.g. steel, water pipe fittings). For many products, however, positive action is required.

In many cases, customers and enforcement authorities need documentary evidence that the products do meet the source country's regulations and appropriate standards, and that those regulations and standards meet equivalent health and safety objectives. This often requires accreditation of testing and certification bodies, and a mutual recognition arrangement (MRA) between bodies testing or certifying a particular product. The 'global approach' to testing and certification was developed by the EC to facilitate this, and the European Organization for Testing and Certification (EOTC) was set up to provide an infrastructure.

If national governments fail to recognize other Member States' products, action can be taken by the EC, leading ultimately to referral to the European Court of Justice. A notification procedure exists (under Directive 83/189/EEC) for new regulations and national standards. From 1997, product withdrawals also need to be formally notified. Complaints about existing regulatory barriers can be brought to the EC by individuals, firms, trade associations or governments. The Commission has handled over 1,200 infringement proceedings, which often result in the withdrawal of regulations or insertion of a specific mutual recognition clause. The cost of these procedures is relatively low, and appears to have been quite successful in preventing new barriers.

1.4.2. The case studies (Part III, Chapters 11 to 17)

Seven sample products were investigated which are not (or not yet) covered by New Approach directives, and where technical regulations apply. Most of these were selected because there was known to be a failure of mutual recognition. They are summarized in Table 1.1.

The case studies indicate that, where there are significant technical regulations, MRP only seems to work if there is either a formal mutual recognition arrangement (e.g. HAR agreement), or mutually recognized standards have been developed (e.g. CENELEC cable standards, ECISS steel standards). Where there are serious concerns about the health and safety hazards (e.g. pesticides, fortified foods and drinks), there tend to be divergent approaches and MRP fails, unless there is a strong industrial logic (dominant multinational firms, strong gains from trade, high economies of scale) in developing voluntary arrangements for common standards or mutual recognition arrangements.

Table 1.1.   Effectiveness of the Mutual Recognition Principle in sample product sectors

Electric cables	Some common (mutually recognized) standards and an MRA exist. Barriers are weak and compliance costs low.
Cement	Regulatory and non-regulatory barriers, and little trade. One Art. 30 case, successful but with little practical effect. Some voluntary harmonization has begun, and cement will come under the Construction Products Directive (CPD) (COM (88) 783).
Pesticides	Strong technical barriers and high costs of compliance: MRP does not work and detailed harmonization has not yet been effective.
Structural steel	Voluntary common (mutually recognized) standards: some non-regulatory barriers remain. MRP functions without infringement procedures.
Carpets	Regulatory (fire testing) and non-regulatory (use of classification and environmental labels) barriers. High compliance costs. MRP not working, but embryonic MRAs exist.
Fortified food and drinks	Strong regulatory barriers and costly conformity requirements. MRP does not work (but some notable MRP successes in opening specific markets).
Water pipe fittings	No regulatory barriers reported, but there are diverse customer specifications.

The Mutual Recognition Principle, and the implantation of MRP into national regulations via the Directive 83/189/EEC procedures, is a necessary condition for developing MRAs, formally or informally, between suppliers, testing and certification bodies, and customers. [The Consultant doubts, however, that the MRP on its own will usually be sufficient to remove strongly entrenched technical barriers to trade, because if customers need information or protection, they (or retailers) will rightly demand recognized testing and certification.]

Mutual recognition has to exist at three levels:

(a)   the high level recognition between differing national sets of regulations, so that their level of protection is recognized (the MRP);
(b)   between accreditation systems for testing and certification bodies, so that the competence of the bodies is recognized (notified bodies for harmonized products; EAC/EAL structures for others);
(c)   between the testing or certification bodies for each specific product, so that attestation procedures and tests are recognized (using the 'global approach' modules for harmonized products; EOTC agreement groups or private arrangements for others).

EOTC is new and has not so far been very successful in developing new MRAs, and has very little resources. Existing MRAs cover about 20% of intra-EU trade (mainly electrical and electronic goods covered by directives) (Section 4.4). One reason for this is the lack of voluntary support from industry, and low priority for public funding. The testing and certification community itself has little incentive to create MRAs because they expect to lose business by the reduction of double testing (although improvements in national market surveillance may create new testing work on behalf of the enforcement authorities).

Sectors where MR generally appears to function (but not investigated in the study) include basic fuels and chemicals, furniture, transport equipment other than motor vehicles, alcoholic beverages, fibres and textiles.

1.5. The New Approach directives

1.5.1. Basis and functioning (Section 4.3)

In cases where the MRP fails, and there are barriers which create significant costs and trade restrictions, the EC acts to harmonize technical regulations. There have been three distinct approaches to harmonization:

(a)   detailed harmonization (the Old Approach) for specific products or characteristics (mainly in food, pharmaceuticals and chemicals, motor vehicles);

(b)   the Low Voltage Directive, which has some similarities to the New Approach directives;

(c)   the New Approach directives.

New Approach directives establish essential requirements, and specified routes for attestation of conformity. They are supported by the development of harmonized standards, so that products manufactured in accordance with these standards have a presumption of conformity (in all directives there are alternative routes to conformity, so standards are not mandatory but they are the easiest and usually the preferred route to the declaration of conformity for manufacturers). This has promoted a successful development of the capacity and efficiency of the European standardization bodies, and a change in the role of national standards bodies. The New Approach directives also require the appointment of Notified Bodies (NoBos) for testing and certification and EC type-examination approval, whose role is defined by each directive. This is leading to development of co-ordination procedures for the NoBos – similar to the role of EOTC in the non-harmonized sphere. The CE-marking arrangements become mandatory after an initial transitional period, as a mark of attestation of conformity. Co-ordination of the enforcement procedures for this is now a priority.

There are now 17 New Approach directives and a number in draft form. Together they cover around 17% of intra-EU trade. It is unlikely that any more will be proposed for new products, but the concept could, in the view of the standards bodies, be applied to other types of regulation, for example in services.

1.5.2. The case studies (Part II, Chapters 5 to 10)

Six case studies of products under New Approach directives were investigated (see Table 1.2).

The case studies show that the New Approach directives already implemented are working well and have removed barriers, both regulatory and non-regulatory. The Machinery Directive, quite recently implemented, and with a very broad scope, needs more supporting standards which may take some time to produce, and meanwhile firms are faced with uncertainties and with higher costs of compliance than would otherwise be the case.

Other directives with a broad scope may face similar problems. In particular, the Construction Products Directive is exceptional in that it requires mandatory standards, but as yet none of these have been decided upon. The fact that they are mandatory may well delay their agreement, but meanwhile in construction no certification at European level is required. The proposed Pressure Equipment Directive, also covering a broad area of national regulation, has not yet been adopted and may be another difficult area.

Table 1.2. Effectiveness of the New Approach directives in sample product sectors

Air reservoirs	Simple Pressure Vessels (SPV) Directive (87/404/EEC) fully functioning. No barriers remain.
Cardiac pacemakers	Active Implantable Medical Devices (AIMD) Directive (90/385/EEC) fully functioning. No significant barriers remain (but some minor complaints).
Dolls	Toy Safety Directive (88/378/EEC) fully functioning. A few regulatory, and some non-regulatory, barriers remain, but the cost is not significant.
Circular saws	Machinery (MD) Directive (89/392/EEC) functioning. However, lack of standards makes conformity assessment costly for producers of some low volume machinery, and coordination of enforcement is needed.
Portable power tools	MD and standards in place. Some minor regulatory and non-regulatory barriers exist, but costs are low. There are complaints about enforcement.
Domestic gas cookers	Gas Appliances (GAD) Directive (90/396/EEC) in place, and some standards. No regulatory barriers remain; there are some non-regulatory barriers, but not significant.

1.6. Economic importance of barriers (Chapter 19)

From the evidence of the case studies, the interview programme, and other sources, the likely incidence of barriers for each three-digit NACE sector of manufacturing and extractive industries has been assessed. This showed that 79% of intra-EU trade in products is potentially affected by regulatory barriers (including those sectors where the single market barriers have already been removed by harmonization), and within this, 55% of trade is also subject to non-regulatory barriers which might remain even when regulatory barriers are removed. Few sectors are subject to purely non-regulatory barriers: usually, if technical specifications and testing requirements are needed, then they are imposed as regulations in at least some of the Member States.[1]

The extent of the application of measures within the regulated and non-regulated sectors is shown in Table 1.3. Harmonization measures apply to over half of intra-EU trade: over a quarter is reliant upon the MRP.

---

[1]   These figures, of course, do not indicate the cost or weight of the barriers for individual sectors. For some products the cost of meeting different specifications and conformity procedures is not high: and if it is, the economic cost of reduced trade may not be high if there are no significant economies of scale or differences in comparative advantage.

Table 1.3.   Extent of application of approaches to removing technical barriers to trade

Type of sector or product	% share of intra-EU trade	% share of EU manufacturing value added
Regulated,[1] relying on mutual recognition of regulations	28	21
Regulated, harmonized by New Approach	17	22
Regulated, with detailed harmonization (Old Approach)	33	33
Total of sectors with regulatory barriers...	79	75
...of which sectors with non-regulatory barriers as well	55	44
...of which sectors also with MRAs	10	7
Non-regulated, with non-regulatory barriers	2	1
Non-regulated, with no apparent barriers	19	24
All products	100	100

Note: Numbers may total 100 due to rounding.

[1] A regulated sector is defined as a product sector where a significant range of products are covered by technical regulations in at least one Member State, which potentially create barriers to trade.

1.7. Review of effectiveness of approaches (Section 19.4)

Table 1.4 summarizes the effectiveness of the various approaches in removing barriers, based on the Consultants' assessment from the evidence of the case studies and other surveys. It shows that measures have been successfully implemented for products comprising 64% of EU trade, but for two-thirds of this (46% of trade) other, non-regulatory, barriers are likely to remain. For around a further 16% of trade measures have been adopted, but are either in a transitional phase or have problems of implementation (including the development of harmonized standards for the machinery and construction products directives, and pressure equipment). Only a negligible 1% of trade is subject to barriers for which no solution has been adopted (this includes hallmarking of precious metals and jewellery).

Table 1.4.   Effectiveness of approaches

	% share of intra-EU trade
Barriers successfully removed	18
Measures implemented and working, but other barriers remain	46
Measures adopted but problems/delays in implementation	7
Measures adopted but not effective	9
Barriers exist, but no measures taken	1
No barriers, no measures required	19
All products	100

1.8. Issues raised by interviewees (Chapter 20)

A number of issues relating to the New Approach were commonly raised by interviewees:

(a) The lack of consistent enforcement of New Approach directives (especially the Machinery Directive), and co-ordination between NoBos. Some firms are seen to take advantage of this to evade conformity requirements, or to make false claims.

(b) There is a general lack of information for enterprises, and poor understanding of the needs of new directives, which causes unnecessary costs.

(c) In the absence of standards, even though these are not mandatory, the costs of attestation are sometimes prohibitive, partly because NoBos (and other third party test labs used by manufacturers) have to devise test procedures for special cases. There is often also a lack of testing capacity and consequent high fees in the transitional period. Some manufacturers are concerned about the liability consequences of self-certification, so they need harmonized standards. Standards are very important to industry, both to designers and to purchasers/specifiers, and the uncertainty caused by the lack of harmonized standards, or incomplete sets of standards, is of concern to some manufacturers and suppliers.

(d) Resources that used to be devoted to voluntary standardization, mainly related to performance and quality measures, are now either diverted to harmonization of standards for the directives (related to essential requirements) or may no longer be provided voluntarily by industry which sees no benefit in terms of competitive advantage or protection from low quality imports.

(e) Many firms, particularly in the machinery sectors (and it will probably be true also in some of the construction products sectors), are concerned that the CE-marking is misunderstood by customers, and abused by competitors, because it is confused with a quality mark.[2] Conversely, some firms in sectors where there are no accepted quality marks are very keen to see CE-marking adopted. Manufacturers like quality marks because they both act as a form of protection, and give competitive advantage.

Few enterprises are really aware of the meaning and functioning of the Mutual Recognition Principle. Few take advantage of it, but a few have been able to use it to enter new markets (e.g. the Austrian energy drinks manufacturers).

1.9. Concluding remarks

The EU's approaches have had a spectacular and widespread impact by setting up the structure for a new system of standards, mutual recognition of regulations and mutual recognition of testing and certification. The approaches are revolutionary and have never been tried in any trading group before. They will, when they are further operational, become a model for the future world trading system.

Industry, when it exports, complains about the costs and inconvenience of the old system of national technical regulations, standards and conformity requirements. But in the past it came to rely on this system of technical protectionism in its home markets. While welcoming the

---

[2] A quality mark is understood to be a mark showing that a product meets certain voluntary performance or safety standards which are beyond the legal obligations and that the product and manufacturer are subject to third party testing and surveillance by the organization granting the mark.

new system, industry is often unprepared for the changes, which entail significant transition costs for some firms, particularly those SMEs which are not involved in trade and have not previously been concerned about attestation nor had to adapt to new standards.

This revolution in the technical infrastructure has been achieved mainly in the short period from 1989 to 1995 (although the seeds were sown in the early 1980s). It includes the development of the New Approach directives, radical changes in the functioning of the European and national standards bodies, procedures for reporting and acting on new national regulations and standards, a global approach to testing and certification, development of accreditation systems based on ISO/EN45000, development of mutual recognition arrangements for testing and certification, the rapid adoption of certification systems for pre-qualification and for marketing purposes based on ISO9000/EN29000, and the beginning of coordination of enforcement arrangements for the regulatory aspects of the system.

These approaches have overthrown systems of national standards built up over a century or more. The major national systems were, intentionally or otherwise, protectionist in nature. Many industry sectors and their trade associations are naturally trying to retain some of the old ways. Most industrialists see only the short-term impact on their own business, which entails transition costs, without understanding the whole system and the benefits of this to industry and customers. They complain about the difficulties of adapting and the uncertainties and lack of information. The slow development of new standards has caused real problems, yet because individual firms have no protectionist interest in contributing to developing common standards, the old reliance on voluntary work by industry cannot cope with the huge volume of new standards required.

It will inevitably take four to five years for most of the new system of European standards to be put in place to support the directives and the conformity attestation system, and even longer for many of the construction products standards. The time for producing individual standards is being reduced and CEN aim to get it down to two to three years. The success of this process might lead to the extension of the system to new products (including the service sectors, in which CEN is beginning to become active). The new standards may also become *de facto* global standards (wherever ISO standards do not already exist). Because the European Union is the world's largest single market, the world's exporting manufacturers will have to use European standards. The standards infrastructure in the USA is less well coordinated than the EU's; and Japan, by operating a largely closed market, has little influence on world standards. So Europe has to get it right, and that will need massive resources and sufficient time. Meanwhile industry faces uncertainty and additional conformance costs.

The main weakness of the approaches seems to be the failure to develop the mutual recognition arrangements and supporting accreditation in the non-harmonized sectors, to make the Mutual Recognition Principle work. This requires much more resources, because of the vested interests involved.

Alongside that, the priorities now are seen to be:

(a)   a strengthening of the procedures for dealing with MRP infringements;
(b)   the development of co-ordination between NoBos paralleling the development of mutual recognition arrangements in the non-harmonized sectors;
(c)   intensifying market surveillance and improving its coordination;

(d)   the quality infrastructure; and in due course, focus needs to be shifted back to performance and quality standards, and quality schemes to improve EU competitiveness.

Part I: Overview

2. Introduction

2.1. Contents of the report

This report reviews the effectiveness of the two main approaches currently being applied by the European Commission (EC) in the context of the single market programme (SMP) to remove or reduce technical barriers to trade (TBTs). These are the enforcement of the Mutual Recognition Principle (MRP), and the New Approach to technical harmonization (NA). The report is divided into sections accordingly.

The report is based on:

(a)   a review of the extensive literature and previous studies;
(b)   interviews with EC officials, national administrations, standards bodies, national employers' organizations and other bodies in the 15 EU Member States;
(c)   case studies of 13 sample products involving interviews with trade associations, manufacturers, traders and users.

Part I of the report reviews briefly the different approaches, the functional processes by which they are implemented, and the complex legal and institutional arrangement on which they are based, as the factual background for the remaining sections. Part II describes six case studies of sample products under the New Approach directives; and Part III describes seven case studies of products where mutual recognition is relied upon to overcome potential barriers (one was found to present no significant barriers and is not included in further analysis). Part IV synthesizes the findings of the case studies with the results of the interview programme and the literature review, to present an assessment of the global economic importance of barriers, the scope of the measures, and their effectiveness and perceived problems.

2.2. Terminology

The terminology of technical standards and mutual recognition is often confusing. Similar terms mean different things to different groups of people, but this report uses the terminology of the European Commission. A glossary is provided in Appendix B, and a few key definitions are set out below.

Technical barriers to trade refers both to:

(a)   *technical regulations:* national regulations which impose (mandatory) technical specifications or testing and certification requirements on goods and services put on the market (this is the area in which the EC has competence);
(b)   *non-regulatory barriers:* other technical barriers arising from (voluntary) standards or testing requirements imposed by customers, trade associations, institutions or insurance companies and the like, or by non-mandatory government advice, guidelines or other documents.

The distinction between mandatory and voluntary requirements is not always clear, however (particularly when the requirements arise from guidelines from a government body). This is discussed in Chapter 3.

Mutual recognition, when used by the EC, refers only to the principles enshrined in the Treaties, interpreted by the ECJ, as set out in the Cassis de Dijon judgment (Case 120/78 [1979] ECR 649). We call this the Mutual Recognition Principle (MRP). This states that national regulations in other Member States should be recognized as equivalent, and goods legally put on the market in the other Member State must be allowed to be put on the market in any other, unless there can be shown to be a lower level of protection (e.g. of health, safety and the environment according to Arts. 30 and 36 as interpreted by the ECJ). The term 'mutual recognition' when used by industry usually refers to the mutual recognition of testing and certification procedures, so that certificates issued in one country can be recognized in another, and usually requires that an explicit mutual recognition arrangement (MRA) has been negotiated between industry bodies or firms and the testing and certification bodies. We will refer to this as mutual recognition of testing and certification. It presupposes the mutual recognition of the accreditation systems for testing and certification bodies.

Harmonized standards means standards developed under a mandate from the EC to support the essential requirements of one of the NA Directives. Otherwise we refer to common standards, European standards or international standards as appropriate. Sometimes the term 'harmonized standards' is used to refer to non-mandated European standards, for example CENELEC standards developed in support of the Low Voltage Directive, which are essentially a compilation of previously existing national standards adapted by common nomenclature and tables of equivalence: this is a means of formal mutual recognition which does not necessarily involve harmonization in the sense used here.

2.3.   Selection of case studies

The case studies described in Parts II and III of the report were selected following the first stage of the study, which included discussions with the government departments or employers' organizations dealing with technical barriers cases, and with the officials of the Commission dealing with Art. 30 complaints and 83/189 cases. In all cases the interviewees declined to reveal names of enterprises involved, or to provide access to databases of complaints, or files or documentation relating to cases, because of the confidentiality extended to enterprises. The Consultants were, however, able to draw an overall impression of the areas in which complaints occurred, and this was one factor in selecting products for case studies.

Six products were selected to illustrate problems (or successes) in the application of each of the two approaches. The main criteria were:

(a)   *for NA products* (these products were proposed by Commission officials): products under directives which have been in force for sufficient time to see the effects, namely:
  (i)   air reservoirs (Simple Pressure Vessels Directive);
  (ii)   implantable cardiac pacemakers (Active Implantable Medical Devices Directive);
  (iii) dolls (Toy Safety Directive);
  (iv)   circular woodworking saws (Machinery Directive – Annex IV product);
  (v)   portable power tools (Machinery Directive– non-Annex IV product);
  (vi)   domestic gas cookers (Gas Appliances Directive);
(b)   *for MRP products* (these products were selected by the Consultants, and agreed by the Commission): products were selected to cover a wide range of NACE categories, from basic materials to consumer products, where national technical regulations were known to exist. Most of these are products where complaints have been made under Art. 30, but

some were selected where no known complaints have been investigated. Some of the products will in future fall under the scope of NA directives (construction products, and the CE-marking requirements of the Low Voltage Directive (LVD)), but these have not had an impact on their trade in the past. The selected products are:

(i)   cement (national standards and testing requirements, recent Art. 30 opinion);

(ii)   electrical cables (non-mandated European standards but national standards persist: a mutual recognition arrangement for testing and certification exists);

(iii)   pesticides (will be harmonized under the old approach, but strong national barriers exist);

(iv)   structural steel (diverse standards and mainly national producers, but voluntary harmonization of standards);

(v)   carpets and rugs (national fire regulations and grading systems);

(vi)   water pipe fittings (national network standards and environmental regulations);

(vii) fortified foods and drinks (partially harmonized under the old approach, but divergent national rules on vitamin content remain).

3. The sources of technical barriers to trade

3.1. Definitions

Technical barriers to trade may occur whenever either an EU producer has to alter his product (legally manufactured in accordance with home country regulations and standards) to comply with industrial standards or legal regulations for commercialization in another EU country, or he must have his product tested and certified by the importing country (for reasons other than the customer's legitimate contractual or quality control requirements). The two principal causes of technical barriers are:

(a) technical regulations imposed by government;
(b) standards (which are voluntary but may be invoked by codes of practice, insurance requirements, quality marking requirements, etc. imposed by non-governmental bodies).

Either of these sources of technical specifications may lead to multiple testing and certification requirements which are not technically necessary, or to the need to adapt products, or both.

In this study we distinguish between *technical regulations,* which result from government or other legal obligations (relating either to technical specifications or testing and certification requirements); and *non-regulatory barriers*, which result from the requirements by customers, industry bodies, insurers or other non-governmental organizations that the exporter use the national standards or testing and certification procedures of the importing country in such a way that the exporting firm is disadvantaged by comparison with national producers (by double testing, or additional approval costs or delays, or product modifications). These may have *de facto* mandatory character, but are outside the scope of regulatory policy.

3.2. The role of standards

In principle, industrial standards, which are voluntary in nature, are intended to facilitate commerce and trade by:

(a) simplifying the process of specification for procurement purposes;
(b) simplifying the design process;
(c) enabling a comparison of prices and qualities to be made, so that markets work efficiently;
(d) ensuring that separate parts, components and equipment work together; and/or by enabling a reference to standards in contracts, to facilitate measurement and pricing.

For their use in international trade and within the single market, it is clearly desirable that exporting and importing countries use the same standards. Different customers may well want to use different standards because of different needs or preferences. Often, however, different standards have no technical rationale, but are just the result of separate standards-making processes reaching different but equally valid solutions. Often, in fact, standards are, explicitly or implicitly, used for protectionist purposes because national manufacturers will request and provide support for standards if they think this will help to keep low-cost goods out of their home market.

It is not the standards themselves which are a barrier, but the requirement that they are used in a way which creates double testing, testing which is more onerous than for national producers, or modifications to a standard product. It follows that technical standards are more likely to be a problem for producers of mass-produced goods. With goods which are normally made to a customer's or retailer's specification (such as bespoke machinery, retailer-label clothing, construction works) the producer is accustomed to making to different specifications, so it is only the testing and certification procedures which are a problem, and this is also usually normal practice and not a barrier for 'bespoke' manufacturers.

The boundary between technical regulations and non-regulatory barriers to trade is not clear-cut. For example, the user of a pressure vessel may have a statutory requirement to be insured and undergo periodic inspection of the plant, and a condition for insurance laid down by the insurers' coordinating body (non-governmental but with government supervision or representation) may be the use only of vessels manufactured to certain standards. There are no technical regulations on the pressure vessels, and the insurers' requirements are non-regulatory, but the insurance regulations make the use of the standards *de facto* compulsory. Similarly, architects may only specify building products with a specific form of approval (e.g. the French *avis technique*) because liability insurance is mandatory, and use of national approved products makes insurance easier.

3.3. Customer requirements

It is also not entirely clear where the boundary lies between customer requirements which constitute a barrier and those which are to be considered normal customer choice. Customers have a right to demand that goods they buy are tested to the standards or specifications they choose, but there is a cost involved (which the customer will pay directly or indirectly). Retailers buying to sell on to less-informed consumers, and manufacturers buying materials for further processing, are particularly likely to require special testing or certification by their suppliers.

> For example, a well known UK retail chain purchases its goods from a wide range of different suppliers worldwide and sells all under its own label, which is marketed as a quality label. Consumers know that the retailer has its own quality control requirements, requires suppliers to test the products it sells, and carries out surveillance of the supplier. The suppliers are pleased because to be an approved supplier also gives the supplier a quality approval. Where the supplier also has to undergo statutory testing or certification, this constitutes double testing. It cannot be a technical barrier to trade because the label and the related testing are an intrinsic part of the product, but in some cases it could discriminate between local producers, for whom the testing requirements of the retailer are also sufficient for regulatory purposes, and importers who may have had to undergo conformity requirements in their home market for similar goods sold locally.

To some extent testing and certification requirements which appear to be technical barriers to trade, as defined, are needed by the market even with mutual recognition of national regulations. Consumers have the right to expect that goods sold by retailers who claim a quality image are legally manufactured (meeting regulatory requirements, such as not using toxic dyes), and meet accepted (voluntary) performance standards (e.g. for the life of clothing, or accuracy of thermostats). The retailer can therefore be expected to call for either its own testing and certification requirements, or proof of meeting the exporting country requirements or standards. The latter would require an agreed form of certificate, by a recognized laboratory with appropriate accreditation, to agreed test procedures. To avoid double testing would therefore require a Mutual Recognition Arrangement to be in place (the case for very few products). This would be construed as a commercial barrier to trade by the exporter, but is a purely voluntary (but necessary) customer requirement and indeed the retail market would not operate efficiently without such requirements.

Retailers' or similar customers' own testing and quality requirements (e.g. for Marks & Spencer, Mercedes Benz) should not be construed as technical barriers to trade if the supplier has, in theory, alternative routes to commercialization of his product, either through other, less discriminatory, retail channels or customers (and therefore at a lower price), by setting up his own distribution channels, by direct marketing or mail order, etc.

Clearly, however, if retailers, original equipment manufacturers (OEMs) or other purchasers insist on *national* standards when equivalent standards or international standards could be used, that is a clear non-regulatory barrier, probably caused by historical precedent and national bias in technical training.

The distinction between barriers and non-barriers must be whether the requirements relate to:

(a)   (minimum) essential requirements for health, safety, moral and environmental protection to which all suppliers must comply, and where national standards or procedures are habitually applied. For these, in theory, inter-governmental agreement on necessary levels of protection might be reached so that common standards or specifications and single testing, conformity assessment and certification could be possible. Differences in these requirements would be technical barriers to trade;

(b)   quality or performance approvals, which might be related either to an end-customer's own requirements, or a retailer's reputation, or a label, or a (voluntary and open) quality mark, and which are not linked to historically derived national standards and procedures. These would be marketing costs but not technical barriers to trade, and would generally result in a higher product selling price or lower distribution costs than available alternative routes.

3.4.   The impact of barriers

Technical barriers to trade do not constitute a total ban or quota on sale of the products, but entail a significant economic cost on suppliers of imported goods in a particular country, which are not faced by domestic suppliers. These costs arise from:

(a)   costs of research and development, design, technical documentation, retooling etc. to produce product variants to meet differing national standards and technical regulations (e.g. pesticides);

(b)   re-labelling costs, either to meet labelling regulations, or to comply with a quality labelling scheme, or to make reference to national standards (e.g. fortified foods) (although it should be noted that where labelling and packaging is important, particularly for consumer goods, then an exporter would normally, in the EU, expect to have to produce multi-language labelling, or separate language labelling for different countries);

(c)   diseconomies of production of several variants in short runs (e.g. metric/imperial dimensions for steel; formulated pesticides) (although it should be noted that the economies of scale arising from the total volume of production may still enable a trading company to be cost competitive with a similar manufacturer serving only the home market – the technical barriers to trade reduce but do not usually remove the gains from trade);

(d)   inventory and spares costs, required to serve a wide range of product variants (although not apparently important for any of our sample products);

(e)   the need for local representation in the importing country to deal with testing and certification (rather than to serve customer service and marketing needs) (no examples from our sample products);

(f)   multiple testing and certification costs. In some cases the actual costs of meeting the testing requirements are higher for a non-resident firm, if for example the testing body in the importing country has to send inspectors in person to visit the supplier's premises to inspect plant and procedures or to take random samples (e.g. cement, pesticides);

(g)   learning and management costs of dealing with multiple standards or regulations (all of our sample products).

It would be wrong to exaggerate the impact of technical barriers on production and selling costs. The costs of meeting standards and testing was not a major concern in any of our case studies. The most significant problems are:

(a)   the lack of information and experience of the target country's procedures, which because of constraints on management time (and language abilities) inhibits attempts to enter new markets in the first place; or

(b)   the time delays in getting approvals, especially where there are allegations that foreign firms are put to the back of the queue by national testing organizations. Where products are made to a customer's specification (e.g. machinery for special uses, pressure vessels) these delays can completely prevent a supplier from meeting the customer's contractual requirements; or where product innovation is important (e.g. pacemakers, hand tools, fortified foods and most consumer goods), they can prevent suppliers from gaining market share and competitive advantage before the innovative product is copied by established suppliers.

3.5. Typology of barriers

For the purposes of this study we have distinguished a typology of barriers within the two categories of technical regulations and non-regulatory barriers to trade, as follows. A third category, pure consumer preference, may in some circumstances be considered to create barriers and is discussed below.

(a)   *Technical regulations*: most technical regulations relate to health and safety and consumer protection. Increasingly they are being used for environmental protection. Some relate to public procurement, where specifications are given the status of regulations.

      (i)   *Technical (design) specifications for health and safety aspects.* Technical specifications define some aspects of the design of a product: for example, the design of electrical plugs, or the cut-off controls on gas cookers. For capital goods, there may be rules on issues such as protective guards on moving parts, electrical insulation, use of toxic dyes and materials, flammability, machinery controls, warnings, breaking strength etc., which are often very detailed. The approach to regulation varies between countries, from total physical protection for even a careless or untrained user of the product to provision of adequate information for a trained user.

      (ii)   *Marketing and packaging rules.* These apply mainly to consumer products (food, pharmaceuticals, toys etc.), requiring specific information on contents, ingredients, nutritional information, recommended ages, origin of the goods and often include requirements that the labelling be in the local language.

(iii) *Approved lists; use restrictions*. These include pharmaceutical approvals, approval procedures for certain foodstuffs, and *agrément* certificates for approved construction products.

(iv) *Purity or quality regulations*. For example, the former German beer purity laws and other recipe rules for foodstuffs; hallmarking of precious metals.

(v) *Installation rules*. These are national regulations which determine the way a product is to be installed, what products are permitted in particular applications or the personnel qualified to install it, which in turn determine the specification of the products even though there is no direct regulation of the product. An example is certification of gas fitters, where the examination for the gas fitter's approval may include examination on the national standards or codes of practice for gas appliances and fittings and an obligation on the fitter to use only those standards or codes.

(vi) *Specifications for public procurement*. One result of the EC public procurement legislation is that tender specifications which were previously proprietary to individual purchasing entities have been made transparent by publishing them as technical specifications under national regulations, or as national standards (although there is unlikely to have been a consultation process to make these proper standards). The development of new harmonized standards in the areas where public procurement is important (e.g. for roads, bridges, air traffic systems, power, gas, water, telecommunications equipment) is being mandated to CEN.

(vii) *Network standards*. Generally a special case of public procurement specifications, network standards also include parameters unique to networks (e.g. gas pipelines, electricity distribution, water and sewerage, telephone cables and mobile networks) such as pressures, voltages, pipe diameters and connections, which cannot be changed to suit products supplied to different standards. The classic and unharmonizable case of electric power sockets is a special case of this, as is left-hand drive on UK and Irish roads.

(viii) *Environmental rules*. This includes rules on recycling arrangements, emissions, use of renewable materials. [It is notable that environmental regulations being adopted by Member States vary considerably in scope, approach and parameters, to a much greater extent than health and safety rules.]

(ix) *Building regulations and urban planning*. This is probably the most pervasive and difficult area of technical specifications, often set by local authorities. They may specify what materials and products can be used, and the dimensions or performance specifications which go beyond the Essential Safety Requirements of the Construction Products Directive.

(x) *Mandatory insurance or liability provisions*. As discussed in the text above, there may be mandatory insurance requirements, or liability legislation or case law, which make it *de facto* mandatory to use products complying with national codes of practice or standards, even if the latter are in theory voluntary.

(xi) *Local bye-laws and regulations*. Local and regional regulations may escape the requirements of EC and international agreements. They are not directly subject to GATT rules and may not be notified to the EC under 83/189 procedures. For example, water bye-laws in the UK prohibit the use of mains water for motive power. This creates a ban on the use of products such as water-powered gates which are marketed in other countries.

(b) *Non-regulatory barriers:*

   (i) *Trade association codes of practice or guidelines:* trade associations, professional institutions and the like often prepare codes of practice which are binding on their members, and may make reference to standards, or include specifications of products and materials to be used, or design or performance specifications for the products produced by the members. This then becomes *de facto* mandatory in the country, and customers will believe it to be mandatory, or at least that they will be exposed to liability claims in the case of faulty products or third party damage if they use non-compliant products. The use by electricians of cables which do not meet national standards is one example. In some Member States membership of a chamber of commerce or a trade association is mandatory, so their codes of practice are, in effect, mandatory. In other cases, firms which choose not to belong to a trade association are forced to operate in a low-cost, low-quality market.

   (ii) *Insurance requirements (where insurance is non-mandatory):* this includes, for example, the requirements by insurers that machinery they insure is built to certain standards, or that construction products used in buildings which are covered for latent damage have national product approvals. In the latter case, it may be the independent technical controllers who take product approvals into account in their risk analysis.

   (iii) *Consumer association requirements:* the product ratings of consumer associations may carry great weight with consumers or with the buyers for major retailers, and consumer associations may take into account whether a product is manufactured in accordance with local standards or their own criteria.

   (iv) *Registration of professions:* architects, chartered engineers of all specialisms, and other design or project management professions which specify products may be required by their registration body or professional institutions to follow codes of practice which refer to national systems of standards, and their professional examinations are likely to require knowledge founded on national standards.

   (v) *Education:* as a more general case of the above, all professional education tends to bias designers, specifiers and purchasers to the use of national systems of standards.

(c) *'Pure' consumer preference:* finally, it is the right of any consumer or purchaser to ask for the testing or certification of safety and performance that he sees fit. Customers with special risks or requirements (because of liability for their own end product, or because of the value of goodwill and reputation in their business, or because of the nature of their use of the products, e.g. in defence, or dangerous sports), are likely to demand special testing requirements. If these are linked to historical national standards or customary requirements they constitute technical barriers (see Section 3.3). Customers are also likely to ask for special testing requirements if for any reason they have insufficient knowledge of or trust in the supplier's own testing and certification. This distrust or preference for national testing or standards may be a result of tradition (e.g. German consumers' trust in the GS mark) or advertising, or simply because they are prepared to pay more for a higher level of quality or security.

Most of the above categories of barriers will manifest themselves in additional or multiple testing and certification requirements. It is usually these testing and certification requirements which constitute the barrier (i.e. the source of additional costs for the importers), but they are only able to exist because there are national standards or technical specifications. The requirements are of three types:

(a) *Local testing and conformity requirements:* requirements for the testing of products against standards or specifications, which may require that specified test labs or classes of test labs are used.

(b) *Certification requirements:* inspection and/or surveillance requirements to be undergone by firms to certify that their systems meet specified standards (the acceptance of European standards such as EN29000 for QA systems or EN45000 for testing laboratory procedures is a solution to remove these barriers) or that their products meet the type approval.

(c) *Accreditation requirements:* procedures required to approve test and certification bodies. Most countries now have one or more accreditation bodies (for testing laboratories and/or certification bodies and/or calibration laboratories), with mutual bilateral or multilateral recognition arrangements between national accreditation systems now being set up under EAC and EAL. Where these accreditation MRAs do not exist firms may have to have multiple testing carried out on their products even if the regulations are mutually accepted or there are common standards, because the test certificates are not recognized. The Notified Bodies arrangement under each of the NA directives is a mutual recognition arrangement, in which the national government accredits the bodies.

4.   EC policies and approaches

4.1.   The overall policy

Removal of technical barriers to trade is not an end in itself, but a means of achieving the free trade objectives of the single market. To assess the effectiveness of the approaches taken to remove barriers, this chapter first reviews why they should be removed.

4.1.1.   Policy objectives

The immediate objective of policy and approaches to removing technical barriers to trade is to ensure compliance with Article 30 of the Treaty of Rome which prohibits all measures having equivalent effect to quantitative restrictions on imports. This was put into effect by a directive in 1969 (70/50/EEC) banning all measures which impose an additional cost or restriction on imported goods. This has a list of 19 measures which constitute barriers, including price restrictions and rules about agents, as well as technical specifications and testing requirements. EC policy also has to conform to the GATT TBT code, which is similarly intended to ensure free trade.

Technical barriers are not unconditionally banned by the Treaty. The removal of barriers 'shall not preclude prohibitions or restrictions on imports, exports or goods in transit justified on grounds of public morality, public policy or public security; the protection of health and life of humans, animals or plants; the protection of national treasures possessing artistic, historic or archaeological value; or the protection of industrial and commercial property. ...' (Article 36).

The effectiveness of the EC measures, however, should be assessed against the overall objectives of the single market, as set out in the EC Treaty and in the subsequent White Papers on the Single Market (the Cockfield White Paper (COM (85) 310)) and on Employment, Growth and Competitiveness (the Delors White Paper (COM (93) 700)).

The EEC Treaty was to 'ensure the economic and social progress of [its] countries by common action to eliminate the barriers which divide Europe'; and ... 'to guarantee steady expansion, balanced trade and fair competition' (Preamble of the Treaty of Rome).

'The Economics of 1992'[3] deduced that the remaining barriers then, in 1988, were essentially:

(a)   differences in technical regulations;
(b)   customs delays;
(c)   public procurement restrictions; and
(d)   controls on financial and transport services.

Removal of these would lead to four types of benefit:

(a)   economies of scale in production;
(b)   rationalization of products or production, increased efficiency and price reductions as a result of increased competition;

---

[3]   See bibliography (EC, 1988).

(c)   restructuring of industry (e.g. plant closures, mergers, reorganization, relocation) to gain comparative advantage;
(d)   innovation, stimulated by the dynamics of the single market.

All of these benefits provide welfare gains for the European consumer by reducing the cost of goods and services or increasing quality, and hence improving value for money and range of choice.

The Delors White Paper in 1993 (COM (93) 700) emphasized the employment problem, and the need to stimulate growth to provide jobs. Growth would come from increasing the competitiveness of European industry, in order to increase exports, increase inward investment and prevent export of jobs. This increased competitiveness should be stimulated by increased intensity of competition in the single market, as a result of removing barriers. (The Delors White Paper added the development of infrastructure networks as a new element in reducing barriers and improving competitiveness.)

4.1.2. The approaches

EU policy relating to standards, testing and certification has two current approaches: enforcement of the Mutual Recognition Principle, or, where this fails, harmonization of national regulations and standards.

(a)   *Mutual recognition of national regulations:* Under 'normal' circumstances, the Mutual Recognition Principle is assumed to apply (as already defined in Section 2.2). With products for which certain aspects have been harmonized by detailed (Old Approach) directives, the MRP also applies to non-harmonized aspects. The Commission has a set of procedures to identify apparent failures of Member States to apply MR principles, and to negotiate with Member States to withdraw or adapt their national regulations (see Section 4.2).

(b)   *Harmonization of national regulations and standards:* Where appropriate, directives are adopted which require Member States to replace national regulations by harmonized procedures and standards. The directives are of two types:

(i)   *Detailed harmonization* ('the Old Approach'): harmonization of national regulations is sometimes carried through by means of directives which substitute existing national regulations by detailed EU specifications applying to specific products and their testing requirements. This is time consuming, and it is very difficult to achieve consensus. The directives often apply only to narrow product groups, and only harmonize some aspects of the products. They may also fossilize technical specifications which take no account of technical progress. The approach is only suitable therefore for certain products, and is only applied to specific health, safety or environmental characteristics. It is still used in the areas of foodstuffs, labelling, chemicals, pharmaceuticals and motor vehicles, but has been replaced in other areas by the New Approach.

(ii)   *The New Approach*: this applies to groups of products which have similar characteristics, or to a set of health, safety or environmental phenomena, and where there has been widespread and divergent technical regulation in many of the EU countries. In these cases a harmonization of the standards, testing and certification requirements is achieved by means of the directives which set out Essential Requirements (ERs), covering all mandatory aspects of the product, and provide a choice of routes to attestation of conformity of products to those ERs. The directives allow manufacturers and testing and certification bodies to refer to harmonized standards, which are developed by the European standards bodies (ESBs) under mandate from the EC (see Section 4.2 below).

The bases of this policy were established in the 1985 Cockfield White Paper (COM (85) 310) ('Completing the internal market', EC, 1985). The essential paragraphs of this are set out below.

'The Commission takes into account the underlying reasons for the existence of barriers to trade, and recognizes the essential equivalence of Member States' legislative objectives in the protection of health and safety, and of the environment. Its harmonization approach is based on the following principles:

'– a clear distinction needs to be drawn in future internal market initiatives between what is essential to harmonize and what may be left to mutual recognition of national regulations and standards; this implies that, on the occasion of each harmonization initiative, the Commission will determine whether national regulations are excessive in relation to the mandatory requirements pursued and, thus, constitute unjustified barriers to trade according to Articles 30–36 of the EEC Treaty;

'– legislative harmonization (Council Directives based on Article 100) will in future be restricted to laying down essential health and safety requirements which will be obligatory in all Member States. Conformity with this will entitle a product to free movement;

'– harmonization of industrial standards by the elaboration of European standards will be promoted to the maximum extent, but the absence of European Standards should not be allowed to be used as a barrier to free movement. During the waiting period while European Standards are being developed, the mutual acceptance of national standards, with agreed procedures, should be the guiding principle.

'The creation of the internal market relies in the first place on the willingness of Member States to respect the principle of free movement of goods as laid down in the Treaty. But it is not sufficient when barriers are justified under the Treaty. Similarly, there will be cases where the introduction of common standards, particularly in the high technology sectors, will encourage and increase the international competitivity of Community industries.' (paras 65, 66)

'Following the rulings of the Court of Justice, both the European Parliament and the Dooge Committee have stressed the principle that goods lawfully manufactured and marketed in one Member State must be allowed free entry into other Member States. In cases where harmonization of regulations and standards is not considered essential from either a health/safety or an industrial point of view, immediate and full recognition of differing quality standards, food composition rules, etc. must be the rule. In particular, sales bans cannot be based on the sole argument that an imported product has been manufactured according to specifications which differ from those used in the importing country. There is no obligation on the buyer to prove the equivalence of a product produced according to the rules of the exporting state. Similarly he must not be required to submit such a product to additional technical tests nor to certification procedures in the importing State. Any purchaser, be he wholesaler, retailer or the final consumer, should have the right to choose his supplier in any part of the Community without restriction. The Commission will use all the powers available under the Treaty, particularly Articles 30-36, to reinforce this principle of mutual recognition.' (para. 77)

4.1.3. The process and functioning of the two approaches

Figures 4.1 and 4.2 illustrate the processes involved in implementing each of the two approaches.

Figure 4.1 shows the scenarios which may apply under the MRP. Member States should accept any product which complies with the regulations in a partner state. If not, and the enforcement authorities (customs and excise, consumer protection bodies, trading standards, health and safety or environmental agencies) deny access to the product, one of three problems may apply:

(a) The authorities cannot tell from the documentation whether the product does in fact comply (no information on the exporting country's rules and requirements, the certificates are not recognized or understood, or the testing and certification body is not recognized as competent). In these cases a number of steps may be needed including dissemination of information, agreement on testing methods, accreditation of laboratories and/or the setting up of a formal mutual recognition arrangement: all of these are complex matters which may take a long time and heavy costs to implement.

(b) The Member State is in fact in breach of the Treaty and applying restrictions for national policy interests; in this case infringement proceedings must be taken (see below).

(c) There are legitimate reasons for not accepting the equivalence of the levels of protection because Member State A requires a higher level of protection than Member State B – perhaps because of new information about hazards (see, for example, the fortified foods and the pesticides case studies). In these cases the MRP is inadequate and a degree of technical harmonization may be necessary – or one may decide to suspend the MRP requirement in the interests of safety and inform all Member States about the requirements so that suppliers may have the opportunity to meet the strictest requirements.

Even when all these requirements are met, and regulatory barriers have been removed, there may still be non-regulatory barriers (see, for example, the cables case study). In these cases a form of mutual recognition arrangement is required for interchangeability of marks and testing and certification results, for which the EC's preferred mechanism is the EOTC arrangements.

In case (c), if harmonization is required, the preferred route is via the New Approach, illustrated in Figure 4.2, the details of which are summarized in Section 4.3.

Figure 4.1.   Functioning of the Mutual Recognition Principle

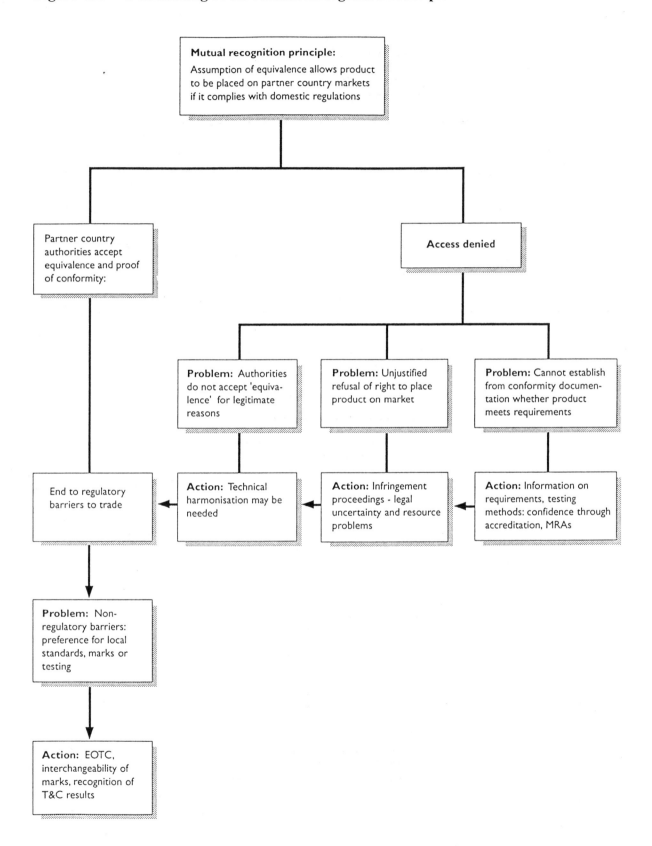

Figure 4.2.   Functioning of the 'New Approach'

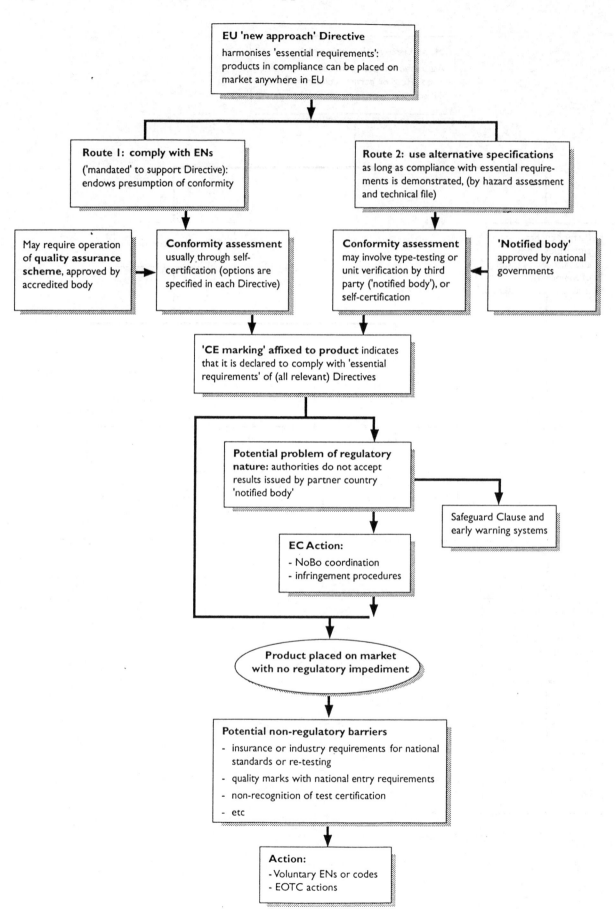

EU 'new approach' Directive
harmonises 'essential requirements': products in compliance can be placed on market anywhere in EU

Route 1: comply with ENs
('mandated' to support Directive): endows presumption of conformity

Route 2: use alternative specifications
as long as compliance with essential requirements is demonstrated, (by hazard assessment and technical file)

May require operation of **quality assurance scheme**, approved by accredited body

Conformity assessment usually through self-certification (options are specified in each Directive)

Conformity assessment may involve type-testing or unit verification by third party ('notified body'), or self-certification

'Notified body' approved by national governments

'CE marking' affixed to product indicates that it is declared to comply with 'essential requirements' of (all relevant) Directives

Potential problem of regulatory nature: authorities do not accept results issued by partner country 'notified body'

Safeguard Clause and early warning systems

EC Action:
- NoBo coordination
- infringement procedures

Product placed on market with no regulatory impediment

Potential non-regulatory barriers
- insurance or industry requirements for national standards or re-testing
- quality marks with national entry requirements
- non-recognition of test certification
- etc

Action:
- Voluntary ENs or codes
- EOTC actions

4.1.4. The spheres of application

The spheres in which these distinct approaches and environments operate are discussed below. The final section of this report will make an assessment of the relative importance of each sphere, in terms of the volume of trade which each affects.

The universe of traded products can be divided into those for which one or other Member State has regulations governing their commercialization (regulated products) and those for which there are no regulations having an impact on commercialization (non-regulated products). Among regulated products, some product groups are covered by the European rules (New Approach directives and detailed harmonization under the Old Approach) for the harmonization of regulations and mandatory specifications. Recent documents (e.g. the recent ECOSOC Opinion referred to in Appendix G) define the regulated, harmonized sector (governed by EC Directives), the regulated non-harmonized sector (governed by national rules and the Mutual Recognition Principle) and the non-regulated sector.

The quality and testing industry, on the other hand, talks about the regulatory sector (where testing and certification is harmonized by directives) and the voluntary sector (where testing and certification is subject to voluntary mutual recognition arrangements between accredited laboratories).

The overlap of these distinct concepts leads to a more complex situation illustrated in Figure 4.3. This shows three sets:

(a)   the set of regulated products, where commercialization is subject to regulations in at least one Member State;
(b)   the set of harmonized products, comprising:
    (i)   Old Approach products,
    (ii)   Low Voltage Directive products,
    (iii) New Approach products;
(c)   products with mutual recognition arrangements for testing and certification in place.

As described before, the boundaries of these sets are fuzzy, because there are grey areas. The spheres are also dynamic. New regulations are created and old ones removed by deregulation; the area of application of the harmonizing directives is extending rapidly as new directives come into force and as the scope of existing ones is widened by interpretations.

The configuration of the diagram indicates the relative importance of each of these spheres in terms of the volume of trade. The harmonized set now (from 1995 and including construction products) covers most of the regulated set (in terms of their importance in trade) and will expand a little more as the remaining, mainly less important, directives are implemented and the scope of existing ones is widened.

The regulated set, however, is expanding at the edges as a result of new regulations or the application of regulations in new areas (e.g. vitaminized foods) so there is always a non-harmonized regulated area to which the MRP must be applied. The number of new regulations notified under the 83/189 procedures (see Section 4.2.2) illustrates the expansion of this area, although the large number of notifications does not necessarily indicate the economic importance of these in trade.

Conversely, the harmonized sphere may cover some products, because of the widely defined scope, which may not previously have been affected by regulations (e.g. complete process lines assembled from used machines). The harmonized sphere also eclipses the regulated sphere – once they have been harmonized, products cease to be regulated by national rules. The MRP area may be seen as a 'corona' around the eclipse, where new regulations flare up and escape the harmonized sphere.

The area of products covered by mutual recognition arrangements for testing and certification is relatively small, covering mainly electrical and electronic products (also under LVD). It has not been growing recently despite the role given to the EOTC to develop this sphere, although many new MRAs are now under consideration and may soon be implemented. Individual MRAs (Agreement Groups) tend to cover narrow product definitions, and a lot of work is required to set up new agreement groups, so that it is difficult for this sphere to grow very rapidly. Some of the existing Agreement Groups may also die as the need for MRAs is removed by new NA directives. (It is interesting to note that there is an existing agreement group for EMC testing, which is now covered by the EMC Directive (89/336/EEC), so this agreement group should now be redundant).

Figure 4.3.   Spheres of application of approaches to technical barriers to trade

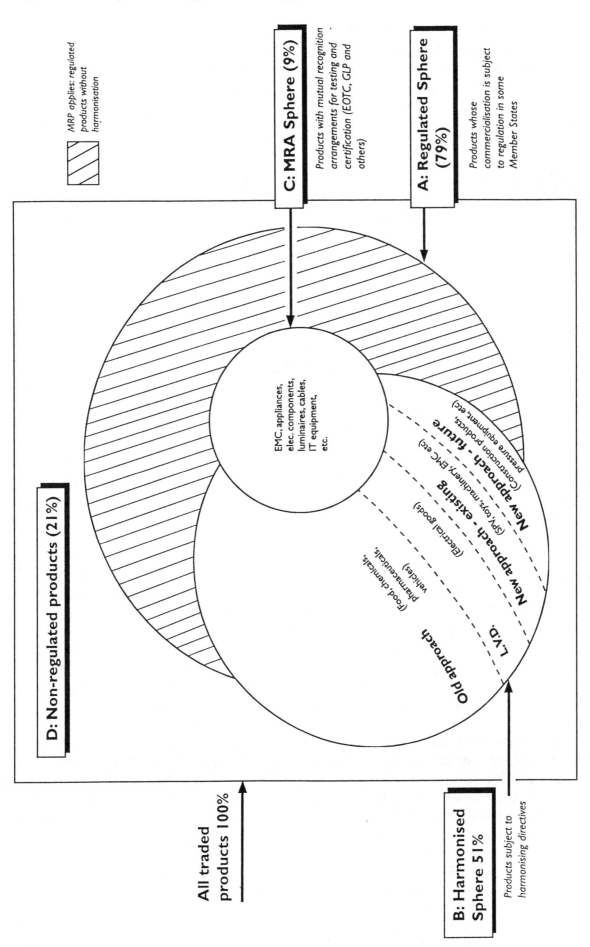

4.2. Mutual recognition

4.2.1. The Mutual Recognition Principle

The Mutual Recognition Principle is the first line of defence against technical barriers in the regulated non-harmonized sphere (as defined in Section 4.1.4). In practice, however, most of the broad product areas where technical regulations are important have now been harmonized either under Old Approach or New Approach directives, or are the subject of draft or proposed directives, which have been introduced for product areas where the MRP was seen to be failing (see Chapter 19).

An important area of application of the MRP is for products within or close to the old approach areas (such as food, pharmaceuticals and chemicals, vehicles), where there are some non-harmonized aspects of the product, or when new regulations arise because of innovative products or new safety, environment or consumer protection concerns. Of particular importance at present are new environmental protection measures, and differences in the approach and level of environmental protection adopted by different Member States.

In carrying out this study the Consultants had difficulty in identifying products which are important to trade, are clearly in the MRP sphere, and where previously existing technical barriers to trade had been removed by Mutual Recognition. The principal examples of success of the MRP are for those regulations which are new and have been notified to the EC under the 83/189 procedures (see Section 4.2.2.), and have then been negotiated away or had specific mutual recognition clauses inserted into the regulations. In these cases there is no removal of a previously existing situation of barriers, but rather the prevention of new barriers. The removal of barriers by the MRP is harder to identify, because it relies on complaints from firms or trade associations. These are often unwilling to raise the issues in the first place (they have vested interests in retaining separate markets unless there are dominant pan-European companies) or if they do, wish to do so anonymously. There are a number of well-known cases, such as the German beer purity laws, and the Italian pasta purity laws, but these are relatively few.

The inherent problem in Mutual Recognition is the effect of Art. 36. This preserves the Member States' rights to restrict or prohibit imports on grounds of health and safety and other policy objectives, as long as this is not 'a means of arbitrary discrimination or a disguised restriction on trade'. This makes it possible for a country having high levels of protection not to recognize as equivalent the regulations of other countries with lower levels. In view of the evident disparity in levels of protection between countries, this will frequently be the case. As protection levels for health and the environment are raised, countries may introduce new regulations and withhold mutual recognition of the lower levels of regulation in others. Many cases handled by the 83/189 procedure, e.g. fortified foods, arise this way.

There are natural philosophical differences between Member States on the level of protection which is desirable for consumers and the environment. Higher levels of protection bring disadvantages: higher priced goods and services, restriction on consumer choice and freedom of action, restrictions on innovation if technical specifications are too rigid, and consequent loss of industrial competitiveness. Conversely, in some cases, high levels of protection and strict standards can stimulate innovation and create new competitive products (e.g. land reclamation services, thermally efficient windows). Differences in levels of protection can also arise from pressure from influential local industries, either to impose strict controls to protect local industry, or to relax them to permit the expansion of local industry.

In practice, nevertheless, the MRP is frequently respected even when disparities in levels of protection are perceived to exist. For example, there is a list published by the German *Bundestag* of 200 types of food products whose import is permitted under the mutual recognition provisions of the German food law (Lebensmittel-Bundesgesetz (LMBG) clause 37) which have ingredients (particularly artificial sweeteners) or processes which are banned for German domestic producers. The German food manufacturers complain that they are disadvantaged, because they have to meet different standards or undergo stricter testing and approvals than imports from other Member States.

4.2.2. 83/189 procedures

Directive 83/189/EEC, which has two parts, established the requirement (a) for Member States to notify proposed new national regulations and (b) for national standards bodies to notify work on new standards. It set up a committee of Member States' representatives (the 83/189 Committee) to consider any issues. Notifications by Member States, which are compulsory, are listed in the *Official Journal of the European Communities* (OJ), and passed on to all Member States so that they in turn can notify interested trade associations or others. It allows for a standstill period, and for the EC to provide comments, or a detailed opinion (*avis circonstancié*) if there is an apparent infringement of Community law, or to propose new Community measures.

An analysis of the notifications of national regulations is given in the Commission's paper 'National regulations affecting products in the single market: a cause for concern; experience gained in the application of Directive 83/189 1992–94' (ref.: III/2185-EN/final 28 Feb. 1996). Table 4.1 shows the breakdown by product sector. Over 90% of notifications are in areas already extensively harmonized, namely:

(a)   four sectors which are the main areas of extensive Old Approach directives: agriculture/food products, transport goods, chemicals, pharmaceuticals;

(b)   three sectors with important New Approach directives which are not yet fully functioning: telecoms, building and construction products, mechanical engineering (which includes machinery and pressure equipment).

In these cases part of the reason for many notifications is the consequence of directives, particularly the Public Procurement Directive, which require specifications to be made transparent by being published as regulations or standards. These reasons are set out in more detail in the Commission paper.

Between 360 and 390 new regulatory proposals were notified by Member States each year from 1992 to 1994 (430–470 including Austria, Finland and Sweden). The number of new regulations is approximately proportional to the size of the economy, for which there is no evident economic explanation other than the number of civil servants and money available to draft the regulations! The number of types of products in circulation and the right to health and environmental protection is the same for all countries irrespective of their size.

The 439 notifications of technical regulations in 1995 were dealt with as shown in Table 4.2.

The number of regulations, however, has no necessary relation to the economic importance of the measures. For example, the UK Department for Trade and Industry (DTI) report that over half of the regulations notified are publications of many existing individual technical specifications for roads and other public purchases to meet the requirement of the public procurement legislation. There has indeed been a tendency to issue regulations rather than rely on developing standards, partly because the requirements of the public procurement legislation required rapid transposition of customary specifications into a published form and regulations are the only way to do that.

Table 4.1.   83/189 notifications by sector, 1992–94

Sector	1992	1993	1994	1995	Total	Share (%)
Telecommunications	89	132	110	119	450	29
Agriculture and food products	77	56	65	58	256	16
Mechanical engineering	29	39	74	103	245	15
Building and construction	56	35	52	49	192	12
Transport	47	53	34	53	187	12
Chemical products	15	22	17	9	63	4
Pharmaceutical products	14	20	14	12	60	4
Products for household and leisure use	10	2	7	11	30	2
Environment, packaging	9	7	2	11	29	2
Health, medical equipment	9	9	4	4	26	2
Energy, minerals, wood	3	6	5	3	17	1
Other products	4	4	5	7	20	1
Total	**362**	**385**	**389**	**439**	**1575**	**100**
Total including new Member States	**466**	**438**	**442**	**439**	**1785**	

Source: DG III, III/2185-EN/final with additional information for 1995 provided by DG III.

Table 4.2.   Reactions sent to EC Member States regarding draft technical regulations notified by them in 1995

	1993	1994	1995
Total number of notifications	**438**	**442**	**439**
Observations under Art. 8(2) of Dir. 83/189			
– by a Member State	136	162	183
– by the Commission	177	266	133
– by EFTA	30	46	4
Total Observations	**343**	**474**	**320**
Detailed opinions under Art. 9(2)			
- by a Member State	75	86	80
- by the Commission	138	114	75
Total Detailed Opinions	**213**	**200**	**155**
Regulations postponed: EC intentions to propose a Directive, Regulation or Decision	5	9	4
EC proposal presented to the Council	5	0	6

Source: COM(96) 286.

The notification procedures are now being strengthened by Decision 3052/95 which requires, from January 1997, the notification by Member States of all products which are withdrawn from the national markets for health, safety or other reasons.

4.2.3.   Article 30–36 complaints procedures

Notifications under the 83/189 information procedures, along with complaints about technical barriers to trade directed to the EC from Member States, trade associations or individual firms, or contraventions identified by the Commission services themselves, are evaluated by Commission services and the Member States, who are also entitled to enter observations or a detailed opinion which blocks other Member States' legislation. This occurs regularly and normally exceeds the number of Commission opinions. Apparent contraventions of the MRP under Art. 30 *et seq.* are methodically pursued through Opinions (*avis*), through meetings with Member States, and ultimately through referral to the European Court of Justice. Problem cases are also referred to the Internal Market Advisory Committee (IMAC) which was dealing with 11 cases in January 1996. At the beginning of 1996 DG XV was handling 1,229 cases. About one-third of these had originated in notifications via the 83/189 procedures, and a few out of cases arising from the General Product Safety Directive (92/59/EEC), but the majority were complaints received from firms or Member States, or from press reports.

Many of the individual cases amongst the 1,229 dossiers are of little economic importance in themselves, and the large number of cases is not an indication of a major problem of Mutual Recognition. For example, there are a large number of complaints relating to personal registration of motor vehicles which have been imported by individual persons or taken with them when moving to a new Member State, and the vehicle is unusual in some way – a kit, or a conversion or a vintage car to which harmonized type approvals do not apply. Similarly, there are very many complaints about the labelling or ingredients of specific food products.

A further 37 infringement procedures were undertaken by the Commission in 1995 on the basis of Art. 169 of the EC Treaty in respect of national technical regulations adopted previously by Member States in violation of the provisions of Directive 83/189.

Thumbnail sketches of a selection of cases of which the Consultants are aware are shown in Figure 4.4.

Figure 4.4.   A selection of Art. 30 cases

A French regulation required that bread labelled *pain au levain* had to be produced in accordance with a specific recipe, which would restrict trade between Member States. The regulation was amended to read *pain de levain de tradition française*, so that bread of other recipes could be marketed as *pain de levain*.

France issued a decree imposing safety requirements on bicycles. A trade association complained. The decree was withdrawn.

Belgium has specific technical requirements for liquefied gas bottles. The technical regulation was required to include an 'or equivalent' clause.

There are differing regulations for licensing of motorized ultra-light aircraft, based on different technical parameters. The UK and Belgian authorities were asked to insert a MR clause.

Fruit juice drinks in Greece had to contain at least 20% juice. This excluded many cordials and squashes. After complaint by a US supplier the regulations were changed so that the concentration was shown on the label but drinks with less than 20% were permitted.

Austria has an approved list of cleaning products for swimming pools, but there is no procedure for approval of new products from other states. A complaint was handled from a manufacturer whose product was approved in other Member States but could not get approval in Austria.

Swedish exhaust emission rules for cars are stricter than those of other Member States. Although this was harmonized in 1993, cars built before then have problems in registration in Sweden.

Sweden and the Netherlands have strict rules about food additives, particularly vitamins which prevent many products marketed in other Member States from entering the market in those countries (see case study in Part III).

Portugal requires labelling information to be in Portuguese, including some elements such as 'Made in France' which are customarily accepted in English or the source language. A trade association complained about the application of this to pictograms on toys.

Italy and France have special procedures for testing approval of foodstuffs for special consumption, such as baby foods, sports drinks, despite the Directive on food labelling which lays down simple procedures for notification to Member States of foodstuffs being placed on the market. The EU position is that they can test products which are already on the market and use the safeguard procedure if they are found to be dangerous, but cannot prevent products legally marketed in other Member States from being placed on the market.

There are many complaints about the Foodstuffs Book in Germany, which lays down specific recipes. Germany in principle respects the MRP, but there are often labelling requirements for foreign suppliers of foodstuffs and ingredients which do not comply with the recipes in the Foodstuffs Book.

A number of cases are related to special marks in Germany, e.g. the Ü-mark for construction products and the H-mark for laboratory equipment.

From interviews with national authorities it appears that the large number of Art. 30 actions force the acceptance of the MRP in a serious way for the first time since the Treaty imposed it. Often Member States include a clause to allow equivalent standards in the proposed national regulations wherever reference is made to a national standard and a similar phrase where there are references to national testing and certification procedures. This incorporates the principles of Art. 30 and the MRP into national regulations, so making them explicit and visible. The process of 83/189 procedures therefore also has a psychological impact.

As an example of a case leading to a mutual recognition clause, a French decree of 1990 required imported cement to meet AFNOR norms and be tested by French laboratories. It was revised to include the clauses 'the tests must be carried out by French or foreign laboratories accredited for this purpose by the Minister for Industry, on the basis of general criteria for the competence of laboratories fixed by standards of the EN45000 series', and a notice was published announcing procedures by which AFNOR would process applications for recognition of the equivalence of foreign standards (see Cement case study, Chapter 11).

4.2.4. ECJ cases

Very few of the Art. 30–36 cases handled by DG XV are referred to the European Court of Justice. Appendix G, however, presents a synopsis of ECJ judgments over the period 1991 to 1994 which relate to Articles 30–36 of the Treaty of Rome and involve technical barriers to trade. The majority of these concern food products or pharmaceuticals.

4.3. The New Approach

4.3.1. The Directives

The New Approach was initiated by a Council Resolution on a new approach to technical harmonization and standards (85/C 136/01). The NA directives apply to groups of products which had divergent technical regulations in Member States, and have sufficiently similar technical characteristics that essential requirements can be devised for all the products. In practice, most technical regulations are directed at protecting the health and safety of the user of the product (from infection, toxins, explosion, cuts or wounds from mechanical parts, electric shock, burning, falls, etc.). The products to which these sorts of hazards apply can in theory be listed by analysing product nomenclatures, although the process of selecting areas for NA directives arose mainly from the strength of industry pressure to remove the obvious barriers to trade and hence took into account the manifest economic benefits (volume of trade, gains from economies of scale) which motivate industry. The list of directives adopted or proposed is shown in Figure 4.5.

The areas where consumer health and safety issues are most evident were already covered by Old Approach directives. This includes most processed foods, pharmaceuticals and cosmetics, chemicals and motor vehicles. These areas have not been brought into the New Approach, but specific aspects of the products not covered by harmonization directives are dealt with under the Mutual Recognition Principle (see Section 4.2).

The Low Voltage Directive (LVD) of 1973 (73/23/EEC), which preceded the New Approach, applies to all electrical equipment and appliances except high voltage industrial process equipment and power generation and distribution equipment. It was successful because the major electrical appliance manufacturers were becoming multinational, and there are large benefits from product differentiation and economies of scale which are realized through trade. A few large European manufacturers were influential in making the directive work with the support of CENELEC. It was not a NA directive because it did not refer to new harmonized European standards, nor have a CE-marking arrangement, but did incorporate safety objectives. Because it did not have explicit essential requirements against which a manufacturer could declare conformity of his products, it required 'harmonization' of existing standards by incorporating common elements, and mutual recognition of the standards and the testing procedures. It led to the development of several Agreement Groups for mutual recognition of testing of electro-technical products, and the establishment of sectoral committees which became the basis for the EOTC later.

The experience with the LVD provides indications of the criteria for the success of NA directives: a strong industrial interest with a number of influential suppliers who have clear gains from freer trade; and supporting mutual recognition arrangements for testing and certification.

Where these conditions are very strong – few global manufacturers and strong testing and certification arrangements – New Approach directives are no longer needed. The aerospace industry is an obvious case where the small number of firms in each segment and the dominance of the US Federal Aviation Association regulations created a global arrangement.

There are areas other than health and safety where the NA might be applied. These include environmental protection (effluents, recycling, etc.), and financial or economic loss (e.g. from financial services, travel services, medical services, building defects). The Directive on hot water boilers (92/42/EEC) deals with an environmental issue (energy efficiency), as do some of the essential requirements (ERs) of the Construction Products Directive (CPD) (89/106/EEC).

The EMC Directive (89/336/EEC) does not respond to differences in health and safety regulations, but to an emerging need for product regulation to protect electrical and electronic equipment (especially communications and control equipment which has a national defence importance) from increasing interference and the possibility of electro-magnetic warfare. It therefore pre-empted national regulations and provided a rapid implementation of a new form of protection. Directive 90/384 on non-automatic weighing instruments and 91/263 on telecoms terminal equipment are also examples of NA directives responding to technical harmonization which does not have a health and safety objective.

Figure 4.5. New Approach directives

Directive	Date of implementation	End of transition period
Low voltage electrical equipment (73/23)	21.08.1974	01.01.1997
Simple pressure vessels (87/404)	01.07.1990	01.07.1992
Toy safety (88/378)	01.01.1990	01.01.1997
Construction products (89/106)	27.06.1991	open
Electro-magnetic compatibility – EMC (89/336)	01.01.1992	01.01.1997
Appliances burning gaseous fuels (90/396)	01.01.1992	01.01.1996
Personal protective equipment (89/686)	01.07.1992	30.06.1995
Telecommunications terminal equipment (91/263)	06.11.1992	
Machinery (89/392, 91/368)	01.01.1993	01.01.1996
Non-automatic weighing instruments (90/384)	01.01.1993	01.01.2003
Active implantable medical devices (90/385)	01.01.1993	31.12.1994
New hot water boilers fired with liquid or gaseous fuels (92/42, 93/68 amend)	01.01.1994	31.12.1997
Explosives for civil use (93/15)	01.01.1995	31.12.2002
Equipment and protective systems intended for use in potentially explosive atmosphere (94/9)	01.03.1996	30.06.2003
Recreational crafts (94/25)	16.06.1996	16.6.1998
Lifts (95/16)	01.07.1997	3.6.1999
Precious metals	draft	
Pressure equipment	draft	
Cableway installations	draft	

4.3.2. European standardization

The New Approach directives' reference to harmonized standards provides more flexibility than detailed harmonization directives, by using the established standardization structures and procedures of CEN, CENELEC, ETSI and the national standards bodies (NSBs) which directly involve industry. The standardization work is achieved in a more efficient way and with greater participation from industry and the standards are easy to update. The great benefit of New Approach directives rather than total harmonization is the choice of attestation routes available when specific harmonized standards are unavailable: by self-certification against the ERs; by using generic standards (which generally have been adopted); or by using notified bodies for type approval and testing of conformity to type.

The ESBs (European Standards Bodies) have had to undergo some radical changes to respond to the pressure of development of harmonized standards. Mandated work (which includes work in support of public procurement as well as the New Approach directives) now makes up a quarter of CEN's standards, and the majority of their current work effort. The volume of the remaining voluntary standardization requested by industry has also grown. At the end of 1995 CEN had 269 active Technical Committees, over 9,000 work items in progress, and 2,403 valid standardization documents (ENs, ENVs, HDs and CRs), with 710 new documents produced in 1995 compared to only 10 per year a decade ago. The rate of production of new standards is still rising. CENELEC and ETSI are rather smaller, but had in January 1996 around 1,800 and 1,100 standardization documents respectively. Many standards are now entering the period when they have to be revised, so the workload will remain high.

CEN and the other bodies have been forced to adapt to the new challenges by the introduction of electronic systems and use of the Internet for transmission of drafts, modifications and voting procedures between the national members of the technical committees and working groups. They are aiming to reduce the production period for standards from around five to seven years to two to three years.

The national standards bodies have also had to change. A dominant part of their work is now in managing the inputs into ESB technical committees and work groups. In the past they derived their revenue from the sale of national standards and technical advice. Now the sale is largely of European and international standards (in which they are in competition with sales from other NSBs), and the volume of sales is smaller in relation to the volume of new standardization work. For some NSBs the deficit has been made up by certification of quality assurance systems under ISO EN29000, and NSBs generally are likely to take a greater interest in testing and certification work to provide income instead of the sale of standards.

Initially great emphasis was placed on the concept of reference to voluntary standards prepared by the European Standards Bodies to 'give technical expression to the essential requirements (ERs) of Community Directives' (quoting from the Green Paper on standardization). As time has gone on and it has become clear that the number of standards required is immense and the procedures difficult and time consuming, more emphasis has been given in the directives (especially in the Machinery Directive (89/392/EEC)) to the choice of conformity assessment procedures and the option of self-certification by manufacturers, or type examination and approval to type by NoBos, without reference to standards. Standards are voluntary except that the Construction Products Directive firmly requires compliance with either harmonized standards or European Technical Approvals (ETAs, which are a variant of the existing *agrément* system) for approval of innovative construction products for which standards have not yet been developed.

4.3.3. CE-marking

Directive 93/465 set common rules for CE-marking of products which fall under any of the New Approach directives and Directive 93/68 modified all the previous New Approach directives so that the CE-marking is incorporated. The CE-marking is affixed by the manufacturer or importer (who must be established in the EU) to certify that the product conforms with all the requirements of all of the relevant directives. The marking may also show the identification number of the notified body involved in the production control phase if that applies. At present a number of directives are in the transition phase and for these the products may still be produced to national rules; so until all New Approach directives are fully in force the CE-marking may only indicate compliance with certain of the directives.

Other national marks continue to be used for some products, and in Germany in particular the GS mark, which formerly performed a similar role to the CE-marking, is still commonly demanded by customers and retailers. It now indicates conformity with similar requirements to the CE-marking, but shows third party testing by one of the scheme's member test bodies.

These now include some test houses outside Germany. The GS mark is still seen as a barrier by many exporters because, although not a mandatory requirement, it has become *de facto* required by customers, and it is still not easy to obtain outside Germany. Safety marks in other countries, such as the Kitemark in the UK and the NF mark in France, do not have such a wide acceptance as the GS mark and are likely to fall into disuse, except for products where they have become firmly established.

4.3.4. The Global Approach to conformity assessment and Notified Bodies

Each of the New Approach directives specifies the alternative routes available to manufacturers and importers for conformity assessment. These vary between products, but since the adoption of the Global Approach to testing and certification (Council Resolution 90/C 10/01 of December 1989 and Council Decision 90/683 of December 1990) they are selected from a clear set of optional modules, applying separately to the design phase and the production phase of a product. The modules are shown in Figure 4.6.

The Global Approach is not limited to the New Approach directives, but also sets a framework for the whole conformity assessment industry in both the harmonized and the non-harmonized spheres. It established the use of ISO EN29000 for quality assurance systems and EN45000 for accreditation, called for the development of the quality infrastructure, and for promotion of mutual recognition arrangements for testing, certification and marks, both within Europe and with third countries. It also called for the setting up of 'a flexible, non-bureaucratic testing and certification organization at European level with the basic role of promoting such agreements and of providing a prime forum within which to frame them.' This was implemented by establishing the EOTC in April 1990 under a charter signed by the EC, EFTA, CEN and CENELEC (see Section 4.4). The significance of this appears not yet to have permeated the collective consciousness of industry, but in establishing this framework and common language the Global Approach should have laid the foundations for a single European testing and certification industry, which in turn could be the model for a world industry.

Each of the New Approach directives requires that Member States notify bodies which are technically competent to carry out the necessary elements of the attestation procedures. These are given an identification number by the EC and the list of Notified Bodies (NoBos) is published periodically in the OJ, showing the competencies of each.

The directives also lay down the necessary criteria for designation of NoBos. These typically include:

(a)   independence of manufacturers;
(b)   competence of staff;
(c)   availability of necessary facilities and staff for the specific tasks;
(d)   impartiality, with remuneration not dependent on the results of tests;
(e)   liability insurance.

There is no specific requirement for the procedure for accreditation, or the responsibilities of the notifying body (usually the ministry of industry or trade or equivalent). This has not been possible because Member States have differing accreditation systems for testing and certification bodies (see Section 4.4.2). These differences in the approach to notification/accreditation lead to the discrepancies in attestation of conformity and the distrust which parts of industry has in the CE marking system.

There seems also to be uncertainty about the liability position of NoBos. It is not clear to the Consultants what, if any, legal liability they carry, if a product which causes damage is found to be inherently dangerous, or does not meet the ERs, but has been attested for conformity by a NoBo. This may vary between Member States. The same issue applies to third party laboratories carrying out testing for quality marks or to meet customers requirements. The actual liability may be limited by the laboratories' or NoBos' individual contracts in some countries, and be set by the Civil Code in others. This is an issue not investigated during the study, but may merit further study.

The New Approach essentially creates a simplified subset of the standards, testing and certification system. There is a small number of broad NA directives instead of very many national technical regulations; a rationalized set of harmonized standards instead of a much larger number of previous national standards; a few hundred Notified Bodies instead of 10,000 testing and certification bodies; a notification procedure by national administrations instead of the independent EAC/EAL accreditation system; and one CE-marking with a limited number of attestation options instead of very many different attestation and marking procedures. This duplication of two systems of testing and certification is in itself seen by some representatives of the testing and certification industry as a transitional phenomenon, and there are calls for 'convergence' of the two regimes – the 'regulatory' regime under NA with notified bodies (approved by governments), and the 'voluntary' regime of mutual recognition arrangements (between independent accredited bodies).

The cooperation between NoBos is now partly funded by the EC. Cooperation committees are being set up between the NoBos notified for each directive, with one of the NoBos holding the chair. Such committees exist and are functioning for those directives which are in full application.

Cooperation between NoBos is obviously essential. This is analogous to the mutual recognition arrangements in the non-harmonized sector, and involves developing criteria for testing and test procedures, and peer-reviewing their competence in order to harmonize the testing and attestation procedures and criteria they use. This creates a problem for the ESBs, because it is essentially pre-empting the normal standards-making consensus procedures. It also duplicates, in the harmonized sphere, the tasks which the EOTC was formed to co-ordinate in the non-harmonized sphere.

Figure 4.6. The modules for conformity testing set out in the Global Approach

CONFORMITY ASSESSMENT PROCEDURES IN COMMUNITY LEGISLATION

	A. (internal control of production)	B. (type examination)	C. (conformity to type)	D. (production quality assurance)	E. (product quality assurance)	F. (product verification)	G. (unit verification)	H. (full quality assurance)
DESIGN	**Manufacturer** — Keeps technical documentation at the disposal of national authorities	**Manufacturer submits to notified body** — Technical documentation — Type					**Manufacturer** — Submits technical documentation	EN 29001 **Manufacturer** — Operates an approved quality system (QS) for design **Notified body** — Carries out surveillance of the QS — Verifies conformity of the design (¹) — Issues EC design examination certificate (¹)
	Aa — Intervention of notified body	**Notified body** — Ascertains conformity with essential requirements — Carries out tests, if necessary — Issues EC type-examination certificate		EN 29002	EN 29003			
PRODUCTION	**A.** **Manufacturer** — Declares conformity with essential requirements — Affixes the CE mark		**C.** **Manufacturer** — Declares conformity with approved type — Affixes the CE mark	**D.** **Manufacturer** — Operates an approved quality system (QS) for production and testing — Declares conformity with approved type — Affixes the CE mark	**E.** **Manufacturer** — Operates an approved quality system (QS) for inspection and testing — Declares conformity with approved type, or to essential requirements — Affixes the CE mark	**F.** **Manufacturer** — Declares conformity with approved type, or with essential requirements — Affixes the CE mark	**Manufacturer** — Submits product — Declares conformity — Affixes the CE mark	**Manufacturer** — Operates an approved QS for production and testing — Declares conformity — Affixes the CE mark
	Aa **Notified body** — Tests on specific aspects of the product (¹) — Product checks at random intervals (¹)		**Notified body** — Tests on specific aspects of the product (¹) — Product checks at random intervals (¹)	**Notified body** — Approves the QS — Carries out surveillance of the QS	**Notified body** — Approves the QS — Carries out surveillance of the QS	**Notified body** — Verifies conformity — issues certificate at conformity	**Notified body** — Verifies conformity with essential requirements — Issues certificate of conformity	**Notified body** — Carries out surveillance of the QS

(1) Supplementary requirements which may be used in specific directives.

4.3.5. Enforcement: the Common Approach

The EC is now beginning the final stage of implementation of the NA system, which is the co-ordination of the enforcement (or market surveillance) procedures by development of a so-called 'Common Approach' to enforcement. This is at an early stage, since even those Member States with well-developed enforcement systems are still developing their own approach to enforcement, and in some Member States enforcement is considered to be ineffective. There seems to be little information about how the enforcement authorities operate in the various Member States. The competent enforcement authorities vary between countries (e.g. trading standards officers controlled by the local authorities in the UK; central government in France; and customs authorities in Finland), and their respective approaches also vary.

The criteria applied by enforcement officers at present is also influenced by the fact that most directives are either in the transitional phase, or are in the learning phase of full implementation when not all standards are available and NoBos are developing procedures. Some enforcement authorities are therefore reported to be adopting a flexible attitude to attestation and CE-marking, as long as the products are seen to be safe.

This initial weakness in some areas of enforcement, and differences in criteria or approach between countries and between product sectors, is one of the main reasons for the distrust in the CE-marking which was evident in many of the interviews for the case studies.

4.4. Testing and certification in the non-harmonized sphere

4.4.1. The need for testing and certification

Testing and certification is carried out by manufacturers and traders at various stages and for various purposes: for quality control of purchased materials and components, for verification of prices of purchased materials, for process control, for compliance with customer's contract specifications, to meet customers' quality assurance (QA) procedures, for quality marking, for research and development, as well as for statutory requirements. Firms are also increasingly undergoing certification (e.g. to ISO 9000 series QA system standards) for prequalification or for marketing purposes, or for management improvement. Some testing is done by in-house laboratories, but increasingly testing, and always certification, is done by independent third-party test houses and certification bodies. The testing and certification industry is large and growing. In the UK, for example, there are about 2,000 UKAS accredited testing laboratories, mostly doing third-party work. A few of these are large organizations with many laboratories, often operating worldwide (e.g. SGS of Switzerland, Norsk Veritas of Norway, Lloyds Register of UK). Other Member States have a less market-oriented and decentralized industry than the UK and in some countries, such as France and Portugal, most testing is done by large government laboratories.

Testing is an essential process in the functioning of the market system. It has become more important as product liability and construction liability laws have become stricter and the commercial systems more litigious. It is particularly important for suppliers to large retailers whose reputation, and often their legal liability, depends on consistent and high product quality; for construction contractors and construction product suppliers; and for suppliers of components to manufacturers of machinery, vehicles and electronic equipment. It is also particularly important in international trade, where distance prevents the customer from inspecting goods in person and where standards, and testing against standards, are required in order to permit fair competition.

There is now an additional growing area of demand for spot testing in enforcement of product regulations, particularly in consequence of increased trade within the EU resulting from the New Approach directives (although this enforcement demand is in substitute for specific customer or statutory attestation of conformity and should, by definition, be a much smaller volume of business than the regular testing it replaces).

The increase in testing related to trade has made mutual recognition of testing and certification bodies more important. This is done through the accreditation systems.

4.4.2. Accreditation

Third party testing and certification only works if the customer recognizes the capability, independence and reliability of the testing and certification body. Most countries have an accreditation scheme, or sometimes separate accreditation schemes for test laboratories, certification bodies and metrology laboratories. These accreditation schemes now have a European standard, the ISO EN45000 series, by which to regulate the procedures for accreditation. In Europe, only Greece has no accreditation scheme, which causes difficulties for the mutual recognition of Greek products. Germany has a more complex arrangement, with no single accreditation body, which also causes some difficulties. France relies on government notification of laboratories with less reliance on third party accreditation. The UK has a fully functional independent accreditation system and the government draws on this for approving notified bodies under the directives.

EAC/EAL

The acceptance of a manufacturer's home country testing and certification requires the mutual recognition of the two countries' accreditation systems, so that in turn the testing and certification bodies can be recognized. This is facilitated by two arrangements: EAC (European Accreditation of Certification Bodies) and EAL (European Cooperation for Accreditation of Laboratories), which are members of the EOTC. These have taken a series of bilateral agreements built up over the past decade and melded them into multilateral agreements covering all the European members. They are in turn members of ILAC (International Laboratory Accreditation Conference). Bilateral MRAs are being set up between EAC/EAL and other countries and regions, in particular with APLAC (Asia Pacific Laboratory Accreditation Council) which is modelled on EAL.

EAC/EAL work by appraising each member's accreditation bodies by teams of expert appraisers drawn from other members' accreditation bodies, with regular surveillance. They are both members of the EOTC which provides them with some support and technical assistance.

This level of mutual recognition arrangement (between accreditation bodies) is essential to the removal of technical barriers to trade, and is just beginning to be implemented. The whole process of mutual recognition of testing and certification bodies is very new. The first bilateral mutual recognition arrangements were made in the 1980s between France, Sweden and the Netherlands. The structure for these agreements was first developed as the Western Europe Laboratory Accreditation Council (WELAC) in 1989 and EAL was formed in June 1994. The equivalent organizations for certification were developed a little earlier – WECC in the 1980s and EAC from 1990 onwards.

GLP

In the field of chemicals, pharmaceuticals and pesticides a successful mutual recognition arrangement has been functioning since 1981, called the Good Laboratory Practice (GLP) Agreement for testing related to international agreements. This was set up by the OECD and is transposed into EU law by Directives 87/18 and 88/320. The GLP is a multinational accreditation arrangement which has a relatively small number of members (34 member labs in the EU and 76 in the world) and is seen to be functioning well. Laboratory inspection and monitoring is carried out by Member States, with joint visits, and has supporting databases for monitoring laboratory practice and enforcement. It is therefore a third system, run by public authorities, in addition to the NoBo system for New Approach directives and the EOTC system of voluntary accreditation and agreement groups.

4.4.3. EOTC and Agreement Groups

The EOTC was set up in 1990 as a result of the decision in the Global Approach to promote mutual recognition arrangements for testing and certification, based on ISO EN29000 and ISO EN45000, and to set up an organization to co-ordinate these arrangements. Its members are the European organizations involved in testing and certification, including EAC and EAL, and a number of sectoral organizations (for IT testing, electro-technical, fire and intruder protection, and water products) dedicated to the development of mutual recognition arrangements in their sector.

The EOTC set criteria for the functioning of Agreement Groups (AGs), which are agreements between testing or certification bodies to provide testing or certification for a specific product area, to agreed standards and procedures, so that their certificates can be recognized by customers in any of their member countries. It took under its wing a number of existing AGs, mainly in the electro-technical field. It has been assisting a number of other potential AGs to set up. The total list of AGs under the EOTC in mid-1996 are shown in Figure 4.7.

Only the last of these has been formed since the EOTC came into being, but there are reported to be around 20 other potential AGs under consideration – NDT personnel, timber, aluminium coating, aluminium building products, air conditioning equipment, quality labelling for house-building products, ceramic tiles, plastic pipes, radiators, fire testing, traffic control, caravans, textiles, sterilized packaging, welders' qualifications, electronic data interchange, nuclear engineering, food inspection, wheels and railways.

A number of AGs exist which have not become members of the EOTC because they do not meet the EOTC's criteria, in particular that the AGs must be open to any laboratory and not closed shops creating a monopoly in each country. Among these are LUMAG for luminaires (light fittings), HAR for cables (see Part II), and CCA for domestic electrical appliances.

Figure 4.7.   Existing EOTC Agreement Groups

under ECITC – the European Committee for IT Testing and Certification:

- OSTC - Open Systems Testing Consortium

- EMCIT - European Testing of EMC of Information Technology Products

- ETCOM - European Testing of Certification for Office and Manufacturing Protocols

- ITQS - Assessment and Certification of Quality Systems in Information Technology

under ELSECOM – the European Electrotechnical Sectoral Committee

- STLA – Short Circuit Testing Group

- LOVAG – Low Voltage Agreement Group (for building wiring and switches)

- EMCEL – EMC Testing

under ESCIF – the European Committee for Intrusion and Fire Protection

- EFSC – European Fire and Security Group

EMEDCA – the European Active Medical Certification Agreement (for active medical devices)

IIEG – International Instrument Evaluation Group

RMAG – Recreational Marine Agreement Group

4.4.4.   Quality marks

Quality marks and labels exist in many forms:

(a)   for product groups (e.g. Woolmark for wool textiles) ;
(b)   as safety marks, tied to national standards bodies and compliance with national safety standards (GS mark, Kitemark);
(c)   as environmental labels (*Grünepunkt*);
(d)   as retailers' labels (St Michael for Marks & Spencer);
(e)   as trade marks, for franchise operations (McDonald's, Dyno-rod);
(f)   as simple proprietary trade marks (Ferrari).

The importance of such marks for customers is evident. They enable the marketplace to function by competition between products of known quality, and hence stimulate innovation and continuous improvement in quality. Without them competitive markets simply drive down prices and quality, potentially to unacceptable levels – as happens in 'cowboy' construction for example.

There is a concern in the EC, however, that quality marks which are based on national standards create technical barriers to trade and, moreover, will be confused with the CE-marking and take away the value of the latter. Equally there is a concern in industry that the CE-marking will be confused with a quality mark, taking away the value of genuine quality marks relating to performance standards and providing a third party guarantee.

The problem with quality marks is that they may create abuses of competition in contravention of Articles 85 and 86 of the Treaty of Rome. Many marks are, by their rules, closed shops which only national firms can join. This is clearly a partitioning of markets which is inconsistent with the single market. The marking schemes run by national standards bodies are likely to cause technical barriers to trade at best, and closed shops at worst. But competition rules could be applied to quality marks, to ensure that any manufacturer who meets the technical specifications can join, and that the marks are independent of any national body or trade association.

At present the only initiative to develop non-national marks is the CEN Keymark, launched in September 1995. This is a new initiative, which at the time of writing this report has only one product ('Scheme Development Group'), plastic piping and ducting systems, approved in 1995. The Keymark is intended to be complementary to CE-marking, but would clearly be appropriate for products which are not under New Approach directives. Its certification requires type-testing, QA systems to ISO EN9002, and surveillance of production. It is within the competence of the EOTC to develop suitable Europe-wide quality marks, but it has not done so. CEN had a former scheme, the CENCER mark, which only had one product group – thermostatic radiator valves – and failed to develop. It remains to be seen whether the Keymark is any more successful. It is possible that active initiatives are required in order to promote international or Europe-wide quality marks.

4.5. The institutional structures

Both of the approaches depend upon a very complex system of standards, testing and certification. It is important to understand the complexity of these institutional arrangements, which are an essential part of the functioning of the approaches to removing technical barriers. The systems are still developing, particularly in the area of mutual recognition arrangements, including accreditation systems, but there is no doubt that the real achievement of the EC measures for removing technical barriers to trade has been the development of the institutional system at EU and at national levels. The development of this has been truly remarkable and involves many thousands of people, as well as the many thousands of volunteers on technical committees developing new EN standards.

The institutional elements of the system are illustrated in Figures 4.8 and 4.9, and include:

(a)   the EC sponsoring departments for the numerous Old Approach directives; the EC sponsoring departments and (in some cases) the Committees for the 17 New Approach directives; and sponsoring departments in the national administrations;

(b)   the European Standards Bodies (ESBs) – CEN, CENELEC, ETSI – with their Associated Standards Bodies (e.g. ECISS for steel standards);

(c)   National Standards Bodies (NSBs) who provide the secretariat of the technical committees;

(d)   test laboratories (some 10,000 in the EU), who test products and materials against standards and specifications. Some of them (approximately 600 in early 1996) are Notified Bodies (NoBos) under NA directives;

(e)   certification bodies (several in each MS), some of which are also NoBos, who carry out certification of firms, mainly to ISO EN29000 quality assurance standards;

(f)   national accreditation bodies, which implement the procedures for approval of the testing and certification bodies, agreed at the European level;

(g)   EAL and EAC, creating and supervising multilateral mutual recognition agreements between accreditation bodies;

(h)   EOTC (the European Organization for Testing and Certification) and its sectoral committees and product Agreement Groups for mutual recognition arrangements between testing and certification bodies for specific products, some under the EOTC arrangement and some outside it;

(i)   Information Procedure of the 83/189 Committee for notifications of standards and regulations (to which will be added from 1997 the notification procedures for product withdrawals set up by Council Decision 3052/95);

(j)   the EC's Art. 30 procedures for handling complaints about technical barriers to trade and enforcing the Mutual Recognition Principle (managed by the European Commission (DG XV)), along with specific complaint channels in some Member States;

(k)   enforcement authorities in each Member State, including customs and excise, health and safety, environmental, and trading standards authorities, which may be controlled by central or local government.

Figure 4.8 illustrates the institutional arrangements involved for products covered by New Approach directives. The essential elements of these are described above in Section 4.3. The involvement of Notified Bodies and certification bodies may be optional or mandatory, depending on the provisions of each directive. Producers may also decide to submit their products to additional testing and certification according to the customers' or insurers' preferences or other non-mandatory requirements, particularly customary quality marks. The latter may involve bodies in the export market, but otherwise all the New Approach directives requirements are fulfilled in the home country (unless the producer chooses to use NoBos in other countries).

Figure 4.9 illustrates the more complex institutional environment in the non-harmonized sphere. Here both mandatory and voluntary arrangements may apply (shown on the left and right of the diagram respectively). In the absence of mutual recognition arrangements producers would be faced with similar structures in each and every country they sell to. The diagram shows, however, the mutual recognition arrangements which should apply (shown outside the shaded sphere of home country arrangements). On the left of the diagram – the mandatory side – are the EU arrangements to ensure application of the Mutual Recognition Principle, namely the 83/189 notification procedures and the Art. 30–36 procedures. On the right of the diagram are the structures which might be in place (but are only in place for very few products) to ensure mutual recognition arrangements for testing and certification, co-ordinated in theory by the EOTC. These are described in Part III.

Figure 4.8.   The testing and certification system in the harmonized sphere

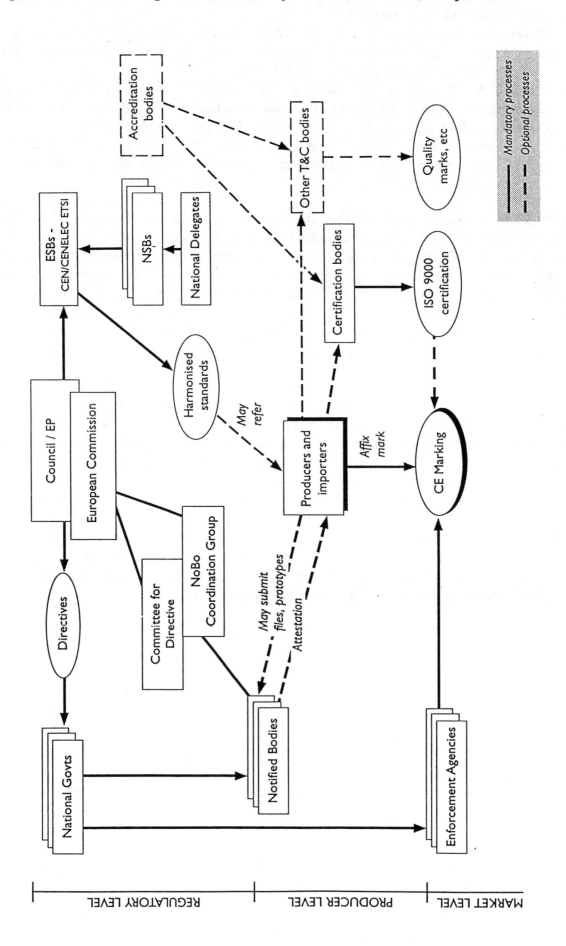

Figure 4.9.   The testing and certification system in the non-harmonized sphere

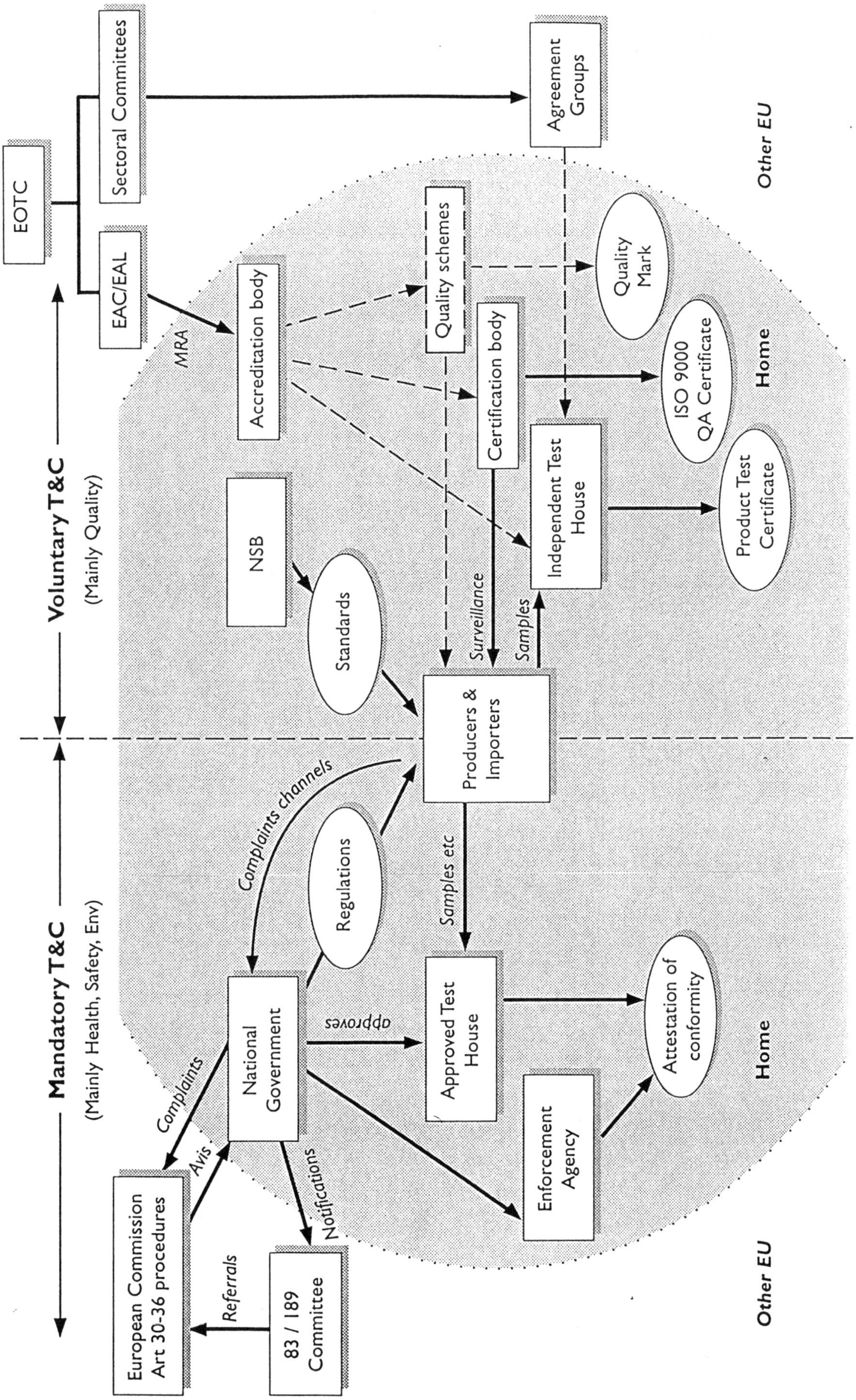

Part II: Sample product sectors – New Approach

5. Air reservoirs

5.1. Product information

NACE codes: 28.2 manufacture of tanks, reservoirs and containers of metal

PRODCOM codes: 28.21.11.10   >300 litre tanks steel
                               28.21.11.70   >300 litre tanks aluminium
                               28.21.11.30   containers for gas iron or steel
                               28.21.12.50   containers for gas aluminium
                               28.21 90.00   repair and maintenance of tanks, reservoirs and containers

5.1.1. Product scope

The Simple Pressure Vessels (SPV) Directive (87/404/EEC) covers standard products manufactured by mass production techniques. These are mainly compressed air reservoirs for vehicle braking systems or for driving compressed air tools and machinery. Specific reference is made in this document to pressure vessels as used by the vehicle industry, but the difficulties and issues described are representative of those faced by manufacturers of mass-produced simple pressure vessels in general.

Air receivers are relatively low value components which form part of braking circuits fitted to most commercial vehicles. These circuits are normally designed by one of the larger manufacturers such as Bosch, Lucas or Teves who also supply the control valves, actuators and electronics. These components are shipped loose to vehicle manufacturers who assemble similar vehicles for most European markets. Testing of braking systems fitted to trucks is the responsibility of vehicle manufacturers who are also primarily liable for functionality and performance. Although air receivers are very similar, individual units are made to the precise requirements of the vehicle manufacturers.

Air receivers are normally welded three-piece constructions made from thin gauge steel or aluminium which is painted to protect it from the elements. The capacity of most air receivers is between 5 and 30 litres and the working pressures range from around 10 bar for the larger tanks to 20 bar for the smaller tanks. Most efforts within the industry are concentrated on reducing the costs of manufacture and improving reliability of supply. The products themselves are not undergoing any radical development, although the use of aluminium has only recently become generally accepted.

5.1.2. National regulations

Prior to the introduction of the SPV Directive, pressure vessels were manufactured in accordance with national regulations covering design, production and in-service use and maintenance.

Because of frequent accidents with early steam boilers in the 19th century, many countries adopted strict rules and regulations governing their manufacture and use. Years of experience and improving technology have turned pressure vessels from dangerous industrial plant into relatively safe products, and all industrial countries can point to exemplary safety records. Lasting concern over the inherent dangerous nature of pressure vessels has, however, meant that health and safety regulators have remained particularly vigilant in this area.

5.1.3. New Approach (and other EC) measures

Air reservoirs are covered by New Approach Directive 87/404/EEC ('Simple Pressure Vessels'), as amended by Directive 90/488/EEC and the global Directive 93/68/EEC. The original directive was adopted in 1987 and came into force on 1 July 1990 with a transition period of 1 year. The second directive was adopted three years later and came into force on 1 July 1991. The transition period for this directive is not specified. This was the first of the New Approach directives, although the Low Voltage Directive pre-dated the New Approach by around 15 years.

The automotive industry operates almost exclusively using the 'old approach' of precisely-defined European technical regulations. There are around 50 such standards at present. As an industry, it is generally outside the scope of the New Approach directives and will probably continue to be so. The SPV is an exception.

The SPV Directive covers SPVs which hold air or nitrogen only, are mass produced, and are of a limited size and capacity. A Pressure Equipment Directive is still in its draft form and will cover larger boilers and pressure vessels that do not fall under the SPV description or are manufactured on a low volume or specialized basis.

The Pressure-Volume multiple (PV) is a measure of the size and danger of a vessel and its contents. Below PV=50, manufacturers of pressure vessels need only prove that they have conformed to general engineering principles when designing and manufacturing tanks. Above PV=50 they have a choice of either:

(a)   obtaining design approval; or
(b)   satisfying a proof test as specified in the Directive.

General engineering principles may, but do not necessarily, include adherence to EN286 and appropriate national standards. In basic terms, the higher the PV, the greater is the involvement of NoBos. The Directive is unusual in including technical parameters and not merely essential requirements, and also in giving companies the opportunity of verifying conformance through testing – known as the experimental technique. The Directive resolved the technical barriers which exists for other pressure equipment because of the fundamental differences in testing methods between those countries, like the UK, which favour an experimental technique and those, like France, which favour an approach based on calculated parameters.

The manufacturer may choose which NoBo to use. Some NoBos are stricter than others when conducting tests. Surveillance or a full factory inspection, for instance, may be recommended by a NoBo once a year or once every three months. Evidently, it will be cheaper and easier for a company to be inspected once every year and most companies would choose this approach.

In the Directive eventually agreed by the European member countries, the traditional prescriptive approach was diluted and some national representatives fought to include aluminium as an allowable material. (Its use and acceptance is now widespread.)

Interestingly, inflated tyres used on almost all vehicles could be classified as simple pressure vessels and their inclusion in the SPV Directive was briefly considered. Tyres are, however, considered safe and already covered by regular government vehicular safety tests and the introduction of additional verification systems was recognized as being unworkable and largely unnecessary.

5.1.4. Development of harmonized standards

The SPV Directive was the first New Approach directive. Problems encountered with it must therefore be put into context since the process provided a learning opportunity for both EU member countries and CEN Working Party participants.

After the SPV Directive was published, the 12 negotiating member countries found difficulties in developing the supporting standard. The difficulties were exacerbated by the addition of a further half-dozen or so members of CEN who were required to contribute to the standards. Few, if any, of these additional members had direct involvement in the creation of the Directive; nor were they affected by it, and in the opinion of some of those interviewed many did not appreciate the requirements and limitations of mass-produced air reservoirs. EN286.2, the relevant standard, represents the views of all CEN members and at Working Group level participation is not weighted. WG2 of Technical Committee (TC)54 thus had to adopt many compromises.

Company representatives on WG2 report that the Swedes and Finns were particularly concerned with low temperature performance. Failure in these conditions is more likely when using low ductile German-style tanks, although the safety record of tanks fitted to vehicles in all European countries is regarded as being very good. The Irish, representing a US-owned manufacturer of tanks, favoured the low ductile approach. The Austrians on TC 54 represented a well-established pressure vessel industry, but it seems that many, being primarily plant engineers concerned with industrial pressure vessels, were used to non-destructive testing, and such methods are impracticable for automotive air receiver manufacturers.

The standards adopted by the WG include a stipulation that aluminium tanks can be included, but that their wall thickness must be 3mm as opposed to 2mm for mild steel. This was a point of contention because, in the opinion of some members of the WG, aluminium performance at 3mm is better than that of steel at 2mm and using heavier gauge aluminium reduces the weight advantages of the material.

5.1.5. Mutual recognition arrangements

There are very few manufacturers of SPVs, and few customers, and as the harmonized standard and adequate notified bodies exist, MR arrangements are not necessary.

5.2. Industry information

5.2.1. Sector representation

The automotive sector is an important component of the European economy. Organizations representing the original equipment manufacturers (OEMs) in European countries include the VDA in Germany, FIEV in France, ANFIA in Italy and SMMT in the UK. In these traditional vehicle producing countries they wield considerable power. In Germany, it is estimated that around one-third of the workforce is directly or indirectly involved in vehicle manufacture. In Italy, the Fiat group turnover alone is variously estimated to comprise between 3 and 5% of gross national product.

Although the automotive industry as a whole is well represented, makers of air receivers do not have their own sub-representation. Within the UK only two are members of the SMMT and although the Consultant has been advised of the existence of an unofficial grouping of European air receiver manufacturers which has met twice, we have not succeeded in making contact independently.

5.2.2. Industry structure

There are only a handful of major manufacturers of air reservoirs, and pressure vessels represent a very small part of automotive sector economic activity. Within a field where many, if not most, products are used across the EU, and where suppliers are increasingly obliged to sell across borders, the SPV Directive has set European standards and opened up the market to greater competition.

Relatively few trucks are sold by European manufacturers direct to the US and Asian Pacific markets. Although Renault, Volvo and Mercedes have interests in American truck makers, vehicles sold in these markets are generally made locally and fitted with air receivers sourced outside Europe.

In this study the Consultant has contacted several manufacturers in the major automotive producing countries who between them supply all the major European truck builders. These include:

Forster & Hales (small UK company),
Wabco (part of the US Wabco Automotive group),
Le Réservoir (French based European market leader),
Linnemann-Schnitzer (major German company),
Equal (Spanish supplier to IVECO Pegaso).

Another former manufacturer, Sillit Werke, a German company, has recently ceased production. Other companies approached either no longer manufactured for the automotive market, or did so only on a sporadic basis in very small volumes.

5.2.3. Output and trade

There are no reliable statistics relating to this sector of the industry. Since all vehicles over 7.5 tonnes gross weight and construction-related road-going mobile machines are normally fitted with air brake systems using at least two tanks, we can, however, estimate the total number of air receivers sold each year to be in excess of 1 million.

Wabco in the UK makes around 150,000 units each year; Le Réservoir produces more than 350,000. There are no figures available for the other large manufacturer, Linnemann-Schnitzer.

Almost all the trade in this sector is intra-EU. Very few air receivers are shipped on an intercontinental basis because of high transport costs. With the possible exception of one manufacturer, all the companies expected to increase supplies to OEMs based in other countries. There is a possibility that suppliers in relatively advanced eastern European nations such as the Czech Republic and Poland may be in a position to compete with established western European suppliers within a few years, but competition from further afield is unlikely.

5.3. Trade barriers

5.3.1. Technical regulations

There are now no national technical regulations or standards for this specific product. Harmonized Standard EN286.2 for air receivers has been in place since 1992.

More complex pressure vessels, however, will be covered by a directive which is still in its draft form, and pressure equipment in general is still subject to many technical barriers resulting from testing and certification requirements.

Once in place, different countries' manufacturers adopted different attitudes towards the standard. Having established EN286.2, some manufacturers of non-automotive tanks (UK, Germany) presumed that all would follow it. Others, though, decided to largely ignore the specification route of the harmonized standards and opted for complying with the essential requirements (ERs) instead. Tanks made in this way still conform, but the quality is regarded by some suppliers and customers as inferior. Since the customers are qualified engineers in vehicle assembly companies who will be well aware of the difference, this does not matter (but it may have implications for consumer products where the customer is not aware of the possible difference in quality between products made to a harmonized standard and those directly manufactured against ERs).

The view of one trade association is that tanks made to EN286.2 by its members are about 15% more expensive to produce than previously, although it claims that there is no recognizable improvement in safety or performance. Industry claims that its own views were outvoted by representatives of non-manufacturing countries on CEN committees, but we are not able to substantiate this.

Before the introduction of the SPV Directive, some manufacturers found it easier to ship vehicles without air receivers to countries which had specific regulations. Once imported, they would be fitted with air tanks made locally. The introduction of a harmonized standard has thus allowed vehicle OEMs to stop this expensive practice and fit tanks while they are still on the assembly line.

Interviewees felt that the SPV Directive is now working, but there is a general desire not to see the scope of the Pressure Equipment Directive, presently in draft form, enlarged to include other automotive components.

5.3.2. Testing and certification

Differences in the approach to attestation, with consequent differences in technical specification, have been referred to above. These do not constitute a technical barrier because in either case the product can be legally marketed, although it is something customers must be aware of. Further examples of differences in testing and attestation are described below.

Pressure vessels present a special problem, however, that most other products do not suffer. Although a pressure vessel may be legally marketed, there are also requirements for in-service testing and surveillance to ensure that it remains safe, especially as regards the long-term effect of corrosion. It is not a problem for vehicle air reservoirs, but can discriminate against imports for some other types of SPV, and an example is given below.

Automotive air reservoirs

Testing of pressure vessels used to be done by the relevant authority in each country. For instance, in France, one company's SPVs were made in accordance with COBAP mechanical engineering design requirements, a French design standard. At the time, the company felt that designing its products to the highest standard was initially expensive but ultimately worthwhile since it gave it a competitive advantage and allowed it to reduce manufacturing costs. Conversely, in the UK, pressure vessels made by a competitor were in accordance with country requirements and general principles, but not to any specific automotive standards. As indicated previously, the Scandinavians were very concerned about performance in cold climates, and German regulations called for TÜV certification of tanks once a year. These differences in approach to testing still persist.

Previous national regulations generally required that tanks withstand a pressure somewhat greater than that encountered in normal service. This multiple did, however, vary substantially. For instance, in Germany, a tank needed only to withstand 1.3 times its working pressure. In France it was 1.5 times working pressure and in Italy a tank needed to withstand 2.4 times operating pressure before failing. In all cases, however, the prescribed failure characteristics were and remain similar. These stipulate that tanks do not burst around welds and that no material becomes detached in the event of failure. In practice, most tanks are designed to fail well above these levels. One major manufacturer states that its products (and those of most other manufacturers) fail with predictable characteristics at around eight times working pressure. It tests its products to destruction regularly to verify this.

For tanks with a pressure volume multiple greater than 50, products must now either be designed in conformance with design and manufacturing principles as laid down by a Notified Body or satisfy a proof test as specified in the Directive. Most companies in the automotive market have chosen to follow the design approval path as this is preferred by their OEM customers.

Some large manufacturers have chosen to self-certify their own products. One company interviewed self-certifies its designs and applies CE-marking in accordance with its status as a manufacturer certified to ISO 9002 by Bureau Veritas, but whilst one of its competitors also verifies its own tanks, it believes it worthwhile to have all drawings checked by Lloyd's Register. When one takes into account that modifications to all tanks are submitted to Lloyd's, this can be an expensive process. There is therefore still no consistent approach to attestation.

Related products

Although companies are free to work to ERs, these are subjective and different Notified Bodies have different views of how an ER is interpreted and what sort of production controls should be in place.

> Example: Some larger pressure vessels used in industrial applications must include an inspection hole which will allow a 'competent' person to inspect the inner surfaces for corrosion and residues in accordance with the manufacturer's directions. The British Standard BS 5169 specifies a 50mm hole. One Italian manufacturer of industrial pressure vessels used in compressors fitted its products destined for Britain with a 19mm inspection cap. Short of using an endoscope, inspection through such a small aperture is nearly impossible. (Air receivers fitted to vehicles are not required to be fitted with inspection ports, but must have drain taps.)

> Example: The Consultant has been told by a leading insurance agency in the UK of an Italian pressure vessel imported into the country with the minimum 2mm wall thickness. The vessels were impounded and a prohibition notice issued by the Department for Trade and Industry (DTI), primarily because a support bracket was welded to the vessel wall without using a doubling plate. This is not regarded as prudent and upon inspection the weld was found to have a 25% undercut eating into the 2mm wall thickness. The vessels in question had CE-marking and had been certified by Italian and German Notified Bodies. For this product, the manufacturer specified an inspection every three months, the cost of which would surely outweigh the advantages of its very low cost (less than UK £220).

The case of the impounded tank described above suggested that a product which is individually type-approved or manufactured in accordance with a NoBo's interpretation of a relevant directive in one country is not always acceptable to another. The position of manufacturers on this point is unclear and there appears to be no redress on the part of a user if a product which has been bought as conforming to regulations is deemed unacceptable by the enforcement authorities in his home country.

In the opinion of safety inspectors interviewed, smaller companies cannot be expected to have expert knowledge of all health and safety issues and many of these companies, keen to spend as little as possible on plant and equipment, will be unaware of life cycle costs. The money saved by purchasing a cheaper tank will, in many cases, be offset by more frequent safety inspections and the possibility that a tank will not be insurable.

It is reported by one insurance group that following publication of the SPV Directive, some European manufacturers exporting to France decided to continue building tanks to tried and trusted methods, conforming to essential requirements, but not using the harmonized standard. The French Government then introduced in-service testing requirements which stipulated more frequent inspection periods for tanks not made to harmonized standards. Although all tanks with the CE mark were legally allowed, those not built to harmonized standards needed to be inspected more frequently at greater cost to the operator. There was a complaint that French manufacturers had prior knowledge of this forthcoming legislation, which was effectively a barrier to trade. As in-service requirements are outside the requirements of the Directive, their complaints were not upheld.

The British Pressure Systems Regulations state that the user of a pressure vessel needs to draw up a plan for inspection using a competent person, but the definition of who is and who is not a competent person is open to interpretation. For this reason, most companies are not prepared to take a chance and employ outside agencies to determine their maintenance requirements. Planned maintenance periods can, however, be of almost any period. Within the UK, the old Factories Act stipulated 14-month periods for boilers and 24 months for SPVs. Most manufacturers of static pressure vessels and boilers in the UK have decided to retain these periods.

5.3.3. Quality policies and marks

The automotive sector has led the way in the introduction of quality systems and company accreditation. Many automobile manufacturers have their own in-house quality control procedures and have adapted these to assess and certify suppliers. Ford's Q1 rating is well known within the industry and the company regularly takes out full page advertisements to announce newly certified suppliers. ISO9000 is almost *de rigueur* in the UK and gaining importance across Europe.

Manufacturers contacted during this study have declared that quality marks issued by independent bodies are rare and in any case take second place to automotive OEM customer quality certification. Organizations such as Ford and Mercedes are well respected and generally speaking, when a supplier is deemed capable of conforming to the requirements of a premier OEM, then its products will be acceptable to others.

5.3.4. Non-regulatory barriers

The remaining technical barriers relate mainly to insurance requirements. The UK Association of Industrial Insurers is particularly concerned about industrial pressure vessels which are difficult to inspect. Following a number of cases similar to those reported in Section 5.3.2, a British Safety Federation (SAFED) position paper published in the UK recommends that simple pressure vessels built for industrial use and featuring an inspection hole that is smaller than that recommended should not be certified. Although conforming to minimum requirements, such products would be very difficult to insure in the UK.

Generally speaking, old prejudices are disappearing although the French authorities are still accused by some of erecting trade barriers such as the in-service inspection requirement described earlier.

Some customer requirements appear to suppliers to be unnecessary, and are held up as technical barriers, but in fact can only be regarded as individual customer preferences.

> Example: Some product attributes demanded by the major customers are more stringent than those set by the European Standard. Resistance to salt spray, for instance, which determines oxidation performance, very often needs to be in accordance with a client's general specification and some set higher standards than others. Nearly all externally mounted components are painted to protect them from corrosion, but although the quality of the paint and finish specified by vehicle manufacturers varies greatly, contractual requirements cannot be regarded as technical barriers.

> Example: A large manufacturer of commercial vehicles recently switched supply of reservoirs from a French to a UK manufacturer. Although the UK company's new etched acrylic information plates conform to the relevant standard and have shown good performance in tests, subsequent to awarding the contract the OEM customer indicated that its French customers were dissatisfied with them and would prefer a metal plate welded to the body or riveted to a supporting bracket. The manufacturer in question is currently looking at automated engraving of the end caps to overcome the problem. The reason for dissatisfaction with the product is not clear, but whatever the case, the supplier is likely to have to discard its newly acquired etching equipment and revert to metal plates to meet its customer's wishes, although its product conforms to the SPV Directive.

5.4. Enterprise strategies

5.4.1. Product range

Sales of air receivers follow demand for commercial vehicles which is closely correlated to economic cycles and swings in interest rates. Recent periods of uncertainty in numerous countries have therefore had an adverse effect on production.

Prior to the introduction of the SPV Directive, most companies were forced to manufacture in accordance with the rules and legislation prevailing in each country governing the design, production and in-service inspection. The costs associated with adherence to these requirements were frequently high and in some cases companies preferred not to conduct business because of the expense.

Whilst some companies appear to regard the introduction of EN286 as unwelcome, other manufacturers believe that the adoption of the SPV Directive has virtually eliminated technical barriers to trade. This means that it is now possible for them to build air receivers to a common standard in one country and export them to any other EU state without difficulty. These companies are now able to invest in production plant and equipment which will enable them to build common products on single manufacturing lines allowing them to reduce unit costs.

5.4.2. Investment

Investment in facilities seen by the Consultant has been substantial. Most companies have moved away from small batch manufacturing operations to product standardization and volume manufacture. More efficient volume manufacture is largely dependent on greater utilization of existing operators, their skills and automation. Some companies visited are thus currently installing more modern welding and painting plant which will increase capacity and reduce unit costs. To some extent this can be attributed to the more competitive market and the departure of some suppliers from the market, as a result of increased standardization, trade and quality requirements.

There has also been investment specifically to improve product quality in the plant used to wash and clean steel and aluminium prior to fabrication. Ensuring that raw materials are free from defects, contamination and protective coatings is essential if high quality welding and painting is to be achieved. Even though one maker of aluminium air receivers sources its metals in three recognized European companies using EN10204 and the strict 3.1.B third party certification process, it still re-checks incoming aluminium using an independent laboratory.

It is difficult to prove, but it is possible that this recent investment is in part a consequence of the increased degree of competition (in vehicle manufacture as well as in air reservoir manufacture) as a result of the single market generally and the removal of technical barriers in particular, and also to the larger market opportunities for the air reservoir manufacturers as a result of the SPV Directive.

5.4.3. Distribution and marketing

Increased competition appears to have encouraged most companies to develop stronger links with existing customers. Within the commercial vehicle sector there are only two truly international full line manufacturers with plants in several countries and around ten smaller manufacturers who concentrate on building a limited range of vehicles in one country. Mobile plant and equipment manufacturers number around 100, but only a handful manufacture large road-going machines using pneumatic brakes. With such a small number of potential customers, many suppliers have concentrated on securing longer term contracts and safeguarding their position against the threat of eastern European competitors.

Stiffer competition as a result of harmonization of the product has encouraged some companies to concentrate on satisfying additional customer requirements. This includes producing more attractive product literature and setting up after-sales service, although the relatively simple nature of the product excludes it from after-sales schemes designed to service more complicated products. It is therefore difficult for suppliers to differentiate their product and service.

Even though the single market has created more competition in the transportation sector, smaller manufacturers are unable to export over large distances because the low value of tanks and their relatively large volume makes transportation costs a high percentage of the delivered price of a tank. Unless manufacturers are able to reduce the price of their tanks substantially, this will remain the case and local sourcing will remain the preferred option of smaller vehicle assemblers, who are unable to negotiate volume discounts.

5.4.4. Organization and management

We have found no evidence of significant impacts of the Directive on organization and management. The growing internationalism of the market and the increased use of English in the automotive field, however, has precipitated more bilingual labelling and information flow. Drawings, specifications and product information are now habitually supplied using English as the prime or secondary language.

5.4.5. Quality and testing

Quality assurance within automotive suppliers is governed by the OEM customer and the route chosen by the manufacturer in satisfying the requirements of the SPV Directive. As explained earlier, these tend to be very similar. OEMs conduct supplier quality approval audits which investigate and score a supplier's performance in key technical and commercial areas. In countries where quality and efficiency was not considered to be a strong point, OEMs originally introduced these audits in an effort to improve the level of service that could be expected from their suppliers. With the possible exception of Germany, suppliers in most countries have now also been forced into complying with ISO9000/1/2 just to pre-qualify as potential suppliers.

The universal acceptance within western Europe of EN286 has, in conjunction with the ISO9000 series, been largely responsible for more consistent technological and trading standards. Although some countries outside the EU, including the Czech Republic, still have their own QA requirements, the once-off costs of complying with the SPV Directive and setting up procedures in accordance with ISO9000 are seen by some companies as acceptable when compared to the cost of ongoing certification required previously.

5.4.6. Impact on competitiveness and customer choice

The large manufacturers visited for this survey report that they have attempted to reduce their costs and increase the efficiency of their manufacturing operations, because the removal of technical trade barriers has created a more level playing-field, increased competition and pushed down selling prices. Any technological advantage that some companies could previously claim to have had has now been eroded if not negated by common adoption of the European Standard supporting the SPV Directive.

In view of this, one manufacturer has stated that it intends to concentrate future efforts on developing technologies that will allow it to make tanks out of composite materials. It sees participation in CEN working groups as critical and believes that adoption of new materials and manufacturing technology will allow it to regain a competitive advantage.

One producer reportedly halted production of air receivers recently because the adopted standard EN286.2 imposed high additional costs which would not be justified internally.

There are also rumours that one other company is considering lodging an objection to the continued use of EN286.2. Despite this, several of the larger companies interviewed had reduced their workforce and, at the same time, increased their output. One smaller company has benefited from a new relationship with a large OEM and has increased its turnover from ECU 100,000 in 1989 to ECU 500,000 in 1995 and increased employment from 3 to 19 over the same period.

The relatively low value and large volume of air receivers means that the cost of shipping them appreciable distances is high and because country requirements have historically differed, air receivers have usually been made and fitted locally. As automotive companies have sought to reduce the number of suppliers, there now appears to be a trend to manufacture larger volumes for fewer customers who may be further afield. Coupled with the fact that there is more competition in the transport sector, successful automotive suppliers are increasingly likely to send products across borders.

The same difficulties that in the past hindered European manufacturers also proved to be a barrier to entry for non-European competitors. However, whilst they too are now able to build standard products which fulfil all legal requirements, the issue of long-distance transportation means that on balance European manufacturers of air receivers are still well placed to defend their territory.

5.5. Conclusions

5.5.1. Effectiveness of approaches

Because of the introduction of the SPV Directive the industry believes that trade is freer, remaining regulatory barriers are minimal (and likely to be resolved soon) and other non-regulatory technical barriers are largely confined to a few issues relating to inspection and in-service testing in the UK and France respectively. Table 5.1 summarizes the existing measures.

Table 5.1.   Effectiveness of measures for simple pressure vessels

Measure	Effectiveness[1]	Comments
SPV Directive	****	issues relating to NoBo interpretation outstanding
EN286.2	****	industry considers it too restrictive
Machinery Directive	***	issues relating to labelling, marking

[1] on a scale of 1-5 where ***** = the most effective
Source: W.S. Atkins.

5.5.2. Remaining barriers

Table 5.2 summarizes the remaining barriers to trade in this sector.

Table 5.2.   Remaining barriers in trade in simple pressure vessels

Issue	Importance of resolving[1]
Insurance requirements of SPVs intended for industry	***
In-service testing requirements	**

[1] on a scale of 1-5 where ***** = the most important
Source: W.S. Atkins.

5.5.3. Measures proposed by industry

No new measures or actions were proposed by industry, other than the normal revision of the standards in due course.

6.   Pacemakers

6.1. Product information

NACE code: 33.10 – Manufacture of medical and surgical equipment and orthopaedic appliances.

PRODCOM code: 33.10.18.50 – Pacemakers for stimulating heart muscles (excl. parts and accessories).

6.1.1. Product scope

Pacemakers are heart stimulators used mainly to treat heart rhythm disorders which occur when disease or ageing have affected the heart's natural pacemaker and the spread of electrical energy. They consist of a pulse generator, which contains batteries and electronic circuitry, and one or more electrode leads. Pacemakers are now so small, they can be implanted under local anaesthetic in a small pocket between the skin and muscle on the chest and the leads are fed into the heart via a vein in the neck or pectoral region.

Because of technological progress, the pacemakers' functions and applications are likely to develop further over the next decade. R&D efforts are currently focused on a further reduction in size as well as extension of battery life of pacemakers and automatic functions.

Pacemakers are not the only active implantable device to have to comply with the Active Implantable Medical Devices Directive but they are the most important segment in terms of size of the market. Other products like defibrillators share with pacemakers the same manufacturers, the same trade association, the same problem issues, etc., and consequently what will be said below about pacemakers is equally applicable to them.

6.1.2. New approach measures

The pacemaker market is regulated in Europe by the Active Implantable Medical Devices (AIMD) Directive 90/385/EEC adopted by the Council on 20 June 1990. The Directive entered into force on 1 January 1993 and the transition period came to an end on 1 January 1995 and since then, by law, should be fully implemented in all the Member States.

There is one CEN/CENELEC standard, EN50061, which was drafted and in use before the AIMD Directive but the standard is now being revised and replaced by prEN45502, a horizontal standard dealing with the general requirements, and will be accompanied by two or three vertical standards. Most manufacturers participate in CENELEC's work. The largest manufacturers attend the meetings more often and in larger numbers than smaller ones but because everyone can comment, even by proxy, everyone's opinion is taken into account.

Article 9 of the AIMD Directive lays out the possible attestation procedures, all of which require some measure of involvement of a notified body:

(a)   The EC declaration of conformity (Module H), Annex II to the Directive. The declaration of conformity is a complete quality assurance system whereby the manufacturer operates an approved quality assurance system (QS) for both the design and production phases. At the design stage, the notified body carries out surveillance of the QS, verifies conformity of the design to the essential requirements or standard, and issues an EC design examination certificate. At the production stage, the manufacturer prepares the declaration of conformity to the approved design and applies the CE-marking, and the NoBo carries out surveillance of the QS for production and testing.

(b)   EC type examination (Module B), Annex III to the Directive, coupled with the EC product verification (Module F), Annex IV. At the type examination stage, the manufacturer submits the technical documentation and a prototype to the notified body and the notified body ascertains conformity with the essential requirements, carrying out tests as necessary and issuing the EC type-examination certificate. At the production stage, under the EC product verification procedure, the manufacturer himself declares the conformity of the product with the approved type (or with essential requirements) and affixes the CE mark, and the notified body carries out checks on products to verify conformity and issues a certificate of conformity. This is appropriate for manufacturers who do not have a certified quality assurance system for either design or production.

(c)   EC type examination (Module B), Annex III to the Directive, combined with the EC declaration of conformity to type (Module D), Annex V. Type examination is as described above but is here associated with the EC declaration of conformity to type which is a production quality assurance procedure, whereby the manufacturer operates an approved quality system (QS) for production and testing, declares conformity with the approved type and affixes the CE mark. Then, the notified body approves the QS and carries out surveillance of the QS to ensure that it continues to be applied. This is appropriate for manufacturers who have a certified QS for production but not for design.

The above attestation routes reflect the two pre-existing European systems, namely, the homologation (or type testing/type approval) which was used in France and Germany, and the quality assurance used in the UK and, to a lesser extent, in the Netherlands.

In accordance with Article 6(2) of the AIMD Directive, a standing committee was to be set up as a forum in which to discuss and solve problems. It was to be composed of the representatives of the Member States and chaired by the representative of the Commission. The committee has not yet been created.

The AIMD Directive obliges the manufacturer to report certain types of incident to the competent authorities and Article 8 of the AIMD Directive outlines the obligations of the Member States upon receipt of incident reports, from manufacturers or other sources, concerning any medical device which carries the CE-mark. This system for the notification and evaluation of adverse incidents is known as the Medical Devices Vigilance System and is detailed in Guidelines produced by the Commission explaining the purpose of the vigilance system, the types of incidents manufacturers have to report and how the authorities should receive and treat the reports.

There are 16 notified bodies under the AIMD Directive, spread in Europe as follows: eight in Germany; two in the UK; two in the Netherlands; one in Spain; one in Portugal; one in Italy and one in France. However, not all notified bodies offer certification through all routes. This is particularly true in the Member States where there is more than one notified body.

An EC coordinating committee has been set up and is trying to bring the notified bodies together to decide on common procedures for testing and a common interpretation of the directive and standards. Manufacturers support this initiative as they believe that the new approach relies on trust and that harmonized testing procedures would help create this feeling.

However, because the notified bodies work in a very competitive environment, this co-operation might prove difficult.

Pacemaker manufacturers who produce other medical devices may have to comply with the Medical Devices Directive (93/42/EEC), with which all implantable or non-implantable non-active medical devices have to comply. Some manufacturers might also have to conform in the future with the In-Vitro Diagnostic Medical Devices Directive (COM (96) 643) which is at the moment with the Council for discussion.

6.1.3. Mutual recognition arrangements

The European Active Medical Certification Agreement (EMEDCA) is a product-oriented mutual recognition arrangement for the certification of non-regulated active medical devices which is recognized by the EOTC. It covers products which fall outside the scope of the AIMD Directive. Its scope is the mutual recognition of test results based on harmonized European standards (CENELEC EN60601, Part 1 and 2) which are themselves based on international standards (IEC) or other commonly accepted normative documents. There are 14 signatories to the agreement drawn from EU and EFTA countries. The chair organization of the Agreement group is VDE PZI in Offenbach, Germany. The agreement was concluded in 1991 and recognized by the EOTC on 16 March 1995.

6.2. Industry information

6.2.1. Sector representation

The pacemaker manufacturers are represented at European and international level by the IAPM (International Association of Medical Prostheses Manufacturers). IAPM was founded in 1978 to serve, at that time, the mutual interest of pacemaker manufacturers. Currently, active implants include many more products such as implantable defibrillators, neuro-stimulators, and other products.

IAPM represents more than 95% of the world-wide active implant manufacturers. The goal of IAPM is to help its members gain access to the market all over the world.

In 1985, IAPM expanded to include manufacturers of other implants, non-active implants. IAPM has been and still is instrumental in the generation and maintenance of all aspects of the AIMD Directive and the Medical Devices Directive.

6.2.2. Industry structure

There are about 20 pacemaker manufacturers world-wide, but the top ten pacemaker manufacturers account for 99% of the world market. Most manufacturers are US-based with distribution and sometimes manufacturing facilities in most European countries.

Although the European manufacturers' market share seems small on the world scale, they each have higher market shares in Europe and particularly high market shares in their home countries. ELA Medical is the leading pacemaker supplier in France and Sorin is estimated to have a 9% market share in Europe and a 30% market share in Italy.

In 1995, the pacemaker market was estimated to be worth US$ 2,500 million and forecast to grow rapidly over the next decade under the double influence of an ageing OECD population and increased health spending in Eastern Europe and Asia.

The top six pacemaker markets are the US (24%), Japan (24%), Germany (8%), France (6%), Italy (3%), and the UK (3%).

Table 6.1.   Top ten pacemaker manufacturers

Pacemaker manufacturers	Country of origin	Estimated world market share (%)
Medtronic	USA	40
St Jude Pacesetter	USA	19
Telectronics	Australia	13
Intermedics	Switzerland	11
Guidant	USA	10
ELA Medical	France	3
Sorin Biomedica	Italy	2
Biotronik	Germany	1
Cardiac Control Systems	USA	<1
Cook	USA	<1

Source: Clinica, December 1995.

6.2.3.   Output and trade

Table 6.2.   Pacemakers: intra- and extra-EU trade, 1988–94 ('000 ECU)

	Intra-EU trade	Extra-EU exports	Extra-EU imports
1988	106,296	35,344	102,828
1989	110,982	44,458	110,922
1990	122,207	51,913	120,993
1991	141,008	57,609	140,896
1992	175,633	62,956	148,974
1993	155,758	55,178	138,092
1994	195,368	76,690	186,416

Source: Eurostat.

6.3.   Trade barriers

6.3.1.   Regulatory barriers

Most players in the pacemaker business agree that there are few regulatory barriers left in the EU. However, they also consider that there were very few before the AIMD Directive. Some manufacturers think that today's situation should not be compared with the previous situation but with what was probably going to happen without harmonization, i.e. the multiplication of national standards and of national certification procedures. The manufacturers believe the Directive prevented new regulatory barriers from being raised and as such is considered a success.

The feeling amongst most manufacturers is that even if there were important technical barriers to trade, manufacturers would not make an official complaint to the Commission (but informal complaints are said to be voiced weekly). Selling pacemakers implies selling to governments more or less directly, so making a complaint would be bad publicity. Complaints have also often been said to be 'not the style of the industry', meaning that discussion and co-operation are preferred methods. Moreover, the complaint procedures are often considered very inadequate and much too slow for industry to be able to rely on them, and the delays and efforts involved to be not compatible with economic realities.

Some barriers still remain. Some relate to the scope of the Directive, and others are non-regulatory barriers or procurement requirements outside the scope of the Directive. The regulatory barriers are listed below.

Non-implementation of the AIMD Directive

The Belgian State was recently taken to the European Court of Justice for non-transposition of the AIMD Directive and was found to have infringed its obligations under the Treaty of Rome in the Court's judgment (Case C-239/95 [1996] ECR I-1459) rendered on 14 March 1996.

Labelling requirements

In Italy and France, there are specific labelling requirements which are criticized by the manufacturers (e.g. the need to specify if the product is made of/contains animal or human tissues and the need to translate the label into the official language of the country the product is intended for). Complying with national labelling requirements of this kind is considered by manufacturers to incur costs without adding real value to the customer. Language requirements are reasonable, however, and in the case of food products for example, the provision of a label in a language understood by the user is a requirement of EC legislation.

Placement on the market

In Spain, all active implantable medical devices have to be registered within 30 days of their being placed on the market. This constitutes an additional requirement not included in the Directive, for which the Commission is currently handling an infringement procedure.

Translations

Manufacturers report that since the early 1990s they have faced increased translation costs because of the AIMD Directive. Although the Directive does not oblige the manufacturer to translate product information, by stating that 'when a device is put into service, Member States may require' these instructions to be in their national language(s), the Directive introduced expectations which did not exist previously. These expectations have been transformed into requirements by the Member States and manufacturers now have to translate not only labels and manuals but also the software into most European languages at a high cost and lengthy delays. Translation costs are particularly resented by the US manufacturers and their subsidiaries in Europe. The European manufacturers tend to understand better national requirements. [It seems perfectly reasonable that medical staff and users should have documentation in their own language.]

6.3.2. Other technical barriers

There are some customer requirements which the manufacturers think create commercial barriers. The two cases mentioned by manufacturers are: excessive tender requirements, and reimbursement procedures. Since these purchasing requirements fall within the scope of public procurement they are considered by manufacturers to be within the competence of the EC. They represent marketing costs for suppliers, but do not require product adaptation or testing, and are equal for all suppliers, so are not really technical barriers. Producers are in fact looking to the EC for harmonization which will reduce their marketing costs, outside the strict field of technical barriers to trade (this might in fact reduce competitive pressures, which would be contrary to the objectives of removing technical barriers to trade).

Excessive tender requirements

Manufacturers complain about excessive tender requirements in several countries: France and Germany were mentioned by interviewees but similar requirements may exist elsewhere. An example is the Marseille region where the main hospital, which can be considered to have a monopoly in the area, has a tender requirement not of the CE-marking but of a full design dossier translated into French. This dossier is said to be as thick and detailed as one the manufacturer would give its notified body for testing and certification. [It is perhaps not unreasonable that a major purchaser, who then becomes a single supplier, should make a very careful technical scrutiny of the devices it selects, since the end-user – the patient – is not able to make a choice.]

The EC has also in the past handled complaints about the register of manufacturers in the UK. As a result of the AIMD Directive this arrangement has been abolished, and neither the IAPM nor the firms interviewed reported problems in the UK. This may be counted as a further success of the AIMD Directive in freeing trade.

Often the situation is complicated because it occurs not at State level but at regional level. This makes it even more difficult for the manufacturers and the Commission to react.

Because throughout Europe the purchase decision is mainly made via a tender, manufacturers expect that forms will have to be filled in, a dossier prepared, etc. It is only when the extra requirements become very costly and time consuming that they feel the spirit of the Directive has been betrayed and wish something could be done at European level.

Reimbursement of purchases in France (and in Belgium and Germany)

Since 1 January 1993, France has applied the AIMD Directive. Thus, all pacemakers bearing the CE-marking can be legally placed and sold on the market without going through the French pre-marketing approval or *homologation*. However, authorization to put a product on the market does not mean authorization for reimbursement. In France, only the products included in the TIPS list are reimbursed by the national sickness insurance schemes. The TIPS list is regularly updated by the Ministry of Health who, together with other Ministries, add health-care products and medical devices which are considered to meet performance requirements and discard the others. The pacemaker performance is assessed on the basis of programmable functions, battery life, price etc. The TIPS list system is outside the scope of the Directive and is not a discriminatory system; no manufacturer is excluded from the TIPS list but some products are. It is therefore not a technical barrier as such, but a 'pre-qualification procedure' which does represent a marketing cost for all suppliers.

Having one's product added to the list is essential for a manufacturer to sell in France (Belgium and Germany have very similar systems) for two reasons. Clinics and private hospitals have their costs reimbursed in arrears by the Ministry of Health and according to the TIPS list. If they buy outside the TIPS list, their purchase might not be reimbursed. Public hospitals, on the other hand, are allocated a budget each year and can spend it as they wish. In practice, however, hospitals do follow the TIPS list as they consider its assessment of products to be a useful guide. The TIPS system existed long before the Directive and regulates the reimbursement of all devices, medicines and medical services.

6.3.3. Testing and certification

Testing and certification procedures seem to have been the only major barriers to trade in the sector before the AIMD Directive. Conformity assessment varied greatly from country to country: there was the French *homologation*, the German type approval, the Italian type-testing, the British quality assurance system, etc. Some procedures were voluntary, but most of them were compulsory. Mutual recognition of certificates was practically non-existent.

Instead of these diverse national regulations and their associated costs and delays, the Directive substituted three equivalent ways to prove conformity. This is considered by all manufacturers as an important step forward.

Manufacturers tend to go to their national notified bodies for testing and certification of their devices. However, several manufacturers have expressed dissatisfaction with their notified body and said that they would consider a change, even to a notified body based in another European country if delays were not shortened. According to some manufacturers and customers, the German notified bodies (TÜVs) are well organized and efficient and have been successful in recruiting non-German customers through their European offices.

As far as testing procedures are concerned, pacemaker manufacturers seem to follow their historical patterns already mentioned in Section 6.1.2, i.e. those based in countries where type testing was used tend to follow the procedures of Annex III (coupled with Annex IV or V) whereas those based in countries where quality assurance was the preferred option tend to follow the Annex II route. Customers seem to be indifferent to the chosen procedure.

6.3.4. Quality policies and marks

There are no quality marks for pacemakers and the feeling in the industry is that there should not be. A quality mark can only be awarded on the strength of a performance standard and performance standards are not efficient or useful when the product is complicated and likely to undergo frequent technological changes.

The customer usually purchases the product through a tender and wants to study its characteristics in detail. Quality marks, however, are only appropriate when the product is intended for the man on the street or for mass production which is certainly not the case of pacemakers. The fact that there are very few manufacturers in Europe (around eight) also makes a difference; all manufacturers are well known by the customers.

Most manufacturers and distributors are certified to ISO9000; some say that the certification helped them gain new customers. However, the customers interviewed said they considered ISO9000 to have little or no importance.

6.4. Enterprise strategies

6.4.1. Product range

Over the past ten years pacemakers have changed in a radical way but manufacturers feel these modifications are due mostly to technological advances and that regulatory issues have had little impact on the development of the product range.

The adaptations of the product to meet the AIMD Directive were very few. The safety features and technical specifications did not change; the product was safe and the market highly regulated before the adoption of the new approach.

Because of the structure of the market there are still some product variants destined to certain European states. Before harmonization, large US manufacturers set up subsidiaries and/or distributors in most European countries. The distance and the lack of supervision from the manufacturer made it possible for subsidiaries to manage their own market in a very independent way. Product variants developed as a result of this division. Thus, they are more the reflection of the lack of a European strategy than of a need for different products in European countries. Today, things are beginning to change and manufacturers are starting to consider the 15 Member States as one single market.

Some customers consider that since harmonization of conformity assessment procedures, product availability has improved. There are more brands on the market and competition is stronger. Admittedly, the highly competitive environment has not brought about a decline in prices; rather it has created ideal conditions for innovation and progress [which further technical harmonization and removal of technical appraisal procedures in procurement, as demanded by the manufacturers' association, would possibly destroy].

6.4.2. Investment

The pacemaker market is forecast to grow over the next five years. The reasons for this growth are mainly an ageing population in the Western world and the increased health-care spending in Eastern Europe which will continue the trend despite the pressure on prices brought about by world-wide healthcare reform. Competition will thus focus on low prices, timely innovations and new markets.

With the single European market and the new approach, selling into Europe is now comparatively easy. This might allow pacemaker manufacturers to concentrate on research and development and direct the bulk of their investment towards the countries where the annual growth rate (for the period 1995–2000) is forecast to reach double figures. These countries are Switzerland (14%), the UK (13%), Austria (13%), Denmark (11%), the Czech Republic (11%), Poland (10%) and the Netherlands (10%).

In the US, the situation has become critical for pacemaker manufacturers. Over the last two years a regulatory bottleneck has developed in the FDA (Food and Drug Administration), the federal organization responsible for granting approval to market new medical products. In

1995 (according to an industry report), there were 510,000 applications pending, four times as many as in 1993. This situation was brought about by stricter regulations on product safety (following the breast implant scandal) and a voluntary lengthening of procedures to limit the proliferation of new technologies in an attempt to curb the cost of healthcare. Thus, introducing new products in the US has become a long and arduous process. As a result, some manufacturers are said to have moved the bulk of their research and development activities to Europe and others are planning to follow. This is a strong indication of the success of the single market.

6.4.3. Distribution and marketing

Pacemaker manufacturers, European and American, have subsidiaries in most European countries. Some have manufacturing bases in several Member States and a European co-ordinating centre based in Brussels. Others (a minority) prefer to organize the sale of their products mainly through independent distributors. This situation has not changed since the 1980s.

A major pacemaker manufacturer mentioned that before the implementation of the new approach, they used to have a manufacturing centre in France because being able to stamp 'Made in France' on the product was an important selling point. Since then, the need has disappeared and the manufacturer has been able to divest and presumably reduce its costs.

The AIMD Directive requires the manufacturer to control closely its distribution activities. This means that the subsidiary structure might be preferred to the independent distributor in the future. For example, a major American pacemaker manufacturer which traditionally serviced northern Europe through wholly owned subsidiaries and southern Europe through independent distributors is planning to restructure its European activities and replace distributors by subsidiaries.

In the pacemaker industry, having one European centre for distribution into the whole of Europe does not yet exist. Some manufacturers think it is the way forward and have started to work in this direction. Others think that the nature of the product requires a close relationship with the customer (for the follow-up and training, etc.), and prevents this development from happening. The customer product requirements are often emergency ones and it is not unusual for a hospital to ask to be supplied with a pacemaker within two hours. Hospitals also tend to order their products at the last moment for financial reasons. These timescales mean that it is essential for a manufacturer to have a national presence/distributor in all the European Member States.

The packaging and labelling of pacemakers have changed slightly with the Directive. However, these changes are seen as pure legal requirements with little or no benefit to the customer.

6.4.4. Organization and management

Some US manufacturers have set up a European centre in Brussels and employ personnel to follow European regulatory affairs. They say this investment of time and resources became necessary when the new approach was implemented in the pacemaker industry. This has been a significant short-term cost, to achieve the benefits of harmonization in the way that suits the US industry.

6.4.5. Quality and testing

The harmonization of conformity assessment is considered by manufacturers as a very important step forward. As a result, many of them are able to save on time and on personnel. They save on time because the procedures carried out by a notified body now take three to six months and are accepted in every European country. This saving can amount to as much as six months' sales. Thanks to the Directive many manufacturers were also able to reduce the number of personnel dealing with conformity assessment procedures. National procedures of which there might have been four or five prior to harmonization have now been replaced by a unique procedure. Reportedly, the number of staff dealing with conformity assessment procedures in the EU has decreased following the same ratio.

The harmonization of testing and certification procedures brought about substantial savings, but manufacturers are unable to quantify these. Most manufacturers consider that overall their total costs are about the same because of increased cost due to the translation demands discussed in Section 6.3.1 and to the need for personnel to follow regulatory activities in Brussels (most manufacturers employ full time regulatory affairs staff).

Most players in the pacemaker market are using a quality assurance scheme according to the requirements of ISO9000. Independent distributors seem to have benefited from the certification and gained customers. Most manufacturers and subsidiaries of US manufacturers now are members of a quality assurance scheme and as a result having ISO9000 does not give them a competitive edge any more.

6.4.6. Impact on competitiveness and customer choice

Compared to ten years ago, manufacturers report no increased economies of scale, no relevant changes of their products (that would be linked with regulatory matters) and no increased exports. Likewise, many customers are not aware of an increased availability of products or of a wider choice of products and as a consequence see very little benefit for them in the AIMD Directive. However, we believe they are now able to chose between ten manufacturers whereas it might otherwise have been two or three. We have also seen that harmonization has brought about increased competition and technological progress.

Another indication of the effectiveness of the New Approach directive, however, can be obtained by looking at what happens outside Europe where regulations have not been harmonized. The US is the largest market for pacemakers with 24% of the world market. It is thus essential for European manufacturers to have access to the US market. However, it is much easier to sell into Europe than into the US, not only for European manufacturers but also for US ones (and European manufacturers are disadvantaged when exporting to the US compared with US manufacturers exporting to the EU). The certification procedures in the US are lengthy and bureaucratic; reportedly, it can take as much as ten years for a product to be approved by the FDA. As a result, in the US pacemakers can be up to two generations behind compared to Europe. This is another strong indication of the success of the AIMD Directive.

6.5. Conclusions

6.5.1. Effectiveness of approaches

The new approach has made intra-European trade become freer. However, being able to place one's product on the market does not necessarily imply selling it successfully.

There seem to be no important problems left regarding the measures that have been taken. The Directive is relatively new; so inevitably there remain details to fine tune, but this should happen within the next two to three years. The enthusiasm of the industry for harmonization will certainly help matters along.

Table 6.3.   Effectiveness of measures for pacemakers

Measure/action	State of implementation	Effectiveness [1]
Essential safety requirements	End of transition period 31 December 1994	*****
Harmonized standards	EN50061 is being revised at the moment	*****
CE-marking	Compulsory except for clinical investigations and custom-made devices	*

[1] on a scale of 1-5 where ***** = the most effective

Source: W.S. Atkins.

Purchasers and even ministries are often unaware of the issues connected with the new approach. Many do not know about the CE-marking requirements and think that if there are abuses of CE-marking in one industry (e.g. toys), there might be in the medical devices industry as well. The industry believes that this lack of information could be damaging, the danger being the resurgence of national quality marks such as GS and NF. There also exists the precedent of breast implants in France; these have been banned despite them bearing the CE-mark.

6.5.2. Remaining barriers

The remaining barriers reported by the industry are assessed in Table 6.4.

Belgium is the only Member State to have failed to implement the AIMD Directive. Since the ECJ judgment in Case C-239/95 ([1996] ECR I-1459) it is hoped the Directive will now be transposed and applied.

As mentioned previously, there exist specific labelling requirements in Italy, France and Belgium. However, they are considered trivial and are complied with without delays or heavy costs for the manufacturer.

Public procurement requirements in Spain are resented by some manufacturers. However, most of them agree that these extra requirements do not result in time consuming, costly operations.

Translations, as mentioned before, constitute a problem for some manufacturers, particularly as they are now said to be requested in 13 different European languages. Before the Directive, the five main European languages were used. Reportedly, many heart surgeons and cardiologists are trained in the US, and most of them actually prefer to read instructions in English as they are already familiar with the technical vocabulary. The translation into the national language(s) asked for by the Member States introduced by the AIMD Directive is claimed by manufacturers to be of little value to the customer.

The tender requirements in France, Germany and the UK are resented by the majority of manufacturers. However, because these issues are not covered by the Directive they would be difficult to solve (if it is considered desirable to reduce the level of technical appraisal by purchasers).

The problem of reimbursement of medical devices in France is particularly acute because of the TIPS list. This list is not illegal; it is not thought to be discriminatory on national grounds, and is said to be used voluntarily, as a valuable and reliable guide by most public hospitals in France. The TIPS list is unlikely to disappear as the reduction of health costs is at the top of the French government's agenda.

Despite this list of barriers to trade, there seems to be a general consensus regarding the Directive. It is relatively recent and the above problems should with time and continued work eventually get solved.

The European industry is working together with the European Commission to try to convince the FDA to adopt the New Approach in the US (mutual recognition discussions have already taken place quite frequently between the FDA and the European Commission). This is perhaps the best proof that the system is considered a valid and effective one.

Table 6.4.   Remaining barriers to trade

Barriers to trade	Perceived importance[1]
Regulatory requirements: within scope of AIMD Directive	
Non-transposition of the Directive (Belgium)	**
Labelling requirements (Italy, France)	*
Placement on the market (Spain)	*
Procurement requirements: not technical barriers to trade and outside scope of AIMD Directive	
Tender requirements (France, Germany, UK)	**
Reimbursement procedures (France, Germany and Belgium)	****

[1] on a scale of 1-5 where ***** = the most important
Source: W.S. Atkins.

6.5.3. Measures suggested by the industry

The manufacturers of pacemakers co-operate well in the context of their trade association, IAPM, and in a group discussion with the Consultants made the following suggestions.

(a)   Most manufacturers would like to see the AIMD Standing Committee set up, which could become a forum for the Commission and the Member States to discuss outstanding/problem issues.

(b)   Education of customers in European matters was considered an important issue which should be tackled by the Member States and the services of the Commission. The industry felt that the Commission does not have sufficient resources in personnel (in this sector) to carry out the necessary information campaign and participate in international industry conferences.

(c)   Many manufacturers would welcome a return to a five-language translation of material destined to physicians.

(d)   As very few technical barriers to trade remain within the EU, manufacturers are keen to tackle extra-EU trade and would welcome:

    (i)   a Commission action with regard to information to the regulatory authorities outside Europe. It is the experience of manufacturers that, in the Middle and Far East and Central and South America, authorities are not aware of the meaning of New Approach and CE-marking and thus regulatory barriers are very high;

    (ii)   renewed efforts to try and convince other countries such as Japan, Australia, Canada and, of course, the US to adopt the New Approach and CE-marking.

7. Toys (dolls and similar)

7.1. Product information

NACE code: 494 – Manufacture of toys.

PRODCOM code: 36.50.11.00 – Dolls representing only human beings.

7.1.1. Product scope

The toy industry is divided among ten different sectors which include:

(a)   toys for babies and young children;
(b)   dolls (all types, in plastic and other materials);
(c)   plush toys;
(d)   mechanical toys;
(e)   automotive toys, including electrical trains and other types of remote-controlled toys;
(f)   toys to ride, including tricycles, bicycles and others;
(g)   games, such as board games and puzzles, cards, dice;
(h)` assembling games, such as models, construction sets;
(i)   other types of toys, which include arms, musical games;
(j)   video games (in 1994, video games were not manufactured in Europe but imported from the Far East).

This study covers dolls and similar toys, including plush toys and other play figures. Dolls or similar items which are battery-operated have not been considered since they may also be covered by the EMC, or the Low Voltage, Directives. The Toy Safety Directive is the only New Approach directive which applies to non-electrical dolls and similar soft toys.

7.1.2. National regulations

In most Member States, toy safety was regulated with national standards before the implementation of the Toy Safety Directive. Most regulations had been progressively implemented before 1990: for example, in the UK national toy safety standards were implemented from 1969, and in Sweden since 1974. These have been replaced by the Toy Safety Directive.

7.1.3. New approach measures

The Toy Safety Directive on the approximation of the laws of the Member States concerning the safety of toys (88/378/EEC) is a New Approach directive. The Directive came into force on 6 May 1988 and was to be implemented by 1 January 1990.

The Directive covers all toys, defined as 'any product or material designed or clearly intended for use in play by children of less than 14 years of age', with the exception of a specified list of 21 products. Toys which are not covered by the Directive are listed in Annex I to the Directive and include, for example, Christmas decorations, air guns and air pistols, detailed scale models for adults, sets of darts with metallic points, etc.

The Low Voltage Directive (73/23/EEC) and the EMC Directive (89/336/EEC) also apply to toys operated by batteries or by mains electricity.

Attestation procedures

Toy manufacturers have two attestation procedures: self-certification (Module A) or EC type-examination (Module B).

(a) Module A: in the case of self-certification, the manufacturer produces toys in conformity with the harmonized standards where these cover all relevant aspects of the safety of toys. The manufacturer may carry out tests in-house or use third-party testing laboratories. The manufacturer is responsible for declaring conformity with the essential requirements of Annex II and affixes the CE-mark. The company keeps the technical documentation at the disposal of national authorities.

(b) Module B: the EC type-examination procedure is legally required where the relevant harmonized standards are inadequate to establish compliance with the essential safety requirements of Annex II. The manufacturer must submit a sample of a toy or model together with other information to a notified body for EC type-examination. The notified body ascertains and certifies that the sample of the toy satisfies the essential safety requirements. The notified body carries out appropriate inspections and tests on specific aspects of the product. The notified body draws up an EC type-examination certificate stating the conclusions of the examination, indicating any conditions attached to it.

Notified bodies

There are 50 notified bodies in Europe which can carry out EC type-examination under the scope of the Toy Safety Directive as listed in Table 7.1. Austria, Belgium, Sweden and Luxembourg do not have national notified bodies for toy safety type-examination.

It was reported by a French notified body that while very few notified bodies actually carry out EC type-examination tests for the CE-marking (Module B), there are many notified bodies which would carry out third party testing against one or two parts of the EN71 standard at the request of the manufacturer, to confirm compliance under Module A.

Table 7.1.   Notified bodies for type examination under the Toy Safety Directive

Country	Notified bodies	Country	Notified bodies
France	4	UK	18
Ireland	1	Netherlands	2
Germany	8	Denmark	2
Italy	8	Greece	1
Portugal	1	Finland	1
Spain	4		

Source : OJ.

Grey areas of scope and definition

Member States have informed the Commission about difficulties they have encountered while carrying out market controls in interpreting the concept of toy within the definition of the Directive. In our discussions several countries' authorities raised problems of grey areas between dolls and collectors' items, and examples have been quoted by the European

Association for the Coordination of Consumer Representation in Standardization (ANEC). These included a Batman figure (Belgium), cheap replicas of porcelain dolls (France), and soft toy animals (Portugal), which had been sold as collectors' items but were clearly toys. [Folk or decorative dolls are excluded from the definition of dolls under the Toy Safety Directive. The Commission's interpretation is that folk, decorative and collector's dolls have very different features from those of toys: for example, dolls with porcelain faces intended as toys for children are cheap copies of dolls for collections and therefore could not be mistaken for the latter.]

> A doll manufacturer based in the Netherlands claims that in France, collector's dolls still have to meet the EN71 relevant technical requirements. The manufacturer claims that the French authorities had defined as a toy a doll which was to be used as a US$ 500 designers' model for a *haute couture* show, so the model had to meet the technical requirements in the EN71 standard. After discussions, the French enforcement authorities accepted the manufacturer's position.

Other directives relevant to the industry

Dolls and soft toys are also affected by a number of other Council directives which include the following :

(a)   the Packaging and Waste Directive, 94/62/EEC;
(b)   the Television Without Frontiers Directive 89/552/EEC which covers a number of advertising issues and the harmonization of European advertising rules;
(c)   the Dangerous Substances (67/548/EEC) and Preparations (88/379/EEC) Directives and Directive 91/338/EEC for the restriction on dangerous substances and preparations;
(d)   Council Directive 80/836/Euratom as referred in the Toy Safety Directive Annex II, relating to radioactive substances (e.g. luminous paints);
(e)   the EU Product Safety Directive 92/59/EEC;
(f)   the Food Imitations Directive 87/357/EEC for any toy that children may mistake for food;
(g)   plastic materials and articles intended to come into contact with foodstuffs which are covered under Directive 90/128/EEC;
(h)   the Cosmetics Products Directive 76/768/EEC and Directive 90/121/EEC, which cover make-up kits that are supplied with certain dolls. Proposal 90/C322/06 for a Council Directive relating to cosmetic products (and various modifications).

7.1.4. Standards

The work of the CEN Technical Committee for the Toy Safety Directive (TC52) is almost completed and is mainly related to updating the standard. The CENELEC Technical Committee, TC61, is working on the standards for electric toys. The study carried out by the OECD entitled 'Consumer product safety standards and conformity assessment: their effect on international trade' (see bibliography) states that it cost manufacturers which participated in the development of EN71 between US$ 10,000 and US$50,000 each.

There is one harmonized EN standard produced under the Toy Safety Directive – EN71, which has six parts (EN71.1 to EN71.6). CENELEC has published EN50088 for electrical toys, and EN55014 which falls under the EMC Directive. The standards are listed in Table 7.2.

Table 7.2.   List of EN standards covered under the Toy Safety Directive

EN71-1 December 1988	Safety of Toys – Part 1 : Mechanical and physical properties
EN71-2 October 1993 (ed. 3)	Safety of Toys – Part 2 : Flammability
EN71-3 December 1994	Safety of Toys – Part 3 : Migration of certain elements
EN71-4 May 1990	Safety of Toys – Part 4 : Experimental sets for chemistry and related activities
EN71-5 May 1993	Safety of Toys – Part 5 : Chemical toys (sets) other than experimental sets
EN71-6 August 1994	Safety of Toys – Part 6 : Graphical symbol for age warning labelling
EN60742 of 1994	Isolating transformers and safety isolating transformers (a harmonized standard under the Toy Safety Directive and the Low Voltage Directive)
HD 271 5S1 CENELEC (EN50088 of 1995 and EN 50088-A1 of 1995)	Safety of household and similar electrical appliances. Particular requirements for electric toys supplied with very low voltage.
EN50082*	EMC generic immunity standard Part 1: residential commercial and industrial
EN55014*	Electromagnetic compatibility – radio disturbance characteristics: household appliances, portable tools and similar

* EMC and LVD harmonized standards.
Source: CENELEC and Laboratoire National d'Essais (LNE): 'The CE-marking of toys the LNE helps you to get over'
(January 1996).

European standards are updated every five years and additional specifications are defined under the same EN reference. For instance, EN71.1, which was recently updated, now includes technical requirements for noise levels: whereas this part used to be 12 pages, the draft for the same part is now over 98 pages.

A new issue is being discussed with respect to dolls and other soft toys with hair. The Commission mandated CEN to update EN71.1 and requested that specific technical requirements concerning hair loss be included. CEN questioned the relevance of these technical requirements, and a study was carried out to assess the risk of suffocation for small children playing with dolls and other toys with hair. The study concluded that there were no real hazards involved, and the latest update of EN71.1 does not cover hair loss issues. The Commission is expected to publish its decision on whether hair loss should be included by 1997.

This raises two issues: on one hand, the toy industry is concerned about the economic impact of the decision on their business and, on the other hand, the industry is also concerned about what testing procedures will be used. No accepted testing methods have been recognized with regards to hair loss, so a standard cannot be agreed; but if 'hair' falls outside the EN71 standard, manufacturers of toys with hair will have to send the toys to a notified body for EC type-examination. Self-certification will not be possible because the presumption of conformity to the essential requirements by manufacturing to the EN71.1 standard will no longer be sufficient.

Some doll manufacturers say they are particularly concerned by EN71.2 on flammability, which still creates problems for them. This EN standard, which was last updated in December 1995, measures how the speed of the flame spreads on the toy. Some textiles used for toys do not pass the relevant flammability tests. This indicates an area where the Directive is creating a real improvement in safety standards, at additional cost to the manufacturer (the manufacturers are probably concerned that some competitors will evade the standard).

Whilst the industry thinks there are still a number of issues to be resolved in EN71, Toy Manufacturers of Europe (TME), which voices the position of most national associations and the largest European manufacturers, states that the EN standards have benefited the industry.

7.1.5. Mutual recognition arrangements and NoBo coordination groups

In theory, with the Toy Safety Directive and the relevant standards in place, mutual recognition arrangements for testing and certification of toys are not necessary. In practice, there is still some concern about the equivalence of notified bodies type approval criteria and tests for conformity with the standards.

In 1993, EUROLAB organized a Europe-wide survey to verify the equivalence of notified bodies' testing methods. Twenty notified laboratories participated in the exercise. The same sample of toys was sent to each notified body, which had to test each product. Test results were compared and, although the tests were fairly simple, results were different, as were the testing methods employed. The EUROLAB exercise proved that close co-operation had to be established between notified bodies in order to ensure homogeneous levels of testing procedures and services. Cooperation arrangements for notified bodies are being set up but are not yet implemented. Some Member States have established similar co-operation arrangements at national level. This is the case in Germany where TÜV has taken the responsibility of being the national coordinator.

Some testing bodies have set up bilateral agreements on testing procedures for specific quality marks. For example, one of the French notified bodies stated that it was entitled to carry out a number of product certification and apply the French NF Toys mark, the German GS mark and the Japanese S and SG marks. It then acts as a direct competitor to other German or Japanese laboratories. It also has an agreement with the British Standards Institute (BSI) to grant the Kitemark: it carries out tests recognized by the BSI, sends the paperwork to BSI, which will return the approved test certificates. This procedure can take up to two months.

Switzerland is currently transposing the Toy Safety Directive and will sign a Mutual Recognition Arrangement, also covering cosmetics and other products. This will be the first bilateral EU Mutual Recognition Arrangement.

7.1.6. The role of importers and traders in CE-marking

Importers and traders are responsible for checking that products bearing the CE-mark meet the technical requirements of the Directive. Importers carry out simple verifications, e.g. checking the certificate which proves conformity to EN standards. They seldom control that the doll or other toy meets the essential safety requirements. The British Importers and Distributors Association would be interested in developing a system to assist Member States and traders in checking toys imported from third countries, and bearing the CE-mark.

A number of products imported from Hong Kong and China are accompanied by test certificates proving that the products have been tested against the EN71 standard by local laboratories. These products do not bear the CE-mark because it is, as mentioned above, the responsibility of the importer/trader to apply the CE-marking either through a notified body or through the self-certification route. It is the choice of the importer to decide whether the supplier's test certificates give adequate assurance of conformity to the essential requirements, or whether further testing is required. A French notified body reported that, in some cases, importers have had the imported product satisfactorily tested against the EN71 standard in the country of origin but when new batches of imported toys were tested again later, some items failed to comply with EN71. The importer therefore has a responsibility to carry out surveillance testing on the products he imports.

> It was stated by a British importer that since the implementation of the Toy Safety Directive, it is possible to trace toys which do not comply with the safety requirements and track the importer and the manufacturer, if it is based in third countries. It was argued by that importer that in his sector, the company must carry out personal visits to the third country factory. Verification and sample testing prior to the orders and the verification of the toys once they arrive in the EU through testing houses, in order to check that the toys meet the EN standards and can bear the CE-mark, is necessary. This British importer also claims that every product which has been on the market more than 18 months will be re-tested. From this, it appears that the Toy Safety Directive has forced importers to develop their own checks and quality systems.

7.1.7. Enforcement and safeguard procedures

Enforcement

Associations, importers and manufacturers report that there are still differences between Member States in the effectiveness and approach to market surveillance and control. For instance, it was reported that in France market surveillance is good, whereas in Italy a number of toys which are placed on the market would never be granted access to the market in the UK. An Italian manufacturer, however, stated that there is a lack of market control in most European countries with the exception of the UK and Scandinavian countries.

Some authorities are concerned that at European borders market surveillance is difficult because certificates produced by third countries' manufacturers may be falsified ones. It was quoted that customs authorities find it very difficult to differentiate between authentic certificates and falsified ones, and toy importers have to learn that paperwork cannot always be trusted. Some further testing may be required, should there be any doubts on the safety of any batch of toys.

In some Member States the controls exercised by retailers are more important than the enforcement which is carried out by the national authorities. Retailers or buyers ask for proof of conformity with the essential safety requirements, particularly in France, the UK and in Germany where some retailers have in-house testing facilities.

Safeguard procedures

Member States are required within their own jurisdiction to remove from the market toys which do not satisfy the safety requirements. Member States must then notify the European Commission of the enforcement action when the non-compliance relates to safety and the toy bears the CE-mark. Where the Commission is satisfied that the action is justified, it is required to send details of the case to the other Member States so that they can consider taking similar action. This is the so-called safeguard procedure. Contacts between the Commission and the Member States occur mainly when safeguard measures are reported by national supervisory authorities, before notifications are passed on to other Member States. These consultations are generally bilateral.

Member States treat the safeguard procedure clause quite differently [ANEC report from meeting with the European Commission (DG XXIV), 21 December 1995], in consequence of national differences in the effectiveness of enforcement. In general, the industry believes there are too few product withdrawals. The two following examples illustrate Member States' position towards safeguard procedures.

There have been very few safeguard procedures undertaken in the UK for dolls. The British Government reports that there were only five notifications on dolls and similar items since 1990. Each notification was made for dolls imported from third countries and especially from the Far East. The British Government claims that there would be more notifications, but manufacturers are usually reluctant to report officially their complaints about competitors' products.

The National Swedish Board for Consumer Policies believes that the safeguard procedure may have flaws because if a manufacturer withdraws its product voluntarily, the country does not have to notify the Commission and therefore other Member States may not be informed of 'unsafe' toys, since matters are seldom taken to court. If there are no systematic notifications between countries, unsafe products may circulate in other Member States where controls are less stringent.

7.2.   Industry information

7.2.1. Sector representation

The European toy industry is represented by two trade associations, the Toy Manufacturers of Europe (TME) and the European Federation of Toy Manufacturers (*Fédération Européenne des Fabricants de Jouets* – FEFJ). TME, which has a permanent secretariat in Brussels, represents some national associations and the largest toy manufacturers, whilst FEFJ represents some national associations and small manufacturers. In 1996, the Spanish association held the secretariat of the FEFJ, which has five members, the Spanish, German, French, Greek and Dutch associations. FEFJ is working closely with TME.

TME had 21 corporate and associate members in May 1996; its total membership accounts for more than 80% of all toys and games manufactured and sold in Europe. TME was set up in order to establish a permanent representation in Brussels for the toy manufacturing industry. It represents the interests of the European toy industry to the European Union institutions.

7.2.2. Industry structure

In 1991, the world's largest toy manufacturers (of all toys, not just dolls) were Nintendo (Japan), Hasbro (USA), Sega (Japan), Lego (Denmark), Mattel (USA), Idéal Loisir (France), Playmobil (Germany), Fisher Price (USA), Tomy (Japan) and Ravensburger (Germany).

Nearly 2,500 manufacturers, most of them small- or medium-sized enterprises, provide direct jobs for 80,000 employees. Almost 80% of the manufacturers in Europe are SMEs with less than 20 employees.

Geographically, the industry is highly concentrated following a restructuring trend due to the globalization of markets. The largest proportion of toy manufacturers are located in Bavaria and Baden-Württemberg in Germany, Lombardy in Italy, Jura and Rhônes-Alpes in France, and Alicante and Barcelona in Spain. Many of the larger manufacturers have manufacturing subsidiaries or major subcontract suppliers in South-East Asia.

7.2.3. Output and trade

The toy industry is relatively small in Europe; total EU toy production amounted to ECU 3,883 million in 1993. In 1991, the European Union was ranked third producer of toys, behind Japan and the USA.

In the EU, more than 90% of the toys manufactured are produced by six countries: Germany (26%), France (23%), Italy (17%), Denmark (10%), Spain (9%) and the UK (7%).

Five countries represent 86% of the market for toys sold in the EU (based on retail sales in 1991). France is the largest market, closely followed by the UK, Italy, Germany and Spain.

In the toy industry, competition is fierce as a result of an increasing level of products imported from non-EU countries such as China. European manufacturers will generally compete on price or on model design. Strategic emphasis is given to merchandising tactics or to R&D and new product development.

Output of certain product lines with high labour cost (such as soft toys and die cast vehicles) are relocated in the lower labour cost countries outside Europe: China, Taiwan, Vietnam and more recently Indonesia. Since March 1994, the import of some Chinese toys into the EU has been restricted. This is expected to result in a 20% decrease of EU toy imports from China. In 1995, it was quoted that approximately 27% of the toys sold on the European market are imported from China.

7.3.   Trade barriers

7.3.1. Regulatory barriers

Manufacturers and importers have encountered difficulties with either national enforcement authorities or with their customers in different Member States. These are described below.

Safety regulations

As described above, most regulatory barriers related to safety have been removed, except for the hair loss issue. However, some problems remain with the mutual recognition of test results of notified bodies.

HD271, which is now EN50088, is a harmonized standard to cover the essential electrical safety requirements of the Toy Safety Directive. But the French interpretation of the above harmonized document is not equivalent to that of other Member States. European manufacturers reported that in France, the authorities test toys with batteries against NF73622. This is in some ways equivalent to HD271; however, HD271 measures the hazard in terms of temperature whereas the French NF will measure it in terms of the electrical current. Before EN50088 was published, the French national enforcement authorities required a specific test by LNE against NF73622 and did not recognize tests to HD271. This problem should now be resolved, but was still of concern to non-French suppliers at the time of the survey.

Television advertising harmonization

The trade association reports that its members complain about the discriminatory effect of restrictions on television advertising. Because they are consumer goods, sales of toys rely heavily on advertising and promotion campaigns. Television advertising rules are harmonized under the European Broadcasting Directive 89/552/EEC, but differences remain in each Member State. For instance, some Member States (allegedly Norway and Sweden) interpreted the Directive in such a way that they implemented national bans on television advertising for children. Greece introduced a law on advertising for children which limits the amount of broadcasting time. Manufacturers exporting to Greece consider that this specific new regulation is a regulatory barrier to trade since the Greek toy manufacturers enjoy the advantage of being established, whereas new imported toys cannot benefit from the impact of heavy advertising campaigns. (This seems to be a weak complaint since toy advertising is allowed in Greece. It may create, however, a rationing of available broadcast time, although this affects all suppliers, domestic or foreign.)

The Broadcasting Committee of TME has developed and established guidelines on advertising to try to pre-empt European legislation which would restrict advertising to children. These guidelines harmonized on a voluntary basis all the existing rules on advertising content. TME is pursuing plans to ensure the adoption of these guidelines throughout the EU.

Advertising restrictions, however, do not affect the product or packaging specification, or testing and certification requirements, and should not be considered as technical barriers to trade.

Recycling marks

Additional regulations and requirements arise from environmental recycling schemes and marks. Germany has the *Grüne Punkt* mark, France the *Point Vert* and Belgium the *Fost Plus*. These are all mandatory schemes. The UK is due to introduce a scheme, Val Pack, in January 1997.

A UK-based manufacturer reported that the schemes are different and therefore the firm had to apply all marks on its products. The complaint of manufacturers is that to sell in other national markets they have to join each of the national schemes: this involves additional administration and levies.

In Germany, packaging must carry the *Grüne Punkt* (Green Point) label, showing that a packaging recycling arrangement is used by the manufacturer. It is governed by the *Töpfer* law, *Verpackungsverordnung*, implemented in December 1991. It covers all types of packaging, so toy manufacturers wishing to succeed in the German market need to subscribe to the *Duales System Deutschland,* which collects a levy to pay for the collection and recycling of packaging from retail outlets. There is a different scheme for packaging which has a plastic window: manufacturers have to subscribe to the German *Gebrauchte Kunststoffverpackungen* regulations, known as VGK. These are legal requirements under the law on waste, the *Abfallgesetz*. There are additional environmental testing requirements in Germany which are apparently not enforced through regulations, and are listed in Section 7.3.2.

In France, manufacturers have to subscribe to the organization *Eco-Emballage* in order to obtain the *Point Vert*. This is implemented through *Décret* 92-377. *Eco-Emballage* uses the same symbol as the German scheme by a mutual arrangement.

Labelling and packaging issues

In France, the recent and controversial *Loi Toubon* (Toubon Law) regulates the use of the French language. Manufacturers and importers claim they are forced to use special wordings for the 'warning' labels. The French decree which imposes texts of safety warnings is the *Décret* 91-1292 of December 1991 which only applies to articles for children and it is comparable to the US regulations where the CPSC has defined official national warning wordings.

Importers and manufacturers also complain about language requirements demanded by retailers, which do not have a regulatory basis. For example, a British importer claimed that French retailers demand that the product description be translated into French. The toys were imported from the Far East and tested against the relevant EN standards in a laboratory based in the Far East. Whilst all toys bear the CE-marking and had the safety instructions translated into French as stipulated in the Toy Safety Directive, so were imported legally, the importer had to re-label the toys' description in French in order to sell in France. [The complaints from manufacturers about their customers' understandable wish for packaging and instructions in their own language seem surprising, and indicate a short-sighted attitude to basic marketing requirements.]

Differences in enforcement procedures

A Convention was signed between the French Toy Manufacturers' association *Fédération des Industries du Jouet* (FIJ), and the French enforcement authorities, the *Direction Générale de la Concurrence, de la Consommation et de la Répression des Fraudes* (DGCCRF) of the Ministry for the Economy and Finance. Whilst the Convention was set up in order to facilitate the enforcement of the Toy Safety Directive and the CE-marking, third parties view the Convention as a new national regulation which is a barrier to trade for non-members of the Convention. The FIJ has presented the Convention to TME as a working document to develop in other Member States. Manufacturers perceive that they have to respect certain unwritten rules in order to sell products freely on the French market: products have to be tested in France, and all documents must be produced in French. Should a foreign manufacturer meet all these requirements, it is less likely to have its products questioned. On the other hand, if the manufacturer cannot demonstrate that its products meet all characteristics and produce certificates in French, the same manufacturer is likely to go through stricter control procedures and could possibly have its product retested by the French authorities.

A Spanish manufacturer reported that in France, the DGCCRF checks its products and requests its technical file at least twice a year. Whilst France is one of its largest markets, this has seldom happened in other Member States which demonstrates that France has a strong enforcement policy. A French soft toy manufacturer reports that it also has to produce the technical file on a regular basis to the French authorities, so it is not a case of discrimination against importers.

7.3.2. Non-regulatory barriers

There were no significant non-regulatory barriers reported by the industry, with the important exception of testing requirements related to safety and environmental aspects of toys in Germany, where these aspects are not covered by the Toy Safety Directive and its associated harmonized standards. The requirements reported by toy manufacturers are described below. Similar requirements may exist elsewhere but were not reported by manufacturers so must be assumed to be insignificant.

National requirements in Germany

In Germany, a number of tests are habitually required by retailers, even for properly CE-marked toys. The precise status of these has been rather unclear. There is no apparent regulatory basis, but the need for them seems to have been promoted by the authorities. It appears that previous regulations may have been withdrawn or amended as a result of the Toy Safety Directive having harmonized safety requirements. Nevertheless, retailers feel obliged to request additional tests and certificates.

Doll manufacturers reported that the azo dyes test (relating to the benzene content in dyes) is required by retailers for all dolls, plush toys or similar toys. There is a national law on the use of azo dyes in consumer products called the *Zweite Verordnung der Bedarfsgegen-ständeverordnung.* The law was published on 15 July 1996, but does not cover toys. The Consumer Protection organization in Germany, the former *Bundesgesundheitsamt,* has published a text recommending that azo dyes should not be used in toys and this influences the purchasing criteria of retailers. A Spanish manufacturer was specifically asked by his German client (a large German retail chain) to produce an 'azo passport'. Without this, the retailer would refuse to pay the invoice. In order to clarify the issue, the TME addressed a letter to the German *Bundesministerium für Gesundheit.* The Ministry replied that toys and entertainment articles (according to para.5, indent1, no.5 LMBG) were not subject to the azo dye regulation. Members of the TME can now contact their clients showing the answer from the Ministry. A manufacturer claimed that the reply from the Ministry solved his problems with retailers and his products were now accepted with no azo certificate. Nevertheless, in the medium term, toy manufacturers will have to try to avoid the use of azo dyes in their products since it is demanded by their clients and it could become an additional requirement within EN71.

A similar requirement in Germany concerns the use of DEHP in plastics. German retailers insist on obtaining the DEHP test certificate. The German environmental agency, the *Umweltbundesamt,* published a number of documents which condemn the use of DEHP. Whilst there is no official regulation, a Spanish manufacturer considers this limitation as a new technical barrier to trade.

The case for the saliva and perspiration test for dolls' clothing is similar to the above examples. It is required by the national authorities and German retailers. Toy manufacturers claim that this specific test is only demanded for the German market. Again, there are no regulations. A Dutch manufacturer claims that he does not comply with this specific requirement although customers have been asking for this test for more than ten years.

A multinational firm stated that whilst its toys meet the Toy Safety Directive's essential requirements, it has to prove to a German retailer that its products comply with the European requirement on cadmium content. This is not part of the Toy Safety Directive, but German retailers enforce it for the customer's health and safety.

In effect, in the above cases, German retailers under advice from national agencies, are requiring tests not foreseen in EN71, and are not accepting the declaration of conformity with essential requirements that CE-marking indicates. It may be that these requirements will become part of the harmonized requirements, by being incorporated in revisions of the EN71 standard or in NoBo test procedures or by a separate directive, but at present German retailers are implicitly challenging the Toy Safety Directive and the credibility of CE-marking by requesting non-regulatory tests (as they are perfectly entitled to do). Retailers are probably afraid that if a toy is later shown by the consumer protection authorities to be hazardous, for reasons falling outside the scope of EN71, it will be withdrawn under safeguard procedures, leaving them with unsaleable stock and costs of disposal.

7.3.3. Testing and certification

Section 7.3.2 above has described a number of remaining national testing requirements which continue to present technical barriers to trade, not removed by the Toy Safety Directive.

As discussed in Section 7.1.4, however, there are also differences in testing procedures and in the control and accreditation of notified bodies which cause concern to exporters. This is due partly to differences in testing tradition and the status of the test houses which have become NoBos. In France the system is centralized with few NoBos and those who are traditionally accustomed to regulatory conformity testing, whereas in the UK there is the greatest number of notified bodies, some private with a background in process quality control or research and others under the local authority, but without a tradition of regulatory testing.

Manufacturers often use the notified bodies in their export markets, thus negating the intended benefit of the Directive, because they are not confident that testing in the home market would be accepted in the export market. Other manufacturers have claimed to shop around seeking best value for money, or the least strict testing. A number of cases were reported to the consultant where manufacturers had to re-test their products either to comply with additional customer requirements or to have the product re-tested by the national notified body. The following examples illustrate several issues on testing and certification.

> The time required to obtain test certificates is an issue which has been highlighted by the respondents. A Spanish manufacturer claims that for similar tests, the Spanish notified body will take up to 25 days, the French laboratory would take up to 35 days. The Spanish manufacturer alleges that the French notified body will give priority to local manufacturers.

> A German manufacturer claimed that in the UK, additional tests are necessary to prove that no more than 0.7g of dolls' hair falls out when combed 28 times with a 20mm comb. This specific case corresponds to the hair loss issue which has not been solved to date.

> A French importer uses either a British or a French notified body for tests against specific parts of the EN71 standards. The importer claims that test results differ.

> It was reported that in Spain, a notified body has met difficulties in having its certificates and the CE-mark accepted in other Member States. Spanish manufacturers of toys had to carry out additional tests in order to keep their toys on the market. As a result, in some cases, mutual recognition of testing between notified bodies is not working since some clients still prefer that test certificates be issued in their country.

An Italian manufacturer claims that French distributors insist on products being certified by their own national notified bodies even though the end consumer is not aware of the meaning of the notified body's reference.

A similar case has arisen recently for a German toy manufacturer with Chinese subcontractors. However, the German manufacturer established a company policy whereby a client wishing to have toys re-tested which had already been tested and CE-marked would have to bear the cost himself. This strong stance is only possible for manufacturers which are well established on the market.

In order to market their toys outside the single market, manufacturers still have to conform to certain national requirements. A manufacturer claims that Switzerland and Croatia, for example, do not accept tests carried out by the French notified body so re-testing is necessary. Other manufacturers claim when exporting to the North American market, toys must comply to the American standard, ASTM F963-92.

7.3.4. Quality policies and marks

The existence of quality marks in the toy manufacturing industry is limited. Multinationals claim that their quality mark is obviously their brand name and that they do not need any other kind of marketing tool. Some national marks still exist, described by the industry as marketing or commercial marks rather than quality marks.

(a)   In France the NF mark is granted by the French standards body, AFNOR, for specific toys.

(b)   In the UK there are two marks: the Lion mark granted by the British Toy and Hobby Association and the Kitemark, granted by the BSI, attesting compliance with BS safety standards, which is used for toys and many other products. The Lion mark is considered as a gentlemen's agreement where no control is carried out. The Kitemark is granted after testing against specific British Standards (or the relevant ENs, where these have replaced BSs, as for toys).

(c)   In Germany, the GS mark was previously mandatory for toys, and is still generally required by customers.

(d)   In Italy, the *Istituto di Sicurezza del Giocattolo* (ISG), also produces a label, Giocattolo Sicuro, which specifies that the toy has been checked by the institute and that it is safe. This label is added after the CE-marking.

(e)   In Spain, the national standards organization which is also a notified body, *Asociación Española de Normalisación* (AENOR), is currently working in cooperation with the national laboratory specialized in the toy industry on a project to develop a national quality mark, the UNE mark. The mark will not be granted unless the manufacturer has obtained QA certification to ISO9000.

Both the Kitemark and the GS mark are, in reality, safety marks and ought to add nothing to the CE-marking other than evidence of third party testing. One interviewee believed that the BSI Kitemark is losing influence. For one manufacturer obtaining the Kitemark costs approximately ECU 1,700 per product – not a large sum, but many manufacturers believe that since many toys have a short life cycle, the investment is not worth the commercial impact.

The industry often alleges that customers can be confused about the CE-marking. Industry seems to favour these national 'quality' marks, which they seem to think give them more protection against low-cost imports than the CE-marking. Nevertheless, the continuation of these national marks leads to double testing requirements.

A Dutch manufacturer claims that in Germany, customers identify with both the GS and the TÜV mark. This implies that a toy which bears the GS mark and the TÜV mark will be preferred to a toy which bears only the GS mark which has been granted by a French laboratory.

Some major retail groups also have their own testing requirements for toys. Some have their own in-house laboratories; others require that tests be carried out by a local test house. A Spanish manufacturer claims that his clients require, on a regular basis, that his product be re-tested. In most cases, manufacturers will adapt to their client's requirements. Only large multinationals are sometimes confident enough of their market power to be able to fight against preconceived ideas about testing requirements which they believe are unnecessary.

7.4.   Enterprise strategies

7.4.1. Product range

Importers and manufacturers interviewed reported that the Toy Safety Directive has not had a strong impact on their production and the product ranges for dolls and soft toys in 1995 compared to 1985. There are still differences in packaging between countries. There had never been national differences in the requirements of the toy itself. For instance, the 'Sindy' doll or the 'Barbie' doll is the same for the whole European market. In addition, multinationals claim that safety is a key success factor for building a brand name, so the Toy Safety Directive itself did not have a strong impact on their product range and production activities.

Nevertheless some manufacturers recognize that as a result of both the essential safety requirements and EN71, new prototypes are designed and created so that the toy strictly conforms to the Directive. This forces manufacturers to try new materials and become more innovative. The toy industry is not a highly technical industry. A Spanish notified body which works closely with manufacturers stated that the Directive has enabled manufacturers to learn and develop new techniques to remain competitive.

7.4.2. Investment

There is little apparent effect of the Toy Safety Directive on inward investment by non-EU toy manufacturers. Companies such as Mattel or Tomy were present in the European market before the establishment of the single market, and conversely EU manufacturers were investing on production in low-cost countries.

The total number of doll and soft toy manufacturers has reduced since 1985. This trend is related to the increased competition in Europe and the high labour costs attached to dolls and soft toy manufacturing activities. European manufacturers have adopted delocalization strategies and have set up production plants in third countries. Others have decided to sub-contract their activities to third countries, mainly the Far East.

Nevertheless a German manufacturer stated that prior to Spain joining to the EU, the country's national industry was well protected. The German manufacturer now has its own production plant in Alicante from which it supplies the Spanish and the Portuguese markets, representing 10% of total company turnover in 1996. This investment was probably facilitated by the general single market opening, though not perhaps specifically the removal of technical barriers.

7.4.3. Distribution and marketing

The EN71 standard has facilitated the harmonization of labelling and made packaging easier. Nevertheless, large multinationals still need to use several different packages and labels to be able to distribute their product throughout the single market. [While manufacturers could clearly save costs by using a single packaging, it is in the nature of consumer products that the packaging should be in the language of the consumer: this is a marketing issue and not really a technical barrier to trade.]

> There has been at least one Article 30 complaint relating to packaging of toys. This was a demand from Portugal that as well as the pictogram, toys in Portugal should bear the words in Portuguese, but since different packaging is needed for different language markets this is not really a major problem, although it is an important precedent. Manufacturers complained about language labelling requirements: they say, for example, that the packaging for smaller toys makes it difficult to allow enough space to print warnings in all European languages [such cases must be exceptional, and not the case for dolls and soft toys].

There is no evident impact on simplification of distribution and marketing channels or methods.

7.4.4. Organization and management

The impact of the single market and the measures implemented by the European Commission are perceived differently by multinationals and smaller manufacturers. Multinationals claim that the single market had no impact on their organizations and management. Smaller firms, however, have been forced to develop better quality management systems.

Some firms have taken on staff specifically to deal with issues relating to the Directive.

> A French soft toy manufacturer claims that he had to employ one person in order to follow up the safety issues and the technical requirements of the Directive. The person used to attend some CEN meetings; this role was passed on to the French Association technical representative.

7.4.5. Quality and testing

One of the important benefits of the Toy Safety Directive, beyond the removal of barriers by harmonization, is an apparent heightened concern about quality assurance and product testing throughout the industry. Manufacturers stated that the Directive has forced them to focus on the EN standards, thereby promoting better quality levels in the European industry. A further consequence of the Directive, reported by a number of manufacturers and trade associations, is that manufacturers have introduced new or stricter testing of their purchased materials and spare parts to ensure compliance with EN71 in the finished products.

Manufacturers acknowledge the benefits of the CE-marking and the Toy Safety Directive in reducing the number of different testing procedures required. A German manufacturer estimated savings at approximately DM 100,000 per year out of a turnover of DM 168 million in 1995.

Manufacturers claim that new investments were necessary with respect to testing equipment, for instance for the in-house flammability test and the strength of dolls' eyes. Nevertheless, such costs were not excessive. Since the implementation of the Directive, a number of systematic safety tests are carried out which had not been tested regularly before. The Toy

Safety Directive has forced manufacturers to establish stricter in-house quality management schemes.

A Spanish notified body confirms that the implementation of the Toy Safety Directive has been beneficial for the majority of manufacturers with whom they work. The implementation of standards and European directives has pushed manufacturers to improve and innovate. For instance, they foresee future environmental trends and have started to research new types of plastics or similar materials. The implementation of European measures forces manufacturers to prepare for changes and adapt.

Few manufacturers, however, choose to obtain the CE-marking through a third party. The EC type-examination test is perceived to be complicated and unreliable since it is the result of technical discussion between a notified body and the manufacturer. They jointly agree on the relevant test methods which would demonstrate that a toy meets the essential safety requirements. Manufacturers are concerned that the chosen testing method can be questioned by enforcement authorities, who may have defined other testing methods and procedures.

> A French importer claimed that notified bodies in France have refused to carry out EC type-examination because they would not accept the liability of certification when the product was not manufactured to harmonized standards.

Most manufacturers interviewed by the Consultant stated that they preferred to manufacture to harmonized standards with self-certification. They perceived this route as being safer. Manufacturers will carry out the simple mechanical tests in-house. However, they seek confirmation through product testing by a third party, which is likely to be a notified body. Self-certification of conformity is viewed as being quicker, cheaper and safer by most manufacturers.

7.4.6. Impact on competitiveness

There has not been a significant impact on manufacturing costs. The technical requirements are not burdensome. It was reported, however, by a British importer that the requirements of the Toy Safety Directive tend to be a burden for SMEs. Whereas large manufacturers dedicate one or more persons to quality management issues, smaller manufacturers cannot afford such a burden. It is often the Managing Director of the company who will carry out the CE-marking test requirements and other quality or safety activities.

> One British manufacturer claims that it is expensive to carry out all the testing procedures for type-examination and to have their products tested against the EN 71 standards. However, the product development manager believes that the CE-marking has helped in making intra-EU trade easier.

We found no evidence of an impact of the Directive on increased competition, enhanced products or consumer choice, or on reducing product prices as a result of increased trade or competitive pressure (although the direct saving in re-testing costs must have had a small impact on prices).

7.5. Conclusions

7.5.1. Effectiveness of approaches

The discussions with importers, manufacturers and distributors confirm that the Toy Safety Directive is performing well. Manufacturers claim that the Directive has brought great advantages and that 'it has saved time, effort and money', but raised some issues which would be solved by updating the EN standards. The harmonization of packaging and labelling standards is also seen to be positive, but the costs of different packaging are still considered to be important for small, regionally-oriented companies who wish to enter foreign markets for the first time.

Table 7.3. The effectiveness of approaches

Approach	Effectiveness[1]
Toy Safety Directive	*****
Harmonized standards	****
Coordination of testing procedures of notified bodies	**

[1] on a scale of 1-5 where ***** is the most effective
Source: W.S. Atkins.

The main concern of manufacturers is continued evasion of the Directive. ANEC reported that several studies have already been carried out into the safety of toys including the annual report of the Dutch General Inspectorate for Health Protection; the investigation carried out in June–August 1993 by the Swedish Board for Consumer Policies into the validity of CE markings; and the study by the Consumer Association of Ireland in August 1994 into whether toys distributed on the Irish market were safe. These studies showed that there are still a number of unsafe toys in these markets and that the CE-marking was not always justified. The national consumer associations are worried about this.

[The OECD has carried out a recent study entitled 'Consumer Product Safety Standards and Conformity Assessment: Their Effect on International Trade'. The final draft which covers toys as a case study is to be published by the end of 1996.]

7.5.2. Remaining barriers

Whilst some differences remain between national markets in customers' preferences, language and cultural issues, which require different marketing approaches, manufacturers and importers believe that the single market is performing well. The cultural differences are a sign of Europe's cultural diversity, not the result of national standards or regulations. The main problems are: the need for local testing because of customers' distrust of NoBos, particularly in France (a transitional problem); and azo and several similar additional testing requirements, particularly in Germany.

Table 7.4.   Remaining barriers in toys

Remaining barrier	Impact on industry[1]
Coordination of testing procedures	*
Customer testing requirements /semi-legal regulations (Germany)	****
Labelling requirements (France)	***
Environmental labels (Germany, Belgium and France)	*
Enforcement differences	**

[1] on a scale of 1-5 where ***** = the greatest impact
Source: W.S. Atkins.

7.5.3. Measures suggested by industry

Interviewees provided a number of views on improvements they would like to see in the functioning of the Directive:

(a)   develop the 'common approach' and ensure that notified bodies and enforcement authorities from each Member State regularly communicate views on implementation and enforcement;

(b)   develop the role of advice and consultancy from notified bodies;

(c)   develop a European standard which would define permitted plastics to be used in manufacturing toys (referring to the existing tight German regulations and cultural sensitivity to health and safety and environmental issues);

(d)   whilst work is underway on an ISO toy standard, the industry is in favour of the harmonization of the US ASTM standard and the Japanese toy safety standards with EN71.

8.   Circular woodworking saws

8.1.   Product information

NACE code: 327.1 – Woodworking machinery.

PRODCOM code: 29.40.42.35 – Sawing machines for circular sawing for wood, cork, bone, hard rubber, etc.

8.1.1.   Product scope

This report covers circular saws for working wood and a range of analogous materials – meat, cork, plastics, etc. In general, these saws are bench- or table-mounted and electrically powered. Hand-held saws are excluded, but the research did cover manufacturers of tractor-driven (non-electrical) saws.

8.1.2.   National regulations

In the past, circular woodworking saws – viewed in most countries' legislation as particularly hazardous products – were generally manufactured in accordance with national standards designed to ensure their safety. National approaches differed in terms of technical specifications laid down in the diverse body of regulations, the approach to testing, inspection and certification, and the body of national standards underlying national regulation and practice. These differences made circular saws (and other woodworking and similar machinery) subject to particularly difficult trade barriers.

Regulations relating to the marketing of products should now have been superseded by the New Approach directives (see below), but some relating to health and safety at work are still in place and are not expected to be replaced in the near future. In France, for instance, circular saws fitted to an optional table unit must comply with specific standards.

In some Member States, national regulation has traditionally been stringent. In the case of France, third party type-testing has been standard practice for many years, but this is not the tradition in other countries.

8.1.3.   New Approach and other EC measures

Three main NA directives apply to circular saws:

(a)   the Low Voltage Directive,
(b)   the EMC Directive,
(c)   the Machinery Directive.

The oldest of these, the Low Voltage Directive 73/23/EEC (LVD) is not a New Approach directive in the true sense since it has been in place since 1973, well before the formal adoption of the New Approach. The CE-marking requirement was introduced to the Directive by Directive 93/68/EEC, and the end of the transition period was 1 January 1997. The LVD was intended to specifically cover products where risk of electric shock was deemed to be the primary danger in use. It would apply to electrically-powered circular saws operating at below 1,000V AC.

The Electromagnetic Compatibility (EMC) Directive 89/336/EEC was first adopted on 3 May 1989 and came into force on 1 January 1992 with a transitional period ending on 31 December 1995. It covers any electrical device which might cause interference.

The Machinery Directive

The newest of the three Directives, and of most importance for circular saws, is the Machinery Directive 89/392/EEC (MD) adopted in its basic form on 14 June 1989. This Directive first entered into force on 31 December 1992 with a transitional period lasting three years and expiring on 31 December 1995. The transition period of the most recent addition, 93/44/EEC, adopted on 14 June 1993, ended on 31 December 1996, and extends the Directive to machinery for lifting people and to safety components sold separately.

The MD applies to a very wide range of mechanical engineering products[4] to which the general ERs apply. Some classes of machinery have additional ERs. The additional requirements for machinery for working wood and analogous materials (which includes circular saws) are described below. Circular saws also belong to a small group – around 5% of the total production of machinery – listed in Annex IV to the Directive, which are covered by specific attestation requirements which reflect their particularly hazardous nature.

Essential requirements

Annex I to the MD lists the ERs, which are set out in considerably more detail than other New Approach directives. The text and commentary on Annex I in the Commission's Guide to the Directive covers 45 pages. Paragraph 2(3) of Annex I sets out the special requirements for woodworking machinery, namely that:

(a) the machinery must be designed, constructed or equipped so that the piece being machined can be placed and guided in safety; where the piece is hand-held on a work bench, the latter must be sufficiently stable during the work and must not impede the movement of the piece;

(b) where the machinery is likely to be used in conditions involving the risk of ejection of pieces of wood, it must be designed, constructed or equipped to eliminate this ejection, or, if this is not the case, so that the ejection does not engender risks for the operator and/or exposed persons;

(c) the machinery must be equipped with an automatic brake that stops the tool in a sufficiently short time if there is a risk of contact with the tool while it runs down;

(d) where the tool is incorporated into a non-fully-automated machine, the latter must be so designed and constructed as to eliminate or reduce the risk of serious accidental injury, for example by using cylindrical cutter blocks, restricting depth of cut, etc.

Point (a) above is proving to be a point of contention since there continues to be disagreement at national level over permissible ratios between blade diameter and table width. The safety

---

4   Machinery is defined as: 'an assembly of linked parts or components, at least one of which moves, with the appropriate actuators, control and power circuits, etc., joined together for a specific application ...'. The Directive also covers 'an assembly of machines which, in order to achieve the same end, are arranged and controlled so that they function as an integral whole' (e.g. an assembly line); 'interchangeable equipment...' (e.g. a circular saw attachment for a tractor, even though it does not have its own power source); and 'safety components' (e.g. controls for a circular saw).

features which are mandatory under item (c) were not mandatory in all Member States before the entry into force of the Directive. In raising the level of safety, therefore, this requirement has also necessitated product modifications in many cases.

Conformity requirements

Circular saws belong to the group of products identified in Annex IV to the MD. Manufacturers of products not referred to in Annex IV need simply to draw up a technical file, as described in Annex V to the MD, and provide the declaration of conformity without the obligation of third party testing. Manufacturers of products which do fall under Annex IV have two options:

(a) if the product is manufactured in accordance with the relevant harmonized standards, the manufacturer may either:
  (i) simply send a technical file to a NoBo (only if the machine is totally in accordance with ENs which cover all the essential requirements), and optionally request the NoBo to verify from the file that the standards have been correctly applied; or
  (ii) submit a sample of the product to a NoBo for EC type-examination (in which case the NoBo takes responsibility for verifying that the machine meets the ERs, whether or not it is built in accordance with ENs).
  Either of these actions will lead to authorization to affix the CE-marking to the product;
(b) if the product is not manufactured to the relevant harmonized standards, then the manufacturer has no option but to submit the product for EC type approval by a NoBo authorized for testing circular saws.

There are currently no harmonized standards for circular saws, although 15 drafts are under preparation, under the management of TC142, and are expected to be ready by the end of 1996. This means that manufacturers of circular saws currently must submit products for EC type approval. This is causing difficulties for manufacturers since even small enterprises can have quite wide product ranges and specialized/custom-built equipment is quite common. This may mean that every single machine produced by a company might have to be type-tested.

There are currently 57 NoBos authorized to carry out type-testing of circular saws in the EU, plus 13 authorized only to receive technical files. The largest number of type testing NoBos are in Germany (14) and Italy (13), a reflection, perhaps, of the dominance of those countries in the manufacture of circular saws. Twelve of the 13 bodies listed as authorized only to receive technical files are in Spain (the other is in Norway).

It should be pointed out that in some countries the concept of mandatory type testing is relatively new, which can mean that the capacity and expertise to undertake type testing may be insufficient to meet demand (even though testing capacity in general is well developed). In others, France being a notable example, there is a long history of third party testing and the infrastructure is already well established.

8.2. Industry information

8.2.1. Sector representation

There are a number of national manufacturers' associations. The international association – European Committee of Woodworking Machinery Manufacturers (EUMABOIS) – has members from Switzerland, the Czech Republic, Germany, Denmark, France, the UK, Portugal and Finland. It is interesting that there is no Spanish or Italian representation on EUMABOIS, although both countries have national associations. This suggests that the industry is not particularly well coordinated at an international level and thus may well not have a common standpoint with regard to standards.

8.2.2. Industry structure

We have not gathered detailed information on manufacturers of circular woodworking saws. Italy is reported as being the dominant manufacturer of 'classical' woodworking machinery and has many enterprises, most of which are SMEs. Very few companies operating in the sector anywhere in Europe can be considered as large.

There are several Member States where circular woodworking saws are not manufactured at all. In others the industry is believed to be dying out. It was reported to us that the industry has almost disappeared in France and the UK (in the latter there is possibly only one manufacturer left today compared with six or seven at the start of the decade) and is under pressure in Germany and Portugal. While we have heard it suggested that some manufacturers dropped some product lines in anticipation of problems arising from Annex IV (particularly type testing of one-off machines) and the lack of supporting ENs, we understand that the larger number of withdrawals have been as a result of simple competitive pressures.

No separate figures for trade in circular saws appear to exist. It was pointed out to us, however, that most of the exhibitors at international trade fairs in the woodworking machinery sector are Italian.

8.3.   Trade barriers

8.3.1. Regulatory barriers

There do not seem to be any significant remaining regulatory barriers to trade.

8.3.2. Testing and certification

It is clear from published and anecdotal evidence that there are significant costs associated with MD compliance, especially in the case of Annex IV machines.

'Compliance Cost Assessment' (prepared for the UK DTI by March Consulting Group, July 1994) identifies both recurring and non-recurring costs arising as a direct result of compliance with the MD. These costs are defined as follows:

Non-recurring

(a)   redesign
(b)   investment in new equipment for manufacturing
(c)   sample production after redesign or respecification
(d)   testing (including transport costs)
(e)   certification
(f)   retraining of producers' employees
(g)   retraining of customers' employees
(h)   preparation of technical files

(i)   rewriting and printing sales and user documents

(j)   planning and implementing the compliance programme.

Recurring

(a)   fitting new or changing to more expensive components

(b)   altering manufacturing processes

(c)   changing to more expensive materials

(d)   CE-marking of the finished product.

The March report calculated that companies producing machinery for working materials analogous to wood and meat (which includes manufacturers of circular saws) would face non-recurring costs of approximately ECU 30,000 and recurring costs of ECU 10,000. These figures are significant, given that the manufacturers concerned tend to be SMEs. In very competitive markets, such as woodworking machinery, it may not always be possible to pass these costs on to the consumer.

The March report also suggests that the additional export sales which might be won through the MD and CE-marking would be unlikely to cover the overall costs of compliance with the Directive.

We were able to obtain several compliance cost estimates during our research. It has not been possible to verify these, and it should be borne in mind that in many cases the NoBos and the manufacturers are still learning how to carry out the attestation efficiently, and that high costs in the early stages may not be repeated. These costs should be compared with typical sales prices of the order of ECU 1,000 to 10,000, and typical batch sizes of one to a few hundred machines per year:

(a)   ECU 2,700 to type test a machine (a one-off cost for each product range) with total cost of CE-marking (product adaptation studies and documentation, new brochures and manuals) of ECU 5,000 (quoted by an SME manufacturer with a turnover of approximately ECU 1.75 million);

(b)   an estimated total cost of ECU 125,000 to achieve CE-marking (quoted by an SME, albeit a highly automated one with an apparently high level of production; the figure may be exaggerated);

(c)   ECU 9,000 for type testing of one-off saws;

(d)   another company claimed it costs ECU 25,000 per machine type to adapt equipment, carry out studies, produce new brochures and manuals.

These sort of type approval costs are evidently prohibitive for one-off machinery, but in practice manufacturers would have families of machines, and obtain type approval for a family, perhaps having only minor checks on variants. The cost of type approval is of real concern, however, for a product which is not of very high unit value.

8.3.3. Quality policies and marks

The use of quality marks does not appear to be widespread although there is evidence that products bearing the GS mark are favoured by customers in Germany, who may even demand the GS mark as well as CE marking. Insurance can sometimes be linked to these marks and achieving some user groups' marks can be effectively mandatory.

ISO9002 quality assurance accreditation is not considered to be important by manufacturers, who appear to think that reputation is more valuable.

Some companies have felt it necessary to bring in outside consultants to assess their products before submitting them to third party type testing.

8.3.4. Non-regulatory barriers

There do not appear to be any serious non-regulatory barriers to trade.

It has been suggested, however, that for commercial reasons related to the structure of the industry it is still difficult for many of the firms to enter foreign markets. A high proportion of manufacturers are SMEs and thus may lack the resources to undertake marketing outside their home base.

8.4.   Enterprise strategies

8.4.1. Product range

Because of the long-standing national regulations, in the main circular saws were safe even before the implementation of EU directives, but additional safety features have been incorporated in many cases as a direct result of the MD and the need for CE-marking. Frequently, manufacturers have been obliged to modify their products in order to achieve conformity with the ERs. Typically this has involved the fitting of additional safety features such as guards and improving braking systems (which bring the blade to a stop more quickly when the machine is running down).

There is no evidence that firms have been able to simplify their range of variants, or extend the range of models, as a result of the removal of previous national regulations.

8.4.2. Organization and management

We have received no evidence that manufacturers of circular woodworking saws have had to undertake any restructuring of organization or management as a result of the MD. It should be remembered that most manufacturers are SMEs.

8.4.3. Impact on competitiveness and customer choice

Manufacturers have noted an increase in trade. For example, there is reported to have been an increasing penetration by Italian manufacturers, which may well be attributed in part to easier trade as a result of the Directive (but they have also benefited from the depreciation of the lira, and other manufacturers complain of unfair pricing by Italian firms). This increased trade will have increased competitive pressures. A significant number of firms have been forced out of the market by the squeeze between competitive pressures and increased conformity costs. Those companies which were already producing to high standards may thus have benefited. A reduction in the number of small manufacturers is likely to have led to increased efficiency. The overall impact on prices, however, is reported by manufacturers to be upwards, as a result of enhanced safety features and conformity attestation costs.

It was suggested by some enterprises that the requirements of the ERs may oblige customers to buy machinery with safety features which they do not want [but clearly this is why legislation is necessary to protect users] or are impractical [which is presumably a design problem]. It was stated by several manufacturers that customers often disable or remove safety features in order to increase productivity. Several also complained that the standards produced for the MD have been written by academics and theoreticians and not by manufacturers.

8.5. Conclusions

8.5.1. Effectiveness of approaches

Before the MD, saw manufacturers needed to make to a variety of national standards if they wished to export to other countries. There was also a requirement for type testing in some countries, e.g. France.

CE-marking has removed the earlier requirement for French *homologation* via INRES and GS marking for German market, although some customers will still demand GS marks. Type-examination is now *de facto* necessary in all markets (not just France), and will continue to be necessary until or unless the forthcoming ENs cover all the ERs, but there should no longer be any requirement to use a French laboratory.

Customization is a problem since one-off products covered by Annex IV are not exempt from type testing (unless the one-off is a variant of an existing product and the alterations do not affect the level of safety of the product). There is a need to clarify the extent to which the MD will restrict customization and product development. There appears to be a divergence of opinion between industry and the bodies involved in setting the standards. The industry is also somewhat unclear how second-hand machinery will be treated in practice by the MD (originating both within and outside the EU). [The legal position is now clear: second-hand machinery has to conform and be CE-marked when it is first put on the market in the EU, but machinery formerly in use in the EU can be sold without CE-marking. Machinery in use, however, has to conform to the Directive on Use of Work Equipment (89/655/EEC), which requires that all machinery in use complies with the MD after 1 January 1997.]

The lateness of the ENs is a problem because it continues to impose a requirement for type testing on manufacturers of machinery covered by Annex IV. It presents a major burden. Because of this, national health and safety authorities are tending to take a lenient and relaxed approach to enforcing the MD, even in the case of imports from outside the EU. They tend only to act where machinery is patently dangerous or is fraudulently CE-marked.

A recent investigation in Sweden showed that only 50% of a sample of machines (including woodworking machines) met the rules for CE-marking. On some of the more dangerous equipment much of the required information was missing. Some 25% did not have a Swedish user's manual and 14% did not have any CE-marking.

Those companies not affected by Annex IV have few problems and are generally in favour of CE-marking and the single market measures in general.

8.5.2. Remaining barriers

No other remaining barriers were reported, now that multiple testing requirements are removed.

8.5.3. Measures suggested by interviewees

From the interviews, the main concern of industry is the lack of consistency of understanding and of enforcement of the Directive. Two main suggestions arise:

(a)   There does not appear to be an equivalent degree of understanding throughout the EU on the implications and workings of the MD. There is a need for a programme of education. This should include a better understanding for industry of the application of the MD and LVD.

(b)   There is reported to be a lack of consistency in the quality of work done by NoBos, both within Member States and when individual Member States are compared. This is an area that needs to be addressed since the system will collapse if it can be seen that NoBos are interpreting ERs in fundamentally different ways, and applying different criteria for attestation.

9.   Portable electric power tools

9.1.   Product information

NACE codes:
>   28.62 Manufacture of tools
>   29.24 Manufacture of other general purpose machinery n.e.c.

PRODCOM codes:
>   29.40.52.17 Other hand drills
>   29.40.52.25 Circular saws
>   29.40.52.27 Other (e.g. jig saws)
>   29.40.52.51 Angle grinders
>   29.40.52.53 Belt sanders
>   29.40.52.55 Others (e.g. orbital sanders)
>   29.40.52.57 Hand planing machines
>   29.40.52.90 Other electric tools

9.1.1.   Product scope

Portable electric power tools include electric hand drills, jig saws, angle grinders, sanders and circular saws intended for domestic use and in the workplace. The variety of portable electric tools has widened considerably in the last 20 years as manufacturers have taken the original concept of the pistol-style electric drill and designed new drive systems which have allowed the simple spindle rotation to be converted into reciprocating and vibrating motions. In addition, companies introduced tools with a percussive action which means that many jobs that were once almost exclusively performed manually or using pneumatic tools requiring an expensive compressed air supply can now be done using electric tools which need only a mains socket or sometimes just a battery pack. It is, therefore, an innovative product where rapid market access with flexible standards is important (and consequently the industry has supported the New Approach which minimizes product approval delays and allows attestation against essential requirements).

Portable electric power tools are split broadly into those which are intended for use in less demanding domestic circumstances and those which are intended for professional or heavy duty work. The domestic 'do it yourself' (DIY) tools are very similar in design and construction to the professional trade and heavy duty machines, generally differing only in their use of less robust key mechanical components such as bearings, gears and motors. The casings of some professional tools are also stronger to withstand knocks and the rigours of frequent use.

Smaller DIY tools such as entry level drills and screwdrivers made by reputable manufacturers are sold in European discount stores for as little as ECU 20–30. More complicated tools utilizing electronic controls and more powerful 500–750 and sometimes 1,000-Watt motors cost up to ECU 200. Standard professional tools are likely to cost around 1.5 times as much, whilst more elaborate and larger tools used, for example, on production lines and building sites can cost twice as much again.

Some manufacturers are active in a number of areas where there is synergy in product technology. Although many aspects of, for instance, electric garden tools, kitchen utensils and household appliances are similar, they are excluded from the scope of this report.

9.1.2. National regulations

Before the adoption of the New Approach, most electric products and especially tools deemed to represent a health and safety threat were governed by a multitude of national regulations, guidelines and certification procedures. Those relating to the marketing of products should now have been superseded by the New Approach directives (see Section 9.1.3), but some relating to health and safety at work are still in place, and are not expected to be replaced in the near future.

9.1.3. New Approach measures

As with circular saws (see Chapter 8), three main NA directives apply to portable power tools:

(a)   the Low Voltage Directive,
(b)   the Machinery Directive,
(c)   the EMC Directive.

The oldest of these, the Low Voltage Directive 73/23/EEC (LVD) is not a New Approach directive in the true sense since it has been in place since 1973, well before the formal adoption of the New Approach. The CE-marking requirement was introduced to the Directive by Directive 83/68/EEC, and the date of compulsory implementation was 1 January 1997. The LVD was intended to specifically cover products where risk of electric shock was deemed to be the primary danger in use.

The Electromagnetic Compatibility (EMC) Directive 89/336/EEC was first adopted on 3 May 1989 and came into force on 1 January 1992 with a transitional period ending on 31 December 1995. It covers any electrical device which might cause interference. Some manufacturers interviewed, however, believed that it covers only industrial products within certain critical environments and that portable power tools used at home, for instance, should fall outside its jurisdiction.

The newest of the three directives which covers portable power tools is the Machinery Directive 89/392/EEC (MD) adopted in its basic form on 14 June 1989. This Directive first entered into force on 31 December 1992 with a transitional period lasting three years and expiring on 31 December 1995. The transition period of the most recent addition, 93/44/EEC, adopted on 14 June 1993, ended on 31 December 1996, and extends the Directive to machinery for lifting people and to safety components sold separately.

The 'overlapping' problem

The electrical machinery industry is very concerned about the potential conflicts which might arise from the parallel application of these three Directives. This overlapping problem is thought by the industry to be of such importance that a two-day European conference on the topic was organized by CENELEC in early 1996. The electrical hand tool manufacturers would like to have it accepted that the hazards presented by their goods are principally electrical – they will then be able to comply only with the LVD, which is seen to be less burdensome.

No specific problems were quoted (except management time in resolving the question of which Directive applies to each product) but the potential problems are seen to arise from:

(a)   the possibility that standards developed under mandates from each Directive might place conflicting technical specifications or parameters on a product; and

(b)   the possible need for multiple attestation procedures.

The first potential problem has been tackled by setting up a joint CEN/CENELEC approach to preparing the standards and arrangements to ensure only one standard for each topic. CENELEC is also developing a cross-reference manual on application of directives and standards to products.

There is, however, a transitory problem for manufacturers because of lack of certainty and lack of information. Within industry associations and companies, managers and engineers disagree about whether their products are covered only by the LVD or whether the MD also applies. Most manufacturers argue that the LVD is sufficient for electrical hand tools and all companies claim that their products conform with its requirements (the LVD covers electrical and non-electrical hazards). The legal position appears to be that if a product falls within the MD's scope, then the MD also applies, unless the only important risks are electrical ones (Art. 1(5) of the MD says 'where the risks are mainly of electrical origin' the machinery is covered exclusively by the LVD). Some manufacturers prefer not to follow this interpretation in case their products have to go through two attestation procedures.

Although neither EN50154 nor the principal elements of the safety objectives of the LVD are expressed in the same way as the essential requirements of the Machinery Directive, most companies claim that their products are as safe as they can be and designed so that they conform to practically every aspect of the safety requirements of all three Directives anyway. Certain elements of the Machinery Directive and the EMC Directive are felt by manufacturers to place unrealistic demands on relatively cheap and simple machines such as power tools. Complying with all aspects of the EMC, especially, is considered by some companies to be expensive and unrealistic, as the following comment illustrates:

> One interviewee commented that his company's electric tools were already adequately fitted with interference suppression circuitry and that most users would not be completing home improvements whilst watching television. He also added that since the introduction of the EMC new forms of data transmission including satellite television, cellular radio and fibre optic cabling had become popular. In his opinion, even if the EMC is a statutory requirement, the related standards would be inadequate since they now failed to take into account these more recent forms of data transmission.

Such comments may be regarded as coming from individuals who wish to absolve themselves of responsibility, but they do serve to underline the difficulties which companies face in this particular area. Theoretically, if the standards are not considered appropriate it is not mandatory to manufacture to the standards, but relying on self-certification or EC type-examination is perceived by some manufacturers as risking potential liability claims.

> Documentation forwarded by one company to the Consultant illustrates the arguments advanced by power tool manufacturers. Its national trade body argues that the LVD is the valid Directive for power tools. It claims that this view is backed up by the text of the Machinery Directive and the guidelines to the LVD (MKY/pm-III/D/1 December 1995). The former states in Article 1 that: 'Where for machinery, the risks referred to in this Directive are wholly or partly covered by specific Community Directives, this Directive shall not apply, or shall cease to apply, in the case of such machinery and of such risks on the implementation of these specific directives (Art. 1(4)).' and also 'where for machinery, the risks are mainly of electrical origin, such machinery shall be covered exclusively by Council Directive 73/23/EEC of 19 February 1973 (Art. 1(5)).' In sections 5(i) and 5(ii) of the LVD guidelines it is stated that electrical goods already sufficiently well covered by the LVD and whose free movement is already

assured by that directive, are outside the scope of the Machinery Directive. The view of the Commission services is that there are important mechanical risks from hand tools, and that anyway free trade is not assured by the LVD, so the MD must apply also. The official advice of the national ministry enforces the Commission's intentions and states that if after conducting a risk analysis there is any doubt on the part of the manufacturer as to the nature of danger posed by its product, then both the LVD and the MD should apply. In addition, the ministry advises that manufacturers should strive to apply both Directives anyway.

Evidently, some of the arguments and opinions presented by industry and its trade associations are based on subjective reading and interpretation of documentation whose meaning may also have changed subtly in translation or whose intention conflicts with their business interests. In practice, however, all companies interviewed are pragmatic and simultaneously follow the LVD, the MD and the essential elements of EMC, but would like to see a simplification of the situation.

9.1.4. European standardization

Harmonized Standard EN50144 is a specific standard for hand-held electric tools, adopted in 1994. National standards are to be withdrawn by December 1996. This ensures that products shall be considered to meet the relevant principal elements of the LVD and gives presumption of conformity with the relevant ESRs of the MD. Some countries have existing standards in place. BS2769, for example, is the current UK standard and is the transposition of HD400, an older European harmonized document from the 1970s. It is, however, regarded by some manufacturers as being excessively stringent for domestic power tools.

Industry is not entirely in agreement with the new standard. Some manufacturers think it has characteristics which are more appropriate to pneumatic tools which are used continuously over longer periods. It was considered helpful, however, that the draft standard was distributed, in Germany at least, to numerous smaller companies before finally being agreed. This practice seems to be an unusual and valuable practice since many of the smaller companies cannot afford to be permanently represented on working groups, but would nevertheless like to be consulted. Some manufacturers interviewed also felt that too many persons from health and safety organizations were involved in the working groups which created an adversarial atmosphere. Companies making power tools indicated that they, as consumer-oriented organizations, wish to make products which customers will want to use and feel safe using, so self-interest would prevent them making products which are or are perceived to be dangerous. It would appear from this type of reaction that industry believes the harmonized standard has imposed stricter safety standards than they think the competitive marketplace would permit, so we deduce that the standards have raised safety levels at the lower end of the market, as well as harmonizing them.

9.1.5. Mutual recognition arrangements

The Consultant was not made aware of any mutual recognition arrangements governing power tools. Any that may have been in place have now been superseded by the New Approach.

9.2.   Industry information

9.2.1. Sector representation

The trade is represented in individual countries by a number of bodies such as the ZVEI (*Zentral-Verband der Elektroindustrie*) in Germany and PETMA (the Portable Electric Tool Manufacturers' Association) in the UK. Surprisingly, in some larger countries such as Spain there is no national association at all and in the UK none of the three companies represented by PETMA are British owned. On a European level, most companies are members of the European Power Tools Association, EPTA.

9.2.2. Industry structure

The industry in Europe is dominated by a few global companies, but with a large number of smaller specialist companies. The number of manufacturers of portable electric power tools has reduced considerably in the last ten years as the larger companies such as Bosch of Germany and Black & Decker of the US have moved to buy smaller companies and consolidated their position as European and global leaders.

The sector is dominated by Bosch and Black & Decker, with a group of upmarket companies such as AEG and Metabo. Japanese companies are increasingly important. A large number of smaller manufacturers represented nearly one quarter of the market. These numbers portray market share in terms of number of units sold but if one takes into account the higher selling price of most German products, the share by value of others, especially Far Eastern products, is significantly lower.

Table 9.1   EU market shares

	Market share (%)
Bosch	35
Black & Decker	20
AEG	7
Metabo	6
Japanese	13
Others	9

On a global level, Bosch and Black & Decker are leaders with 23% and 22% respectively. The relevant importance of Japanese manufacturers is now more apparent. Makita, a company with a significant presence in Europe, holds 18% of the world market and Hitachi and Ryobi have 8% and 5% respectively.

There has been significant recent internationalization of the sector. Bosch recently acquired SKIL, a Dutch company which sells primarily through discount warehouses, and Qualcast, a UK manufacturer of powered garden tools. The AEG brand name was recently bought by Atlas Copco of Sweden. AEG's electric power tools continue to be made in Germany but are now marketed by Atlas Copco alongside their own pneumatic range of tools catering primarily for the industrial market. Black & Decker has two Italian and one UK factory producing tools which are primarily aimed at the large number of light DIY users. The brand is particularly strong in the UK. It is interesting to note that the relative importance of the DIY market changes significantly from country to country. Although DIY is popular in the northern part of

Europe, southern Europeans spend far less on home power tools. Black & Decker reports that in Italy 95% of power tools sold are for the professional market. In the UK, on the other hand, nearly all the power tools sold by Black & Decker are for use in the home.

Smaller companies with a stronger regional presence such as Casals in Spain and Peugeot Outillage Electrique in France are much more dependent on their home markets. Increasingly, they feel themselves squeezed between the multinationals and cheap low quality products from the Far East. Although in the past Far Eastern and primarily Chinese products were not well regarded, the number of products has multiplied considerably, and Asian manufacturers have set up an office in Germany to research the market more thoroughly and to establish business contacts. The increased presence of these Asian importers represents the major threat to the established European companies.

9.3.   Trade barriers

9.3.1. Technical regulations

Despite the difficulties in agreeing which directives are applicable to portable electric power tools, the directives themselves are well established and universally recognized. The existence of a specific harmonized standard enables them to function well.

Only a few regulatory barriers remain. One of the most frequently quoted is the need to fit BS 1363 ASTA or BSI approved three-pin plugs to all 240V consumer appliances sold in the UK (Plug and Socket Safety Regulation 1994-1768). Many EU companies, which are normally required to fit the standard two-pin plug to their products, used to supply without plugs. This is no longer possible because plugs must now be fitted and wired on all consumer appliances before placing on the market. (Black & Decker avoid this problem by fitting a unique Black & Decker plug and selling extension leads separately with the appropriate plug for each market). In practice the original manufacturer needs to fit the plug, because if it is done by the importer or retailer, they become liable as a manufacturer. Apart from the need to fit a special plug for the Swiss market, the fitting of different plugs does not present a problem in other EU markets. Manufacturers accept the need to comply with historic differences relating to voltage and earthing which they do not regard as trade barriers. Although most of their products are designed for use in countries where the electricity supply is 220V at 60Hz, manufacturers (with the exception of one Spanish company) have not indicated that the UK's 240V 50Hz supply presents any practical difficulties.

Throughout Europe, health and safety bodies have resisted the introduction of lock-on switches for many types of industrial power tools and most saws. Lock-on switches allow an operator to continue using a piece of equipment without the need to hold the trigger which, over longer periods, can induce fatigue. Lock-on switches are allowed for certain types of power tool, but must be designed in such a way that they can not be activated accidentally. In France, for instance, there is a specific regulation that covers belt sanders over 124mm diameter requiring the lock-on switch to be placed in such a way that it cannot be reached easily without moving the hand. Manufacturers are sympathetic to the reasoning behind restrictions on lock-on switches, but claim that customers would prefer a lock-off switch to prevent accidental operation.

> One major manufacturer complains that the tool made for the French market must incorporate a design change to the lock-on switch at significant extra cost.

Another major company states that although a lock-on switch is generally allowed in Germany, products sold in Finland are not allowed to incorporate it. A company sales representative claimed, however, that many workers disliked having to depress a trigger for long periods and sometimes used adhesive tape to hold the trigger down, preferring instead to switch a machine off at the mains supply. He also noted a difference in attitudes towards health and safety generally, with older workers in many factories resisting attempts to introduce health and safety regulations. Although younger workers were keen to work with better enforced rules and regulations, a high proportion of older colleagues were prepared to accept risks that would allow them to maintain higher piece rates. If accidents happened some workers believed that they would receive generous compensation.

Two manufacturers have indicated specific problems with semi-portable circular saws, because it is not clear whether the harmonized standard for hand-held tools is sufficient for saws that are fitted to a small table or are semi-portable, which would then fall under Annex IV to the MD.

Hand-held saws, when fitted to an optional table were no longer deemed by the Finnish health and safety inspectorate to meet the ESRs of the MD [we believe this is because they require a different type of guard when mounted in an upside-down position] although the product was freely sold in Germany. The manufacturer was not, however, barred from selling the saw and table separately in Finland, but had to declare the combination of saw and table not to have the CE-marking. [The Finnish position may be reasonable: the question then is whether the same restrictions on sale of an unsafe product should be applied everywhere.]

In another case, a company wished to make a range of semi-portable circular saw benches for the European market. They were deemed to fall under Annex IV to the MD (see chapter on circular saws) and the standards for portable tools were not considered to cover all the ERs. The manufacturer used available DIN standards as a guide and contracted one of the TÜV agencies in Germany to undertake an EC type-approval. The TÜV found the saws to be in accordance with the essential requirements, and saws were exported to, amongst other countries, France. The French authorities stated that for certain models the relationship between the saw blade diameter and the table area did not conform to a fixed ratio prescribed in a prEN. The manufacturer believes that as the saw is type-tested by a notified body and the prEN is not yet a valid document, the table is legally saleable and it is resisting attempts to have the saw table banned [in fact, if it was indeed properly given EC type-approval by a NoBo, it is not mandatory to follow harmonized standards]. A French users' group is monitoring the situation and, maybe surprisingly, its German equivalent has indicated that it would not find the tables acceptable. In light of this, another manufacturer has taken note of the prEN and is making its tables to the new dimensions.

9.3.2. Non-regulatory barriers

Electrical hand tools are now widely and freely traded, and as we have seen most manufacturers are multinational and sell world-wide. Market shares vary somewhat between countries and regions, but the same manufacturers are present in all markets, and usually with the same ranking of shares. This is evidence that whatever other barriers remain, they are not significant in impeding trade. Industry nevertheless raised a number of perceived problems, which may require further development of the standards, but are not strictly barriers to trade.

Voltage is another issue. The UK Health and Safety Executive used to require that electrical plant and equipment destined for use on UK construction sites operate on 110V, which was perceived as being safer than the standard 240V used in domestic situations. Under the Use of Work Equipment Directive (89/655/EEC) this is no longer mandatory, and there is only a recommendation that it does so. The fact that the UK's construction industry is very safety conscious and that 110V is 'preferred' by insurance companies has, however, forced companies to continue to offer tools which work at a lower voltage.

Of particular concern to the industry is Raynaud's phenomenon, more commonly known as Vibration White Finger (VWF). Subsections of EN50144 stipulate permissible noise and vibration levels but all manufacturers are worried about this problem and other vibration-related ailments. One interviewee working for a major manufacturer expressed doubts over the degree to which competitors actually adhered to this aspect. Another smaller company believed that noise and vibration were well covered by the EN and that there was no problem in this area. A recent court ruling reported in a British journal indicates that the problem may, however, be significant. In the case brought by ex-miners, the judge ruled that the employer should have been aware of the risks of VWF resulting from power tools (these cases would have occurred before the MD and the EN50144 were in force). It is estimated that in the UK alone there could be 100,000 potential claimants [but no evidence of this causing a technical barrier were given].

One area which potentially presents a problem to manufacturers, but is not really a technical barrier, is in the tool hire sector. In the UK particularly, many tools are sold to hire companies who then rent them out on a daily or weekly basis to professional and domestic users. Rental equipment generally has to conform with standards laid down by the biggest companies in the sector or their trade association. One such company, HSS in the UK, demands a flash test, designed to verify electrical insulation. This 3000V insulation breakdown test was originally designed to be used on a one-off basis to ensure the insulation properties of new products, but it is now supposedly used after every hire to verify continuing insulation performance. This does not represent a cost to the manufacturer *per se*, but one manufacturer has indicated that the ongoing use of such a test might actually begin to damage the product and undermine the insulation that it is supposed to check [and so might require product adaptation in response to this additional testing, and perhaps need a development of the standard]. The UK's electrical engineering body, the IEE, does not recognize the need to flash-test.

Some manufacturers reported that the biggest barriers to the use of power tools were workplace rules frequently laid down by trade unions influential in local authorities.

Other issues raised by the industry appear to be of relatively minor importance. Council Regulation (EEC) No 880/92 (OJ L 99, 11.4.1992, p. 1) covering eco-labelling of products has not yet been adopted by certain countries including Spain and Italy and there is at present only limited agreement on how associated costs of recycling packaging are to be paid. These issues are general, though, and not limited to the power tool sector.

9.3.3. Testing and certification

Manufacturers agree that there have been significant savings as a result of the removal of multiple testing requirements, but a few special requirements still exist.

Some government organizations and user groups require additional testing. In the UK, the Ministry of Defence specifies the BSI Kitemark and compliance with NATO standards [but it is not clear whether there are NATO standards applicable to hand-held power tools], although only one company interviewed indicated that it sells to the military. In France and Germany user groups are influential, especially in the woodworking sector. One such group in Germany specifies its own technical standards and sets maximum requirements for dust particle concentration within breathable air.

The cost of testing can be high, especially if conformance with different directives must be conducted by different agencies.

> One Spanish company reviewed the performance of testing institutes in its own country and found them to be inefficient. It now ships its tools to a laboratory in Germany to be tested for adherence to EMC and to Italy and Denmark for testing MD and LVD compliance. The company in question estimates that it has spent PTA 10 million (ECU 60,000) in new equipment for in-house testing and must pay around PTA 45,000 (ECU 280) for each appliance to be independently tested. For larger customers in Spain, the company is also required to offer further proof of conformity in which case it presents a document known as the NTR which summarizes the standards with which the tool complies. This costs around PTA 200,000 (ECU 1,250) but is regarded as being worthwhile. [It should be noted that none of these requirements are mandated by the Directives: the first case is the choice of the manufacturer to ensure himself that his products comply; the second case is a requirement of his customer, and the costs should perhaps be considered part of the normal costs of doing business, not additional costs caused by technical barriers, or by compliance with the MD itself.]

When the MD was first introduced some domestic manufacturers and importers of power tools experienced difficulties with the Spanish enforcement authorities, having to explain testing procedures, prove conformity and replace labels which did not include appropriate reference numbers. Early problems related to these procedural issues have, however, now been clarified and the system in Spain works well.

> A French company interviewed in this survey reported that prior to the introduction of CE marking it had to certify its products in accordance with national requirements using, for example, INRS in its home market and GS in Germany. This was a lengthy process often taking up to 18 months. Today, it certifies its products in-house and applies the CE marking itself, also using it on the packaging, because many Chinese products still do not have CE marking and the company believes it can differentiate its products effectively in this way.

> Not having to comply with Finnish regulations demanding electrical tests has saved one multinational the 2% of annual turnover in power tools that used to be levied. The mandatory FI marking service has been made redundant by CE marking.

Companies report transitional costs in adapting their testing policies and procedures to the requirements of the Directives. In the opinion of one larger manufacturer, it and many other companies in the British engineering sector are still not well acquainted with the requirements of the MD and associated CE marking, and it spent a considerable period of time researching the issues before acquiring a degree of confidence that it was properly meeting the requirements. It now uses the BSI to independently test all its products (even when EC type-examination by a NoBo is not required). Companies in other countries have described similar experiences and most have followed the same pattern of designing products to conform with the safety requirements of the three Directives, and then having the tools tested by independent bodies (not necessarily NoBos, and although this is not mandatory under the MD). One smaller German company regards independent testing to be a form of insurance.

9.3.4. Quality policies and marks

Although not a legal requirement in EU countries, many companies continue to use quality marks awarded by recognized bodies. Foremost among these are the Kitemark in the UK, GS in Germany and the French INRS, especially important for woodworking tools. An attempt by one of the German woodworking tools users' groups to introduce its own quality mark is being resisted by the German government who fears that this would be regarded unfavourably by its EU partners.

Despite the requirement for some sector-specific quality marks, the overall trend is to reduce dependence on quality marks. On the whole companies are not convinced of the benefits and find that they are expensive. The Kitemark, for instance, is the exclusive property of BSI which operates the marking service under a Royal Charter, but its worth is debatable, especially since it is more expensive than an equivalent GS/TÜV mark which is internationally better known. Another mark, the IMQ Mark, awarded by the Italian organization and used by a multinational on its products sold in Italy, is also losing favour and the company doubts that it will continue to apply it.

In Switzerland, the USA and certain former Soviet Union states, quality marks can be mandatory and companies selling to these markets will have to continue using them for the time being.

9.4.   Enterprise strategies

9.4.1. Product range

Opinion differs on the effect that the single market and associated directives have had on product range. Because electric hand tools were already covered by the LVD, most companies have pointed out that cost of conformity has not dropped substantially, but that rules and country requirements have been significantly simplified. Using a single conformity assessment procedure, they can now obtain the CE marking and sell similar or identical products throughout the EU. Simpler tools such as drills were and continue to be exported without any difficulty and these products have been little affected by the adoption of the New Approach.

With single certification procedures now in place, more complicated tools such as planers, circular saws and angle grinders can now be made to an almost universal standard. In conjunction with in-house strategies to globalize R&D and develop a modular approach to design, companies should now be able to reap the benefits that one-stop certification can bring. As most companies have steadily enlarged their product range over the years, any simplification in design and lower tooling costs should result in appreciable savings.

9.4.2. Investment

The New Approach has probably helped European companies achieve economies of scale in some areas, but major investment decisions amongst the larger companies are usually driven by the cost of logistics and local labour. Makita, Bosch and Black & Decker all have numerous plants throughout the world with mostly centralized R&D facilities in the home market. In some cases, they have also made use of investment grants to establish low-cost assembly plants that can compete with those in the Far East. Each of the major firms, however, serves the whole EU market from a small number of plant locations where investment is concentrated.

The industry now clearly benefits from economies of scale from selling in a European market, and this has, to a large extent, been facilitated by the closure or acquisition of less efficient manufacturers.

Smaller companies such as Peugeot Outillage Electrique, Metabo and Casals have either relied on their home market or concentrated on upmarket or specialist machines. The smaller

German companies, especially, are forced to charge higher prices than their competitors and tend to market only premium products.

9.4.3. Distribution and marketing

Because harmonization began with the LVD, it is difficult to identify any changes in marketing policy. It is clear, however, that design, packaging and marketing policies of the major firms are increasingly similar across all countries.

Packaging is dependent on company policy. Whilst some companies customize their marketing approach and packaging to perceived or actual country requirements, other manufacturers, particularly the larger ones, have adopted multilingual or visual based instruction sheets and packaging intended to serve all EU markets. Where necessary, translations carry local certification, but for the most part products and packaging are becoming uniform.

European regulations covering recycling are being introduced at different speeds across the EU and whilst some companies have decided to do the minimum necessary, others have decided to conform to the most stringent requirements and use this packaging in all markets.

9.4.4. Organization and management

The removal of barriers has enabled this industry to be led by global firms with a global management outlook whose R&D centre might be in Japan, the USA or Germany, but whose plants may be in Italy, the UK or Switzerland.

One consequence is that the major firms dedicate considerable time and resources to regulatory and trade issues. At least two of the interviewees in the larger companies visited were or had been engaged in regulatory matters full time. Small manufacturers in particular were concerned that they were disadvantaged by not being able to devote staff to investigate regulation and market-oriented quality issues on the same basis as their larger competitors.

9.4.5. Quality and testing

The increased demands of the three Directives, the LVD, MD and EMC, have placed additional requirements for testing, certification and quality assurance on all companies, especially those whose testing was previously limited to ensuring conformity with local requirements. The impact has been disproportionately high on smaller companies with a lower investment budget. The large firms have significant in-house R&D and testing facilities, and while we have no direct evidence, it is likely that there has been increased investment in in-house testing facilities which will enable manufacturers to improve the quality of their product and reduce the dependency on third party facilities.

9.4.6. Impact on competitiveness and customer choice

In theory, following the implementation of the New Approach and the long-term savings associated with it, the consumer might have expected the cost of domestic and professional power tools to fall. Whilst none of the companies interviewed have declared that their selling prices have reduced as a result of the single market and lower design and production costs, they have spoken of a downward trend precipitated by more competition from non-EU countries.

The Chinese, in particular, have spent much time in improving their portable tools. Several years ago, Chinese exports, although cheap, were of poor quality and not likely to last. Now, many are close to conforming with all directives and have much better performance. [An interviewee alleged that there are still Chinese tools on the market which are CE-marked and do not conform with the ESRs, and that some claim to have had tests done by EU test houses – we have been unable to verify these allegations. Some Chinese tools on the world market are also alleged to have designs, logos and packaging which are close imitations of those of EU firms.]

In Shanghai there is apparently a large central R&D centre which is working on improving the design and production of power tools destined to be sold in large numbers on the world market. The engineers employed there are highly regarded, some of them having visited European companies to award a mandatory certificate necessary for export to China. Inevitably, this certificate costs money and must be renewed yearly. Although smaller companies cannot always afford such annual fees, because of its sheer size China is viewed by many to be an important market, but their inspection and testing of imports is seen by manufacturers as a way of obtaining technical data about their competitors' new products.

Several years ago and on behalf of its trade association, an EU manufacturer bought some imported machines sold in discount chains which, when subjected to the usual tests, overheated and were considered unreliable and unsafe. A short while ago, however, the company purchased some 580W angle grinders for less than ECU 10. These were found to be of quite adequate quality and lacking only in certain areas. The equivalent machines in the EU manufacturers' catalogue, although of better quality and with full service back-up, would be two or three times more expensive.

9.5.   Conclusions

9.5.1. Effectiveness of approaches

After many years in which manufacturers of portable power tools looked to the LVD and HD400 as a guide to design and manufacture, the introduction of the EMC and Machinery Directives has caused some initial confusion. Manufacturers claim that official guidance has been inadequate and is more likely to lead to further debate than a satisfactory outcome.

Despite this, the evidence from the market is that harmonization has been very effective, with common products across the EU, and noticeably improved value for money and choice, and very innovative products.

Table 9.2.   Effectiveness of measures for power tools

Measures	Effectiveness[1]
Low Voltage Directive	****
Machinery Directive	****
EMC Directive	**
EN50144	****

[1] on a scale of 1-5 where ***** = the most effective
Source: W.S. Atkins.

9.5.2. Remaining barriers

For the most part, non-regulatory barriers are not a problem within the market for DIY tools, although tools sold for use in the workplace are subject to certain restrictions arising from health and safety in the workplace guidelines. The fact that some insurance companies offering cover in, for instance, the UK construction sector and the French and German woodworking industry prefer 110V tools or tools which have been accredited by user groups, effectively makes these requirements mandatory: but it is not viewed as a problem [manufacturers have to make 110V tools anyway for other markets].

Companies interviewed in this survey have not, however, complained vociferously about these requirements and are far more concerned with the cost and difficulty of complying with directives.

Remaining technical barriers are indicated in Table 9.2.

Table 9.3.   Remaining barriers to trade for power tools

Remaining issues	Importance of resolving issues[1]
Hire tool test requirements	**
UK construction site 110V requirements	**
German, French user certification	***
Lock-on switches rules	***
Semi-portable saws	**

[1] on a scale of 1-5 where ***** = the most important
Source: W.S. Atkins.

9.5.3. Measures suggested by industry

The remaining issues which industrialists are concerned about are:

(a)   the industry still seeks clarification on the application of the MD and LVC Directives;

(b)   enforcement needs to be improved so that products which do not conform are not sold.

10. Domestic gas cookers

10.1. Product information

NACE code: 29.72 – Manufacture of non-electric domestic appliances

PRODCOM codes: 29.72.11.13 – Cooking appliances, plate warmers, for gas fuels with oven
29.72.11.15 – Cooking appliances, plate warmers, for gas fuels without oven

10.1.1. Product scope

This study deals mainly with one type of gas appliance, the common domestic gas cooker. However, wherever possible and relevant, mention will be made of other gas appliances such as gas heaters and gas fires in order to assess the impact of the New Approach on the gas appliance industry.

10.1.2. New Approach measures

Domestic gas cookers have to comply with the Appliances Burning Gaseous Fuels Directive (90/396/EEC), commonly referred to as the Gas Appliances Directive (GAD), adopted by the Council on 29 June 1990 and amended by the CE Marking Directive 93/68/EEC. The GAD entered into force on 1 January 1992 and the transition period came to an end on 1 January 1996. All domestic gas cookers must now bear the CE marking prior to being placed on the market.

In addition to the GAD, domestic gas cookers also have to comply with the Low Voltage Directive (LVD) and Electromagnetic Compatibility Directive (EMCD).

Standards

There are two draft harmonized European standards for domestic gas cookers: the prEN 30.1 dealing with safety and prEN 30.2 dealing with efficiency. There is also a harmonized document, HD 1003 dealing with surface temperature. The elaboration of standards for gas cooking appliances is carried out by CEN's Technical Committee TC49 in which the representatives of the main European manufacturers participate actively.

Conformity assessment

Manufacturers of domestic gas cookers have to apply one of the following conformity assessment procedures (as described in Annex II) which all involve a notified body:

(a) EC type examination with EC declaration of conformity to type (Module C) which involves on-site random testing of appliances by a notified body;
(b) EC type examination with EC declaration of conformity to type (Guarantee of production quality) (Module D) whereby the Quality Assurance System for production and testing is approved by a notified body;
(c) EC type examination with EC declaration of conformity (Module E) whereby the Quality Assurance System for inspection and testing is approved by a notified body;
(d) EC type examination with EC verification (Module F) which involves checks by a notified body on each appliance or on a statistical basis.

At present, there are 19 notified bodies under the GAD. These are located in Europe as follows: six in the UK; three in Germany; two in Italy; one in Ireland; one in Austria; one in Belgium; one in Denmark; one in the Netherlands; one in Spain; one in Portugal and one in France.

The Gas Appliances Directive Advisory Committee (GADAC) was recently created as the notified bodies' coordination group. The GADAC works in very close co-operation with the experts from each Member State and the industry representatives and endeavours to harmonize notified bodies' testing procedures.

10.1.3. Mutual recognition arrangements

There are no mutual recognition arrangements for testing of domestic gas cookers in Europe. With GAD in place and working well, such arrangements are not necessary.

However, the negotiations currently taking place between the EU and the USA to reach a mutual recognition agreement were often mentioned and eagerly anticipated since the US remains a very difficult market to penetrate.

10.2.   Industry information

10.2.1. Sector representation

Gas cooker manufacturers are represented at European level, through their national trade association, either by the *Confédération Européenne des Fabricants d'Appareils de Chauffage Domestique* (CEFACD) or by the European Committee of Manufacturers of Electrical Domestic Equipment (CECED). Originally, the CEFACD was the sole representative of the gas appliances manufacturers and the CECED that of the electrical appliances industry. Today, because of the evolution of the industry, such a differentiation is no longer as clear cut since the associations have members who manufacture both gas and electrical appliances.

At national level, some countries have a single trade association representing both gas and electrical domestic appliance manufacturers, as is the case for example in Italy and France; others offer two associations, corresponding to the two different energies used, as for example in the UK.

The European trade associations' roles include: participation in CEN's standardization work, co-operation with the Commission regarding the legislation and representation of members' complaints to European institutions. Many manufacturers keep in very close contact with their national trade association for updates on the standardization work in order to conform as soon as possible with the latest projected standards.

10.2.2. Industry structure

Since the 1980s, the white goods industry has undergone a number of mergers and acquisitions. In 1996, as Table 10.1 shows, the European market was almost entirely dominated by multinationals.

Table 10.1.   The top five European domestic appliances manufacturers and their share of the European market

Domestic appliances manufacturers	Country of origin	Estimated European market share in 1994 (%)
Electrolux	Sweden	23
Bosch-Siemens Hausgeräte	Germany	17
Merloni	Italy	10
Brandt Electroménager	France	9
Candy	Italy	n.a.

Source: Panorama of EC industry, 1995.

In terms of the world market, the largest producer of domestic appliances is Whirlpool (US), which has marketing links with Philips.

The mergers and acquisitions trend is expected to continue over the next five years, albeit at a slower rate. The SMEs that remain in the market usually have a particular niche and/or manufacture very sophisticated goods. Relocation of production facilities to low-cost countries (mainly in Asia) is also part of the multinationals' low manufacturing costs strategy. Such relocation is made possible by the fact that white goods are relatively low technology products.

European white goods manufacturers are looking increasingly to expand into the newly industrialized and developing regions since the market in industrialized countries has reached maturity and offers limited prospects. The greatest potential lies in South-East Asia, Central and South America, the Middle East and Eastern Europe.

10.2.3. Output and trade

As Table 10.2 shows, Europe is a main producer of gas cookers with ECU 172.2 million traded within the EU and ECU 172.3 million exported to non-EU countries. Since the adoption of the GAD in 1990, intra-EU trade has increased steadily and so have extra-EU exports, albeit at a much slower rate. Extra-EU imports reached a peak in 1993 of ECU 73.3 million and then decreased in 1994 to ECU 57.7 million. This figure should decrease further as Sweden, one of the main producers of domestic gas cookers, has joined the EU.

Table 10.2.   Gas cookers: intra- and extra-EU trade, 1988–94 (million ECU)

	1988	1989	1990	1991	1992	1993	1994
Intra-EU trade	110	111	106	119	121	141	172
Extra-EU imports	18	21	25	43	67	73	58
Extra-EU exports	111	136	112	141	148	168	172

Source: Eurostat.

10.3.   Trade barriers

10.3.1. Regulatory barriers

Domestic gas cookers are one of the products of the GAD for which very few technical barriers to trade remain. Manufacturers of other appliances such as gas heaters or gas fires have to face more stringent national regulations, particularly regarding emissions of CO_2.

The following barriers still remain:

Germany

The installation of a flame safety device (FSD) on each burner of the cooker is a regulatory requirement in Germany whereas in other Member States, the UK for example, generally only one flame safety device is installed per cooker. According to manufacturers, this FSD requirement adds ECU 65 to the production cost of a gas cooker. However, for many manufacturers and particularly SMEs the export market more than the home market has been driving production. Moreover, FSDs seem to have become a world-wide trend and a customer requirement.

Austria

Austria demands additional features, particularly with respect to ovens, which have to be fitted with a special thermostat to control temperature when working below 100°Celsius.

Permitted levels of NO_x and CO emissions are not fixed in the GAD, but a harmonized document on the environment and gas appliances was adopted and circulated by CEN in 1994. Despite this document, some Member States continue to determine unilaterally very low levels of emissions which constitute a barrier to trade for manufacturers. This is the case of Germany and Austria which recently passed new legislation fixing much lower levels of NO_x and CO emissions than those recommended in CEN's harmonized document.

Belgium

EN437 is a harmonized standard dealing with horizontal issues such as appliance categories (1, 2 or 3 depending on the gases the appliance can work with). Belgium has been trying to impose its own classification of appliances, different from the one set in EN437, thus creating confusion within the industry. Although this problem does not on its own constitute a big obstacle to trade, manufacturers feel the attitude behind it needs to be opposed if further fragmentation of the market is to be avoided.

Faulty implementation of the Directive

The diversity of gas distribution, gas types and gas pressures remains an impediment to the manufacture and trade of a cooker that could be used throughout Europe. The pressures at which gas is supplied vary greatly not only in Europe but also within Member States. Manufacturers need to adapt their product for each market and use different gas fittings. A Belgian customer could not use his/her cooker in Italy; it would be at best inefficient, at worst it could potentially be quite dangerous. The Directive tried to ease the problem by stating in its Article 2(2) that Member States must declare what gas and what pressures they use. This would allow manufacturers to adapt their products accordingly. However, this requirement of the GAD has not been fulfilled, and the differences in gas network standards remain a technical barrier to trade.

The harmonization of gas types, distribution and pressures is often compared to the harmonization of plugs in Europe and is not considered a cost-effective measure to take. Moreover, harmonization would require gas distributors to invest in new equipment and systems, without there being a direct benefit to them. Gas distribution in Europe is still very much in the hands of state-owned or local authority monopolies (with a few notable exceptions, such as the UK).

10.3.2. Testing and certification

The harmonization of conformity assessment is considered by manufacturers to be the main benefit of the Directive. Before the introduction of the Directive, manufacturers had to repeat product testing and certification in each country of export. This was time consuming because the design and technical dossiers had to be provided in the language for each model and personnel were required to follow national regulations and procedures.

However, after the publication of the GAD it became increasingly obvious that notified bodies interpreted the Directive and conducted the tests in very different ways. The GADAC was created as a forum for notified bodies, at which the Commission and manufacturers could agree on an interpretation of the essential requirements of the Directive and on the procedures and tests to assess conformity with them. To date tests are still not harmonized and discrepancies between testing procedures of notified bodies can be wide, creating a feeling of mistrust.

Conformity assessment procedures have been harmonized with the Directive, but it is still the case that several tests and certifications remain necessary in order to obtain national quality marks.

10.3.3. Quality policies and marks

Since the implementation of the Directive and the compulsory CE marking, testing and certification bodies are said to have lost two-thirds of their income. As a result, in an attempt to regain some of the lost income, national quality or performance marks have proliferated. In almost every Member State a mark or label has been introduced or reintroduced. This is particularly the case in the fields of efficiency and eco-friendliness. There is the HR label in Belgium (which stands for *haut rendement* or efficiency), the Blue Angel in Germany (environmentally friendly), and the French efficiency label.

The German mark DVGW is said to be the strongest quality mark in the gas industry. DVGW contains performance as well as environment-related specifications. Most German retailers refuse to sell products which do not bear the DVGW label. Some manufacturers consider this to be protectionism, others think that the national quality mark is so popular with customers that it would be a bad marketing strategy to try to abandon it.

All these marks deal with an aspect of performance, not of safety, this being covered by the CE marking. The national quality marks are thus permitted under the Directive. National quality marks correspond to national voluntary standards with which manufacturers do not have an obligation to conform. However, national quality marks can be very strong locally and are often more meaningful to the customer than the CE marking (still largely unknown or misinterpreted). Certification to national quality marks standards is therefore seen as a commercial requirement by most manufacturers.

Moreover, the strength of national quality marks is sometimes reinforced by the attitude of national organizations. This is the case in Belgium, for example, where quality mark appeal to customers is reinforced with special incentives. Customers are offered a rebate from the gas supplier when they buy a cooker which achieves a particular working efficiency (corresponding to the 'HR' standards).

A certain amount of pressure from the notified bodies can also be exerted on manufacturers to apply both markings since some notified bodies certify both for the CE marking (under the GAD) and for strong national quality marks.

Testing to national standards can only be carried out by the national organizations. There are no mutual recognition agreements between testing and certification bodies which would allow them to conduct tests for one another's quality marks.

The value and importance of quality marks is recognized by the industry. The problem is that they have been developed with an exclusive national character by national standards bodies. The ideal would be to have a single set of performance standards supported by an open European mark.

10.3.4. Non-regulatory barriers

There are still a number of product adaptations required to market in different Member States. The two areas mentioned were translations and customer preferences, both of which result from cultural differences of the target population, and are not a result of standards or testing required by third parties like trade associations, insurers or retailers. We would hesitate to class them as technical barriers.

Customer preferences

Cooking techniques vary from country to country, often requiring different appliances. For example, in the UK, grilling is a very important cooking method and for this reason the grill is usually separated from the oven and situated at eye level. On the other hand, in Germany as in most other European countries, the grill is seldom used and is almost always integrated into the top part of the oven. Customer requirements in different member countries therefore can constitute an obstacle to manufacturers wanting to produce a standard European cooker. Such national cultural variations, however, cannot be considered to constitute technical barriers to trade.

In addition, many countries have special requirements dictated by customer preference. For example, cookers sold in Sweden must be height adjustable, have wheels and be fixed to the wall.

Translations

Since the implementation of the Directive, manufacturers claim that they have to face increased translation costs.[5] One manufacturer mentioned that translating the documentation for one type of gas cooker costs about ECU 4,500 and this expense needs to be repeated for every model in each product range. It is felt to constitute a barrier to trade, particularly by SMEs, but cannot be considered a significant barrier to major multinational manufacturers. It is not only a requirement of the Directive, applicable to all suppliers, but is an obvious market requirement for any manufacturer.

10.4. Enterprise strategies

10.4.1. Product range

Domestic gas cookers were mass produced by multinationals and traded successfully throughout Europe before the GAD. Multinational companies do not believe their products are safer now than they were ten years ago. Smaller companies said the Directive allowed them to improve the safety and the efficiency of their products and that after the initial investment into new product design their products became more competitive.

Since the Directive there has been no significant reduction in the number of models produced. For reasons already mentioned the manufacturers of gas cookers believe that Europe remains 15 individual national markets, each with its own gas distribution system, cooking methods and customer requirements. The products sold are many, and often are country specific.

10.4.2. Investment

The New Approach in the field of domestic appliances has not brought about any significant inward investment into Europe. If anything, the European appliances industry is entering a period of divestment as factories close down and personnel are laid off. Market competition being ever fiercer, multinationals have been concentrating on cost reduction strategies by means of mergers and acquisitions and relocation of production facilities. Many are trying to relocate their production facilities to regions where labour costs are low, such as in Eastern Europe or in South-East Asia.

In countries where national brands and quality marks are very strong, for example in Germany, the best strategy for a company wanting to sell into that market is to buy a local company and thus circumvent any nationalistic issues. However, the whole of the Western European market is now believed to be saturated and is considered by the industry as a 'replacement market', i.e. white goods penetration per household is so high that sales only depend on replacement rates.

---

[5] The essential requirements of the Directive specify that all appliances must be accompanied by technical instructions for the installer, instructions for use and servicing for the user, and appropriate warning notices, which must all 'be in the official language or languages of the Member States of destination'.

10.4.3. Distribution and marketing

Gas cooker manufacturers tend to sell to big distributors, or distribution chains, who carry stocks and market to consumers. These tend to be national organizations. Manufacturers therefore have had little opportunity to change the marketing strategy or distribution chains as a result of harmonization brought about by the Directive.

It was noted by manufacturers, however, that the distributors and retailers are not yet always aware of the meaning of the CE mark. Distribution networks are often more interested in seeing the national quality mark on a product than the CE mark. Because of their size and their contact with mass consumers, distributors can dictate their conditions to the manufacturers. To eliminate the strength of national marks, therefore, an information campaign aimed at consumers and retailers is necessary.

10.4.4. Organization and management

The research did not indicate that any changes in organization and/or management had taken place as a result of the New Approach.

10.4.5. Quality and testing

Most players in the domestic appliances market are members of a quality assurance scheme according to the requirements of ISO9000. Some SMEs still active in the market find the cost of ISO9000 an obstacle. However, if they do decide to obtain the certification, they tend to benefit. A small Belgian company recently managed to sell its cookers to Chile and Argentina because of its ISO9000 certification.

There was no evidence that the Directive has had any effect on manufacturers' already extensive in-house testing requirements.

Impact on competitiveness and customer choice

In general, the New Approach directives and harmonized standards comprise a benefit for the industry as a whole. However, they have not prevented the resurgence of national standards, national conformity assessment procedures and national quality marks.

Compared to the situation ten years ago, multinationals report no economies of scale, and no relevant changes in their products (which could be linked directly with regulatory issues). The New Approach has had a more visible impact on SMEs. Likewise, customers are not aware of significant changes in product range or choice of manufacturer. Manufacturers remain the same well-recognized multinational companies. Concentration through merger and acquisition in the industry has, if anything, brought about a streamlining of brand names.

10.5. Conclusions

10.5.1. Effectiveness of approaches

There seem to be some important interpretative issues left outstanding with regard to the measures that are covered in the Directive (they are discussed below). However, the Directive is relatively new and there inevitably remain details which require fine tuning.

Table 10.3.   Effectiveness of approaches

Measure/action	State of implementation	Effectiveness[1]
Essential safety requirements	End of transition period 1/1/96	**
Harmonized standards	prEN 30.1 and prEN 30.2	***
CE marking	Compulsory from 1/1/96	*

[1] on a scale of 1-5 where ***** = the most effective
Source: W.S. Atkins.

The essential safety requirements contained in the Directive are often criticized for their lack of clarity, their vagueness or inaccuracies. The GAD is under review at the moment and manufacturers' trade associations hope that greater clarification of certain terms will result. For example, the meaning of 'heating' is to be redefined as well as the original intentions of the GAD regarding 'reconditioned' appliances and the requirements 'to minimize the risk of explosion'. The interpretation of the essential safety requirements is an important point as manufacturers need to ensure that they work to the same parameters as their competitors and the notified bodies which will carry out test procedures.

The problem of interpretation has been partly solved by the drafting of harmonized standards, but prEN 30.1 (safety) and prEN 30.2 (efficiency) have not been adopted and published as yet; they remain drafts. Manufacturers participate to a large extent in the CEN's TC49 but the technical work is slowed down by the divergence of interests and the difficulty of reaching a compromise.

Despite the fact that prEN 30.1 and prEN 30.2 are not fully in place, most manufacturers, multinationals and SMEs alike, tend to apply them and modify their products as each modification is drafted. Other harmonized standards (EN 30.3) are in draft form and are expected to be completed by the end of 1997.

The CE marking has, as we have already seen, harmonized testing and certification in Europe. The GAD however, only allows third party conformity assessment which is a more stringent requirement than self-certification. It is time-consuming and expensive. For this reason, part of the gas industry, represented at the European level by the CEFACD, supports the adoption of Module H from Council Decision 90/683/EEC. For manufacturers, the introduction of Module H would bring the possibility of setting up in-house facilities for testing and self-certifying their products after having operated an approved quality system for design, manufacture and final product inspection and testing.

Article 8(4) requires gas fittings to be sold with a conformity certificate and to bear the CE marking. The article has been interpreted in different ways by Member States and some of them apply the requirement to all gas fittings, including spares. Enclosing a fittings certificate with every spare is very impractical and has created a rather heavy administrative burden. The manufacturers hope that the requirement of Article 8(4) of the Directive will be redrafted to exclude spares.

10.5.2. Remaining barriers

As mentioned previously, there are a number of factors which have impeded the implementation of the Directive, and therefore act as an obstacle to the free movement of gas cookers in Europe. Some of these factors relate specifically to Member States which have not yet fulfilled all the requirements of the GAD, particularly those relating to the publication and dissemination of information (types of gas, pressures, toxic gases, etc.). Other factors relate to delays in the adoption of harmonized standards and harmonized procedures for testing and certification (see Table 10.4).

Table 10.4.   Remaining barriers

Barriers to trade	Importance[1]
Non-implementation of the Directive	***
Customer requirements	*****
National quality marks (DVGW etc.)	***

[1] on a scale of 1-5 where ***** = the most important
Source: W.S. Atkins.

10.5.3. Measures suggested by industry

From the interviews it is clear that the industry would like to see improvements in a number of areas:

(a)   a clarification by the Commission of certain terms and articles of the Gas Appliances Directive;
(b)   to add Module H to the list of possible conformity assessment routes to permit in-house testing;
(c)   full application of the GAD, i.e. Member States must provide information regarding types of gas and pressures used as well as lists of toxic gases used and all other obligatory information according to the GAD;
(d)   separation of the activities of those national testing and certification bodies which have responsibility for both the CE marking and strong national quality marks.

Part III: Sample product sectors – mutual recognition

11. Cement

11.1. Product information

NACE code: 26.51 –Manufacture of cement.

PRODCOM code: 26.51.12/10/30/50/90 – White Portland cement/Portland cement/Aluminous cement and other hydraulic cements.

11.1.1. Product scope

Cement is a basic material for buildings and civil engineering work.

Cement production consists of two essential stages:

(a)   manufacture of semi-finished product, the so-called 'clinker', obtained from the calcination and sintering in a high-performance kiln $(1,450^{\circ}C)$ of raw materials (clay, limestone, etc.);

(b)   manufacture of cement as a finished product, obtained by grinding the clinker together with calcium sulphate and including (or not, depending on the type of cement) one or more additional components: slag, fly ash, pozzolana, filler, etc.

This produces a wide range of cement types described in terms of their composition and chemical, physical and mechanical characteristics. This report deals with common cements as opposed to specials, such as white finishing cement.

Although cement falls under the Construction Products Directive (CPD) (89/106/EEC), this is not yet in practical application because necessary harmonized standards are not yet in place. At present, the product is sold according to national cement standards and in a legal sense relies on the mutual recognition principle. However, in preparation for the production of CPD harmonized standards, the cement industry has helped the development and adoption of a range of standards on the test methods which will be needed for a European cement standard and has supported the development and adoption of a pre-standard for common cements.

Cement may present potential health hazards as a fine dust and is categorized as an irritant by some Member States (although, in practice, this aspect is not often a source of technical barriers).

11.1.2. Product standards

Before the work on European Standards began, there were distinct standards in each Member State defining cement categories, technical specifications and performance parameters, test methods, and test requirements. Although a final mandate for development of harmonized standards under the CPD has not yet been given, CEN has been working on developing common European standards with the support of the European industry, and a number of standards and pre-standards have been introduced from 1992.

There are European experimental pre-standards (ENVs) for common cements; ENV197-1 was adopted in 1992.[6] Since then, many national standards have voluntarily been adjusted to meet the ENV197-1. Some countries have fully adopted the ENV as a national standard.

There are five main product categories:

(a)   CEM I   Portland cement,
(b)   CEM II   Portland-composite cement,
(c)   CEM III Blast furnace cement,
(d)   CEM IV Pozzolanic cement,
(e)   CEM V   Composite cement.

Depending on the type of additives used in Portland-composite cements, this group is further subdivided as follows:

(a)   Portland-slag cement,
(b)   Portland-silica fume cement,
(c)   Portland-pozzolana cement,
(d)   Portland-fly ash cement,
(e)   Portland-burnt shale cement,
(f)   Portland-limestone cement,
(g)   Portland-composite cement.

ENV197-2 'Cement Conformity Evaluation' was agreed by CEN in 1994. It sets out a European scheme for cement certification by setting the requirements for attestation of conformity to the ENV197-1, i.e. it specifies the tests that have to be carried out for each of the properties of cement, defines quality systems for the tests which have to be carried out, and defines how the results should be interpreted. Until such time as it is adopted as an EN, ENV197-2 works in parallel with national standards.

The standard which defines testing procedures for cement has now been adopted as EN196, so any conflicting national standards should have been withdrawn. Testing procedures were previously very different in EU countries, so since its introduction as ENV196 the standard has greatly reduced the complications and costs of testing.

The existing standards, pre-standards and drafts currently published are shown in Table 11.1.

Differing national geographic and climatic conditions and differing construction practices have hindered the production of European harmonized standards. For instance, in Germany fly ash and limestone have not yet been accepted. Portland cement contains only clinker as a main constituent, but some countries have a tradition of using other constituents in cement, e.g. industrial pozzolana, fly ash (which affects the freeze-thaw resistance); calcareous fly ash (which affects stability); slag and limestone (which also affects stability in proportions

---

[6]   ENV pre-standards differ from European Standards (ENs) or Harmonized Documents (HDs) in that the ENV standard is experimental: it is intended for voluntary use with a view to becoming an EN later. Member States are obliged to make the ENV 'available in appropriate form at national level' but 'existing national standards which are inconsistent with the ENV may continue to be implemented ...' (Nicolas, 1995, p. 47).

exceeding 20%). Because these affect the technical characteristics of cement in use, their acceptance in different climates and construction practices has involved lengthy assessment.

Nevertheless, CEMBUREAU report that the European cement industry wants a European cement standard and is participating in the working groups to transform ENV197-1 into an EN standard. It is currently engaged in the preparation of the Mandate which will allow CEN to prepare the harmonized standard.

Table 11.1.   European standards for cement

Standard	Subject
EN196-1	Determination of strength
EN196-2	Chemical analysis of cement
EN196-3	Determination of setting time and soundness
EN196-5	Pozzolanicity test for pozzolanic cements
EN196-6	Determination of fineness
EN196-7	Methods of taking and preparing samples
EN196-21	Determination of the chloride, carbon dioxide and alkali content
EN196-XX	Determination of total organic carbon (TOC) content in limestone (paper in Zement-Kalk-Gips 43 (1990), No. 8, pp. 409-412 to be converted to an EN)
Draft standard prEN933-12	Tests for geometrical properties of aggregates; Part 12: Assessment of fines – Methylene blue test
ISO/DIS 9277	Determination of the specific surface area of solids by gas adsorption using the BET-surface
ENV197-1	Standard for common cement categories
ENV197-2	Conformity procedures

11.1.3. National regulations

There are specific national regulations for cement in several EU countries. Interviewees in this study commented mainly on problems they had encountered in France and Germany. The precise status in other countries was not known to them, but most countries deal with structural requirements for cement through the building approvals and building control processes which vary from country to country, but usually involve design and construction approval either by local authority building inspectors or by registered professionals (architects or engineers).

France

In France the *Code de la Construction* and the *Code Civil* include a range of regulations relating to construction products, as *lois, décrets, arrêtés* and *circulaires*. These apply to all goods sold in France regardless of their domestic or foreign origin. One important characteristic of the French *Code Civil* is the system of decennial responsibility and insurance, which confers a lot of responsibility on the *maître d'oeuvre* (independent project manager – often an architect or consulting engineer – acting for the *maître d'ouvrage* or owner) to enforce standards and reduce exposure to claims. This results in conformity to standards and certification being given a high priority in France.

Under French law, cements, like many other products, have until recently been required by law to conform to French standards (*arrêté* of 15 October 1990 and decree of 26 January 1984). In 1993, following an Art. 30 investigation by the European Commission, the French authorities issued a new *arrêté* introducing mutual recognition clauses into the regulations. This allows cement to AFNOR (*Association Française de Normalisation*) or equivalent standards, and for testing to be carried out by French or foreign laboratories which have been approved by AFNOR, and setting out the approval procedure. So far only one foreign laboratory has been approved (CRIC in Belgium – see below). It should be noted, however, that there is no mutual recognition arrangement in place: the foreign laboratories must be approved by AFNOR.

Cement certification also comes under a 1978 law which governs certification generally and which establishes a legislative framework for the approval of certifying bodies. For cement, AFNOR issues the NF certificate and confers the NF quality mark according to the *Réglement Particulier Marque NF-Liants Hydrauliques*. There is a reference in this document to foreign standards and mutual recognition stating that requests for certification of products with foreign standards 'will be managed taking into account existing mutual recognition arrangements', but it seems that existing mutual recognition arrangements are not successful (see below).

Regulatory barriers in France also arise because of regulations on ready-mix concrete (*Calcul du Béton*).

Germany

One of the characteristics of Germany is the emphasis on detailed building regulations which ensure quality and conformity in construction. There are both safety and product standards which relate to the use and application of products including cement. Tests are required not only for products but also for components, so that, for instance, cement used in the manufacture of concrete beams has to comply to DIN standards. Until recently TÜV certification was required; now Ü-marking is necessary (which can be given by other certification bodies). Understanding the requirements and the procedures for testing is important and often affects the decision to trade.

Germany has introduced a new quality mark for both domestic and imported construction products, the Ü-mark, to be used until the Construction Products Directive is functional, and in response to the large flow of imported products to supply the construction boom in certain areas of the eastern *Länder*. This mark conforms to DIN1164 standard which includes ENV197-1, and this is discussed in more detail in Chapter 14.

11.1.4. New Approach measures

Cement comes under the Construction Products Directive 89/106/EEC. Although the Directive is formally in force (transposed into most Member States), its implementation makes use of EN standards or technical approvals mandatory, and the standards have not yet been adopted. There was a delay in CEN starting work on construction products standards because (unlike other New Approach directives) the Commission had to adopt interpretative documents, which translate the generic essential requirements for construction into a basis for the mandates to draw up standards for products. A mandate is expected to be issued to CEN soon to prepare the documents which lay the basis for harmonized European standards for cement and allow the selection of the conformity attestation procedures.

11.1.5. Mutual recognition arrangements

Industry problems relating to trade are mainly about certification, testing and quality control. Mutual recognition arrangements between testing and certification bodies are, therefore, valuable to industry and one might expect to find more mutual recognition arrangements in place, set up as result of industry pressures to facilitate testing and certification. However, there seem to be few such arrangements in place, confined to the Benelux, Germany and France.

1986 Accord BDLN

The *Accord BDLN* between Belgium, Germany, Luxembourg and the Netherlands is a legal text (published in the *Moniteur Belge*) dating from 1987. It is a legal framework which has been initiated and negotiated at ministerial level (not through the EOTC), designed to provide the basis for mutual recognition in construction products, to overcome barriers to trade and to advance the principle of mutual recognition until such a time as the Construction Products Directive could be implemented. It is implemented by a series of protocols, including:

(a)   general protocol in matters of quality assurance *(Protocole général d'exécution en matière de procédures d'assurances de qualité);*

(b)   principles of procedures and execution *(Traitement des demandes de base de l'article 16 de la Directive communautaire relative aux produits de la construction);*

(c)   harmonization model for mutual recognition of quality and testing in construction products. This is a general protocol on construction products which creates the conditions for close co-ordination between certification institutes of each country to prepare protocols for categories of construction products;

(d)   1996 harmonization model for mutual recognition of quality and testing in cement. This protocol on cement is being drafted and will be in force shortly;

(e)   Belgium-Netherlands protocol (1988). This protocol does not include Germany, only the Benelux countries. Under the General Secretariat of Benelux, its members have arguably gone further than any other countries through a protocol which implements full mutual recognition of certification bodies in construction products. The protocol is likely to be in force within the Benelux countries in the coming months;

(f)   protocol between Belgium and France (1991). The Belgian cement industry research association CRIC (*Centre de recherche de l'industrie cimentière*) has an agreement with AFNOR in France. In principle, both institutes which issue national certificates can contract laboratories to test cement and issue NF and BENOR certificates.

11.2. Industry information

11.2.1. Sector representation

National associations of cement producers are represented at European level by CEMBUREAU, the European Cement Association in Brussels, which is the representative organization. Its full members are European Union and European Economic Area national cement associations plus Switzerland and Turkey. The Czech, Slovak, Hungarian and Polish cement associations are associate members. Efforts to develop harmonized standards in cement have been managed through CEMBUREAU, which disseminates a wide range of information for the industry itself and for policy-makers, including annual reviews with statistics and technical papers. In addition, it lobbies on behalf of the cement industry and co-ordinates with other European representative organizations to promote the use of cement.

11.2.2. Industry structure

Although there are nearly 300 plants in the EU, belonging to some 64 groups, the industry is highly concentrated with less than 10 major cement groups world-wide. Allowing for the differing definitions of turnover and capacity, which impact on the ranking of cement companies, Holderbank (Switzerland) and Italcementi (Italy) are generally regarded to be the largest companies, each producing in excess of 40 million tonnes of cement. Other large firms with interests in the EU are Cemex, a Mexican company with interests throughout Latin America, Lafarge Coppée (France), Blue Circle (UK), Scancem (following the merger of Swedish, Norwegian and Finnish companies) and Heidelberger (Germany). There are a few large Asian companies such as Chichibuonoda and Indocement, which do not have European interests. The largest five firms account for around 20% of world production.

The process of concentration dates from the 1970s when European companies, having little need to invest in new capacity in their home markets, started acquiring cement companies in the US and elsewhere. The industry turned in the 1980s to strategies designed to reduce exposure to the cyclical nature of construction demand, on the one hand, and to control cement production in neighbouring markets as a defensive measure, on the other. These strategies of acquisition, restructuring and market positioning of the leading companies will probably continue.

11.2.3. Output and trade

Output

Cement consumption is linked directly to activity in the construction sector. Public sector investment has a major impact on construction activity and cutbacks in government spending have had an negative impact in many countries. There has been a long-term decline in cement consumption in Europe since the mid-1970s (apart from a substantial growth period in the late 1980s). Consumption in the EU rose by 3.3% in 1994, but in 1995 declined by 1.3% and the outlook for 1996 was pessimistic. The long-term decline in output, combined with heavy investment needs for environmental protection and energy conservation, account partly for the high degree of concentration which resulted from rationalization of the industry, and the concern the industry has about dumping and unfair competition as a result of state aids.

In 1995, the main producers in the EU were Italy (34 million tonnes), Germany (33 million tonnes) and Spain (28 million tonnes). Turkey was the largest producer member of CEMBUREAU with almost 35 million tonnes. Exceptional growth is occurring in Turkey, where four new cement plants creating an additional 2.4 million tonnes clinker capacity have been built, partly to supply a mammoth development scheme in the Tigris and Euphrates river basins for 22 dams and 19 power plants. Production data are shown in Table 11.2.

Table 11.2.   Production of cement,[a] 1984–94 ('000 tonnes)

Country	1984	1989	1994
Austria	4,852	4,735	4,600
Belgium	5,708	6,766	8,412
Denmark	1,450	1,597	1,928
Finland	1,645	1,598	869
France	24,025	26,827	21,184
Germany [b]	26,224	26,505	36,130
Greece	13,460	12,392	14,300
Ireland	1,377	1,869	1,623
Italy	38,891	40,487	33,192
Luxembourg	973	1,241	1,200
Netherlands	3,176	3,479	3,180
Portugal	5,483	6,743	7,977
Spain	26,643	28,217	26,661
Sweden	2,360	2,327	2,153
United Kingdom	13,552	15,764	12,238
EU [c]	**168,380**	**177,144**	**175,647**
Iceland	114	116	81
Norway	1,459	1,417	1,721
Switzerland	4,297	5,461	4,370
Turkey	15,735	24,061	31,897
Czech Republic	na	na	5,363
Hungary	na	na	2,793
Poland	na	na	14,942
Slovak Republic	na	na	2,700
CEMBUREAU	**189,985**	**208,199**	**239,514**

[a] including exported clinker
[b] for 1984 and 1989 West Germany
[c] totals include intra-trade clinker
Source: CEMBUREAU.

Trade

European harmonized statistics on trade for 1995 show that 39.0 million tonnes were exported and 24.3 million tonnes were imported, which is 16% and 10% of output respectively. Trade data for previous years are shown in Table 11.3.

Germany sees the most trade in cement and imports increased by 325% between 1986 and 1995. National statistics for 1995 show that of the 8.6 million tonnes imported, 3.2 million tonnes came from Poland, 1.1 million tonnes from Slovakia, 1.0 million tonnes from the Czech Republic, 0.41 million tonnes from the Benelux and 0.32 million tonnes from France. Clinker is also imported by Germany in considerable quantities from Poland (0.8 million tonnes) and the Benelux (0.5 million tonnes).

Some interviewees claimed that cement trade is being inhibited by technical barriers. This claim would seem to contradict the common argument that cement is a bulky low-price product with commodity characteristics, not worth transporting more than about 150 km by road. However, behind that argument is the assumption that supply and demand are always in rough balance in each region, that road as opposed to other transport costs apply, and that perfectly competitive market pricing is applied.

In practice, cement is traded quite widely, sometimes over very long distances, particularly by sea or rail. Nevertheless, cement is most often delivered to markets close to the point of production, and world trade accounts for only 5% of world cement production, plus 2% of clinker.

However, fluctuations in cement demand do arise at national, regional and local levels through seasonal factors, reflecting the phasing of large construction projects, the purchasing decisions of major users or competitive pricing strategies. Changes in supply also occur due to technical breakdowns in cement plants, interruptions in supply due to transport factors or shortages in certain types of cement. There are also imbalances in supply caused by state aid and investment. In the absence of price controls, shortages lead to price increases which would make trade profitable. In the past, there have been price controls which prevented trade (and there still probably are in non-EU countries), but led to unwise local investment which eventually led to excess capacity. With fewer cement plants in Europe now, due to closures over the last 20 years, cement must be traded increasingly over longer distances.

The statistics show that EU imports (Table 11.3), most of which are intra-EU trade but with some from Turkey and other non-EU exporters, have risen from under 4% of production (Table 11.2) in 1984 to 13% in 1994, and that internal trade in the EU has tripled over 10 years. We believe that this is in part due to the success of the industry in developing standards and bilateral testing agreements described above. There is still some way to go before this process is complete. We would still expect there to be more trade in cement within Europe if technical barriers simply did not exist (see Section 11.3).

It should be noted, however, that some trade is created by the distorting effects of state aid and transport subsidies. This is probably a factor in the trade from some Central European countries into Germany, which would not otherwise be economic.

Table 11.3. Trade in cement and clinker, 1984–94

Country	1984 Exports	1984 Imports	1989 Exports	1989 Imports	1994 Exports	1994 Imports
Austria	14	39	29	79	30	946
Belgium	1,094	263	1,907	342	3,069	661
Denmark	74	33	335	135	1,020	260
Finland	8	14	3	238	5	167
France	2,389	409	1,564	637	2,437	1,506
Germany [a]	1,623	1,860	2,149	2,227	2,339	9,020
Greece	7,332	0	5,115	0	7,662	40
Ireland	81	69	545	236	273	310
Italy	120	252	105	2,400	678	2,454
Luxembourg	679	0	848	0	801	54
Netherlands [b]	98	2,983	46	3,538	490	330
Portugal	23	0	78	4	447	na
Spain	10,248	55	3,270	1,329	4,970	2,250
Sweden	767	200	196	135	1,018	108
United Kingdom	137	400	49	4,285	410	1,607
EU	**24,684**	**6,577**	**16,239**	**15,585**	**25,649**	**22,683**
Iceland	na	1	na	na	na	na
Norway	106	66	na	98	705	109
Switzerland	17	134	21	538	48	225
Turkey	1,932	0	1,098	503	5,204	51
Czech Republic	na	na	na	na	1,600	164
Hungary	na	na	na	na	134	233
Poland	na	na	na	na	4,264	12
Slovak Republic	na	na	na	na	1,400	na
CEMBUREAU	**26,742**	**6,778**	**17,358**	**16,724**	**39,004**	**23,477**

[a] for 1984 and 1989 West Germany only
[b] excluding export to Germany
Source: CEMBUREAU.

11.3. Trade barriers

11.3.1. Regulatory barriers

Those in the cement industry that are involved in international trade do not readily distinguish between regulatory barriers and non-regulatory barriers because their impact on trade is the same, and because of the complicated status of barriers. Manufacturers naturally follow the requirements specified by their customers, or the guidance of their associations, and do not usually enquire about the legal status of the requirements.

Exports, as we have seen, are relatively low, at around 15% of production. All the EU countries register some exports; the main exporters are Greece, followed by Spain and Belgium. Most companies interviewed did not place a priority on increasing exports, and European producers seem generally content to accept the *status quo*. However, there are a number of traders trying to develop a trade in cement, who stated that they encounter certain barriers to trade which may be attributed to regulations. These mainly concern product certification but also include quality control certification of cement plants.

As one example of a regulatory barrier, the Swedish Ministry of Health is reported to have set a maximum content of chromium of 2 ppm (parts per million) in cement, in order to protect those handling cement from developing dermatitis. This is the type of understandable health and safety regulation which creates barriers which cannot easily be removed by mutual recognition, and harmonized standards may not remove them.

11.3.2. Non-regulatory barriers

For cement, besides the regulations referred to above, there are at present specific barriers resulting from the nature of the construction process, and the building controls related to it, which are different in every Member State. These relate to:

(a)   the design codes and the specific training of engineers and architects who design the structures and specify the cement to be used. They are knowledgeable about and trained only in the cement standards and construction codes of their home country and will always specify cement using national standards until and unless European Standards replace them;

(b)   the requirements of building approval and construction control, whether by local authority building inspectors, architects, independent engineers and *Prüfingenieure*, who must approve construction and accept liability for defects and structural damage: their guidelines, rules, technical recommendations and their own training only permit them to accept cement of specific, usually national, standards;

(c)   latent defect or decennial insurance requirements. These are particularly strict in France (which has mandatory decennial insurance for certain classes of building) and Belgium. The insurance system, and the technical controllers (*bureaux de contrôle)* who evaluate the risk, only permit the use of approved products (e.g. with NF certification or with an *avis technique* from the CSTB in France).

For these reasons, it is virtually universal at present for cement users to specify national standards. The development of Eurocodes, and the adoption of harmonized standards under the CPD, will permit changes in the education of engineers and the rules of the insurance and the local authority building control systems, but this will take a long time, and will not necessarily lead to common rules on construction (which the CPD does not envisage as at present formulated).

There have also been barriers caused by public procurement requirements, particularly for public works contracts, where in the past most countries had standard contract clauses and technical specifications based on national standards. The public procurement legislation has now made it compulsory to use European or international standards where these exist, and to accept standards equivalent to national standards where European or international standards do not exist. The general absence of European product standards for cement and concrete means that this element of the Public Procurement Directive cannot yet take effect.

There are difficulties with French practice on standards used in procurement. The *Cahiers des clauses techniques* (CCT) and the *Cahiers des charges spéciales* (CCS) apply contractually. Sometimes, in private contracts, these documents name the supplier, and sometimes also the cement plant. In public contracts, this is no longer permitted by the EC public procurement legislation, but previously suppliers had to meet special standards, the *normes homologées*, which are NF standards whose use was obligatory for products and services supplied under public contracts. Although the public contracts should now specify EN standards or say 'NF or equivalent', the fact that there are as yet no ENs means that foreign cement suppliers would in practice need to get AFNOR certification. We did not find any non-French cement manufacturer who had attempted to supply the French public sector, although some 800,000 tonnes of Belgian cement was sold to France in 1995 and most Belgian cement has an NF certificate.

11.3.3. Testing and certification

The most common issues reported by interviewees as barriers concern certification or more specifically the procedures required to gain certification in destination markets. Even where there are no regulatory barriers, they often see significant administrative barriers. Unfortunately, these barriers are magnified because of inadequate information, due to language or, in some cases, due to unrealistic expectations in dealing with unfamiliar systems and procedures.

It must be recognized that although these may merely be perceptions, and the problems are not barriers to trade so much as a lack of understanding of foreign standards and certification systems, the perceptions exist nonetheless. Few sales managers possess a detailed understanding of national systems and procedures in other countries. What appears to one supplier to be a major barrier to trade appears to another as a mere administrative formality: for example, a cement testing requirement in Germany was perceived as a barrier to trade by a British cement supplier, but is perceived as a mere formality by a Swedish supplier who had previous experience of, and thus understood, the German system. In both cases, the testing had to be done by a German lab. Because the testing of cement is a routine and not very costly process which is universally required for building control, it is not usually considered a barrier unless national requirements cause delays.

A pattern emerges which suggests that problems are mostly faced by suppliers wishing to export to countries where they have limited previous experience. Hence, northern Europeans complain about long procedures for certification and testing in Italy, Spain and Greece, and southern producers complain about delays in certification in northern Europe (e.g. a Spanish request for a Danish certificate took five months), whereas Portuguese suppliers report no problems in obtaining Spanish certification and Dutch suppliers have no problems obtaining certification to sell in Belgium. In some cases, barriers have been overcome through mutual recognition arrangements (e.g. between Belgium and the Netherlands) but in most cases, suppliers are simply more familiar with the market requirements.

Some specific problems of testing and certification were reported by interviewees, as described below.

UK

EU or non-EU manufacturers exporting to the UK are not legally bound to certify conformity of their product to British standards, but often they seek certification to have credibility as suppliers. They certainly do need to label their products with the appropriate BS classification or grade so that contractors can use British codes and follow British architects' and engineers' instructions. Architects and engineers will check that the correct grades of cement are being used on site, and will expect to see the Kitemark on the bags. The BSI Kitemark is issued to manufacturers who operate a system of production control and a system of sample testing for conformity. The sample evaluations are reported to BSI. These procedures have to be in the company's Quality Manual. Initial certification can take time to obtain but once the process of sample testing and plant audit has been followed, there are no problems.

France

Despite the amendment to the French regulations permitting testing by approved foreign laboratories, AFNOR has only (as far as we are aware) approved one foreign laboratory, CRIC in Belgium (the testing requires 12 samples plus an audit of the cement plant). The cost to Belgian producers is a flat fee of BFR 40,000 (ECU 1,000). This is on the basis of a mutual recognition arrangement so that CRIC also recognizes French tests. AFNOR uses the *Laboratoire d'essais des matériaux de la Ville de Paris* (LEMVP).

There were complaints from Belgian, British and German firms about problems of certification in France. One UK cement manufacturer had not attempted to export because of his perception of barriers to trade. Even Belgian manufacturers exporting to France, who benefit from a mutual recognition arrangement, reported that certificates can be difficult to obtain and on occasions even the normally routine renewal of established certificates is arbitrarily suspended. The Belgian view is that the established cement industry wields too much influence in the process of issuing certificates (which is managed by AFNOR). Also, there is not enough independent input in the final decision on whether to issue a certificate of conformity to the NF standard to a foreign product. It is also alleged that deregulation has led to a diminished role of government institutions, which previously might have provided some form of arbitration.

The mutual recognition clauses inserted into the French regulations after the Art. 30 procedures are not seen to have had any significant effect. The cement companies interviewed were not aware of this change, and the interviewee at CEMBUREAU was not aware of it either. In practice, it has little real effect because the recognition of the equivalence of foreign standards to AFNOR standards, the approval of foreign test labs, and the ratification of foreign test certificates are all carried out by AFNOR itself. It is therefore more straightforward, but in practice still difficult, to try to get the testing done by a French laboratory to AFNOR standards, and obtain the NF mark.

In theory, Belgian producers ought to experience less difficulty than other producers because there is a mutual recognition arrangement on cement and concrete testing between *Centre de recherche de l'industrie cimentière* (CRIC) in Belgium and AFNOR in France. Both institutes are able to contract laboratories to test cement and concrete and issue NF and BENOR certificates, but in practice the Belgians complain that they still encounter difficulty selling in France with the certificates issued in Belgium. [These difficulties presumably result from the preference of clients, contractors, technical controllers and insurers for NF certificates and NF standards because of decennial liability, rather than any restriction on placing the product on the market.]

Belgium

Swedish traders indicated that testing requirements of Belgian certification institutes were stricter than other certification institutes, such as those in Lithuania, but this was the result of informal recognition arrangements for testing with Lithuania. German suppliers also observed that Belgian certification involves more testing of products than many other countries. This has a significant impact on costs, although it does not indicate discrimination, as Belgian cements require the same procedures. There is a tradition of more testing in Belgium because of the absence of mandatory building control inspection.

Spain

Complaints about long and costly certification procedures in Spain were made by British, Norwegian and Swedish companies, and the testing requirements were attributed to mandatory regulations. However, Portuguese companies report that they export to Spain and obtain certification without difficulties. There is a requirement for Spanish inspectors to visit the exporter's works for on-site inspection every six months, and for samples to be taken and tested in Spain.

Austria

Certificates of conformity to sell cement in Austria were said to be difficult to obtain and involve long delays. The certification requirement is regulatory. The requirements are also reflected in public procurement tenders, and complaints have been taken up under the Art. 30 procedures against Austrian specification of national standards and testing of cement in public tenders.

Germany

Importing cement into Germany is reported by interviewees to involve considerable administration and delay. A French request for one type of cement certification through the *Institut für Bautechnik* in Berlin submitted in November 1988 took almost three years to September 1991 before being issued, but this may not be typical of the present situation. Indeed, one interviewee stated that he now found Germany the most open EU country in terms of its acceptance of tests carried out in other Member States.

Denmark

An interviewee reported that certification is slow and costly in Denmark.

Italy

In Italy, there are no mutual recognition arrangements on testing, and procedures (which apply equally to Italian cement) are cumbersome and usually take six months or more. For example, we were told that a Belgian exporter requires someone from the Italian certification institute to travel to Belgium each month to take 12 cement samples and for the cement plant to be audited by a designate of an Italian institute, before a certificate of conformity is issued. Apart from long delays, the supplier incurs initial costs of about ECU 7,000 per grade of cement, which may be a significant disincentive for small export contracts, although it is a small sum for a large cement producer. (For comparison, to sell Belgian cement to the Netherlands, the certification and testing can be done in Belgium and is recognized by KOMO in the Netherlands, at a cost of approximately ECU 1,000.) The Italian Government has established that certification may be issued by 'approved official laboratories' in the EU producer country, but the exporter interviewed did not follow this process.

In all of the above cases except between the Benelux and France or Germany, testing is in practice required to be done in test houses in the destination country because there are no mutual recognition arrangements, and tests are required to the target country's standards.

11.4. Enterprise strategies

Measures to remove technical barriers to trade have so far had no significant effect overall on the level or ease of exporting within the EU, so there has been no measurable impact on enterprise strategies. The general strategy of cement firms in fact has been to protect and defend their existing markets and customers, and only to seek exports and new markets as a marginal activity. This section gives some consideration to what impact a removal of barriers and a change to a more open trading environment would have.

The cement industry is characterized by markets that are predominantly regional for the reasons mentioned previously – high transport costs and low price per unit volume. Coupled with the maturity of European cement markets, characterized by flat demand, adequate production capacities and distribution centres covering most of the European market, this significantly influences the strategy of European companies. The penetration of new markets outside natural markets (i.e. a predominantly regional catchment area) usually requires investment in a cement distribution terminal serviced by rail or river with silos for storage and equipment for unloading and loading.

Notwithstanding these reasons for the predominantly regional nature of cement trade, international cement trade has developed over the last decade. Most European cement companies face stagnating or declining regional cement markets and consider international cement trade as a way to maintain or ensure their production level.

The costs for cement exporters resulting from technical barriers are of three types:

(a)   the need for multiple testing due to differing national technical standards. The cost of this testing is not significant compared to the turnover of most cement plants, and the removal of this cost cannot be expected to have any significant impact on trade;

(b)   the need to make different cement types or grades to meet different standards. This cost is probably more significant, but is still not a major impediment to trade, since different blends can be made from the same basic clinker and materials, and a single cement blend may meet several technical specifications;

(c)   the requirement to have testing and certification carried out by approved laboratories or certification authorities in the importing country (even where the theoretical provision exists for approval of bodies in the producing country but none have been approved or the cost and delay in using them is prohibitive). This is of special significance because it creates delays and learning costs for the first export to a new market, and so inhibits the first penetration of a market, and could prevent low-volume occasional exports in response to temporary market opportunities, but is not so important for regular exporters.

The effect on trade is therefore not as great as in products such as machinery, where the test procedures are more expensive, and the wide range of models require a lot of repeated testing. Our interviews have indicated, however, that the testing and certification requirements are a significant factor preventing firms from exporting to new markets, and we would expect the removal of these barriers to have both a direct and a psychological impact on increasing trade.

The delays in particular can make exporting for special customer orders impossible, but cement is normally shipped to a distribution and storage point, so delays are a cost but not always an impediment.

11.4.1. Product range

Cement is a uniform commodity product and there is no significant difference in essence between the products sold in different Member States (although the mix of products may be adapted to local climate, aggregates or soil conditions). The effect of technical barriers to trade is to increase testing costs, against different minimum or target values for the technical parameters, rather than to affect the range of products produced, or the cost of production.

There are five main types of common cements – Portland cement (CEM I), Portland composite cement (CEM II), blast furnace cement (CEM III), pozzolanic cement (CEM IV) and composite cement (CEM V) as well as a number of special cements (e.g. sulphate resisting cement) to particular specifications. All manufacturers are in a position to make CEM I cement (Portland cement) and most can make a number of other cements as well as a range of strength classes.

Manufacturers normally work in campaigns, e.g. a three-month period producing one type of clinker, with different grinding and blending of components to give different specifications. Sometimes a plant will run a special campaign for a major customer or a large export order. There is no significant cost penalty for this since the various grades are produced using a standard clinker. A more open market without technical barriers to trade might lead to some marginal specialization of production, enabling longer and fewer campaigns; it might also remove some of the special campaigns by harmonizing standards; but the effect on cost and efficiency would be marginal.

11.4.2. Investment

A major concern of the industry is unfair import competition from firms, outside the EU, which are state owned or have significant state aid. With the present industry ownership and state-aid regime, it is indeed possible that removal of all technical barriers to trade would favour exports from and further investment in these subsidized plants.

Cost advantages in cement come from such factors as low-cost energy; low cost of environmental protection in quarrying, e.g. outside the EU where local regulations do not always apply; or pre-eminently from economies of scale. The latter usually relate to local and regional market size, which will have the main economic impact. The cost of technical barriers is relatively insignificant compared to these production cost factors, but the general increase in trade which might result from removing barriers could lead new investment to lower cost locations.

This might lead to more acquisitions and mergers in an already concentrated industry, and also to more rationalization of plants by the existing major companies which have plants in many countries. The five major cement groups operate less than 20% of total world capacity, which opens the door to further concentrations.

Acquisitions in central and eastern Europe have in some cases been driven by the desire to limit the impact of low-priced imports and to control neighbouring markets, so it is possible that similar actions within the EU may also take place. Recent acquisitions within the EU, for example Italcementi's acquisition of Ciments Français, show that the process of integration in the cement industry is continuing. The prospect of more open competition may be one cause of this quite considerable reorganization and increasing cross-border ownership is creating pressures, which are likely in the long term to lead to dismantling of technical barriers to trade. This may also lead to pressure from the industry to remove barriers with third countries, where European manufacturers are investing – for example: Poland's 15 million tonne capacity is now 65% controlled by foreign firms including Lafarge of France, CBR of Belgium and new players such as the Irish CRH group and Rumeli, the large Turkish group. The Czech Republic has become a major exporter to the EU. Portuguese manufacturers are looking to acquire plants in Morocco (CIMPOR has recently invested there) and Brazil, and European groups are interested in cement plants throughout the Maghreb and Mashreq regions of the Mediterranean. European groups are also seeking to benefit from expansion in South-East Asia.

11.4.3. Organization and management

Technical barriers to trade or their removal are not seen to have any impact on organization or management of firms, but removal of barriers would have an impact on merger and acquisition activity.

Impact on competitiveness and customer choice

It is clear that competitive forces in the EU would be greater without technical barriers to trade, but it is also likely that the past effect of dumping and subsidized imports would have put much of the EU capacity out of the market in past periods of low demand. Similarly, in the periods of high demand the price increases which give cement companies a periodic boost in profitability would have been reduced by imports and not allowed EU firms to survive the recessions. Discussions with the industry suggest that it would probably argue that the extremely cyclical nature of construction justifies some protection of cement producers.

Analysis of cement prices throughout the EU would be very complex, but it is clear that freer trade would bring benefits to consumers. The wide price differences that may occur when there are shortages show that there is scope for increased trade, leading to price reductions in many regions, especially during periods of high demand.

There is no impact of technical barriers to trade on customer choice: the range of cement grades is always available and there is little product differentiation. But the existing situation does restrict the choice of suppliers for most customers.

11.5. Conclusions

11.5.1. Effectiveness of approaches

The approaches used by the European Commission in tackling barriers to trade in cement are:

(a)   Mutual Recognition procedures through Art. 30. This has been exercised only in France, which was the clearest case of regulatory barriers, but the inclusion of mutual recognition clauses in the French decrees is not seen to have any practical effect;

(b)   the Construction Products Directive, which does not yet work for any products, and has not yet produced a mandate for harmonized standards for cement;

(c)   Public Procurement legislation, which is having an impact by requiring public bodies to redraft their technical specifications.

There is a consensus that the testing standard ENV196 has given a boost to trade and relieved industry of time-consuming administration. Apart from improved testing, however, there is a general consensus among respondents that improvement has been too slow in the last 10 years.

The report of the Chairman of the SLIM Panel on Construction Products (15 October 1996, page 6), which analyses the implementation of the European Directive on Construction Products, recognizes that 'the functioning of the single market through this Directive requires the adoption of technical specifications, either Harmonized Standards or European Technical Approvals or Recognized Technical Specification' but deplores that 'eight years after the adoption of the CPD, none of these are available although substantial financial resources have been engaged'. (ECU 29 million from the Commission budget ...)'.

This process represents a difficult task in the case of the cement industry. This is due to the fact that the cement industry is characterized by the coexistence of a number of regional markets for the reasons described above.

The European cement industry, however, is now very much in favour of the adoption of European Standards for cement and is participating actively in the standardization process. A pre-standard ENV197-1 was thus adopted in 1992. The European cement industry has also participated in the development of the European standards for cement listed in Table 11.1. Since 1992, national cement standards have been adjusted to meet the ENV197-1 requirements. Some countries such as Italy have fully adopted the ENV as their national standard.

As this report is being written, considerable progress has been made in the process to transform the present ENV197-1 into an EN standard. The mandate which will allow the preparation of a harmonized European standard received a positive opinion by the Standing Committee on Construction, of Directive 89/106, and was sent to the Standing Committee of Directive 83/189 for final approval before being officially issued to CEN.

Once a harmonized European cement standard is in place (expected to be at the end of 1999) CE marking will be possible and will assist intra-country trade. This will be welcomed by the cement industry. The effectiveness of past measures, however, has been limited, as shown by the albeit qualitative assessment in Table 11.4. Consumers could well benefit from additional action.

Table 11.4.   Effectiveness of measures for cement

Measure	State of implementation	Effectiveness[1]
MRP: Art. 30 procedures	action against France	*
Public procurement legislation	implemented	**
Construction Products Directive	implemented, but no harmonized standards	n.a.
Harmonized standards	pre-standards, but no HS mandates	*

[1] on a scale of 1-5 where ***** = the most effective
n.a. = not applicable
Source: W.S. Atkins.

11.5.2. Remaining barriers

Manufacturers of cement contacted stated that there are some barriers to trade in Europe, but did not complain vociferously. This appears to be because, given the regional nature of markets, they do not see exports as part of their core business. Traders of cement were more outspoken and stated that serious regulatory and other barriers of uncertain status are affecting the market, and they report that these include national regulations in France and Germany, and to lesser extent in Nordic countries. The main barriers, however, will remain the influence of codes of practice, training, and product approval procedures for building control and latent defects insurance, and the supervision role of architects and engineers in most construction projects, which will be difficult to overcome. In the absence of CPD harmonization these create a need for testing in every destination market, and this multiple testing need is combined with delays, administrative hassle and cost, particularly in countries where a technician from a designated government lab has to visit the exporter's plant in person to collect samples and inspect procedures. It is the testing requirements, and not differences in standards, which create the reported problems.

Table 11.5.   Remaining barriers in cement

Barrier	Importance[1]
Regulations and national testing rules	***
Delays and cost of testing	**
Building regulations and control	***
Decennial/liability insurance (France, Belgium)	****
Construction codes and standards	***
Engineering/architects' training and procedures	****

[1] on a scale of 1-5 where ***** = the most important
Source: W.S. Atkins.

11.5.3. Measures suggested by industry

No action was suggested by the industry, although traders would like to see national testing requirements removed. The European cement industry is working actively to establish the EN for cement so that when the CPD is properly implemented, national testing will no longer be required. In the meantime, consumers need protection, but acceptance of appropriate documentation of producer country testing could suffice.

12. Electrical cables[7]

12.1. Product information

NACE code: 341 insulated wires and cables.

PRODCOM codes:31.30 covers the whole range of insulated wire and cable of which 31.30.13.70.A, 31.30.13.73.B and 31.30.13.75.B are the low voltage groups.

12.1.1. Product scope

The insulated electrical cable category, for use below 1kV, was chosen for review because the sector is subject to both national regulations and different national standards. This category excludes telecoms and computer cables, insulated or enamelled wires for winding and other manufacturing applications, and high voltage power cables. The products are typically used in wiring buildings and in the manufacture of cable harnesses and wiring for electrical equipment and appliances.

Many of the simpler electrical cable types have European CENELEC standards (HDs and ENs) and these are a significant category of cable product in terms of volume, and thus impact across Europe.

The sector is covered by a multilateral recognition arrangement between testing and certification bodies in several countries, the HAR agreement, which has not been accepted as an agreement group by the EOTC. The HAR agreement is, in effect, a mutually recognized set of national quality marks relating to CENELEC harmonized cable types and is thus something of a hybrid between a quality mark and a testing and certification agreement group.

This report covers cable only (i.e. as delivered from a cable making factory, before being used in a manufacturing process or in wiring a building or appliance).

According to manufacturers, the cables market divides into three segments according to the clients' technical requirements:

(a)   the utilities market, with large long-term contracts, using utility companies' own technical specifications, now based mainly on European harmonized standards;
(b)   the industrial market, mainly using industrial standards, increasingly harmonized;
(c)   the special cables market, using special private specifications, and supplied mainly by smaller manufacturers in local markets.

This report deals principally with the industrial segment.

---

[7]   This product was included later in the study and responses from many firms were received too late for them to be visited. The chapter is largely based on interviews in the UK with the UK subsidiaries of major EU cable firms, and written questionnaire responses from several continental EU firms.

12.1.2. National regulations

The cable manufacturing industry is rarely subject to control at a statutory level. Standards bodies we have contacted are not aware of any cable design or testing procedure being incorporated in national law in any Member State.

Trade associations and professional bodies have had a long-term role in the development of technical standards for the industry. In the UK, for example, a trade association has existed for 94 years and procedures and requirements have been developed within the industry.

By contrast there are differing national regulations for installation, including, for example, regulations on what cables are permitted for use in particular house-wiring applications, or in the leads for domestic appliances. 'Traditions' and building regulations vary between countries – the latter also between regions within Member States. No efforts have been made to harmonize in this area, partly because no single country's method is considered to have special technical or health and safety merits, and so there is no obvious benefit in attempting to standardize them. However, as each Member State generally bases its regulations on the international specifications outlined in the International Electrotechnical Committee document IEC 364 (which has been incorporated in a harmonized document HD 384), there is already some consistency across countries.

For example, in the UK requirements for electrical installations have been produced by the Institute of Electrical Engineers (IEE) for supply up to 1kV. These were converted to British Standard 7671 in 1992. They have statutory power as part of the Scottish building regulations and compliance with them is deemed to be statutory compliance in the UK Act that covers the installation of electrical power. The UK Electricity Act has a section requiring the Health and Safety Executive to monitor the electricity supply industry for compliance with the IEE regulations in the installation of electrical supply cables.

For higher voltage cables, the electricity supply industry in each Member State enforces its own specifications and standards. As these utilities are covered by the EC public procurement legislation, their specifications are now generally based on harmonized European standards (and if not, tenders must not specify national standards unless they permit equivalent standards).

12.1.3. New Approach (and other EC) measures

Cables are covered by the Low Voltage Directive (73/23/EEC), which applies to 'any equipment designed for use with a voltage rating of between 50 and 1,000V for alternating current and between 75 and 1,500V for direct current'. 'As a result, any cable which complies with the provisions of the LVD may be legally placed on the market in any EEA country. A wide range of CENELEC standards for cables have been referenced in the OJ as harmonized standards within the terms of the LVD. Consequently, Member States' authorities are required to consider products which comply with such CENELEC standards as being in conformity with the safety objectives of the LVD. In such cases, they are required not to impede their free movement for reasons of safety.'

The CE-marking requirements are now incorporated in the LVD, with a transitional period from 1 January 1995 (entry into force of Directive 93/68 on CE-marking) until 1 January

1997. Some manufacturers do not intend to apply the CE-marking to their products until the end of the transition period, so it is not yet in effective application for cables.

12.1.4. The HAR agreement[8]

The cable industry launched the voluntary HAR agreement in 1974. HAR is described as 'a gentleman's club' with 16 members (the 15 EU Member States and Switzerland). An application from Hungary is currently being reviewed. The agreement covers certain categories of electrical wires and cables which conform to European CENELEC standards. These were not drawn up under the New Approach procedures and so they are not harmonized standards in the sense of the New Approach (see below, Section 12.1.5).

The HAR agreement requires a single third party (non-manufacturer) certification body per country. Because of this it does not meet the rules for EOTC Agreement Groups which must be open to any testing body. This structure for the certification of HAR standards is a consequence of the mechanism for development of 'harmonized' standards used in the Low Voltage Directive, which is different from the New Approach. Harmonized standards under the LVD are established by common agreement by bodies notified by each Member State to the other Member States and the Commission. At the time of creation, most countries had one dominant, frequently state subsidized, standards body for electrical products and the German VDE and French UTE (electrical standards bodies) were particularly powerful. The UK cable industry created a specific cables standards authority, Basec, although originally it remained a section of the UK national standards organization BSI. The standards bodies became the certification bodies under HAR.

The agreement allows for the issue of a single European mark (HAR) accompanied by the national logo awarded by each certification body, with this mark being mutually recognized by all the signatory bodies of the participating countries. Thus, the HAR agreement covers both the mutual recognition of the accreditation of differing certification bodies and mutual recognition of test results and certificates by the uniform use of special standards for testing and the related quality systems.

The HAR agreement is administered by the HAR-CENELEC group, made up of representatives of the member certification bodies, and there is a HAR Advisory Group made up of manufacturers' representatives. The harmonized standards are drawn up by CENELEC Technical Committee TC20. There is also a Committee for Operating Systems and Methods, OSM, with members from the testing laboratories.

The range of cables covered has been stable since 1991. HAR covers five categories of cable, all of which are subject to European harmonized standards adopted by CENELEC. The categories currently covered are:

(a)   PVC insulated cables up to 450/750V;
(b)   rubber insulated cables up to 450/750V;

---

[8]   Note: throughout this chapter we refer to Basec as an example of the functioning of the HAR scheme, since the Consultants interviewed Basec for information about the scheme. The HAR member testing and certification body in other member countries of the HAR scheme are believed to perform in a similar way.

(c)   mineral insulated cables up to 450/750V;

(d)   flat PVC sheathed flexible cables;

(e)   rubber insulated lift cables for normal use.

Conformity tests are carried out on the basis of standards adopted by CENELEC and the agreement requires that by mid-1996 inspections and monitoring of the quality assurance systems of production units on the basis of standard EN ISO29002 is also required.

In 1994 some 222 enterprises had been issued with 1084 HAR mark licences. Each certifier can only certify firms with manufacturing facilities in their own country for HAR. For example, the UK body Basec has issued HAR licences to ten firms in the UK, but it has also issued Basec licences, whose quality requirements it claims to be identical, to around 40 firms, some in the UK and some in 11 other non-EU countries. Firms in HAR member countries are not allowed to apply for certification by the approved body in another member country.

12.1.5. Standards

There are different standards for cable design according to the function of the cable. Even for cables with similar functions, different Member States have developed different technical solutions. As a result there is a wide range of different types and hundreds of different standards. Some standards simply specify the design and materials necessary, others include a description of the required manufacturing process and others lay down testing requirements and their required frequency and necessary support documentation.

Most CENELEC harmonized cable standards have been published as Harmonization Documents (HDs). These differ from ENs in that although they must be announced, and conflicting national standards must be withdrawn, Member States may also retain national standards as long as they do not conflict and the HD allows for national divergence, for example if there are differences in national regulations.

Most harmonized cable standards were developed by compiling existing national cable standards (formerly only recognized at a national level) into a single standard, with a common nomenclature and codes, which is accepted by all members. This is a sort of formal mutual recognition of (some) different national standards. Any cable manufactured to those standards can then be legally placed on the market in any member country. The standards do not correspond to a harmonized set of essential requirements as in the New Approach directives, and because of different installation rules, not all cable types covered by the harmonized standards can be used interchangeably in all Member States. In other words, although the CENELEC standards produced so far are called harmonized standards, they are not harmonizing in the sense of introducing a single common specification used interchangeably throughout Europe.

Many national standards still exist, outside the scope of the harmonized standards, for products used commonly only in one or a few Member States, and many cables are manufactured to customers' own specifications, some of which (e.g. the major electrical engineering firms or motor manufacturers) may have important market power.

It is expected that by 1998 all common cable types will be covered by HDs, but some interviewees commented that progress seems slow. One company commented the industry has no incentive to work for real harmonization because if a particular Member State's standard is adopted, that country would have a commercial advantage, yet setting a completely new standard would simply add cost to Europe as a whole.

Manufacturers' preference is to develop their own design and sell it exclusively using their own reputation and certification as guarantees of quality. When a number of customers make it clear that they wish to multi-source a cable type the manufacturer will approach their national standards body, e.g. VDE, to apply for a standard. The manufacturer has more influence at a national level than at CENELEC. The manufacturer will try to influence the standards body committee to use its design. If it is not successful and a new design is chosen at least there is a level playing-field for everyone. In the majority of cases the market regards conformity with a standard as a sufficient indicator of quality. Manufacturers claim that the disadvantage of a standard is that it freezes the design technology.

12.2. Industry information

12.2.1. Sector representation

The European industry is represented by the European Confederation of Associations of Manufacturers of Insulated Wires and Cables (Europacable). Most of the Member States have a trade association of their own, but not all firms are members.

12.2.2. Industry structure

According to Europacable (quoted in *Panorama of EU Industry*) there were over 100 firms producing cables and wires in the EU in 1993 with around 250 production sites. There were around 71,000 employees. It is probable that the number of firms and employment is rather larger than this, as the example of the UK below suggests. There are production sites in all Member States apart from Luxembourg.

> In the UK the British Cable Makers Confederation (BCMC) has 15 members and claims to represent 90% of the industry. The BCMC acknowledges that there are eight other manufacturers in the UK of which one is substantial but with a limited product range aimed at the 'wholesaler' market. The UK Central Statistical Office gathers returns from 85 'manufacturers'. The big discrepancy is in employment figures where for 1984 BCMC members had 10,500 employees while the CSO figures indicated the industry had 23,500. The certification body, Basec, has 22 manufacturing licensees in the UK and believes there are up to 20 other firms not accredited, including specialist firms making small runs for the aerospace industry. The British trade association would thus seem to be reasonably representative in terms of production volume but is skewed to the larger firms making the volume products. Relative to the other large Member States, the UK is characterized by the relatively high concentration of the industry.

Within Europe the large manufacturers produce both electrical and telecommunications cables as well as winding wires. There are more manufacturers of electrical cables than of other types. Between 1986 and 1993 information cables share of production rose from 23% to 35%. Harmonization has concentrated on electrical cables and the HAR scheme is orientated to electrical cables. Their share of the market fell from 70% to 56% between 1986 and 1983. As a result of these trends, the relative importance of electrical cables below 1kV has declined in the industry.

Compared with other capital products used by the electrical industry, production of cables is unusually fragmented. This arises from the substantial levels of manufacturing carried out by relatively small companies who service their national and regional markets. It is probable that many firms described as cable manufacturers are in fact making up cable harnesses, leads, or special applications from purchased cable and wire, as opposed to integrated cable manufacturers commencing from wire drawing and extrusion or coating of the insulation.

Table 12.1.   Main world manufacturers by sales[1] of wire and cable, 1992–93

1993 rank	Company	Country	1992 sales US$M	1993 sales US$M
1	Alcatel Cable	France	6,224	5,890
2	Pirelli	Italy	3,259	3,558
3	BICC	UK	2,687	2,866
4	Sumitomo Electric	Japan	2,997	2,865
5	Furukawa	Japan	2,429	2,429
6	Fujikura	Japan	1,660	1,503
7	Siemens	Germany	1,297	1,351
8	Hitachi Cable	Japan	1,417	1,275
9	ABB	Sweden	1,203	874
10	Nokia	Finland	526	864
11	Goldstar Cable	South Korea	794	831
12	Mitsubishi Cable	Japan	679	626
13	Showa Electric	Japan	678	608
14	Ericsson	Sweden	508	596
15	Phelps Dodge	USA	544	566
16	Delta	UK	465	516

[1]   Sales values include installation and consultancy work and cover mains distribution cable, building installation cable and winding wire.

Source: Goulden Reports: *The World Manufacturers of Insulated Wire and Cables*, 1996.

The major manufacturers reflect the pattern of local manufacture by producing in a large number of geographically distributed factories (e.g. Nokia cover Europe from the Netherlands, Germany and Finland; ABB have factories in Sweden, Ireland and Germany; BICC serve the EU using factories in the UK, Germany, Italy, Spain and Portugal and many products are made in all the factories). In France, Italy and Germany, in addition to four of the top five large European producers being present, there are many small specialist producers.

In the EU as a whole, around 10% of production volume is accounted for by small and medium-sized companies.

Eastern Europe and the CIS have been the major focus of attention in company expansion plans in the early 1990s but the emphasis is beginning to move to South-East Asia. In addition, a number of new companies are being formed, particularly in South-East Asia.

Cable making is a mature technology, although subject to much innovation in both process technology (e.g. use of robotics) and products (e.g. fibre-optic applications). It is easy for new entrants to invest, with off-the-shelf equipment, and for existing low-cost producers, for example in eastern Europe, to upgrade their technology and quality. It is also a competitive and often low-margin business (for example, judicious buying in the copper market is a significant source of profitability). There is therefore a fear of low-cost competition, and a tendency to favour protective, rather than market-opening measures.

12.2.3. Output and trade

Cable is a product which is traded extensively. Exports outside the EU make up 20% of production, and imports are of a similar magnitude. Data for intra-EU trade is not available, but because there is significant intra-firm trade resulting from production specialization by the large firms, the level of intra-EU trade is believed to be high. One major manufacturer estimates this as 25–30% of consumption for the industrial market.

The volume of intra-EU trade and world trade is reported to be increasing dramatically because of the opening up of markets. This is particularly the case with the utilities market, as a result of the Public Procurement Directives. Italy, the UK and Spain in particular are reported to be opening up quickly and pre-qualifying many non-national suppliers. Trade in the industrial market is also increasing.

The largest producer, with about one-third of EU production, is Germany, and Italy, France and the UK are also large producers.

Table 12.2.   European insulated wires and cables: production data by country, 1993 (million ECU)

Country	Production
Germany	3,223
France	1,704
Italy	1,568
UK	1,311
Spain	545
B/DK/NL	886
GR/IRL/P	419
Total	**9,656**

Source: Europacable (the smaller countries are usually dominated by one manufacturer, so for commercial reasons Europacable consolidates the figures).

Apparent consumption fell each year during the early 1990s although it has now bottomed out over Europe as a whole. Exports grew as the industry tried to compensate and keep factories loaded.

Because the influence of former national standards still dominates, a lot of exports follow historical trade patterns. For example, UK manufacturers tend to export to areas where BS standards have been recognized, such as Ireland, the Middle East, Hong Kong and the Commonwealth: the exports of Pirelli UK are mainly to areas outside the EU, and intra-EU exports from the UK went mainly to Ireland and the country of the parent, Italy.

Table 12.3.   European insulated wires and cables: 1993 trade data

	ECU million
Production	9,655
Extra-EU exports	1,861
Imports	1,782
Apparent consumption	9,576

Source: Panorama of EC Industry 1995.

12.3. Trade barriers

12.3.1. Regulatory barriers

Although there are regulations concerning cables and wiring installations in several countries, no one interviewed considers these to create regulatory barriers to trade. Where different cable types are customarily used in different countries, this is not seen as a problem either: they can manufacture to any standard without significant additional manufacturing cost.

Any cable that has been successfully harmonized at the CENELEC level must, by definition, be legally permitted to be placed on the market in each EU country. In some cases, however, local installation regulations are an obstacle to the use of the cable, but in many cases regulations have been adapted without a problem. For example, to achieve harmonization for PVC flexible cable it was only necessary to agree changes to colour codes in Member States (this took place before the single market programme).

National cable design has been driven by local regulations and so where this has led to the development of specific designs, harmonization is difficult, but is not considered to be a barrier to trade. In order to sell a 'local' cable design a non-local manufacturer must simply design its cable to the relevant local standard, test it as necessary and get it approved by the customer. Because the cost penalty is not great, the existence of local requirements is not seen as a barrier to trade in itself. There is no evidence of Member States generating new local regulations for either consumer or market protection.

The only exception to this is that some manufacturers have expressed concern about a potential future barrier in Denmark. Denmark notified other states about its desire to change its technical regulations to allow both PVC and lead-free PVC cables. No Member State objected and now the change is in place. Currently only local manufacturers supply lead-free cable, so if Denmark were to make ordinary PVC illegal, manufacturers would regard that as a barrier. However, currently there are no plans to do this.

In cases where local requirements have led to the development of new products, the industry does not feel that there are any barriers to exporting that product within the EU. For example, fire disasters in the UK led to London Underground (LUL) specifying stringent new requirements for low smoke and zero halogen cables. UK manufacturers feel that sales to Austria and Germany are possible because the LUL standard is recognized as being state of the art. Each operator/buyer will want to carry out its own tests and may even seek to modify a product to its own precise requirements but that is not seen as a barrier. British firms comment that whilst German national standards are different in some cases, their main problem in serving the market is the entry cost of supplying a full range at competitive prices. Other non-EU markets are simply more attractive to them.

12.3.2. Non-regulatory barriers

Problems related to insurance and liability

In the construction industry, specifiers and contractors face potential liability claims in the event of damage or injury due to electrical fires or electric shock. For this reason, they follow recommended codes of practice, which will refer to standards, and in the case of French decennial insurance, the technical controllers will require that cables either follow a standard or have an *avis technique*. In most cases they will have a strong incentive, therefore, to use HAR-marked cables. For reasons discussed previously, the HAR mark issued by the purchaser's national testing body is usually preferred, even though, by its nature as a mutual recognition scheme, the HAR agreement means that the HAR mark granted by another national testing body should be viewed as equivalent. For example, in the UK Basec cable is chosen by the vast majority of electricians for twin and earth, armoured power cables and fire resistant low smoke and fume (LSF) cables. Failure to do so would invite litigation in the event of failure as they could be accused of knowingly fitting an uncertified grade of cable, or one suspected of having testing requirements less rigorous than the national scheme.

National preferences of customers

Understanding of the HAR mark is extremely low in some sectors of the buyer community. Non-German manufacturers of HAR appliance cable for OEM use say the quality mark is well understood but they still get German customers requesting VDE HAR, not understanding that only a German firm can supply that product. No non-German manufacturer said they had ever lost an order because of this once the HAR system was fully understood by the buyer, and the HAR certification bodies in each country undertake to explain to national customers that the testing carried out by other HAR members is equivalent to that of the national body. [We understand that exceptions to this strict domicile requirement have occasionally been made, e.g. when an Italian manufacturer wished to make cables to a standard only used in the UK, so that testing provisions for it were not available in Italy.]

Other barriers: recycling needs

The provision of cable drums to customers is a major cost to manufacturers. These drums are usually made of wood or plastic. The recirculating or recycling system for cabling drums in Member States, apart from Germany, is manufacturer specific and local and this will add cost for new entrants into the market unless they can arrange a cost-effective returns system, i.e. any importer needs a regular flow of business with empties recirculating rapidly to overcome start-up costs. In Germany an independent organization owns all the drums and recirculates them amongst manufacturers. This is not regarded as a barrier by anyone interviewed, although importers may have a cost disadvantage.

12.3.3. Testing and certification

No substantial problems relating to testing and certification have been mentioned by manufacturers. Testing is cheap, and is done on a sample basis anyway, so testing multiple products to different standards is not a cost penalty. Testing in the destination country is not normally required. The HAR agreement is largely responsible for removing double testing requirements (but some manufacturers still carry out voluntary double testing for marketing reasons).

Manufacturers normally supply buyers with a certificate with each drum stating that they have tested a sample for conformity to either a national standard (usually now implementing a HD or EN standard) or an in-house standard. This certificate is effectively treated as a guarantee, enabling a purchaser to return the goods if they subsequently prove to be below the stated standard.

In Scandinavian Member States, because of local conditions, there is a need for certain cables to perform at -40° C rather than the -15° C test set by CENELEC. (This is a special national condition (SNC), and is therefore permitted. SNCs must be modified as early as possible during the public enquiry stage.) Compliance with this requirement in practice requires local testing of the cable and the use of local marks in both Finland and Sweden, since the tests are not carried out by testing labs in other Member States, and the standard is not included in the HAR agreement. (Legally, of course, Finland or Sweden could not impose regulations making local testing mandatory and there is no suggestion that they would. Indeed, any laboratory could offer the low temperature tests if it chose to, but it would not be able to award the HAR mark licence unless it belonged to a certification body participating in the HAR scheme.)

Other problems that exist are due to customer preference rather than technical barriers.

In the UK, France and Germany in particular, local customers prefer cables which conform to the previous national standards (which have now mostly been incorporated into HD or EN standards). Other types now permitted in the common standard are not generally specified, even though they can be legally sold. The former standards arose originally because of differing building regulations or traditions. This will slow down the pace of real harmonization and reduction in the number of cable types as consumers (i.e. the specifying engineers) are reluctant to change, however minor the change may be, to achieve harmonization (and the cost saving to manufacturers is small).

12.3.4. Testing by the HAR mark scheme

The HAR agreement for mutual recognition of quality marks has its own testing requirements. It should be recalled that HAR is a voluntary agreement, which not all manufacturers use, and has no mandatory requirement. (The Portuguese association APETCE reports that in a recent survey of cables available on the Portuguese market, 72% had the HAR mark, and 15% had CE marking.)

The HAR-CENELEC Group, made up of representatives of the HAR certification bodies, determines the tests necessary and the frequency of tests for a product to be granted the HAR mark. There are four categories of test ranging from those required for every sample taken to those to be carried out on every twentieth sample. The tests cover:

(a)   F100   markings, construction, core (colour and size), insulation and sheathing;
(b)   F50   twisting, tensile strength, stretchability;
(c)   F25   elongation (not a safety test);
(d)   F05   cold tests to -15°C (not a safety test).

As mentioned above by contrast, national standards which are still in use set a variety of tests, or none, depending on the particular cable type. It is not possible to generalize within countries.

The costs of complying with a national standard or user's specification are not significant enough to be a problem to manufacturers. For quality marks, however, prices are higher. Based on the Basec charges in the UK, the ISO 9000 certification costs between ECU 25,000 and ECU 35,000 per year per site. Testing costs from ECU 125 per year for a simple single-core cable to ECU 500 per year for an armoured power cable.

The HAR process effectively means that 16 different certification bodies are deemed able to meet the HAR testing requirements. Mutual recognition works perfectly well in this case. Within a country, however, manufacturers have no incentive to promote the HAR mark because that would encourage imports and anyway public awareness is low. They prefer to promote the local marks. Importers from non-HAR countries cannot use the HAR mark and so refer to their product as harmonized or as harmonized VDE etc., depending on the accreditation their source has. Of course, a harmonized product that is manufactured in a non-HAR country with a certificate from one of the test houses which happens to be a HAR member cannot carry the HAR mark, because the country of origin and local testing requirements have not been met. Most customers appear not to be aware or concerned about this, but the HAR members are trying to raise awareness of the scheme. (Basec has issued full page advertisements in trade press stressing the third party testing and performance requirements, and contrasting it with the CE-marking.)

The HAR system prevents competition amongst testing and certification bodies because the manufacturer has no choice but to use the national 'approved' body – of which there is only one per country. In this it acts as a cartel arrangement by market sharing, with national monopolies. This may well add costs to the process. For example, Basec claim their fee structure for product testing is up to five times cheaper than the Swedish equivalent (because the latter has lower testing volumes over which to recover the capital and overhead costs) but Swedish manufacturers cannot shop around for the best deal. QA certification fees, on the other hand, are believed to be fairly similar, since this is a more competitive business. In an ideal world fewer organizations each with a Europe-wide remit would almost certainly reduce costs. Manufacturers would appear to be in favour of a more rationalized and therefore cheaper certification and testing system but the 'conversion costs' in terms of the promotional campaign needed to make consumers understand the change would be very high. Agreement would also require a degree of consensus amongst testing and certification bodies that has not been shown to date.

The operation of the HAR scheme can be illustrated by the example of Basec.

> Basec was created in 1971 with the aim of policing product quality in the UK. In practice, by raising standards the industry also hoped to reduce the risk of import penetration. This would seem to have worked well for most of that decade. In the 1980s Basec was advertised well to the industry with the advertisements paid for by the UK industry. Irish Cable and Wire (an Alcatel subsidiary) was Basec

accredited but the impression of a British Quality Standard was created. Basec continues to promote its 'principles of safety' – 'Tested to the highest possible standards of durability, strength and efficiency; assured reliability and quality; no unnecessary risks'. Today most electricians insist on Basec approval for BS6004 twin and earth cable. At the lower end of the market for other applications Basec is not so strongly preferred. EU importers know that the BS mark carries commercial weight and if they are selling sufficient volumes the Basec mark might be worth getting to reinforce the quality image. It is unclear whether Basec certification commands a price premium.

Basec is a non-profit organization with a turnover of £1.2m. Half its revenue comes from ISO 9000 certification and the rest from product conformity testing. Only about 20% of their customers for product testing and marking are subscribers to the HAR scheme. The rest (some UK manufacturers but mainly foreign) will display the Basec mark without the HAR mark.

A Basec certified product is subject to superior sampling than a cable that merely conforms to a British Standard. Basec sample 200 units per million, thus ensuring a failure rate of not more than 2% (for contrast, if the UK BSI sampling rate were used – five per million – the risk would be 10%). Sites are visited every three months and up to 150 samples per year are taken. Basec say that consumer protection is not the formal aim of Basec but they regard it as important. Basec are themselves unaware of the sampling frames used by other Member State bodies. Manufacturers claim that the advantage of Basec is that the QA and test procedures provide a formal set of rules to be adhered to by all manufacturers and this also helps them in setting internal management targets. Basec say that their certification procedures are the same for both Basec and Basec HAR marks.

It would seem that the decline in the UK industry has led to a commercial need for Basec to sell its services in other countries. This is one reason why the number of foreign licensees for Basec has grown from one in 1980 to four in 1992 and now stands at 10 with number 11 currently being assessed. This has opened up the UK market to imports of quality product and it seems that the UK manufacturers, who remain one of the guarantors of Basec via the BCMC, would rather that fewer non-UK manufacturers had been licensed.

Now that they are competing for non-HAR customers, the certifying bodies try to establish their own quality image. Basec claims that some other European certification bodies do not have the testing methodology and quality mark image that Basec and VDE, for example, have created in the UK and German markets respectively, although under the HAR scheme the testing procedures and criteria are supposed to be identical.

Many customers in the EU retain a preference for familiar (non-mandatory) local marks, and it is difficult for foreign manufacturers to sell cable with their own national marks, even when the HAR mark is also used showing the equivalence of the testing procedures. In the UK, for example, the Basec mark exists as a local quality mark independently of HAR, and it was reported by one respondent to be common for an EU company which already has HAR certification for products sold in the EU to need also to have a Basec licence for products to BS standards which are sold only in the UK market. (There is no repeat testing of the product, but the ISO 9000 certification may need to be repeated or verified, and *de facto* they have to deal with the testing body in the UK as well as their home certification body.)

Likewise in the UK a company with Basec ISO 9001 certification will find that it needs KEMA ISO 9001 certification as well if it is to sell Dutch standard product in the Dutch market. The companies regard this as a cost of market entry, not a trade barrier. Basec also requires ISO 9000 and prefers this certification to be undertaken by themselves. This certification adds considerable cost which could be an entry barrier if the company concerned does not need ISO 9000 for its home market, but within the EU now this is most unlikely. (It is interesting to note that manufacturers regard ISO 9000 as a cost, not a benefit.)

ISO 9000 has gained rapid acceptance in the UK. Many wholesalers are certified and they believe a price premium is attached to cable produced using an ISO 9000 system although it is not specified by buyers in the wholesale market. Household appliance manufacturers express a preference for ISO 9000 but none of those interviewed by us actually required it. In the UK Basec has required manufacturers to have ISO 9000 for many years. The HAR scheme has only required this from mid-1996. As a result, buyers are not generally aware that HAR now requires both ISO 9000 certification and product testing.

12.4. Enterprise strategies

12.4.1. Product range

Harmonization (i.e. the development of common or compatible standards, although convergence of product specifications has not yet taken place) and the mutual recognition of quality marks has increased trade but is not thought to have had much impact on availability of products, or on rationalization of product ranges. Common standards should in time lead to potential economies of scale through rationalization of product variants, but so far only the relatively simple electrical cables (low voltage installation) have been covered, and differences in the cable types actually used in Member States (permitted under the HD or EN standard) still persist.

For rubber insulated cables in Finland, three former national cable types have been replaced by six harmonized types, with one type covering the special low temperature resistance needs of northern countries. However, it was reported that one clear success of the HAR mark for rubber cables has been that for machinery manufacturers. Machines can now be completed in the factory, whereas previously differing standards meant that customers had to complete cable installation themselves, incurring significant additional safety risks.

12.4.2. Investment

Investment plans have not been altered by the existence of some mutual recognition, but there is a suggestion that investment by EU firms may be diverted to lower cost areas to supply the EU market. One company has for many years supplied cable from Greece, Turkey and Ireland to the UK. In all cases conformity with the British Standard is the key criterion. All that is necessary is a good distribution and warehousing facility. Established European producers believe that further harmonization can only increase import penetration in the EU by factories from lower labour cost economies. [For this reason, manufacturers prefer to promote the HAR mark which is only available to producers from other HAR countries and not to those located in lower cost countries.] One company commented that EU manufacturers' future must lie in added value higher technology products. In the open market, now that standard compliance and quality assessment is widely available, non-EU imports are bound to increase in importance.

Recent years have seen investment for distribution by central European companies in the EU.

> One Polish company has acted to secure improved distribution. This Group's cable operations have a turnover of £300m and EU markets (particularly Germany) are now more significant than their home market. The company has VDE and Basec certification for relevant products. In the UK, the company is price competitive despite transport costs of 8% of product value. In the UK, a joint venture company has begun to supply electricity distributors with cable up to 11kV capacity.

12.4.3. Distribution and marketing

The main impact of removal of barriers came from the HAR scheme, and was mainly felt nearly 20 years ago. Interview respondents provided examples of the way their HAR cable activities had been affected:

> A subsidiary company of a large European group manufacturing HAR marked cable for use on appliances and as part of cord sets confirmed the success of HAR in intra-EU trade. They can now sell cable in any CENELEC country, but their own commercial issues make them concentrate on France, the UK and Switzerland. HAR solved their trade problems 20 years ago, but power cords remain more complicated because of differing standards for moulded plugs. Even so with one factory the company is able to serve five EU countries with cord sets. The group also has a single factory to serve the European market for basic wiring.

> One UK manufacturer shut down its dedicated HAR cable factory in 1995. They relocated some of the machinery and continue to supply the UK wholesale market but have withdrawn from OEM supply. HAR cable was chosen for the cutbacks because market prices were low, commercial product variations (colours and finishes and thus wastage) were high and other products offered better opportunities. However, they have to keep some capacity as they would lose wholesale customers if they could not supply a full product range.

We have seen, however, that trade now appears to be increasing, partly as a result of the entry of new low cost competitors. Some EEA producers may also be concerned that customers will pay less attention to the HAR marking, which only they are able to affix, when CE-marking of cables becomes more widespread. This should happen next year, once the CE-marking amendments to the LVD come fully into force. The main response of manufacturers seems to be attempts to promote and defend the HAR scheme as a protective measure. There may also have been an increase in advertising expenditure, but we have no hard evidence of changes in companies' marketing strategies.

12.4.4. Organization and management

The industry is not transnational to any great degree, but increasing trade is forcing some firms to become more international in outlook. One multinational's experience is indicative of the major firms' current ambitions. It is making attempts to internationalize and improve language ability amongst its managerial staff. A number of middle managers have served one to two years in three countries or more. Since 1995, it sends six managers per year on global strategy business courses and it recruits around 25 multilingual graduates per year.

12.4.5. Quality and testing

Manufacturers' attitudes and practices for testing have been covered elsewhere. Since testing has always been a necessary part of business operations there has been no significant change in procedures, but the HAR scheme's requirement for ISO 9000 certification is making QA system certification universal.

12.4.6. Impact on competitiveness and customer choice

There is no doubt that import penetration of the EU market, and trade within the EU, has increased greatly during the last ten years and particularly during the last five.

For example, one UK importer estimates growth in the 'wholesale' sector in the UK to have been from £12m in 1986 to £125m in 1996 (i.e. to 10%+ of the market). However, the OEM market is much less affected. The main sources of imports are Poland, Italy, Greece and Turkey. There was much less imported product in 1980. Because of the use of ring mains in the UK the two most popular products for installation wholesalers are UK and Ireland specific – PVC twin and earth cable to BS 6004 and single core double insulated PVC cables to BS 5467.

UK manufacturers say that their home market has become more penetrated by imports because of high prevailing prices and because the Basec quality mark is no longer a shield – Basec is actively promoting the mark to non-UK (and non-EU) producers. (It is not clear why UK cable prices remain relatively high, but this must indicate that despite the claims of HAR and the development of CENELEC standards, a significant level of protection has persisted – but is apparently now breaking down.)

Increased competition is reported to have led to lower prices and fewer manufacturers of rubber sheathed cables.

Whilst the importers interviewed tend to feel choice has increased, OEM customers have not experienced any change over the last 10 years. This may be because although the former national standards are now incorporated in the HD or EN standard, which has then been transposed back into national standards, they can continue to use the customary cable products. As new end products are designed, particularly products for EU markets, it is to be expected that there should be a gradual drift to specifying new cable types, leading eventually to some rationalization of specifications.

For most buyers there is now a wider choice of higher quality product, brought about by increased competition and the growth of ISO 9000, and accreditation of factories in lower labour cost countries.

12.5. Conclusions

12.5.1. Effectiveness of approaches

The CE marking provisions of the LVD have not yet reached the end of the transition period, and are as yet hardly being used, partly because of resistance by some major manufacturers. For this reason, mutual recognition in the wider sense can be said to be the approach which has applied.

The CENELEC standards, mainly HDs, have been a formal mechanism establishing mutual recognition of previously existing national standards and creating a degree of harmonization of nomenclature and colour coding, but not of safety and performance specifications. This has been successful in freeing trade and preventing new regulatory barriers. There has been no need for 83/189 notifications or Art. 30 procedures.

It should be remembered, however, that there are still many national standards not covered by CENELEC standards, and many proprietary customer specifications.

Within the limited range of products covered, the HAR scheme has been effective in creating mutual recognition of testing and certification, and largely, but not completely, eliminating the need for multiple testing to meet customer requirements. Now that CE-marking is about to become mandatory as a safety mark and open to all suppliers, HAR is being marketed as a quality mark, distinct from CE-marking.

Given the difficulty that the manufacturing industry is facing from increasingly high quality competition from low cost non-EU sources, their adverse reaction to the CE marking is not surprising. The CE-marking is viewed as a threat, by opening up the EU market and undermining the protective aspect of the HAR mark.

12.5.2. Remaining barriers

There are few remaining barriers to trade in both the perception of manufacturers and customers. The industry is at great pains to stress that trade is free (they propose this as an argument that the CE-marking is not needed), with no significant regulatory barriers. Nevertheless, national preferences reinforced by liability concerns perpetuate customer requests for national standards.

A rating of the identified barriers is shown in Table 12.5.

Table 12.4.   Effectiveness of approaches

Measure	State of implementation	Effectiveness[1]
LVD	since 1974	****
HAR scheme as a Mutual Recognition Arrangement	since 1976	****
HAR scheme as quality mark		***
Harmonized standards	over 100: mostly HDs, still being developed	***
CE marking (LVD)	end of transition period 1997	**

[1] on a scale of 1-5 where ***** = the most effective
Source: W.S. Atkins.

Table 12.5.   Relative importance of remaining barriers to trade

Barrier	Importance[1]
Remaining national standards	*
Residence requirements of the HAR scheme	**
Cost of recycling cable drums	**

[1] on a scale of 1-5 where ***** = the most important
Source: W.S. Atkins.

12.5.3. Measures suggested by industry

The industry is not enthusiastic about further harmonization in general and CE-marking in particular, and interviewees had no suggestions for increasing market access. It would be fair to say that there is a strong difference of view between the European Commission, the industry, and the testing and certification community on the desirable way forward.

Differences in specification, and the cost of testing, are not important issues to the industry, since machines can be reset quickly to new products, and testing is routine and an accepted part of business. Although the industry is dominated by multinationals, the EU players are mainly EU firms which welcome the measure of protection for the EU market (and to some degree to national markets) that the HAR scheme provides. They are concerned about low cost imports, because the technology is mature and plant and equipment is available off the peg to new entrants. They therefore oppose the CE-marking introduced into the LVD, because it is open to any world manufacturer, does not require independent testing, and has only safety and no performance elements in the essential requirements. They fear that consumers will be confused between the mandatory CE-marking (which denotes that the product meets all requirements deemed necessary, in terms of electrical safety, for the products to be legally placed on the market) and the voluntary HAR mark (which denotes that certain performance standards have been attested by one of a limited number of third-party testing bodies). Consequently, they have been promoting HAR as a quality mark.

12.5.4. The Consultants' suggestions

To increase market openness, the Consultants suggest that the following measures are needed:

(a)   development of mandated harmonized standards related to the safety objectives of the LVD, to replace the HDs, which will give presumption of conformity to LVD for (mandatory) CE marking;

(b)   development, if necessary (we have not made a technical assessment of the need), of separate and identifiable EN standards related to performance aspects, against which the (voluntary) HAR quality marks can be awarded (e.g. a scheme of usage categories);

(c)   action to remove from any quality marking scheme nationality or residence requirements, either for the certified firms or for the certifying bodies, and restrictive trade agreements such as sole supplier status for certifiers.

This would create a truly European quality mark, complementary to the CE-marking, open to non-European suppliers, with a more readily understood definition of quality for the buyer, remove all commercial or regulatory need for double testing, and by introducing real competition between certifiers would lead to lower costs for industry and the consumer.

13. Crop protection products: pesticides

13.1. Product information

NACE code: 24.20 – Manufacture of pesticides and other agrochemical products.

PRODCOM codes: 24.20.11/12/13/14/15 – Insecticides/herbicides/plant growth regulators/disinfectants/ fungicides and rodenticides.

13.1.1. Product scope

Pesticides are part of the agrochemical industry which can be defined as the manufacture of chemical products for agricultural purposes. There are two major branches within agrochemicals: chemical products for crop protection, and fertilizers. This report is concerned with the first of these, crop protection products, commonly referred to as pesticides. Plant protection products include four major product sub-groups: insecticides, herbicides, fungicides and plant growth regulators.

This product was selected for the study because there have been complaints against some Member States about the failure of mutual recognition with respect to parallel imports.

13.1.2. National regulations

In most European Member States, stringent legislation is in place to regulate the placing on the market and the use of crop protection products, because they contain toxic ingredients and can represent a hazard to man, animals, or the environment. The legislation regulating pesticides is very similar to that regulating pharmaceutical products. As toxic or dangerous products they are subject to specific national legislation for the placing on the market but also for transportation, waste disposal, packaging and labelling; they are mentioned in environment and wildlife protection acts, in water supply regulations, health and safety at work, etc.

Each new product, or new use of an existing product, has to be registered or homologated by the competent authorities in order to be sold on the Member State's territory. In a first stage the active ingredient or chemical has to be authorized, then each product formulated with the active ingredient has to be in turn registered.

Applications for registration must provide enough technical data to enable an assessment of whether the product may be used safely. The safety data requirement will normally depend on the nature of the pesticide, the activity of its breakdown products and its proposed uses. In most European countries, applicants must also provide efficacy data to enable an assessment of the ability of the product to fulfil the label claims. Registrations have to be renewed every five to ten years in all European countries, except Italy where the approval is given for an un- stipulated period of time, and Portugal where approval has to be renewed every 12 months.

13.1.3. EC harmonization measures

On 15 July 1991, the European Council adopted Directive 91/414/EEC concerning the placing of plant protection product on the market, referred to as the Agrochemicals Registration Directive or Authorization Directive. The Directive is aimed to harmonize the agrochemicals registration within the EU and provides for the following:

(a)   the establishment of a European list of accepted active substances referred to as a positive list (Annex I to the Directive, not yet established);

(b)   a system for the authorization by Member States of different preparations or products containing an accepted active substance of the positive list, in accordance with the requirements laid down in the Directive and according to uniform principles prepared by the Commission;

(c)   mutual recognition of authorizations by Member States with respect to comparable products already authorized in another Member State. Art. 10 states: 'At the request of the applicant ... the Member State must refrain from requiring the repetition of tests and analyses already carried out in connection with the authorization of the product.' However, the principle of mutual recognition is immediately followed by several conditions and restrictions such as '...to the extent that agricultural, plant health and environmental (including climatic) conditions relevant to the use of the product are comparable in the regions concerned...' and '...authorization may be also accompanied by restrictions on use arising from differences in dietary patterns...';

(d)   arrangements for the provisional authorization of preparations by Member States, pending the EU decision to include a new active substance in the positive list;

(e)   a 12-year programme to evaluate the 700 active substances currently on the market which have to be included in the positive list;

(f)   harmonized rules concerning labelling and packaging;

(g)   harmonized rules concerning the development of plant protection products;

(h)   provisions on the exchange of information between the Member States and the Commission.

The deadline for national implementation of the Directive was July 1993 but a few Member States have yet to do so. The provisions on mutual recognition contained in the Directive were due to be implemented one year after the adoption of the uniform principles. The Uniform Principles Directive (94/43/EEC) establishes Annex VI to Directive 91/414 and sets harmonized evaluation and decision-making criteria for registration of agrochemical products by Member States. Directive 94/43 was adopted on 27 July 1994 and came into force on 1 September 1994. Member States were due to incorporate the provisions into national law by 31 August 1995 which most Member States have done.

Other regulations and working documents were issued by the European institutions in order to deal with the different aspects of Directive 91/414 in more detail, e.g. data requirements (revision of Annexes II and III to Directive 91/414 which aims at establishing harmonized detailed data requirements and trigger values for determining when certain data are required for active ingredients and formulated products).

In practice, the implementation of the Agrochemicals Registration Directive and other EU legislation is not considered possible until the completion of Annex I to the Agrochemicals Registration Directive which will contain the positive list of active ingredients.

Pending the completion of all Annexes mentioned in Directive 91/414, and particularly Annex I, and according to the principle of subsidiarity, all national regulations remain in place. It is believed that another ten years are needed before mutual recognition can take place for pesticides. Moreover, it will be limited to toxicity data and not biological data as environmental conditions, agricultural practices and dietary patterns have to be taken into account when authorizing a pesticide.

Another important legislative area, apart from the placing on the market of products, concerns the pesticides residues, regulated at European level by the Pesticides Residues Directives which aim to harmonize maximum residue limits for pesticides in food. Three main directives are in force: 86/362, covering cereals; 86/363, meat and dairy products; and 90/642 other plants (fruit, vegetables and pulses). These directives have been amended by subsequent directives, adding more pesticides and produce categories to the legislation. Although some maximum residue levels (known as MRLs) have been set, most are to be established by various deadlines running to the end of the century.

Other directives and documents regulating aspects relevant to pesticides are: the Drinking Water Directive, the Biocides Directive, the Supplementary Protection Certificate Proposal, and the Registration Fees Directive.

13.1.4. Mutual recognition arrangements

The mutual recognition principle, as established by the jurisprudence of the Court of Justice of the European Communities, does not function well as the basis of the free movement of pesticides in the EU. National authorities refuse to recognize other countries' products without the full testing and registration procedures, on the argument that the same pesticides cannot be used for different geographic areas, because the thickness of the topsoil, the amount of rainfall and the type of pests or diseases that affect crops will influence greatly the composition and dosage of a formulated pesticide product. However, as mentioned above, Directive 91/414/EEC, Article 10, establishes the basis upon which mutual recognition is to be implemented by the Member States.

It is notable that Directive 91/414 is intended to impose mutual recognition by way of the directive, but this requires a long and active programme of harmonization, and particularly the agreement of a harmonized positive list of accepted active substances, but Member States still invoke national differences to avoid mutual recognition.

The OECD Crop Protection Project was launched in 1992 and is seeking to establish harmonized test guidelines for crop protection products, i.e. agree on one set of standards across all OECD countries to accurately measure the environmental and safety performance of new crop protection products. Industry scientists are working with OECD experts in the Joint Chemicals Management Committee. Once agreed, the OECD guidelines will become mandatory in all Member States of the EU and will be accepted for the Agrochemicals Registration Directive. The work is likely to continue for at least the next two years.

The Good Laboratory Practice (GLP) Agreement providing for mutual recognition of laboratory tests in a number of OECD countries, which is a success in the pharmaceutical sector, is now being set up in the pesticides sector.

13.2. Industry information

13.2.1. Sector representation

The sector is represented at European level by the European Crop Protection Association (ECPA) and at national level by one association usually dealing exclusively with pesticides, such as the British Agrochemicals Association (BAA) in the UK, Phytophar in Belgium, UIPP in France or Agrofarma in Italy. Membership of ECPA is open to all manufacturing companies and national trade associations that are based in any European country which is a member of the Council of Europe (27 countries in 1996).

ECPA's declared mission is 'to promote the interests of the crop protection industry as an innovative, responsible and progressive constituent of European industry and agriculture'. The ECPA takes a very active part in the drafting of EU legislation and is seeking, through education and information, to change the perception the public has of the industry.

13.2.2. Industry structure

Pesticides manufacturers can be divided into manufacturers who produce the active ingredients, i.e. the chemicals which represent 5–10% of the finished product as well as the formulated product, and manufacturers of formulated products only who buy the active ingredients and combine it with other ingredients to obtain what is known as a formulated product. Manufacturers of active ingredients devote on average 10% of their turnover to R&D efforts and are multinational companies (see Table 13.1).

The agrochemical sector is relatively concentrated, with the top 11 companies controlling more than 80% of the market.

Novartis, a merger (which took place in April 1996) of the agrochemicals sectors of Ciba Geigy and Sandoz, is the undisputed leader with 16.5% world market share, while eight companies have a market share of between 7 and 9%. Competitors of Novartis complain that the merger gives Novartis an unfair advantage and should have been prohibited in the EU on the basis of Articles 85 and 86 of the Treaty of Rome (competition law).

Table 13.1. The top world agrochemicals manufacturers and their share of the world market

Agrochemicals manufacturers	Country of origin	Market share in 1996 (%)
Novartis (Ciba + Sandoz)	Switzerland	16.5
Monsanto	USA	8.6
AgrEvo	Germany	8.6
Bayer	Germany	8.5
Du Pont de Nemours	USA	8.5
Zeneca	UK	8.4
Rhône Poulenc Agro	France	7.7
Dow Elanco	USA	7.2
American Cyanamid	USA	7.0
Basf	Germany	5.3
Sumitomo	Japan	2.3

Source: Rhône Poulenc Agro, 1996.

13.2.3. Output and trade

Representing close to 40% of the world's production, the EU is the largest region for agrochemical production, ahead of North America, Asia and Eastern Europe. As the table below shows, the European Union is a major exporter of crop protection products. The countries with the highest export levels are Germany, France and the UK. These three countries account for nearly 80% of the total export values of pesticides from the EU. Extra-EU exports are 30% of sales. No data is available for intra-EU trade: it may be expected that intra-EU trade is also quite high, but mainly in active ingredients, with limited trade in formulated products.

Table 13.2.   Plant protection products: sales by area and product, 1993 (million ECU)

	Herbicides	Insecticides	Fungicides	Others	Total
USA	4,666	1,517	430	351	6,964
W. Europe	2,275	929	1,588	466	5,258
Japan	1,149	1,274	1,216	80	3,719
Far East	781	1,199	340	162	2,482
Latin America	1,059	660	426	99	2,244
E. Europe	314	323	144	27	808
Others	156	900	106	48	1,210
Total	**10,400**	**6,802**	**4,250**	**1,233**	**22,685**

Source: Panorama of EU industry 95/96.

Table 13.3.   External trade for agrochemicals in current prices (million ECU)

	1985	1987	1989	1991	1993
Extra-EU exports	1,733	1,380	1,404	1,479	1,530
Extra-EU imports	426	392	572	636	449
Trade balance	1,307	988	832	842	1,081

Source: Panorama of EU industry 95/96.

13.3.   Trade barriers

13.3.1. Regulatory barriers

Regulatory barriers arise from four sources: parallel import bans, banned ingredients, banned formulated products, and tax differences.

Parallel imports

A parallel import is the import of an equivalent or comparable product to one which is already registered or in use in a Member State. Parallel imports become very attractive to wholesalers and farmers' co-operatives (the main distribution channels for pesticides) when the tightly controlled trade in pesticides, and differential pricing strategies by companies, make the price of a formulated product vary between Member States. Moreover, when farmers themselves purchase direct by driving over borders, there are large differences in VAT and eco-taxes as well.

In some European countries parallel imports are considered illegal and are stopped at the borders. Complaints have been put to the Commission concerning Austria, but it probably is not the only country to stop parallel imports (during interviews with manufacturers, Belgium and France were mentioned). The ban does not stop some farmers from driving across borders to bring cheaper pesticides back when wholesalers are prevented from doing so. This situation entails a certain amount of risk as labelling which contains essential information such as use precautions, health warnings and instructions for use will often be in a different language and might not be understood by the consumer, whereas wholesalers who legitimately imported parallel products would be able to relabel them.

According to the principle of mutual recognition of regulations, and provided an equivalent product is already legally sold on the market, parallel imports should not be impeded. Furthermore, legalizing parallel imports would allow Member States' authorities to regulate and control them, e.g. impose repackaging and relabelling of the product before putting it on the market.

> Differences in VAT and eco-taxes have exacerbated the problem of parallel imports in Europe. In Belgium, parallel imports existed before eco-taxes were introduced because VAT is higher (12%) than in France (3%) or in the Netherlands (3–4%). Belgian farmers have been found to drive to these neighbouring countries and fill their lorries with cheaper pesticides. With the introduction of eco-taxes, the practice has been reinforced. Denmark and Belgium have recently introduced eco-taxes on pesticides which can be as high as 37% (insecticides) of the retail price in Denmark and add BFR 50 to the price of one litre volume of pesticide in Belgium. In Denmark, the taxes are calculated on the retail price of pesticides, but they are collected at manufacturing or imports levels. Environmental taxes correspond to the 'polluter pays' principle as the charge affects each pesticide user according to the quantity used. The taxes have been introduced to help the government achieve their targets in reduction of pesticides usage, which aims at a 50% reduction in Denmark. The manufacturers of pesticides and their trade association have complained to the European Commission against both Member States. The Commission approved the taxes as they fall in line with the Community's and the consumers associations' environmental concerns and their objective to reduce chemical usage and promote sustainable agriculture. As a result, some major manufacturers of pesticides are thinking of moving out of Denmark or stopping to export to Denmark as the activity has become less/not profitable.

Banned active ingredients

Most Member States have negative lists of banned ingredients. These differ, creating regulatory barriers and failure of mutual recognition. Three examples cited to us where there have been important recent additions to the list of banned ingredients are listed below:

(a)   Sweden has completed its national re-registration programme (1990–95) before joining the EU on 1 January 1996. It banned 21 active ingredients, imposed use restrictions on 18 and withdrew 18 from the market. Since the 1960s, 45 active ingredients have been banned in Sweden, 23 have been subject to use restrictions and 33 have been withdrawn.

Reportedly, Sweden is determined to maintain the same level of stringent evaluation criteria in the future irrespective of what happens at EU level, i.e. the Uniform Principles Directive.

(b)   The Danish Environmental Protection Agency (EPA) of the Ministry of the Environment and Energy has recently added 10 active ingredients to the list of pesticides it proposes to ban. The 17 active ingredients now on the list, affecting some 100 products, are currently under scientific evaluation. A final decision will be made by the Ministry next year. The EPA's proposal to ban the pesticides is based on the identification of risks of ground water pollution, persistence in soil, or risk to aquatic organisms, birds and mammals. The Danish Agrochemical Industry Association (DAF) believes the Danish criteria for risk assessment are much stricter than those laid down in the EU's Uniform Principles and that there is no political will to adjust legislation to EU regulations.

(c)   The active ingredient MCPA, which is a selective herbicide, is banned in Italy. Some Italian customers go to France where the active ingredient is registered and buy formulated products which contain MCPA.

Banned formulated products

It is often the case that an EU country bans a formulated product on health and safety grounds while it is used freely in other Member States. The Uniform Principles Directive already mentioned harmonizes the evaluation criteria used to grant or refuse authorization, but the Directive has not yet been implemented by all Member States.

> A pesticide manufacturer had been selling its lawn feed and weedkiller combined product in Germany for ten years when their registration was due for renewal in 1989. Because Germany had changed their registration procedure and their requirements in 1987, the registration of the product failed to be renewed. Since then, the company has been unable to sell the product in Germany, although it is a top-selling product in many other EU countries, including the UK and France.

13.3.2. Testing and certification

For pesticides, testing and certification takes the shape of registration or homologation. The authorization of the active ingredient which enters into the composition of the pesticides as well as the registration of each formulated product and each extension of the use of a product is compulsory in every Member State prior to placing the product on the market. This involves heavy administrative burdens which usually have to be repeated every ten years, with the testing carried out in each one of the target countries.

The new EU legislation establishes the registration of active ingredients at European level, but leaves the registration of formulated product to each individual Member State.

13.3.3. Quality policies and marks

There are no quality marks for pesticides as they are mostly destined to farmers and not to the mass market, and the stringent registration requirements make them unnecessary.

13.4.   Enterprise strategies

Since mutual recognition does not work, and there has been no harmonization so far, it is not possible to see any change in enterprise strategy from removal of barriers. This section identifies the main costs for enterprises from the existence of barriers, and the possible consequences of removal.

13.4.1. Product range

The product range is vast as different formulations of the same active ingredients are devised to deal with special crops under specific conditions. Typically, a pesticide will be formulated to eradicate a pest (insects, diseases or weeds) which is specific to a crop and to a given region. Thus, formulations differ between countries but also often within a country; e.g. a herbicide devised for a cereal crop in northern France might not be suitable for southern France but might be appropriate for Belgium.

It is unlikely in this market that perfectly free trade and mutual recognition would enable manufacturers to reduce their range of products very much – but it would undoubtedly have some effect. It would also enable manufacture to be rationalized, since a manufacturing presence in each country would not be seen to be necessary.

However, some manufacturers deliberately produce different variants of each formulated product for each national market in order to protect themselves against parallel imports, and support a price differentiation policy. According to the Agrochemicals Registration Directive, parallel imports are only considered legal if the comparability of the products can be proved. This strategy can be a double-edged sword for the manufacturer as costs are multiplied, but as long as the rules on parallel imports are rigidly applied there will be a proliferation of formulations.

13.4.2. Distribution and marketing

Large manufacturers usually produce their active ingredients in a few large-scale centres and ship them around the world to be combined with locally produced ingredients and transformed into highly differentiated and biologically specific products. Distribution and marketing is thus done on a national basis and this is reflected on national pricing policies which bring about the problem of parallel imports.

Despite the need for many variant formulations it is probable that full mutual recognition and implementation of the EU pesticides legislation would enable producers to adopt an EU-wide marketing, packaging and advertising strategy, even with formulation variants to suit each market and crop.

13.4.3. Quality and testing

Because registration of a pesticide product is essential in order to sell into any market, manufacturers dedicate a lot of resources to the registration of products. A top multinational said they employ hundreds of people in order to overcome the different regulatory difficulties. Registration departments are heavy cost centres and registration procedures time-consuming. The removal of these multiple registration requirements will lead to significant cost savings.

13.4.4. Impact on competitiveness and customer choice

The full implementation of the EU legislation on pesticides will have a beneficial impact for pesticides customers as mutual recognition of equivalent products will force prices down and

European registration of active ingredients (i.e. mutual recognition of toxicity data) combined with the Uniform Principles will prevent Member States from banning active ingredients and products unilaterally on grounds of toxicity. It is at present a very protected industry because of the registration requirements, and increased competition would undoubtedly benefit farmers and consumers.

13.5. Conclusions

At present there is no harmonization, and mutual recognition does not work for pesticides, because of the very specific nature of the hazards, which are dependent on geography, climate, crop and diet patterns.

The Agrochemicals Registration Directive is intended to enforce mutual recognition of toxicity data, along with a substantial programme of harmonization of positive ingredient lists. It is early days to assess the efficiency of the Directive, but because it also allows national approval to take into account different environmental conditions and agricultural practices, many manufacturers believe that the Directive gives no guarantee of free movement.

13.5.1. Effectiveness of approaches

It is worth noting that the effectiveness of approaches is measured here as of June 1996, at a time when the Agrochemical Registration Directive and its annexes are not fully implemented or into place. Table 13.4 summarizes the effectiveness.

Table 13.4.   Effectiveness of approaches

Measure/action	State of implementation	Effectiveness[1]
The Agrochemical Registration Directive 91/414/EEC	End of transition period 31/08/95 but very few active ingredients have been registered at EU level yet	*
Mutual recognition principle		*

[1] on a scale of 1-5 where ***** = the most effective
Source: W.S. Atkins.

The mutual recognition principle has failed to work for pesticides because Member States consider pesticides as dangerous, polluting products and therefore want to control tightly their placing on the market. National registration systems vary greatly which does not promote trust between Member States. For example, the number of experts involved in registration differs enormously: there are 120 in Germany, 100 in the UK, 30 in France and eight in Belgium.

The fact that agrochemical firms are large and influential, and despite being international in marketing are still national in ownership and in general in their location, is no doubt also a factor inhibiting more rapid harmonization or mutual recognition. It is in their interest to retain separate national markets for the formulated products. It is interesting that each of the top ten global firms (before the merger of the two Swiss firms) had between 7% and 8.5% of the world market.

As a result of the failure of mutual recognition and before the full implementation of the new directive, technical barriers to trade remain very high (Table 13.5).

Table 13.5.   Remaining barriers

Barriers to trade	Importance[1]
National registration	*****
Banned parallel imports	*****
Banned active ingredients and formulated products	*****

[1] on a scale of 1-5 where ***** = the most important
Source: W.S. Atkins.

13.5.2. Measures suggested by industry

From the interviews it transpires that most manufacturers are expecting improvements in the future through the full implementation of the Agrochemicals Registration Directive and other EU legislation. No further measures were proposed.

14. Structural steel

14.1. Product information

NACE code: 27.10 – Manufacture of basic iron and steel and of ferro-alloys.

PRODCOM codes: 27.10.70.13/15/23/25 – Parallel flanged heavy I sections, heavy H sections, heavy sections for mining frames, other heavy sections of non-alloy steel.

14.1.1. Product scope

A wide range of steel products are used in construction. These can be grouped according to basic shape or forming process, although within each group there are also many possible variations in size and other characteristics. The principal groups are:

(a)   beams and columns (including joists);
(b)   channels;
(c)   angles;
(d)   plates and flats;
(e)   structural hollow sections (hot finished and cold formed);
(f)   galvanized products;
(g)   tubes.

This report deals mainly with hot rolled sections (items (a)–(c) above), and in particular with the heavier sections (item (a)), which are used almost exclusively in steel framed buildings, bridges and other large structures. It thus concentrates mostly on PRODCOM codes 27.10.70.13/15/23/25. It also covers the constructional steelwork industry, as there are factors that, while not impeding the free movement of steel products themselves within the EU, affect trade in the finished products (fabrications). Although heavy sections are able to move fairly freely within the EU, steelwork fabricators often find it difficult or unattractive to win and carry out work in other Member States.

14.1.2. National regulations

No national regulations on import or marketing of structural steel sections are known. The mutual recognition principle, as related to national trade regulations, is therefore not a problem. National and local building regulations may be a problem (see comments on Ü-mark). There are also *de facto* national specifications for structural steel (e.g. the BCSA National Structural Steel Specification in the UK) which cannot be legally required for public sector contracts, but which can be used freely in the private sector.

14.1.3. EU Directives

Heavy sections will eventually fall within the scope of the Construction Products Directive (89/106/EEC). A draft mandate for structural metallic sections is in the early stages of being produced and is expected to be ready within the next few months. It will then need to pass through the various committee stages. The industry does not appear optimistic that anything will happen quickly: work on the standardization of steel products has already been going on for over 40 years (the precursor of the European Committee for Iron and Steel Standardization (ECISS) was established in 1953).

14.1.4. Product standards

The steel industry is long established, international trade is very common and the products themselves are largely commodities. Steel products can generally be described in terms of their chemical and mechanical characteristics and dimensions. Thus the equivalence of many BS and DIN standards, for example, is well known and documented. Few modern steelmakers have difficulty in producing to the main international norms, or in obtaining the accreditation that will enable them to export world-wide, and because of this a fairly high degree of product standardization already exists.

The Stahlschlüssel ('Key to Steel'), for example, provides tables showing a comparison of international steel qualities (grades). In the case of construction steels, it demonstrates the interchangeability of: W.-Nr/DIN (D), NBN (B), AFNOR (F), BS (UK), UNI (I), JIS (Japan), SS (S), GOST (SU), UNE (E), AISI/SAE/ASTM (USA).

European standards are already in place in many instances and most particularly in the case of steel quality. The European Standard Designation System for Steels – EN 10027 – comprises two parts:

      Part 1: steel names,
      Part 2: steel numbers.

Within Part 1 there are two groups of names. The first is a designation according to mechanical and physical properties and the name includes a letter signifying the application (e.g. S for structural steels, P for pressure purpose steels) and a value of some property specific to the application. Thus, a typical structural steel may have the name EN 10025 S185, where S identifies this material to be structural steel and 185 specifies the minimum yield strength in N/mm^2.

This system is now widely used within the EU and its equivalence to national standards is highly transparent. British Steel, for example, uses it in its structural sections price list, where the basis price cites the steel quality: e.g. BS EN 10025 1993 Grade S275 JR (Equivalent to BS EN 10025 1990 Fe430 B and BS 4360: 1986, Grade 43B).

EN 10027 Part 1 also contains a second group of names based on chemical composition. Part 2 comprises a system for assigning steel numbers. Neither of these systems merits further description in this report.

EN 10020 describes steels according to their main property or application characteristics and forms an element of the EN 10027 Part 2 numbers. EN 10052 covers product forms and includes heat treatment.

Product dimensions are not fully standardized. In all of the EU, other than the UK, heavy sections are produced to standard metric sizes (HEA and IPE ranges). In the UK, sections have traditionally been produced in imperial measurements (BS 4) and continue to be so. Although UK steelmakers now list products in millimetres, the measurements are a direct conversion from inches and the products themselves are not the same size as their European counterparts. ECISS, an associated body under CEN, is looking at the production of common standards for product dimensions. It is anticipated that these will not come into force before the year 2004, at the earliest. In the Consultant's view, their introduction is likely to face opposition from UK steel producers (i.e. British Steel), who will lose a degree of protection from imports into their domestic market and could also face substantial retooling costs, while being welcomed by stockholders, who at present must often carry double stocks (both UK and continental sizes), and fabricators who will no longer face the barriers posed by different national systems.

Imperial measurements remain in common use in many parts of the world (generally in Commonwealth countries); the USA has its own set of dimensions and still uses inches. The major European suppliers of heavy sections, and steel products in general, thus produce imperial sizes, not only for the UK, but also for sale into the much larger world-wide market. Very few steelmakers produce exclusively for their domestic markets. Thus, even after harmonization of European dimension standards, there may still be a need to produce sections in sizes other than those used in Europe.

With regard to product dimension tolerances, I and H sections are now covered by EN 10034. Different national standards remain for other sections (e.g. channels and light sections).

14.2. Industry information

14.2.1. Sector representation

The structural steelwork sector comprises the steelmakers and processors, traders and stockholders, fabricators and contractors. It thus represents a substantial element of EU industry and employment – the stockholding sector alone employs well in excess of 100,000 persons and there are probably another 300,000 directly involved in steelmaking. There are, not surprisingly, numerous national and international trade associations and research organizations, as well as federations of trade associations.

Steelmakers usually organize at a national level, for example BISPA (UK), Comité de la sidérurgie (B), Fédération française de l'acier (F) and Federacciai (I). These national organizations tend, in turn, to be members of Eurofer. As far as trade is concerned, Eurofer is concerned mainly with third countries and with competition issues, and has had little involvement in single market issues. Steelmakers will often have close working relationships with stockholders' associations, frequently as a result of forward integration into steel distribution.

Steel traders do not appear to be extensively represented. By its own admission, the London-based International Steel Trade Association is mainly a forum for discussion and social activities.

Steel stockholders (and service centres) are represented by national associations. Quite often, there is more than one association in each country. Separate associations may exist for different product groups (carbon steels, stainless and special steels, tubes, etc.) and for both mill-owned and independent stockholders. The levels of membership of individual associations, and thus their resources and influence, vary widely from country to country. This affects the range of activities they undertake. The larger associations, for example in the UK, Germany, France, Italy and Spain, typically have an involvement in political lobbying, technical and commercial training, quality assurance training, collection of statistics, promotion, handling members' complaints, organizing conferences and providing a forum for discussion.

The national associations tend also to be members of FENA (*Fédération européenne du négoce d'acier*), which is based in Brussels and which acts as a lobbyist to the European Commission. Another organization, FIANATM (*Fédération internationale des associations de négociants en aciers, tubes et métaux*), includes the members of FENA as well as associations in EFTA countries. The USA and Japan are members of FIANATM but play little active part. FIANATM has hitherto had a limited role. Other than holding an annual conference, its meetings have tended to coincide with those of FENA. In addition, its non-EU membership has precluded it somewhat from making representations to the Commission. To all intents and purposes, FENA and FIANATM can be considered as one body.

Reports from the 1996 FIANATM conference suggest that stockholders and steelmakers intend to co-operate much more closely in future. The aim is to produce much more detailed and co-ordinated statistical information on stock levels, which can be fed back to the mills to enable more efficient production planning.

The *constructional steelwork* (fabrication) industry is highly organized at both national and European levels. A good example of the range of activities undertaken by national associations is the British Constructional Steelwork Association (BCSA), which is involved in the following areas:

(a)   contractual and commercial (industry representation, law and policy, voluntary registration of contractors);
(b)   technical (codes and standards, advisory services, computer applications, new developments, education and training);
(c)   marketing and membership services (industry statistics, promotion, marketing, design awards, education, recruitment);
(d)   quality assurance (certification, development of quality management standards).

Its members include fabricators, steel stockholders, consultants, academics and specialist service providers.

The depth and breadth of its activities is further evidenced by its representation on a number of national and international bodies, the most pertinent of which are: BSI; CEN; UK Department of the Environment committees; ECISS; and the European Convention for Constructional Steelwork (ECCS).

Associations elsewhere in the EU will have activities broadly similar to those set out above, but levels of involvement may vary since steel construction is less common in some countries than in others.

All the EU associations belong to the ECCS, based in Brussels, which also has associate members from EFTA countries, the USA, Japan, Canada and Korea. The role of ECCS is to promote the use of steel in construction. Its work includes technical publishing, conferences, research, certification and registration issues, contractual and commercial terms.

14.2.2. Industry structure

There are four main producers of heavy sections in the EU: Preussag (Germany); Arbed (Luxembourg); Ensidesa (Spain); and British Steel (UK). The dominant among these are British Steel and Arbed. The ownership of all four is national, either public or private sector.

A few other companies produce heavy/medium sections on a limited basis and there are a number of light section producers and re-rollers. Most of the leading steelmakers have trading or stockholding arms in other Member States and, indeed, throughout the world.

A high proportion of the heavy sections entering the market pass through stockholders, whose main role is to break bulk (although many are increasingly looking to add value by offering additional processing or other services). It is quite rare for an end-user to place an order large enough to be of interest to a steel producer.

The stockholding sector has traditionally been localized with regard to client base. In recent years, however, major steelmakers have been acquiring stockholders in other countries as a means of market entry. They have also taken a stake in the distribution channels in their domestic markets. British Steel is a prime example of this practice, having acquired two of the largest British stockholding groups during the 1980s.

The end-users of heavy sections – fabricators and contractors (typically acting as sub-contractors) – are many in number. Their activities vary widely, as do their size and geographical area of operation, but most operate exclusively or mainly in their domestic markets.

14.2.3. Output and trade

The production of constructional steelwork is a major industry, amounting to over 6 million tonnes in 1994 (Table 14.1). This figure includes all structural steel products (sections, plate, tubes, etc.) and thus disguises the dominance of the UK and Luxembourg in heavy sections.

Trade in constructional steelwork is much smaller than production, reflecting the domestic nature of most of the work undertaken (Table 14.2). The relative lack of international trade in steel fabrications appears to stem from:

(a)   the difficulties inherent in transporting steel structures over long distances at competitive prices (structural fabrications, even when broken down, can be very large);

(b)   problems associated with contracting practices and conditions in different countries (the costs of translating tenders and unfamiliar contract terms and labour laws, for example, can often be powerful disincentives to trading overseas, particularly for smaller firms).

The vast majority of steelwork contractors work in the national and local markets. BCSA considers that UK fabricators have 99% of the domestic market (this figure probably refers to single storey buildings; international competition for large buildings and infrastructure is likely to be more intense) and exports from the UK are less than 10% of total output. The UK is among the most active in the international market.

One of the largest and most active international steelwork contractors, a British company, claims that 75% of the bids it submits are for UK work, and that only 25% of its overseas bids (i.e. around 5% of the total) are for projects in the EU.

We understand from discussions with steelmakers and suppliers of sections that problems related to VAT and delays at borders have been largely eliminated by the SMP.

Table 14.1.   Production of constructional steelwork ('000 tonnes)

Country	Actual					Forecast	
	1990	1991	1992	1993	1994	1995	1996
Austria	81	72	69	77	79	70	70
BLEU	359	385	300	304	308	310	315
Denmark	105	97	92	78	88	98	106
Finland	150	125	95	90	95	105	115
France	751	697	641	550	544	556	567
Germany	1,215	1,621	1,706	1,637	1,698	1,730	1,764
Italy	1,200	1,120	920	801	790	725	725
Netherlands	516	561	583	504	533	535	540
Norway	42	40	39	40	44	47	47
Spain	1,269	1,184	1,014	860	900	905	910
Sweden	83	78	72	67	61	62	65
Switzerland	81	82	76	60	55	60	60
UK	1,132	903	833	858	937	1,019	1,052
Total	**6,984**	**6,965**	**6,441**	**5,926**	**6,132**	**6,222**	**6,336**

Source: ECCS.

Table 14.2.   Exports of constructional steelwork ('000 tonnes)

Country	Actual					Forecast	
	1988	1989	1990	1991	1992	1993	1994
Austria[1]	-	-	-	-	-	-	-
Belgium	45	40	38	40	32	30	31
Denmark	14	15	17	19	17	18	22
Finland	50	49	43	27	25	30	35
France	30.6	34.6	36.4	46.9	50	50	50
Germany (W)	-	-	n.a.	-	-	-	-
Italy	-	-	n.a.	-	-	-	-
Netherlands	-	-	n.a.	-	-	-	-
Norway	1.2	1.2	2	3	2	3	3
Spain	-	-	n.a.	-	-	-	-
Sweden	2	1	2	3	2	3	3
Switzerland	2.2	4.2	2.8	7.3	1.4	2.8	2.8
UK	46	49	54	57	65	62	55
Total	**191**	**194**	**195.2**	**203.2**	**194.4**	**198.8**	**201.8**

[1] Estimated at 30–40% of production.

Source: ECCS.

14.3. Trade barriers

14.3.1. Regulatory barriers

The barriers reported by interviewees typically refer to public procurement problems (see Section 14.3.2) rather than regulatory barriers to trade. Complaints about free trade problems of any type appear to be quite rare. The steelwork contracting industry in the UK, for example, considers that complaints are not worthwhile as the process takes so long that contracts are lost. Complaints to the DTI are not deemed to be an effective route and there is considered to be a lack of commitment at the level of individual governments to co-operate with investigations launched by other Member States. The view is shared by the DTI itself. Its single market branch, which covers all sectors, deals with only about 60 individual cases per year, with a success rate of only some 20%. Officials are not aware of any complaints about regulatory barriers being made except:

(a)   problems with welding certification in Germany; and recently
(b)   the German γ-mark.

It states that enterprises may not bother to complain because they think it is pointless.

14.3.2. Public procurement problems

Most complaints are about public procurement obstacles. For example:

(a)   There is some evidence that qualification and registration procedures for public sector projects can cause problems for steelwork contractors wishing to bid for work in other Member States. For example, the costs of translating technical and commercial tender documents can add considerably to the overall cost of submitting bids, significantly increasing the risks associated with bidding and thus reducing the attractiveness of international work.
(b)   There appear to be pre-qualification practices aimed at preventing foreign competition. An example quoted was that of a UK contractor who wished to pre-qualify for work on the French state railways. The contractor was required to submit a sample bid. The terms of reference for this sample bid were for a type of work in which the contractor had little experience, not for the type of work for which the contractor wished to pre-qualify. The application failed and the contractor was consequently not able to qualify for the type of work in which it *was* experienced.
(c)   Other contractors claim that tenders published in the *Official Journal of the European Communities* are issued too late, or contain insufficient detail, for foreign bidders to have much chance of success. We do not have sufficient evidence to confirm or deny this suggestion.
(d)   One international steelwork contractor claimed that some Member States do not appear to put out public sector contracts to international tender.

A common cause for complaint in the industry is the lack of an EU-wide system of qualification and registration of steelwork enterprises. The lack of control over essential requirements (e.g. certification) means that fabricators in countries where controls are weak may be able to undercut significantly fabricators in other Member States where standards are high. As there are not yet any EU-wide standards for structural steelwork, the quality of work being carried out can vary significantly.

In the UK, BCSA has introduced the Register of Qualified Steelwork Contractors. The register indicates the category of steelwork and the class of project which companies are registered to undertake. It is not compulsory, although some sources in other Member States seem to believe that it is, but registration is likely to endow a company with quasi-official approval, which clients may look for as a basic requirement. In some ways the register may thus act as a barrier to trade.

In view of the difficulties created by differing national systems of registration for public sector contracts, the European Commission (Directorate-General for Industry) has mandated CEN and CENELEC to produce common standards for the qualification of construction enterprises. The mandate (M84) calls for the preparation by the end of 1996 of draft standards and the adoption of ENs by mid-1998. These will then be transposed into national standards. Once in place, the ENs will enable enterprises to qualify for particular classes of work in their home country and be automatically qualified for the same type of work in all Member States. The proposal has been generally well received by the industry but its success will clearly depend on the registration procedures being properly controlled in each Member State.

In the past, different national design codes for steelwork construction caused some problems when fabricators attempted to win work in other countries. The development of Eurocodes 3 and 4 appears to have removed many of the barriers to trade caused by national codes, even though the Eurocodes have yet to be finalized and may not be for some years. One source suggested that the Eurocodes are only a partial solution since they do not address more serious barriers, such as registration.

14.3.3. Testing and certification

Testing and certification are areas where barriers to trade continue to exist and may even be increasing. The most commonly cited barriers are:

(a)   the Ü-mark (relates only to construction products sold in Germany),
(b)   the CIPACAS (F) and Decreto Ministeriale (I),
(c)   the German requirement for welding certification and lack of mutual recognition.

The Ü-mark system was introduced at the beginning of 1996 and was expected to enter into full force in October after a transitional period granted to allow the necessary certification work to be carried out. It is a requirement that all products used in construction projects in Germany must bear either the CE-marking or the Ü-mark. As the CPD is not yet able to be applied in practice, the only realistic option is Ü-marking.

Foreign steelmakers wishing to sell into Germany were originally obliged to have their products tested to specified DIN standards and marked accordingly, since German stockholders and users would otherwise be unwilling to buy them. While meeting the standards themselves was not viewed as a major problem – modern steelmakers are generally able to produce to DIN – obtaining the Ü-mark was more difficult since the recognized bodies were all German (with the exception of the Benelux countries, where a mutual recognition arrangement exists). It was thus necessary for British Steel, for example, to approach the German authorities directly.

The Ü-mark has been the source of numerous complaints to the Commission under Article 169 of the EEC Treaty. These include representations by individual companies (mainly stockholders) and both national and international associations (e.g. BISPA and FENA). One major point of contention was that the DIN prescribed standards were unnecessarily demanding.

Recent contacts with the industry suggest that the difficulties caused by the Ü-mark are rapidly diminishing. It is reported that Germany is no longer rigorously imposing the requirement for third party testing and that works' certificates showing conformity with DIN standards are acceptable.

There are a number of theories about the purpose of the Ü-mark. Some view it as an attempt to protect the market from imports from eastern Europe. Others saw it as a general act of protectionism. It has also been suggested that it was an attempt to influence the planned CE-marking. Our interpretation of the German point of view is that the γ-mark was introduced as a stop-gap measure and that it would be discontinued as soon as the relevant ENs were in place and CE-marking could begin.

In any case, not all interested parties would view the Ü-mark as a bad thing. A common complaint about the ERs and supporting standards for other products is that they are a lowest common denominator, which enable low-cost but poor quality producers to operate in markets that would not previously have been available to them. Anything which raises the level of the ENs being developed to support the directives could thus be of benefit to manufacturers in countries where national standards are already high.

Several industry contacts have also pointed out that the Ü-mark is not as onerous as existing systems operated by France (CIPACAS) and Italy. The latter of these is viewed as particularly cumbersome since it requires annual or biannual visits from Italian inspectors and the provision of up to 90 samples of steel. The costs in terms of preparation time alone may be considerable.

Welding certificates and mutual recognition are also a major point of contention. There is currently no mutual recognition of welding testing and certification, although some progress is being made via the European Welding Federation, which was set up by the national welding institutes to create a common syllabus for welding qualifications. To date, only the qualification of 'welding engineer' has been recognized across Member States. The qualification for welding technicians remains to be recognized. Our research did not indicate that this Federation is well known by the industry.

The lack of mutual recognition for welding causes problems when fabrication work is sub-contracted to other Member States. As an example, work for German clients must be accompanied by a German welding certificate. As there is no mutual recognition of testing and certification bodies, fabricators must go to the expense of bringing in German inspectors. It should be pointed out, however, that German fabricators face certification procedures that are equally as stringent as those imposed on foreign companies.

14.3.4. Quality policies and marks

Quality marks are not generally used in the structural steel industry.

Most steelmakers have quality assurance accreditation to internationally accepted norms and awarded by well-known bodies (Lloyds Register, Norske Veritas, etc.).

14.3.5. Other non-regulatory barriers

There are relatively few serious barriers to the free movement of steel sections within the EU. Trade can, however, be limited by the costs involved in transporting steel, particularly where multiple handling is involved, the time factor, which impacts on stock policies, and national preferences. One fabricator stated that the preference was to buy from the national steelmaker even though the products of other (EU) mills were considered to be just as good.

Steelwork fabricators are often discouraged from tendering for international work by the difficulties presented by, for example, a requirement to submit documentation in a foreign language. Translation costs can be very high for detailed technical documentation and drawings and cause delays which prohibit bidding against tight time scales.

Differences in contract law can also be a disincentive; contractors are wary of becoming involved in countries where they do not have an understanding of the relevant contract law, or where the law may be weighted against them.

Opinion varies as to the extent to which differences in the range of product dimensions act as barriers to trade. The UK's National Structural Steelwork Specification for Building Construction, which is not compulsory (although often believed to be so) and which cannot legally be required for public sector projects, specifies EN standards for steel quality but British Standards for product dimensions. Some observers – typically steel traders and stockholders – claim that the standard UK dimensions present a barrier to trade since they are not compatible with those for sections produced elsewhere in Europe (when the UK switched to the metric system, the products themselves were not changed) and steelmakers must thus go to the expense of retooling if they wish to sell into the UK (one source quoted a figure of ECU 300,000).

In reality, the main EU steelmakers selling into the UK have sufficiently large sales in the market to justify the expense of rolling to UK standards. We estimate that Preussag and Arbed sell a total of 150,000 t/y of heavy sections in the UK; retooling costs would therefore amount to only a very small proportion (<1%) of sales revenue. European mills also have sales into other countries that still use the imperial system. Fabricators operating in the UK market – domestic or foreign – have little real difficulty in obtaining the steel they need, regardless of specification.

14.4.   Enterprise strategies

There has been no recent significant change in the degree of openness of the market, either from harmonization or from actions to impose mutual recognition. There is, therefore, no relevant impact on enterprise strategy.

14.4.1. Product range

Development of harmonized (i.e. mutually recognized) standards has not had any evident effect on steel companies' product ranges. They continue to roll a wide range of grades and dimensions, to all national standards and to many specific customer specifications.

In the case of fabricated steelwork, an opening up of public procurement and general single market effects are increasing transborder activity, and promoting some innovation and competition in the market, particularly in the Mediterranean countries where steel construction has been less popular than concrete.

14.4.2. Investment

The main producers of heavy sections in the EU are nationally owned, but are not necessarily in the public sector.

It appears that attempts to establish international joint ventures or other alliances in the steelwork fabrication sector have typically been unsuccessful. The reasons for failure are generally associated with differences in culture, labour law and working practices.

It seems unlikely that the removal of technical barriers *per se* will have an important impact on ownership, mergers and acquisitions and investment, but action on state aids, privatization and changes to previous European Coal and Steel Community industry policy are increasing competition, and leading to transborder acquisitions as the less efficient firms restructure.

14.4.3. Distribution and marketing

In the stockholding sector, cross-border ownership is common. Very often, subsidiaries are intended to be a means of distributing the parent company's products in foreign markets (e.g. British Steel Walter Blume, in Germany). In other cases, the foreign subsidiary is largely free to trade on its own account (e.g. ASD, UK, which is owned by Arbed/Usinor, but which is one of British Steel's largest domestic customers). Standards and removal of technical barriers are not significant factors in this policy.

14.4.4. Organization and management

The research did not indicate that enterprises have had to make any significant changes to their organization and management as a result of technical barriers to trade or their removal.

14.4.5. Quality and testing

Enterprises' responses to quality and testing issues have been covered in Sections 14.3.3 and 14.3.4.

14.4.6. Impact on competitiveness and customer choice

There has been increasing intra-EU trade over a long period, but not, on the whole, due to removal of technical barriers. Harmonization of standards has been a factor, however.

Heavy sections have long been commodity products and are becoming more so as harmonization of standards continues. Customers, e.g. fabricators, rarely face problems in obtaining the products they want (except in cases where genuine shortages occur) and very often they buy from stockholders who typically, but not always, operate multiple sourcing policies.

Steelmakers typically achieve higher prices in their domestic markets than for export sales. In the past, this was a function, at least in part, of protectionist measures such as production controls, and outside the EU, import quotas and tariffs. Today, the differentials are maintained more by customer preference for buying locally and logistics (related to lead times, higher delivery costs when importing, established relationships, etc.).

The economics of steelmaking demand certain levels of output (although this has become less of an issue with the growth in electric steelmaking, where variable costs are a higher proportion of total cost than is the case with the BF-BOF route). Where the domestic market is not sufficiently large to absorb all of a producer's output (and it rarely is), exports must be made to maintain mill throughput. It follows that exported products must be more keenly priced than those produced in target markets. In the past, this has given rise to unfair trading practices – dumping and the beam cartel of a few years ago – but these are not the subject of the present study.

Even though steelmakers must often accept lower prices in export markets, and even after retooling costs are taken into account (e.g. for sales into the UK), their competitiveness is reliant upon production volumes. Market conditions are thus far more of an influence than any real or perceived technical barriers to trade.

14.5. Conclusions

14.5.1. Effectiveness of approaches

Structural steel products have become commodity products, and are thus easily traded, with very little pressure from the EU or other official bodies. The few remaining technical differences that might impede trade are disappearing. The SMP has been successful in removing problems that arose from border delays and VAT, but EC approaches have not had a direct impact on technical barriers to trade. There have been no formal complaints about regulatory barriers to trade.

The effective implementation of the Construction Products Directive is likely to have an impact on harmonizing the standards and customary specifications for steelwork construction, and may lead to simplification of the very complex range of steel specifications and steelwork construction codes.

14.5.2. Remaining barriers

Some barriers to trade in heavy sections and fabrications remain.

Although the effects of the Ü-mark on trade in sections seem destined to be short lived, similar systems exist elsewhere (e.g. France and Italy) and there is clearly potential for other Member States to introduce their own similar barriers, either as pure protectionism, or in retaliation.

Some national differences remain in standards for product dimensions and tolerances. These can make it harder to sell into other Member States. The absence of European standards for qualification of construction enterprises (public sector projects) remains a barrier to international contracting. This is compounded by continuing problems that arise from the lack of mutual recognition of welding certification, and from national contract terms.

14.5.3. Measures suggested by industry

The process of harmonization of standards for heavy sections is ongoing but work remains to be done in the areas of dimensions and tolerances. This work should be encouraged and accelerated, although resistance from some steel manufacturers seems likely since it will be able to argue that it is being prevented from making product sizes for which there is an existing sizeable market.

The introduction of CE-marking for heavy sections is a priority as it will remove the potential for barriers such as the γ-mark. Most steelwork contractors seem to be in favour of an EU-wide system of registration for steelwork contractors operating in the public sector, possibly in conjunction with mutual recognition of welding certification. At the same time, there will be a need for adequate safeguards to ensure that registration procedures are consistently applied in all Member States.

15. Carpets and rugs

15.1. Product information

NACE code: 17.51 – Manufacture of carpets and rugs.

PRODCOM code: 17.51.11/12/13/14 – Knotted carpets/woven tufted/needlefelt and other carpets and textile floor coverings.

15.1.1. Product scope

The industry defines two main types of textile floor coverings: woven and non-woven. Woven carpets are divided into Axminster, Wilton and Brussels. Non-woven carpets include four categories: tufted, needle punched, bonded and knitted.

There are two market segments, the domestic (or residential) market and the contract market for public places.

15.1.2. National regulations

There are no regulations which rule the residential market, whereas the contract market for carpets is heavily regulated in most Member States. Rugs are defined as a decorative item, and the consultant is not aware of any technical regulations or quality standards applying to them.

There are two types of regulations for carpets used in public places: regarding fire safety, and regarding recommended use classification.

Fire safety regulations

Fire safety regulations exist in most Member States. Because testing methods are seldom comparable, there are no mutual recognition agreements. For example, Scandinavian authorities require the 'pill (tablet) test' whereas other Member States, such as France or Belgium, would apply the 'radiant panel test'. Both of the above test methods have an ISO standard (ISO 6925 and ISO DIS9239), but there are different national standards. In Germany, for instance, the fire testing standard is DIN4102-B1, in Belgium, the NBN S21-203 and in France, NF P 92 506.

In France, the *Ministère de l'Intérieur* regulates fire safety procedures, and fire safety (for all products) is classified into six categories: M0, M1, M2, M3 and M4 and 'non-classified'. M4 is the most flammable class of product permitted for use in public buildings; M0 non-flammable products (carpets are normally M3 or M4). Carpets for public buildings must be classified, and for high-rise buildings they must be classified M3 or higher.

Austria (N38 – Part 1), Germany (DIN4102 – Part 14), Scandinavia (Nord Test NT007) and the Netherlands (NEN6066) require additional fire testing related to smoke density. In France, smoke tests are also required, but are related to the toxicity of fumes in case of fire, not to smoke density. There is a French *Arrêté Ministériel* which specifies that if the carpet has been tested and classified M3, the additional smoke test is not required.

In most cases, the community fire brigade of each local authority will give the final authorization with respect to the installation of carpets, so to some extent the barriers are outside the scope of national regulations.

Use regulations

Regulations for recommended use of carpets exist in some Member States (such as France) but not all (such as Belgium and Spain).

In *France*, the national construction regulations, the *Documents Techniques Unifiés* (DTU) define the buildings and the category of carpets authorized. The French system which regulates the use of carpets in public buildings is known as the UPEC/ITR. There are five classes: U2 P2; U2S P2; U3 P2; U3 P3 and U3S P3. UPEC is both a classification for products and for the buildings. U stands for the usage, P for the hallmark (or *poinçonnement*), E corresponds to the water resistance and C to the chemical agents content. A figure from 0 to 4 is associated with each letter. It defines the resistance class of the carpet (class 4 is the highest resistance). For instance, carpets for public buildings will bear the U3S P3 UPEC classification. Two French laboratories can grant the above labels, the *Centre Scientifique et Technique du Bâtiment* (CSTB) and the *Centre de Recherches et d'Etudes Techniques du Tapis* (CRET). The *Décrêt 73-357* of 14 March 1973 (*appellations textiles*) also requires carpets sold in the French market to carry a label describing the textile contents.

15.1.3. Standards

In other Member States, use categories are based on standards which are, by definition, voluntary. The use classifications accepted in Europe are shown in Table 15.1.

Table 15.1.   Use classifications for carpets

Scheme	Countries using scheme	Organizations involved in scheme
ICCO	France, Belgium (also used in the Netherlands, Scandinavia)	Manufacturers' associations
UPEC/ITR	France	Certification body and government labs
ICC	Germany, Switzerland, Austria (used in Italy, Spain)	German manufacturers' association with labs in Germany (DTFI), Switzerland (EMPA), Austria (OTI)
BCMA	UK	Manufacturers' association with self-certification
NCC	Denmark, Finland, Norway, Sweden (now little used)	National bodies
IWS-CCS	All except France (little used in the UK)	International Wool Secretariat

In Germany carpet manufacturers label their products with specific standards (see Table 15.2). The flammability standard is, however, compulsory for carpets that are to be installed in public places.

Table 15.2. Non-exhaustive list of German carpet standards

Technical aspect covered	Standard reference
Electrostatic behaviour	DIN54345
Impact noise rating	DIN52210 (22dB)
Sound absorption coefficient	DIN52212, 1,000 Hertz
Thermal insulation rating	DIN52612
Flammability	DIN66081T-a/DIN4102-B1
Light fastness	DIN54004
Abrasion resistance	DIN54021
Water fastness	DIN54006

Source: German manufacturer's label.

In the UK, the British Carpet Manufacturers' Association (BCMA) carpet grading scheme classifies carpets' expected performance in use, based on BS 7131. Membership of the BCMA grading scheme (which is optional for BCMA members and may also be used by non-members from anywhere in the world) requires that the tests specified in BS7131 be performed by an independent NAMAS approved test house, and that one-tenth of all graded carpets are randomly tested each year. There are four classes: class one, for sleeping areas; class two, dining/study; class three and class four, living areas. There is a distinction between a domestic and a non-domestic grade: a non-domestic grade would apply to carpets which are installed in small contract locations. A distinction is drawn between these and carpets which are specially constructed for heavy or major contract locations. Whilst these classifications are not obligatory for carpets for the domestic market, retailers use them as a marketing tool and often request them (see Section 15.3.3).

15.1.4. New Approach directives

Textile floor coverings fall under the Construction Products Directive, 89/106/EEC, published in OJ L 40 of 11 February 1989. The Directive theoretically entered into force on 27 June 1991. The date for the end of the transitional period is not fixed. Since the Directive makes the use of harmonized standards or technical approvals mandatory, and these do not yet exist, the Directive is not in practice being applied, and products are still dependent on mutual recognition to remove barriers.

Under the Construction Products Directive, carpets have to meet essential safety requirements for fire resistance, impact noise rating, thermal insulation and specific slipperiness requirements.

15.1.5. European and international standards

The European Commission has issued a horizontal mandate to CEN Technical Committee TC127 (building fire safety) to develop an EN standard for reaction to fire which covers textile floor coverings. Recent working documents have been produced such as the N1026 for the radiant panel fire testing procedures.

Euroclasses were defined by the Commission. These establish the status of construction products with respect to fire resistance (OJ L 241, 16.9.1994, p. 29). There are six classes (similar to the French classification) from class A, which represents the class of product with no contribution to fire, to class F, where no performance level is determined. Whilst carpets are not likely to fall under class A or B (construction products with little or no contribution to fire), no official decision was made with respect to which class carpets should fall under.

CEN has also begun work on a standard for measuring slipperiness of carpets – one of the essential requirements.

No other Commission mandates have been issued to cover properties for floorings under the Construction Products Directive. Nevertheless, the industry has initiated work. Standards related to properties for floorings are to be defined by CEN Technical Committee, TC134, which is to publish the prEN1307 on textile floor coverings before the end of 1996. This standard will harmonize the existing national standards for recommended use classification.

Two ISO standards have been adopted with respect to fire safety: the 'tablet test', ISO6925, and the 'radiant panel test' method known as the NBS (ASTM E648, NFPA253), to be adopted as ISO DIS9239. An ISO Technical Committee is currently working on an ISO standard for carpets' recommended use and classification, which is likely to be based on the future EN1307.

15.1.6. Mutual recognition arrangements

There are no Europe-wide mutual recognition arrangements yet for textile floor coverings, but the European Carpet Association (ECA) is developing a laboratory agreement group through which laboratories commit themselves to recognize one another's certifications and testing procedures. Ten laboratories, which are not all accredited under EN45000, have signed the agreement. This agreement group is expected to come into force by the end of 1996. Its activity will be limited to the recommended-use classifications defined by the prEN1307. The ECA will control the group and review the applications of new test houses wishing to join the agreement group.

Only two arrangements already exist between testing laboratories:

(a)   A Belgian testing laboratory, Centexbel, is authorized to carry out specific tests for carpet manufacturers who wish to obtain certification to AFNOR standards. The process takes up to three weeks. The testing documents are forwarded to AFNOR which verifies them and sends Centexbel a certificate confirming the NF mark.
(b)   The German TFI laboratory, the British BTTG, the Belgian Centexbel and the Austrian ÖTI are members of the GÜT scheme, an environmental label.

15.2. Industry information

15.2.1. Sector representation

The industry is represented at a European level by the Brussels-based ECA. The association is very active, and with the support of national associations is participating in the harmonization of recommended use classification requirements through CEN TC134, and CEN TC127 in the development of the fire safety standards. ECA is also involved in developing a European image for the European carpet industry.

EU members of the ECA are national associations which are more or less active depending on the size of the industry in their country:

(a)   Fachverband der Textilindustrie Österreichs (Austria);
(b)   Febeltex (Belgium);
(c)   Union des Fabricants de Tapis de France (France);
(d)   Verband der Deutschen Heimtextilien e.V. (Germany);
(e)   British Carpet Manufacturers' Association (UK);
(f)   Vereniging van Nederlandse Tapijtfabrikanten (Netherlands);
(g)   Asociación de Fabricantes de Moquetas de España (Spain).

Members of the ECA also include:

(h)   the American association, CRI, based in Georgia; and
(i)   the Swiss association, VSTF, based in Zurich.

The textile industry has a long history of managed trade. Carpets fall under multinational rules such as the Multi-Fibre Agreement (MFA), which was negotiated under the previous GATT agreement. Unlike most textile products, carpets are not subject to import quotas but they were subject in 1990 to an administrative monitoring mechanism known as the 'basket extractor'. Under this agreement quantitative limitations can be applied, following consultations with the exporting countries, if imports grow faster than a predetermined rate, depending on the product category and the country of origin. The new GATT Agreement administered by the World Trade Organization will eliminate all existing quantitative import quotas by 2004.

15.2.2. Industry structure

The European carpet industry is made of a large number of SMEs. Belgium and the Netherlands are significant floor covering and carpet producers, Belgium being the largest carpet producer in Europe, and second largest in the world after the United States. In 1991, the three largest European carpet producers were Belgian. Table 15.3 shows the ten largest European producers.

Table 15.3.   Europe's ten largest carpet manufacturers in 1991

Company	Home nation
Beaulieu Group	Belgium
De Porteere	Belgium
Balta/ITC Group	Belgium
Sommer / Besmer	France
Associated Weavers / Prado	Belgium
Dura Tuft	Germany
Desso	Netherlands
Forbo	Switzerland
C.V. Carpets	UK
DLW	Germany

Source: Carpet Management / Intercontuft.

Mainly for climatic reasons, Italy, Spain and Portugal are small producers and consumers of carpets and rugs. Germany, the UK and France are the largest European markets for textile floor covering, as is shown in Table 15.4.

Table 15.4.   World top ten: consumption of carpets (million square metres)

Country/Region	1992
USA	970
Germany	226
UK	170
Japan	142
Canada	78
France	61
Australasia	45
Latin America	44
Eastern Europe	39
Saudi Arabia	36

Source: ICCO.

15.2.3. Output and trade

Between 1989 and 1994, total European production of carpets and rugs has grown by approximately 10%. Belgium/Luxembourg has remained the largest European manufacturer, followed by Germany, the UK and France representing respectively 16%, 12% and 11% of European output.

Table 15.5.   Production of carpets and other textile floor coverings (million square metres)

Country	1989	1991	1994
Germany	159	175	168
France	65	80	109
Italy	28	27	27
Netherlands	82	85	89
Belgium/Luxembourg	393	452	468
UK	156	143	125
Ireland	3	3	3
Denmark	20	17	14
Greece	7	6	4
Spain	-	-	-
Portugal	7	7	6
EU	**923**	**999**	**1,020**

Source: C.I.R.F.S; C.I.T.H; EURATEX (the European Apparel and Textile Organization which compiles industry statistics).

Table 15.6. Intra-EU imports of carpets and other textile floor coverings (million ECU)

Country	1989	1991	1994
Germany	591	836	549
France	457	442	316
Italy	91	99	75
Netherlands	339	366	238
Belgium/Luxembourg	194	212	164
UK	503	481	447
Ireland	55	63	54
Denmark	39	40	33
Greece	32	44	44
Spain	23	43	44
Portugal	16	29	22
EU	**2,344**	**2,660**	**1,990**

Source: C.I.R.F.S; EURATEX (the European Apparel and Textile Organization which compiles industry statistics).

Table 15.7. Extra-EU exports of carpets and other textile floor coverings (million ECU)

Country	1989	1991	1994
Germany	207	192	163
France	39	42	76
Italy	28	20	28
Netherlands	89	84	108
Belgium/Luxembourg	391	390	643
UK	127	102	127
Ireland	14	7	11
Denmark	69	44	32
Greece	11	13	15
Spain	26	20	19
Portugal	11	10	7
EU	**1,016**	**929**	**1,233**

Source: C.I.R.F.S; EURATEX (the European Apparel and Textile Organization which compiles industry statistics).

Intra-EU imports reached ECU 1,990 million in 1994 which represents a 15% drop compared to 1989. In 1994, Germany, the UK and France were the largest importers of carpets representing respectively 27%, 22% and 16% of intra-EU imports in value.

EU exports to third countries have increased by over 20% between 1989 and 1994. The largest exporter is Belgium/Luxembourg, representing over 52% of EU exports to third countries in 1994 and 38% in 1989. Germany and the UK came a long way behind, with 13% and 10% of extra-EU exports respectively.

15.3. Trade barriers

15.3.1. Regulatory barriers

As described in Section 15.1.2, there are a number of regulatory barriers related to fire performance classification in the contract carpet market, but only in France and Germany. These barriers to trade will be dismantled with the development of harmonized EN standards and the implementation of the Construction Products Directive, but this will take several years. In the domestic market, there are no regulatory barriers to trade.

Manufacturers believe that the single market has enabled them to develop exports with other Member States. A Spanish manufacturer which exports more than 40% of its turnover claims that without the single market his company would have gone bankrupt.

It was reported that the carpet industry and the European Commission have differing priorities: the industry's priority is to develop European standards and classifications of carpet durability and fitness for purpose in order to facilitate intra-EU trade for manufacturers, but the EC requires that the industry meet the essential safety requirements under the Construction Products Directive, which cannot be done until the standards relating to the ESRs are developed: this leaves the harmonization of use classes out of the programme.

In Germany, sales of carpets containing specific dyes (such as PCP) are banned, and limits defining the use of dyes are included in the requirements for the GÜT label (along with tests for many other contaminants). This labelling is available to British, Belgian and Austrian carpet makers, who have labs which are members of the scheme, but is more difficult for other countries.

15.3.2. Testing and certification

Because the only mutual recognition arrangements are for specific tests between AFNOR and Centexbel, and between Centexbel, TÜV and USI for the GÜT mark, most trade still requires double testing, either for regulatory fire testing requirements, or non-regulatory use category testing.

> Example (a): When a Belgian carpet manufacturer wishes to export to Germany, his carpets must be tested against the use classifications. The manufacturer can either carry out the testing procedures in-house or contact a third party in Belgium such as Centexbel. The manufacturer then has to contact the *Teppich-Forschungs-Institut* (TFI) in Germany in order to receive the German certificate. The interviewee believes there is only one laboratory in Germany which produces this certificate. The German laboratory will retest the Belgian products. There is no mutual recognition between the laboratories. The manufacturer has to bear the cost for both tests.

> Example (b): One manufacturer claimed that he had to withdraw from competitive tenders in Germany because a client would not recognize the French M3 certificate and required the B1 test. The time and financial investment involved in the testing requirements for fire safety in Germany (B1 certificate) are arduous. The manufacturer claims that it can take up to one year to obtain the certificate, even when tests are carried out quickly. In that case, the manufacturer did not complain. Complaints are tedious and manufacturers prefer to concentrate their efforts on the market opportunities rather than wasting time in administrative procedures.

> The Belgian agent of a British carpet manufacturer reported that products had to meet fire safety regulations (BS476 Part 7 and NBN21203 which incorporates the BS standard). In that case, the local fire brigade stated that Belgian law required the production of a Belgian fire certificate. The British Carpet Manufacturers Association alleges that Belgian authorities prefer a Belgian test house and Belgian documentation. It is mandatory in Belgium to obtain A2 or A3 pass level of the above-mentioned standard for textile floor coverings installed in public areas, in either an escape route or hotel, office or theatre. It is argued in the industry that Belgian standards were fixed 20 years ago as a result of a big store fire in 1967 where 250 people were killed. The standard has not been updated since then and British manufacturers claim that it hinders their export opportunities in Belgium. Carpets which reach a B1 Class to DIN4102 and Class 1 to ASTM E648 are known to fail the NBN S-21203 Belgian

flammability requirements for use in public areas. This case indicates that the Belgian carpet industry, which is the largest in Europe, is protected by this tight fire safety standard from foreign competitors.

The Belgian agent of a German manufacturer also complained about the need to retest their carpets when exporting to Belgium. He also alleged that Belgian test houses are less strict when it comes to checking locally-made carpets than in checking foreign ones (such allegations are not easy to substantiate).

Technical requirements for the Dutch NBS radiant panel (NEN1775 which stipulates '30 sec' requirement and >0.45 Watt/cm2) differ from the ÖTI Austrian radiant panel (ÖN3810 requiring for a B1 category >0.4 Watt/cm2). Trade between these and other pairs of countries with differing test methods require testing to both standards.

Manufacturers report that there are also special testing requirements when exporting to non-EU countries, especially the USA. Testing requirements for exports to Pakistan were also mentioned.

15.3.3. Quality policies and marks

In the European carpet industry, manufacturers and associations have developed several different quality labels, each of which has its own regional influence.

(a)   In Germany, the German Federation of Carpet Manufacturers (*Europäische Teppich Gemeinschaft für Deutschland* (ETG)) has created the 'ETG' commercial label. It only applies to carpets and excludes rugs.

(b)   In France, there are two systems for quality labels: the UPEC/ITR system which is mandatory under national law regulating carpets for public places, and the voluntary T-ICCO system. The UPEC/ITR system is also used by retailers and distributors as a commercial tool, as described in Section 15.1.2. The voluntary T-ICCO system was developed by the International Carpets Classification Organization (ICCO), an international association for rug and carpet manufacturers. This label is a usage classification system for carpets which is well recognized in France and Belgium. It has five classes (T1 to T5) and tests are specified on thickness, uniformity of manufacture, usage performance, and office chair resilience. ICCO carries out regular controls at the point of sales. The organization was set up in 1975 and currently has members from France, Belgium, Egypt and Turkey. The T-ICCO label was boosted by a heavy promotion and advertising campaign in France, and the French association UFTF is looking at developing the T-ICCO label as a European Quality label.

(c)   In the United Kingdom, the BCMA has created a labelling scheme based on the BS classification (as described in Section 15.1.3). Carpets are independently checked for performance and they are subject to periodic testing. The BCMA has created a distinctive label showing recommended use locations and the British Standard grade number.

(d)   In the Netherlands, the PIT labelling scheme is universally applied and all exports to the Netherlands need to join it.

Some quality marks have a wider scope and apply internationally. This is the case for the woolmark, a label which applies to 100% pure wool products. It is an additional quality label which certifies the origin and quality of the wool according to the definitions given by the International Wool Secretariat (IWS). A new label similar to the woolmark was recently created, the New Zealand woolmark, which is perceived to be stricter and therefore preferred by manufacturers. A Spanish manufacturer claims that the woolmark has lost control over its members and therefore they prefer to use the new New Zealand woolmark. Both wool labels are now competing against each other.

Fibre manufacturers' brand names and labels are important in the market: for example, the NOVAL brand from Rhône-Poulenc or ANTRON from Du Pont de Nemours. Other trade marks define the treatment against stains, such as the Scotchguard label which is a proprietary trade mark of the 3M Products company, and the STAINMASTER, the trade mark for a proprietary process by Du Pont de Nemours. These clearly do not constitute barriers if the fibre or process and use of the trade mark is freely available to all carpet manufactures.

The German market is very sensitive about environmental issues and pollution. A German organization, *Gemeinschaft umweltfreundlicher Teppichboden e.V.*, known as the GÜT, created an environment label which bears the same name, GÜT. German retailers require that all carpets bear the label. The ECA has been active in lobbying against national requirements and labels and succeeded in promoting the GÜT as a European label in co-operation with the German organization. GÜT membership now represents more than two-thirds of European carpet manufacturers, and approximately three out of every four carpets manufactured in Europe today are produced under the control of the GÜT, with tests carried out by its approved laboratories (TFI in Germany, BTTG in the UK, Centexbel in Belgium or DTI in Denmark).

In general, the final customer in the domestic market segment is not well informed about existing quality marks unless they are heavily promoted through advertising. After the promotion of the T-ICCO label in French households, final customers specifically asked for a T-ICCO label, but this is no longer the case since advertising promotions were stopped.

15.4. Enterprise strategies

Because there has been no harmonization or effective mutual recognition, there is no impact on enterprise strategies. Future harmonization will undoubtedly have some impact, considered below, but probably of limited extent.

15.4.1. Product range

Producers do not expect harmonization to have any impact on product range because barriers are not related to technical specifications but rather to testing requirements.

The market naturally requires a large range of product variants. Carpets are decorative items and sales depend on fashion and market preferences. Manufacturers exporting to several Member States produce a wide product range, according to national tastes, but the product range is not affected by testing or quality marking requirements.

> With respect to size, Switzerland and Austria, for instance, tend to purchase five-metre wide carpets, whereas France, the Netherlands, Spain and Belgium prefer the four-metre wide carpets. In addition, carpet texture also varies from one Member State to another: in the UK, buyers prefer curl type carpets; Scandinavian countries prefer velvet type carpets. A Spanish manufacturer stated that they exported eight references from their product ranges but only one can be sold in most Member States because of design and colours utilized, but it cannot, however, be sold in Spain because of the market price.

Specific treatment on carpets is, however, needed in the contract market to meet fire testing requirements. With the implementation of the Construction Products Directive and a harmonized fire safety standard, carpet manufacturers hope they will no longer have to use different treatment on carpets.

15.4.2. Investment

The European carpet manufacturing industry has been rationalized and large groups have been acquiring smaller manufacturers. This may be the result of generally increased trade and competition in the single market, but not specifically to removal of technical barriers. Future harmonization and mutual recognition arrangements, by increasing trade and competition, are likely to lead to extensive rationalization, however, because the industry is generally fragmented.

15.4.3. Distribution and marketing

Since the creation of the single market, carpets and rugs for the domestic market are more freely traded within Europe. Some carpet distribution chains have developed their distribution networks and acquired distribution companies in other Member States. This is the case for the Belgian company, Home Market, which was acquired by the French distributor Saint Maclou.

Manufacturers which exported before the opening of the single market claim that distribution and marketing strategies have not changed as a direct result of the European Commission measures. Nevertheless, a German manufacturer produces promotional tools presenting carpets and collections in three languages, using German relevant standards and pictograms presenting suitability and applications of carpets. A medium-sized French manufacturer has set up administration offices in Germany and the UK. The company has also set up a distribution outlet in Denmark in co-operation with their forwarding agent. The same manufacturer has invested in translation and publishes brochures in four languages. It has also set up a new marketing department which develops carpet designs and colours for the EU market.

15.4.4. Organization and management

Because of its origins, the European carpet industry, which is dominated by Belgian manufacturers, has always been trading in Europe and with third countries. Manufacturers argue that the single market has not had an important impact on their organization and management strategy.

15.4.5. Quality and testing

Most manufacturers have in-house quality control systems with internal laboratories to control the quality of threads, and the technical parameters of the final product. As a result of the opening of frontiers, manufacturers report that they have had to improve product quality and meet higher standards. Manufacturers have thus implemented new or stricter testing procedures and have invested in new testing equipment.

Carpet manufacturers for the automotive industry often need to have QA systems certified to ISO 9001. Achieving the certification is easier for these manufacturers since car manufacturers often have their own quality assurance programmes and provide assistance to their suppliers. Other carpet manufacturers do not perceive the necessity to obtain the ISO 9000 certification.

Nevertheless, most of the respondents confirm that they have been enquiring about the certification process.

15.4.6. Impact on competitiveness and customer choice

The removal of barriers to trade has affected costs related to testing procedures required in each Member State but it has not enabled manufacturers to achieve economies of scale. Nevertheless, respondents confirm that the single market has supported their sales development in other Member States.

> A Spanish manufacturer claims that exports saved its company from bankruptcy, and the opening of frontiers has enabled the company to export over 40% of its production to other Member States; it did not export in 1986. A French manufacturer which exported on a sporadic basis in 1986 claims that it exported in 1995 approximately 70% of its turnover.

> A Belgian manufacturer reported that as a result of the single market, it has been able to improve quality and sell to German car manufacturers which previously only used German supplies.

15.5. Conclusions

15.5.1. Effectiveness of approaches

Mutual recognition has not had an impact on removing the barriers caused by fire testing in France and Germany, because the approach is very different and the authorities do not accept their equivalence. These are the only national regulations which apply, but in other countries the local authority or private building inspectors, the fire brigades or insurers are likely to insist on fire testing to the divergent national standards.

The other technical barriers relate to quality marks and use classifications, which except in France are non-mandatory and outside the scope of MRP, but the ECA is trying to eliminate these by backing T-ICCO as a European scheme, and supporting voluntary CEN activity.

Table 15.8 summarizes various measures having an impact on the removal of technical barriers in carpets.

Table 15.8.   Effectiveness of approaches for carpets

Approaches	Effectiveness now[1]	Likely effectiveness[1]
Mutual recognition principle	-	-
Construction Products Directive	-	****
Harmonized EN on fire safety procedures	-	****
European standards on carpet use and classifications (to be published)	**	****
Mutual recognition arrangements for testing and certification	*	**

[1] on a scale of 1-5 where ***** = the most effective
Source: W.S. Atkins.

15.5.2. Remaining barriers

There are no remaining barriers to trade for carpets aimed at the domestic market. With respect to the contract markets, barriers to trade still hinder free trade between Member States and reduce market opportunities for other manufacturers. These are summarized in Table 15.9.

Table 15.9.   Remaining barriers for carpets

Remaining barriers	Impact on industry[1]
Fire testing procedures and certificates	*****
Use labelling schemes	*
Environmental rules in Germany	**

[1] on a scale of 1-5 where ***** = the greatest impact
Source: W.S. Atkins.

16. Water pipe fittings

16.1. Product scope

NACE code: 25.21 – Manufacture of plastic plates, sheets, tubes and profiles.

PRODCOM code: 25.21.21/22 – Tubes, pipes and hoses/fittings for tubes, pipes and hoses of plastic.

Couplings and pipe fittings were selected as sample products, to examine whether technical barriers to trade in the water sector have been removed through the functioning of the principle of mutual recognition. This product group was recommended by several industry contacts as one where intra-EU trade is significant.

16.2. Technical barriers

16.2.1. Regulatory barriers

Discussions with manufacturers have revealed that there are virtually no problems of technical regulations in this sector. Manufacturers were keen to stress, however, that this has always been the case, and that the principle of mutual recognition has not been invoked to remove barriers.

16.2.2. Non-regulatory barriers

Water pipe and fitting specifications are traditionally set by the water company engineers, not by industrial standards. A variety of forms of water company exist throughout Europe, from public enterprises, through local authority agencies, to private companies. There is thus a wide range of specifications and dimensions, but these are neither regulations nor national standards.

Standards for external pipe dimensions differ between countries, so a range of differing dimensions of pipe fittings are needed to meet international markets. For example, Switzerland has no national pipe manufacture and all pipes are, therefore, imported. This has led to a range of pipe dimensions being used in this market and, therefore, a variety of coupling sizes are required. These is not seen as a significant cost factor by manufacturers of fittings, but it must create some additional tooling, stockholding and marketing costs.

Key trading difficulties appear to be related to currency movements affecting companies' competitiveness and culture and tradition acting as limiting factors in the choice of product/supplier. One German company mentioned that its key trading impediment is the strength of the Deutschmark. It has difficulty selling to Italy, not because of any technical barriers, but because Italy has a number of low-cost producers whose products (albeit of a more simple design) are up to 40% cheaper. Previously water company engineers had a greater say in the selection of products, whereas today price and market availability is becoming increasingly important.

German water companies request that all products have DVGW (a technical gas and water association) approval. German produced couplings and fitting which have this approval are reported to be accepted throughout Europe. Products imported into Germany are required by water companies to have this. Although this approval is not mandatory, a German water company would be unlikely to purchase a product without it.

16.3.   Enterprise strategies

There is evidence of investment in other EU countries but this does not appear to be linked to the removal of technical barriers. One company owns a manufacturing plant in Spain but this was established in the 1960s.

Companies active in this sector also tend to produce fittings for the gas sector. There are more potential hazards in this sector and products intended for use in this sector are subject to more stringent requirements, particularly for pressures above 16 bar. The gas sector appears to have a number of barriers to trade ranging from certain EU customers allegedly demonstrating clear preferences for domestic suppliers, to differences in national regulations which are mandatory.

17. Fortified foods and drinks

17.1. Product information

NACE: Division 15 – Manufacture of food products and beverages.

17.1.1. Product scope

This report covers all fortified foodstuffs and drinks, i.e. products to which vitamins and/or minerals have been added. When examining this sector it is important to differentiate between restoration, an industry term to describe the process of restoring the nutrients which are destroyed through processing, and fortification or enrichment, which refers to the addition of nutrients in order to provide a certain proportion of the Recommended Daily Allowance (RDA).

There is no commonly accepted definition of fortification in Europe. The Codex Alimentarius offers the following definition of fortification:

> Fortification, or enrichment, means the addition of one or more essential nutrients to a food, whether or not it is normally contained in the food, for the purpose of preventing or correcting a demonstrated deficiency of one or more nutrients in the population or specific population groups.

The main products which are fortified are:

(a)   breakfast cereals (seven vitamins and iron);
(b)   dairy products (calcium and Vitamins A and D);
(c)   drinks;
(d)   margarine (mandatory fortification).

It is estimated that 5% of all foodstuffs in Germany are fortified, followed by the UK with 3.5%. Table 17.1 shows the proportion of fortification occurring in certain product sectors in selected countries.

Table 17.1.   Fortification levels in Europe (% of value of sales which are fortified)

	Germany	UK	France	Spain
Breakfast cereals	50	76	80	100
Margarine	60	100	100	50
Baby food	75			
Fruit juice	18	5	6	3
Chocolate powder			63	6
Confectionery	5			
Dairy products		20	7	1
Potato crisps		5		
Oil			3	
Biscuits				2
Bread				3

17.1.2. National regulations

There is currently no agreement between Member States with regard to the best approach to food and drink fortification. Member States currently have very differing legislation ranging from a complete ban on all fortification; restoration permitted but enrichment prohibited; maximum permissible levels for certain vitamins; mandatory classification of enriched products as dietetic products; and in some cases, mandatory fortification.

Differences in legislation are justified by the fact that dietary habits and practices vary across Member States, as do the profile of target groups and their likely dietary deficiencies. For many years debate in the European food and drink industry has focused on the issue that fortification at best may provide the consumer with no benefit and at worst may represent a risk to health. The concern of national governments is that consumers often believe that 'natural' and 'harmless' are synonymous, when in fact certain vitamins can, when consumed in excess, have adverse effects on health.

It is not within the scope of this study to discuss or appraise the arguments for and against fortification. It is sufficient to establish that differences in approach exist, and this has led to differences in national regulations, which naturally create regulatory barriers to trade. There is no definitive scientific evidence on potential benefits and dangers of vitamin additives, and national policies are firmly held but different.

An ECJ judgment in 1983 (Case 174/82 *Sandoz* [1983] ECR 2445) accorded Member States the right to place restrictions on imports of fortified foods and drinks on the grounds of Article 36 (i.e. public health). The judgment, however, also makes reference to the principle of proportionality, i.e. any Member State taking action against a product must be able to prove that the action is in proportion to the risk. Taking this into account, outright prohibition of a product should be justified only in rare cases.

Arguments for fortification include the following:

(a)   the population is increasingly sedentary;
(b)   fast food intake is increasing;
(c)   changes in food intake such as:
       (i)   move from butter to margarine (compulsory fortification with vitamins D and A);
       (ii)   milk consumption decreasing (flour fortified with calcium in 1943 in the UK);
       (iii)   decreasing consumption of bread and starchy foods.

17.1.3. European policy measures

There is no European legislation which addresses specifically the issue of food and drink fortification. However, there are a number of 'Old Approach' directives and papers which are relevant to the sector. Four of these are:

(a)   Discussion paper on diet integrators (no longer valid);
(b)   Directive on nutritional labelling of foodstuffs;
(c)   Draft Claims Directive (now withdrawn);
(d)   Directive on foodstuffs for particular nutritional purposes.

Discussion paper on diet integrators

A discussion paper on the subject of diet integrators was put forward by the European Commission in December 1991. This paper covered foods to which vitamins and minerals have been added and also products with 'health giving' properties and concentrated sources of nutrients. The paper concluded that there is no scientific evidence to suggest any adverse effects in countries where fortification is common practice. This paper, however, is no longer valid and a new paper is under preparation by the EC.

Directive on nutritional labelling of foodstuffs (90/496/EEC)

All products which make a nutritionally-related claim or statement fall under this Directive. Fortified products are, therefore, subject to this legislation. The labelling relates to the total nutrient content of the food/drink and not just the fortification. The Directive stipulates what constitutes a significant quantity of vitamins (natural or added) from the nutritional viewpoint. Annex I to this Directive defines this as at least 15% of the reference value of the vitamin per 100g or 100ml product. The reference is based on Recommended Daily Allowances which are minimum intakes estimated to ensure that adequate amounts of the nutrient in question are consumed in order to maintain good health.

Since publication of this Directive, the EU's Scientific Committee for Foods (SCF) has issued a new publication on the subject of nutrient and energy intakes, which could be used as a basis for updating Annex I to the Directive.

This Directive, whilst fixing a minimum fortification level necessary for the product label to be able to make reference to fortification, does not fix a minimum level of actual fortification. However, it is unlikely that a manufacturer would want to fortify to a lower level if it meant no reference could be made to fortification on the label.

Draft Claims Directive

A Claims Directive relating to food has been discussed since 1993, but has now been withdrawn and the European Commission's Directorate-General for Consumer Policy and Consumer Health Protection (DG XXIV) is considering amendments to the Misleading Advertising Directive (84/450/EEC). The first draft of the Claims Directive contained different possible forms for nutrient contents claims and the criteria for their use. A revision of this document contained only principles, and did not include specific limiting values as did the first draft. This Directive would automatically have included fortified products and was intended to harmonize the basis for claims such as 'rich in Vitamin X'.

Directive on foodstuffs for particular nutritional purposes (89/398/EEC)

This Directive applies to specific categories of food targeted at meeting the particular nutritional requirements for the population for which they are intended, such as baby foods or diet products. Some fortified products may fall under this Directive and are, therefore, subject to certain provisions regarding product composition, labelling and advertising. The Directive should have removed regulatory barriers resulting from national ingredient rules for the specialist products which it covers, which may be manufactured by the same suppliers as fortified foods and drinks for general consumption. The latter, however, are not affected.

17.1.4. Mutual recognition arrangements

There are no known mutual recognition arrangements between laboratories for the testing of food additives.

17.2. Industry information

17.2.1. Sector representation

This sector is covered by many different trade associations in each country as fortified foods and drinks cover different sectors, such as drinks, cereals and dairy, for which there are separate trade associations. At European level, the interests of the sector are represented by the umbrella organization *Confédération des Industries Agro-Alimentaires* (CIAA). The CIAA has been assessing the views of European industry on the desirability of some degree of harmonization, and has been conducting a survey amongst its members to establish:

(a)   which nutrients should be restricted;
(b)   if nutrients should be authorized for all foodstuffs or in specific foodstuffs;
(c)   how restricted harmonization should be laid down;
(d)   if minimum levels should be introduced;
(e)   if so, what levels (levels specified in the Nutritional Labelling Directive or the Codex);
(f)   what maximum levels should be introduced;
(g)   how quantities should be expressed.

At least one European trade association is known to have submitted a paper to the EC in 1993, stating that it had serious doubts as to the functioning of the principle of mutual recognition and, therefore, requesting a partial harmonization for the addition of nutrients to foodstuffs.

17.2.2. Industry structure

The structures of the fortified food sector and the drinks sector are different. In the area of fortified cereals or margarine, there are large pan-European companies such as Unilever, Nestlé and Kelloggs. In the field of fortified and energy drinks, companies are frequently smaller and active in niche markets (this is partly due to the fact that transportation costs are high and producers tend to operate close to their main market).

For energy drinks, Austria is the dominant producing Member State. Although the concept of an energy drink was launched by one Austrian company, there are estimated to be around 60 different suppliers of energy drinks (mainly in Austria) today. Most suppliers subcontract production to soft drink manufacturers.

In general, companies add a fortified product to an already well-established product range in order to create a higher value product, or smaller manufacturers specialize in foods which are both fortified and intended for special niche markets.

There tends to be a correlation between countries which have stringent legislation regarding fortification and the number of manufacturers. For example, there are few manufacturers of fortified products in Italy since stringent legislation exists in this field, which is preventing development in the sector.

17.2.3. Output and trade

Output and trade data do not separately identify fortified foods. Feedback from manufacturers, however, indicates that intra-EU trade has increased, partially as a result of mutual recognition but also because of increased demand relating to changes in lifestyle and diet, as well as heavy advertising.

17.3. Trade barriers

17.3.1. Regulatory barriers

Most Member States have their own national legislation governing fortification. These differing regulations are summarized in Tables 17.2 to 17.4 and a more detailed description by country follows. All Member States now recognize the legitimacy of fortification with at least some vitamins in at least some food products; but significant variations exist regarding the nutrients which are authorized; the notification procedures required; and whether fortified foods are permitted to be sold for general consumption or have to be classified as dietetic foods or foods for particular nutritional purposes.

As examples of the differences in approach, a few special cases may be quoted. On the whole, Germany is considered to be liberal where vitamins are concerned but strict with regard to minerals, whereas in the Netherlands the addition of minerals is permitted but not vitamin enrichment; France is the only country to clearly differentiate between restoration and fortification, with fortification being strictly regulated; and the Netherlands is the only country in Europe which currently bans all fortification of normal foods, except margarine, where fortification is mandatory [although a new regulation covering vitaminization of foods is in preparation in the Netherlands].

Table 17.2 summarizes the legislative environment in each country with regard to fortification. Table 17.3 lists fortification which is currently mandatory in the EU and Table 17.4 shows the divergent levels of maximum fortification permitted in each Member State.

In some countries it is necessary to notify fortified products. Notification requirements are also shown in Table 17.2. Some countries, such as Belgium, are reported to request a manufacturer to place the product registration number on the product labelling. Industry considers this requirement to be contrary to the Labelling Directive (79/112/EEC).

France

In France, enrichment of foodstuffs for general consumption with Vitamin D is prohibited (only allowed in baby's milk, meal replacements). By comparison, Vitamin D can be added to foodstuffs in Spain, the UK, Belgium, Ireland and Portugal. In Italy and Germany, Vitamin D can be added to dietetic products. In France, iodine can only be added to dietetic products.

France is reported to be reticent to allow fortification. If a nutritional benefit cannot be proved, fortification is prohibited. In France, all fortified foodstuffs are considered as dietetic products which must be for special use with a claim that can be substantiated and are, therefore, subject to a notification procedure before being placed on the market.

Fortification guidelines are currently being reviewed by CEDAP, the committee for foods for particular nutritional uses.

Table 17.2.   Legislative environment

Member State	Legislation in force	Requirement of notification?
Austria	Maximum levels stipulated in list adopted in May 1994	Yes
Belgium	Decree on nutrients of March 1992	Yes
Denmark	Strict approach. Fortification only permitted if it can be justified from a nutritional point of view	Yes
Finland	Strict approach – no legislation	Yes
France	Strictly regulated and only permitted in certain dietetic products. Must be justified from a nutritional point of view	For dietetic foods
Germany	Permitted up to 3 x RDA (except Vitamins A & D)	
Greece	Maximum 2 x RDA (except Vitamins A, D & K)	For dietetic foods
Ireland	No legislation	
Italy	Follows Codex guidelines. Products classified as dietary	For dietetic foods
Luxembourg	No legislation	Yes
Netherlands	Strict approach. *Warenwet Levensmiddelen* of 1992 prohibits fortification (new legislation in process)	
Portugal	max. 100% of RDA	
Spain	max. 100% of RDA	
Sweden	Rules laid down in SLV 1983:2	Yes
UK	Fortification permitted provided the addition of substances does not cause a risk to health	

Table 17.3.   Mandatory fortification

Country	Foods	Nutrients
UK	Margarine	Vitamins A and D
	Wheat flour	Thiamine, niacin, iron, calcium
Netherlands	Margarine	Vitamins A and D
Denmark	Margarine	Vitamin A
Sweden	Margarine	Vitamins A and D

Table 17.4. Maximum levels of fortification or supplement

Country	Maximum level of fortification
Belgium	In % RDA per serving: - 300% Vit. B, C, E, H, K - 150% Vit. A, D - 150% Cr, Cu, F, Mg, Mn, Se, Mo, Zn, I - 200% Ca, Fe, Cl, P, Na
France	40% RDA per 100 kcal
Denmark, Sweden, Norway	Maximum levels set per food category
Germany	300% RDA per serving
Greece	50% RDA per serving. Above this level a specific authorization from the pharmaceutical organization is necessary
Italy	150% RDA per serving
Netherlands	100% RDA per reasonable daily serving
Spain	No maximum levels
UK	No maximum levels

Netherlands

The fortification of foodstuffs for general consumption is prohibited at present. The Netherlands has, however, now notified the Commission of a new decree which will ease the ban on imports of fortified foodstuffs into the Netherlands but which will still prohibit certain additions, such as Vitamin D, folic acid, zinc and iodine. The new legislation is due to be adopted in the summer of 1996.

The new legislation also contains certain restrictions regarding quantitative nutritional claims. For example, the allegation 'rich in' can only be used for nutrients naturally present in the raw materials and not added during the manufacturing process. In the Netherlands, a reasonable daily serving is considered to be 15% of the RDA, yet a 20% content can be marketed as 'high in vitamins'. A product may be fortified by 15% but would not be able to carry this claim even though it is only marginally lower.

New regulations regarding the addition of nutrients to foodstuffs have been drafted, and publication is pending. In the meantime, the Ministry of Health will allow marketing of products in line with draft regulations.

Enrichment is allowed for all nutrients except Vitamins A, D, folate, zinc, copper and selenium at levels ranging from 15–100% RDA per reasonable daily serving. These additives are allowed, however, for substitution and restoration. Fortified foodstuffs must have the claim 'with added vitamins and minerals'.

One EU manufacturer submitted a complaint to the Dutch authorities on 22 October 1993 for refusing to allow fortified products onto the market. The result of this complaint was negative.

A complaint was also made to the European Commission stating that it was impossible to export vitamin-enriched breakfast cereals produced in Germany or the UK to the Netherlands.

Belgium

The addition of elemental iron is prohibited in Belgium (it is permitted in France, the UK, Ireland, the Netherlands, Italy, Germany, Spain and Denmark).

Fortified products are also subject to a notification procedure in Belgium (*Service d'Inspection des Denrées Alimentaires du Ministère de la Santé publique et de l'Environnement*). A Royal Decree of 3 March 1992 also stipulates that it is mandatory for the notification number to appear on the label.

Complaints were made to the Commission regarding this on 14 May 1993 by the *Syndicat Français des Céréales Prêtes à Consommer*; and on 4 January 1995 by a EU manufacturer. This manufacturer is furthermore being pursued by Belgian courts for not having placed the notification number on the product labelling.

Germany

The addition of Vitamins A and D as well as minerals such as zinc and iodine are prohibited in products for general consumption.

Spain

New regulations regarding the addition of nutrients to foodstuffs have been drafted. Publication is pending.

Enrichment is allowed for all nutrients except elemental iron, at levels ranging between 15 and 30% RDA per recommended daily serving and at a level of 25% for Vitamins A, D and E.

Claims referring to preventive, therapeutic or curative properties are not permitted, nor is the use of terms such as 'healthy' or 'recommended by nutrition specialists'.

Italy

In Italy fortified foodstuffs are classed as dietetic products and are, therefore, subject to a notification procedure.

Scandinavia

Regulation of fortified foodstuffs is complex in Scandinavian countries. A distinction is made between mandatory and voluntary enrichment. In the case of voluntary enrichment, notification to the National Foodstuff Agency is necessary both to put a product on the market and to remove a product from the market. Legislation is defined by product groups (e.g. breakfast cereals, flour, pasta, rice, milk, etc.). For each product there is a list of nutrients which are allowed to be added to each product category.

In *Denmark*, examples of voluntary enrichment (content per 100g) are:

(a)   fortification of breakfast cereals is permitted for Vitamins B1 (1,0mg), B2 (1,0mg), PP (10mg), iron (7mg);
(b)   fortification of wheat flour is permitted for Vitamins B1 (5,0mg), B2 (5,0mg), calcium (2mg) and iron (30mg);
(c)   fortification of fruit juices and drinks is permitted for Vitamin C (40mg).

An example of obligatory enrichment is the fortification of margarine with Vitamin A (840mg).

In *Finland*, voluntary enrichment is limited to three categories of food:

(a)   breakfast cereals – Vitamins B1 (1– 1.4mg), B2 (1– 1.8mg), PP (6.5mg), iron (6.5 mg);
(b)   fruit juices and drinks – Vitamin C (20–60mg);
(c)   margarine – Vitamins A (500–1,000mg) and D (5–10mg).

17.3.2. Enforcement procedures

In countries with the most stringent legislation, market surveillance is reported to be keen. For example, in Italy it is reported that ministerial surveillance is tight and if 150% RDA is exceeded by manufacturers, they risk penal prosecution.

> One Italian manufacturer is currently in legal proceedings as a result of a USL (the local authority body which carries out controls of products on display in shops) establishing that one of the company's products exceeded the RDA. The company reports that the potency of vitamins weakens over time, and since some products have a shelf life of three months, it is necessary to over-fortify at the time of manufacture. In this manufacturer's experience, other countries do not control fortification as tightly; for example, it reports that it is not uncommon to find products in the UK fortified to 300% RDA.

France is also reported to be fairly strict on enforcement. The *Direction Générale de la Concurrence, de la Consommation et de la Répression des Fraudes* (DGCCRF) is responsible for enforcement in France. For example, the DGCCRF considers that some ingredients found in energy drinks (e.g. taurine) are not beneficial to the consumer. In addition, the *Conseil Supérieur de la République Française* has carried out a study which demonstrates that certain vitamin levels are potentially a risk to health. Energy drinks are, therefore, prohibited from sale on the French market and the DGCCRF enforces this decision in spite of the principle of mutual recognition.

In various countries, it would appear that retailers sometimes import products which do not strictly meet national regulations but have been purchased under the principle of mutual recognition. Sometimes local manufacturers object to this. The food and drink sector in the EU is highly competitive and it is not uncommon for national manufacturers to carry out careful examination of competing imported products to identify non-compliance with national regulations. Where non-compliance is established, the company will report the imported product to the enforcement authorities and request withdrawal of the product from circulation. It can, therefore, be seen that policing is often motivated by competitive considerations.

17.3.3. Parallel imports

Some manufacturers are concerned about potential liability problems arising as a result of parallel imports. One EU manufacturer reported that retailers in its home market are importing its products, which are legal for sale in another EU market but which actually contravene the do not respect the mutual recognition principle). This is reported to be increasingly common practice as food retailing becomes more global and large retailers become more active across borders. The problem of parallel imports is likely to happen when retailers bring surplus stock from one country into another, where it is then, technically speaking, not legal to sell. Alternatively, it may be a strategic decision to source in another country for competitive reasons in order to exploit relative price differences.

The problem reported by producers is that consumers may complain to the relevant authorities and the complaint will land on the door of the manufacturer (because MRP does not work), even though the product may have been sold via an intermediary. It is probable that the more real concern of manufacturers is the impact on differential pricing policies: in other words, that the MRP *is* successful in combating trade barriers.

17.3.4. The impact of mutual recognition

Mutual recognition of fortification is only partially taking place, because what is considered to constitute a public health risk differs greatly, and Member States have fundamentally different approaches to controlling the fortification of food.

To summarize the previous section: in some Member States a 'positive' list exists (e.g. France) which is a list of vitamins and nutrients permitted, whereas in other countries (e.g. Spain) there is a 'negative' list of what is prohibited. In some countries (e.g. the UK) vitamin fortification is not regulated by specific legal texts, but by provisions relating to nutritional labelling. Differences also exist in the status of vitamin-enriched foodstuffs: systematic allocation of the status of 'foodstuffs for particular nutritional use' to foods which are fortified is considered by manufacturers to constitute a barrier to trade. Lastly, the labelling and permitted claims of vitamin-enriched products vary from country to country, causing confusion and added expense to manufacturers. Certain countries permit enrichment but do not allow a manufacturer to make any nutritional claims concerning added vitamins and minerals.

Although the principle of mutual recognition is not functioning completely, so that suppliers have to change product formulations, undergo repeated notification and testing procedures or not sell at all into certain markets, it would be incorrect to draw the conclusion that mutual recognition is not functioning at all. Discussions with manufacturers have revealed some (but few) examples where mutual recognition is functioning and how this eases exporting, as compared with a time when mutual recognition did not exist. Figure 17.1 shows practical examples of benefits experienced by manufacturers as a result of MRP.

The principal example of successful mutual recognition is the case of energy drinks (see Case 1 in Figure 17.1). The original German manufacturer of a taurine-based energy drink was unable to produce and market in Germany, or to market into other major EU markets. He therefore set up in Austria, which had more liberal requirements. When Austria acceded to the Union, the firm was able to export to Germany, the UK, and other markets which accepted the product under mutual recognition, even though it would not have been acceptable under national regulations. Austria, by this process, became a dominant producer of these products, with over 80 suppliers.

It may be argued that in this case (and the case of other food additives and ingredients) the application of MRP is properly restricted by Art. 36. The scientific evidence on the potential value or danger from excessive dosage of vitamins and certain minerals is unclear. As new products and new applications are introduced, new research is needed. Some countries may adopt a cautious approach; some countries may find new evidence of potential harm and introduce controls. Consumers may rightly be concerned if products, particularly soft drinks and convenience foods aimed at children, are freely available because one or more Member States have a liberal policy, particularly since Member States are under continual pressure from manufacturers to relax controls on what are often high profit margin goods. It may be argued that for certain products like fortified foods there is an argument for the strictest controls to be universally applied, rather than, as with MRP, the most liberal.

It may be noted that manufacturers of fortified products also report benefits from harmonization as a result of the Nutrition Labelling Directive (90/496/EEC) which has brought benefits through a reduction in the number of different labels required to sell a product throughout the EU. The Products for Particular Nutritional Uses Directive (89/398/EEC) has also brought benefits to manufacturers selling into the French market (not in other countries, however, as fortified foodstuffs are not classed as dietetic foods in most other markets). When one manufacturer launched fortified products into the French market in the late 1980s, it was necessary to have analyses carried out by a French laboratory, whereas analysis carried out in the country of manufacture is now accepted.

It should be noted also that manufacturers are not usually aware of whether improved market access which they achieve is a result of harmonizing directives or mutual recognition (the legal basis of MRP in the Treaty is, of course, unknown and of no interest to them). Most examples of mutual recognition quoted by firms were in fact due to detailed harmonization and labelling rules. This is the approach which has most generally been applied in the case of processed foodstuffs: there has been no detailed harmonization yet for fortified foods because many of the products (e.g. energy drinks) are new, and there is evolving scientific research on the benefits and risks, as well as the different dietary patterns and national approaches mentioned previously.

17.3.5. Other regulatory barriers affecting food and drink manufacturers

Besides the problems of acceptance of vitamin and mineral fortification dealt with in this section, the manufacturers of fortified foods and drinks interviewed raised a number of problems related to permitted additives (preservatives and antioxidants), labelling requirements, food names (such as the use of the terms fruit juice, fruit drink, nectar) and packaging. These are all being dealt with by other EU harmonizing directives and actions. In some cases EU rules already exist but were not effective at the time of the survey; these should become effective in due course. They can be taken as examples of related areas where mutual recognition failed to be effective, and specific harmonizing legislation was or still is required.

The mini case studies presented in Figure 17.2 give examples of the practical problems reported by manufacturers in this sector, which appear to remain even if mutual recognition or harmonization of the fortified products occurs.

Some of these cases are in fact examples where harmonization measures have recently been taken or are being taken, but the effects have not been realized by the manufacturers concerned. This may be because the enforcement authorities continue to enforce old rules because new training, procedures or information have not been provided or the EU directives have not been transposed and implemented; or simply because the manufacturer does not know that the rules have changed and continues to produce the existing range of different products and packaging. There may indeed be a real cost in simplifying an existing range of product variants. This may involve closing some lines, investment in new, higher capacity lines, changing packaging, and more importantly for fast moving consumer goods (FMCG), changing a brand, mounting a new advertising and marketing campaign and changing consumer tastes. Complaints from manufacturers about the need for product variants therefore have to be qualified somewhat in the case of foodstuffs.

Figure 17.1. Examples of benefits experienced by manufacturers

Case 1: An energy drinks supplier believes that increased marketing of its products throughout the EU is mainly a result of natural commercial development which would have happened if the single market did not exist. However, it was conceded that EU-wide marketing of products would have been significantly more difficult without the help of Article 30.

When the founder of the company decided to set up a company in the field of energy drinks, Germany was the first choice to locate the new venture. On closer examination it was found that German law would prohibit the manufacture of such a product. For this reason, the venture was started in Austria.

As the company began to grow from its home market in Austria, it tried to penetrate the German market but the German authorities would not authorize the product as it contravened national law. As Austria was not then a member of the EU, the company was unable to benefit from the principle of mutual recognition in order to gain access into Germany. The company, therefore, decided it needed to penetrate one EU market first and use this as a springboard from which to enter other EU markets under the principle of mutual recognition.

This strategy has been successful for penetrating other EU markets. The company states that the principle of mutual recognition is functioning in half the Member States. For example, although the product contravenes Belgian law, the Belgian authorities are accepting the product on the grounds of mutual recognition.

A further benefit cited by this manufacturer is the fact that a manufacturer is able to approach the EC with problems experienced in placing products on other EU markets and have the confidence that the complaint will be investigated and that the European Commission is committed to finding a solution.

Case 2: A dairy products manufacturer stated that they have been able to reduce the number of different recipes which are necessary to sell into the full range of EU countries. Since the accession of Austria, they are able to sell products there which were previously banned. This is partly a result of harmonizing directives on additives and colourants, but mutual recognition is thought to play a part. Whilst this manufacturer is recognizing certain benefits brought about by mutual recognition, they are keen to underline that if mutual recognition was functioning properly in all markets, it would be possible to make one basic product, thus reducing unit prices by approximately 20–25%.

Case 3: A soft drinks manufacturer has no problems in exporting to Portugal, Spain, Sweden and the Netherlands, where they only need to place a sticker on the bottle listing the ingredients in the local language. The company believes that their success in these markets can be attributed to the single market and the principle of mutual recognition, without which they would have to produce different products for each market. Mutual recognition is working much better today than several years ago. Some countries are reported to try to put up barriers initially but usually back down. Previously, there were countries which the company did not attempt to sell into. The German market used to be considered too difficult, but access is much improved today.

Figure 17.2. Examples of other technical barriers faced by manufacturers of fortified foods and drinks

Case 1: A breakfast cereal manufacturer experiences certain restrictions in EU legislation which prevent it from selling fortified breakfast cereals produced in the UK in certain other Member States. Special production runs are required with changes in vitamin profiles, because:

(a)   fortification of food with vitamins is not permitted in the Netherlands or Norway;

(b)   Vitamin D is not permitted in France, Germany, Belgium and Austria;

(c)   only thiamine, riboflavin, niacin and iron can be added in Denmark, Sweden and Finland.

Other problems include:

(a)   some Member State authorities require notification of fortified products, e.g. Belgium and Greece, creating additional costs and delays in getting products to market;

(b)   in Italy, France and Greece breakfast cereals are allowed to be fortified but are classed as dietetic foods. In these countries, a notification procedure is in place and manufacturers must be able to substantiate their claim that fortification is beneficial to its target market segment (e.g. pregnant women, growing children). It is then difficult to market it for general consumption.

Case 2: A manufacturer of dairy products exports products which are manufactured according to local German regulations and are accompanied by a certificate of the chemical analysis undertaken by a third party laboratory. The company believes that this should suffice to export to all EU countries. In practice, however, this is not the case.

The company manufactures a fortified buttermilk drink. For exporting to France and the Netherlands, it has been necessary to change the product formulation to give a lower vitamin profile. The decision as to whether it was economically feasible to do this for two markets was a borderline one. Attempts to sell into Scandinavian markets have been abandoned due to the stringent legislation in these countries.

This manufacturer also experiences problems with its products in areas other than fortification which are worth mentioning. Italy has differing requirements regarding the bacteria content of yoghurt than those in the country of manufacture. The Italian authorities have stated that unless the bacteria content is changed the product can no longer be marketed in Italy as a fruit yoghurt and will have to be renamed as a yoghurt based fruit dessert.

With regard to ascorbic acid alone, three different recipes are necessary. [In fact rules on ascorbic acid have now been harmonized, but this does not yet seem to have made an impact on the manufacturer.]

Case 3: A manufacturer of soft drinks produces a multivitamin juice and a sports drink. He did not report problems with vitamin content, but produces different packaging and labelling for Belgium, Austria, Germany, Luxembourg and the Netherlands due to differences in the definition of what is a fruit juice, fruit nectar and fruit juice drink. [These definitions have now been harmonized at EU level, but do not yet appear to have removed the need for different packaging.] For their sports drink they purposely chose ingredients which would not be contentious in order to increase export chances.

The company also sells a throat drop which contains Vitamin C. In France, these are not accepted as a throat drop, but have to be sold as a dietetic product. The manufacturer does not really want to do this as it has image and marketing implications. Problems are also encountered with throat drops in the Belgian market. As they contain Vitamin C, they must first be registered and the registration number placed on the package. Even if only small modifications are made to the product, re-registration is necessary and labels with the new number must be printed.

Case 4: An energy drinks manufacturer reports that although mutual recognition is functioning in around half the Member States, some countries, namely Italy, France, Greece and all Scandinavian countries, refuse to accept imports of their energy drinks.

In Italy, legislation prohibits soft drinks with a caffeine content of more than 125 mg per litre (the firm's energy drinks contain 320mg per litre). The manufacturer complains that its drinks have only a caffeine content equivalent to a cup of filter coffee. [There is an SCF opinion on the safety of caffeine: limits are justified because children may drink large volumes of soft drinks in a day.] In 1995, this manufacturer managed to obtain authorization to sell energy drinks into the Italian market as dietetic products. In 1996, the Italian Ministry of Health is reported to have requested all products to be withdrawn from the Italian market due to concern over potential health risks.

France prohibits the import of energy drinks. There are also problems selling into Greece. This manufacturer has, therefore, decided not attempt to sell into these markets for the moment.

Case 5: *A soft drinks manufacturer* reported problems in exporting to the following countries:

(a)   *Greece:* This company has a soft drink product which it markets with the claim 'rich in Vitamin C'. The product is contract packed in Greece for the Greek market. The product formulation is identical to that for other EU markets but the claim 'rich in Vitamin C' cannot be made. Another soft drink which the company sells into the Greek market has a yellow colouring (sunset yellow) which was not previously approved in Greece, but rules on additives have now been harmonized.

(b)   *Denmark:* In Denmark the same problem exists when making the claim 'rich in Vitamin C'. [This is in line with EU legislation: the Fruit Juice Directive states that when ascorbic acid (vitamin C) is used as an additive – preservative or antioxidant – which is the case for fruit drinks, no claim relating to vitamin C content can be made.] In addition to this, the company cannot sell certain ready-to-drink products in Denmark, as Danish environmental law prohibits the use of cans and compels manufacturers to set up a bottle collection system.

(c)   *Germany:* The German notification process is reported to be lengthy and can be difficult. One of this company's products contains the preservative SO_2 which is on the German blacklist and for which the company had tried to obtain approval under mutual recognition. This application started in December 1995 and approval has still not been granted. The German authorities are now reported to be questioning details such as the fact that PLC in the company name appears on the label twice, once in upper and once in lower case! [As above, additives have now been harmonized but this had not yet helped the company.]

(d)   *Italy:* The company has tried to market a fruit juice drink in the Italian market. Italian legislation requires that such a product must have a minimum fruit juice content of 12%, whereas this company's product has only 5%. After careful consideration, it was decided that alteration of the formulation was not economically feasible for just one market.

A particular area of concern which affects manufacturers of fortified foodstuffs, as well as other food products, is permitted claims. To sell into the Norwegian market, for example, with the claim 'sugar free' a product must contain absolutely no sugar, whereas in the UK a product can contain up to 0.2 gm and still make this claim. These differences have marketing implications for companies; either the product formulation must be changed or separate labels with differing claims such as 'less sugar' used.

Where mutual recognition allows products to be imported which do not comply with local labelling and claims rules, domestic discrimination can occur: for example, in most EU countries manufacturers are permitted to make claims such as 'recommended for diabetes', but this is not permitted in Italy. Claims such as 'this product can help as part of a low sugar diet' can be made. This claim is considered to be a weaker one, thus placing a product manufactured in Italy at a potential competitive disadvantage when placed on a supermarket shelf next to an imported product making a stronger claim.

17.4.   Enterprise strategies

17.4.1. Product range

Manufacturers have to some degree been able to reduce the number of product formulations as a result of the partial functioning of the principle of mutual recognition, but in some cases vitamin profiles must still be adapted.

> One leading European breakfast cereal producer states that it has been able to reduce the number of vitamin and mineral profiles of its products. For example, for the UK and Irish markets this manufacturer used to fortify all products with Vitamin D. Since the addition of Vitamin D is not permitted in other countries, it was decided to remove it for the UK and Ireland, apart from special products which are manufactured exclusively for the UK market.

Important costs are incurred if product formulations need to be adapted, with direct impact on production, scheduling, production runs, packaging, stocks etc. The stage at which the vitamin/nutrient is added in the manufacturing process can have a considerable impact on the cost incurred through the different profiles for each country. For example, folic acid, iron and zinc are added to the cooker and, therefore, the inclusion or removal of these items from the product profile will necessitate smaller and therefore more costly production runs. Other vitamins can be added at a later stage in the process via a spray. Since the sprays can be turned on and off, these items have a less crucial cost impact.

Manufacturers try to sell one standard product throughout the EU with minimal need for adaptation. Several manufacturers stated that for new products they endeavour to choose ingredients which are accepted in the majority of EU countries, in order to minimize the costly need to adapt the product and invest valuable management time on long and complicated discussions with the local authorities.

> One Danish retailer with outlets in other EU countries has considered launching an own-brand range of breakfast cereals but has realized that the differing national regulations concerning the fortification of foods would make it impossible to have a single product. However, adapting the product for local markets would make the own-brand concept uncompetitive.

17.4.2. Investment

The research did not identify any impact on investment from application of the principle of mutual recognition. On the other hand, the example of the Austrian energy drink manufacturers clearly shows an important impact on the location of investment caused by operation of the MRP: companies have invested in a country (initially outside the EU) which had looser controls than the main market, Germany. This has led to development of an important sector in Austria with a concerted voice pressing for removal of controls.

There is evidence of companies investing in manufacturing/sales operations in other EU markets, but these appear to be driven by local market demand rather than optimizing production in the single market. Because food products have a limited shelf life, they are normally produced close to market anyway, so for many products there are few benefits from rationalizing production on a Europe-wide scale.

> An EU yoghurt producer set up a manufacturing plant in the UK in 1992. It believes that although the single market may have facilitated establishment of this cross-border operation, it would have happened as part of the company's development strategy anyway. There have been no benefits by rationalizing production as the product has a shelf life of three weeks and, therefore, the UK plant produces the full range of products in order to be able to be close to its local market, thus reducing transport costs and wasting valuable shelf life. Technical regulations played no part in the investment decision.

17.4.3. Distribution and marketing

Most manufacturers agree that mutual recognition, together with harmonization of packaging and labelling rules through the Labelling Directive, has brought considerable benefits by enabling them to simplify packaging and branding. The unified approach to labelling means that for many products multilingual packaging and labelling is acceptable.

We found no evidence, however, of companies changing their distribution methods, logistics or sales organization, or their advertising strategy directly as a result of the application or failure of the MRP. There is evidence of a general Europe-wide approach to branding and marketing. The Austrian energy drinks, for example, tend to have English language brand names used throughout the European market.

17.4.4. Organization and management

There is evidence that many of the larger food manufacturers employ full-time staff to examine the legal differences for marketing products throughout the EU. One large drinks manufacturer in the UK recently advertised a vacancy at director level for somebody to be responsible for keeping abreast of the legal differences among Member States. This clearly demonstrates that mutual recognition is not functioning adequately and that differences between countries cause concern and extra costs to industry.

In markets where the barriers are high or difficult to circumvent, the main cost for a manufacturer can lie in the area of management time, and the cost of flights and legal expenses. These often substantial costs are incurred while a manufacturer is trying to assess the economic feasibility of entering a market in which the principle of mutual recognition is clearly not functioning.

17.4.5. Impact on competitiveness and customer choice

Mutual recognition and harmonization have increased the range of products available to consumers in processed foods generally, and fortified foods in particular. For example, many German customers are reported to have discovered energy drinks while on holiday in Austria, but were unable to buy the product at home because German legislation prohibited the sale of energy drinks. Today, Germany allows energy drinks to be sold in the German market under the principle of mutual recognition, thus demonstrating how mutual recognition brings wider choice to the consumer.

In other countries with strict national legislation, the choice of products for retail buyers and consumers is restricted. This can also limit the degree of competition, and keep prices at non-competitive levels.

> In Denmark, one retailer stated that their own internal regulations were even more strict than the national regulations and they did not, therefore, feel restricted by the national requirements. They believed that the Danish consumer, who likes a product to be as pure as possible, would not feel that his/her choice was restricted. Another retail company in Denmark, however, considered that the national regulations were definitely restrictive and stated that there were products which they would welcome trying to introduce into their retail outlets, but were unable to as they contravened national regulations. Current legislation in Denmark banning the sale of drinks in cans would be a further restriction on the import of energy drinks. Both retailers agreed that the very specific regulations made parallel imports impossible and they felt that due to the requirement to adapt product specifications for the Danish market, they were more at the mercy of the pricing strategy of their suppliers than their counterparts in other countries might be, ultimately having an impact on their competitiveness.

Some manufacturers consider that the differing legislative requirements affect their competitiveness when their manufacturing base is in a country with stringent regulations. 'Domestic discrimination' occurs when imported products which do not meet domestic legislation are permitted onto the national market under the principle of mutual recognition, while domestic manufacturers are not permitted to deviate from national legislation. This may have a cost impact or alter the image of the product, both of which may make a domestic product less attractive than an imported one. Differing rules on claims may also cause domestic discrimination as described in Section 17.3.5.

None of the companies interviewed were benefiting from the potential economies of scale which they could achieve by manufacturing for a fully open EU market. One UK soft drinks manufacturer, however, has recently invested in a highly automated UK plant. From this plant it now wishes to expand its share of the EU market, and in order to benefit from economies of scale, it is endeavouring to sell one standard product, with ingredient stickers provided in other languages.

Where differences remain between Member States and products are not accepted under the principle of mutual recognition, the problems reported by industry can be summarized as follows:

(a)   manufacturers have to invest time and money in understanding the different requirements throughout the EU;

(b)   product recipes are sometimes adapted, which results in a loss of production efficiency and the need to tie up capital in higher levels of stocks (although this is limited by the need for local production for many short-life foodstuffs);

(c)   for some countries notification is necessary, which can be both time consuming and costly;

(d)   differences in permitted claims and status of products (e.g. classification as dietetic products) can result in a product losing its specific appeal in some markets;

(e)   domestic discrimination leads to a loss of competitiveness for some national suppliers *vis-à-vis* their foreign counterparts;

(f)   in countries where legislation is particularly stringent, buyers are restricted in their choice of product; and in these countries buyers feel that they have less economic bargaining power with their suppliers due to the specificity of products required for their markets.

17.5. Conclusions

17.5.1. Effectiveness of approaches

It can be concluded that the principle of mutual recognition is functioning only partially in this industry sector. Several cases quoted earlier in the report testify to the fact that recognition of another Member State's products is increasing and assisting manufacturers to standardize their products, rationalize their labelling and enjoy longer production runs.

There remain, nonetheless, many cases where products are not being accepted. Manufacturers complain that they do not always know why some products are permitted and others prohibited. Some countries appear to adopt much stricter approaches.

Research indicates that companies are reluctant to pursue a complaints procedure through the Commission, and this reduces the effectiveness of MRP procedures. Companies feel that the procedure takes too long, and they are reluctant to be seen to be complaining (and perhaps fear that the controls in stricter countries would be upheld or even made into harmonized requirements). Companies in general prefer to find their own solutions to trade barriers, either by entering into discussions directly with the relevant national authorities, or by adapting their products or by deciding to stay out of a market where the necessary product changes would render the market economically unattractive.

Large groups have subsidiaries in other EU countries, making negotiations with the relevant authorities easier than for an SME which does not have this facility.

17.5.2. Remaining barriers

The conclusions of this case study may be summarized as follows. There are wide differences in regulations and controls on certification on justifiable health grounds, but exacerbated by differences in approach. Mutual recognition functions to some extent (e.g. Austrian energy drinks), but is strictly limited by Art. 36 justifications. If these barriers were removed, manufacturers still face other regulatory barriers (labelling, claims, packaging and recycling), but these are being tackled by harmonization measures. Non-regulatory barriers are relatively unimportant: they principally concern differences in national culinary and dietary custom and tradition (e.g. breakfast habits) rather than standards or institutionalized testing and certification requirements.

17.5.3. Measures suggested by interviewees

The majority of companies interviewed expressed the view that they would like the Commission to increase promotion of the principle of mutual recognition and prevent certain countries from erecting what industry sees as unjustified barriers to trade. [It is not in the Consultants' competence to discuss the health and scientific justification for controls, but the argument for control in this sensitive and uncertain area were outlined in Section 17.3].

Discussions with manufacturers and buyers alike suggest that industry would welcome a degree of harmonization, to simplify product formulation and marketing for manufacturers and give buyers a level procurement playing-field, since mutual recognition is not seen to be working. In 1995, the European Scientific Committee commissioned the TNO in the Netherlands to conduct a study which would assess the nutritional contribution and safety of fortified foods. The results will be used to produce a discussion document on the way forward for the European fortification industry, i.e. whether a limited amount of harmonization would be desirable.

Ceereal, the European breakfast cereal trade association, is reported to believe that the principle of mutual recognition should suffice to allow free circulation of fortified foodstuffs, but as this does not appear to be the case, due to Member States justifying national legislation on public health grounds, this trade association advocates a limited amount of harmonization restricted to the definition of maximum levels for those nutrients presenting a potential public health risk.

Part IV: Effectiveness of approaches

18. Effectiveness of approaches

18.1. Characteristics of the sample sectors

The 13 sample product sectors described in Parts II and III of this report were selected to cover a range of different industry sectors in terms of their technology, industry structure, markets and regulatory regime. All were selected because they are subject to regulation which constitutes potential technical barriers to trade, usually because they present health or environmental hazards. Half of them are subject to harmonization through New Approach directives, of which some show successful harmonization and some less successful. Half are not (or not yet) harmonized, and are therefore dependent upon national governments' mutual recognition of divergent regulations. This is illustrated in Table 18.1.

Table 18.1. Classification of sample products

	Barriers not yet removed	**Barriers partly removed, with some problems remaining**	**Barriers mainly removed**
New Approach harmonization	[cement*] [carpets*]	Portable power tools Circular saws	Toys Air reservoirs Cardiac pacemakers Domestic gas cookers
Mutual recognition	Pesticides Cement	Fortified foods Carpets	Cables Water equipment Structural steel

* subject to the Construction Products Directive (89/106/EEC), not yet functioning.

The characteristics of each of these sectors are described in the relevant chapters of Parts II and III, and are summarized in Appendix C.

18.2. Summary of effectiveness of approaches for the sample sectors

The effectiveness of the approaches in each of the 12 sample sectors is summarized in Table 18.2. This shows:

(a)   what measures have been taken and the status of European standards;
(b)   whether regulatory barriers have been removed, and if not what regulatory barriers remain, in terms of:
    (i)   technical regulations,
    (ii)   conformity requirements,
    (iii) differences in enforcement procedures leading to barriers;
(c)   whether, once regulatory barriers have been removed, there will remain other, non-regulatory, barriers to trade;
(d)   what characteristics of the sector have either favoured or prevented the removal of barriers.

18.2.1. Mutual recognition case studies

Not surprisingly, the case studies have illustrated difficulties in the application of the MRP: they were selected because there are differing technical regulations between Member States (except for structural steel). There are, however, notable differences in the strength and impact of the technical barriers, ranging from a total absence of technical barriers to the placing of products on the market in the case of structural steel products to absolute bans on some ingredients with costly notification rules and other regulations for fortified foods and drinks. In most cases there were also non-regulatory barriers (except for fortified food and drink, where all the barriers are of a regulatory nature).

In most cases, therefore, even if the MRP were completely successful in removing the impact of regulatory barriers, significant non-regulatory barriers would remain. In fact, in the context of the Treaty of Rome the MRP has not been widely successful in eliminating barriers in our case studies. That does not mean that mutual recognition has not been an important factor in removing barriers: there is evidently a continuous process of challenge and negotiation which prevents new barriers, moderates existing barriers to the level that Member States think is essential for the protection of citizens, and generates a few notable successes in removing existing barriers. The entry of Austrian energy drinks into the German market where they were previously banned is an example to add to previous well-known successes, such as beer in Germany and pasta in Italy.

Neither must it be forgotten also that mutual recognition in the wider sense is very important. The mutual recognition schemes for carpets and for cables are important, even though they have drawbacks, are still too narrow in coverage, and are amongst the relatively few examples of much-needed mutual recognition arrangements for testing and certification. The mutual recognition of formerly differing national standards through the non-mandated activities of European standards bodies – illustrated by cables and steel – is another important mechanism which does not involve detailed harmonization.

In our three industrial products – cement, cables and steel – the cost to industry of the barriers, which create some additional testing requirements, is relatively low. Testing is a normal part of the business process, and the testing is cheap. Although the information requirements and the management costs related to it would deter some small businesses from entering export markets for the first time, the costs are unlikely to inhibit trade seriously. These three sectors are, on the face of it, led by very large firms. In the other three products, which are aimed at mainly consumer users, the costs of barriers can be high, and include potential bans on products which are permitted in the exporter's home country.

Rather than drawing universal conclusions, the case studies illustrate that each product sector has different characteristics in terms of the type and mix of technical barriers, the impact of these in terms of costs to industry and the impact on trade, and the ease of removing the barriers. An important factor in removing barriers is the motivation of industry itself. The fact that regulators must rely on technical advice from industry enables industry's own objectives to be reflected to some extent in the form of regulation. Removing the barriers is easiest where the industry is led by multinational firms who see sales to the whole European market as necessary to maintain their growth or to achieve the economies of scale which provide competitiveness. It is most difficult where firms have protectionist motives or where there is a dominance of SMEs serving local markets relying on differentiation of products to meet local tastes and market characteristics as a means of maintaining competitiveness against imports.

18.2.2. The New Approach products

In the case studies selected, the New Approach directives have generally been very successful in removing and preventing barriers. Few barriers were identified, and the cases cited were usually causes of lost management time and therefore perceived important, but of little long-term cost to industry.

Some difficulties were noted in the machinery sectors where it is clear that there is still a transitional stage, with some minor national regulations (or guidelines) and national preferences remaining, and particular concern to industry about the additional costs of testing and certification in areas where standards are still not available or widely accepted. In some cases new hazards have been identified which have given rise to national requirements in those countries which have identified the hazard, such as hair loss in dolls in the UK, and AZO dyes in Germany.

It is clear, once again, that the motivations of industry are important, and that the removal of barriers is easiest in those sectors with a number of important firms who have global or Europe-wide markets. It is noted, for example, that the product sector among our sample where there were most complaints about the difficulties is circular saws: although there are many machinery producers who are keen to see a harmonization of standards and the removal of barriers, the machinery sector has a great number of SMEs, and circular saws in particular are an example of a product with no dominant multinational producers, and generally small batch production.

For the NA products, two problems repeatedly noted are the lack of coordination of NoBo testing and type-examination criteria, and the lack of a common approach to enforcement (meaning market surveillance by the relevant national authorities). These in turn give rise to two concerns, although in practice few concrete examples were found: firstly, the fear of unfair competition from low-cost non-complaint products, particularly from non-EU countries with less stringent controls (of particular concern for electric hand tool manufacturers); and secondly, the fear that products which have been tested or examined as part of the conformity assessment procedures may be rejected nonetheless by the enforcement authorities in the importing country (as has happened in the case of air reservoirs).

Table 18.2.   Effectiveness of approaches in the sample sectors

	Air reservoirs	Pacemakers	Dolls
Measures in force	Simple Pressure Vessels Directive	Active Implantable Medical Devices Directive	Toy Safety Directive
Are EN standards in place?	yes	yes	yes (revisions being prepared)
Are there still regulatory barriers?	no	not significant (but non-transposition in Belgium)	yes
- technical regulations	no	labelling requirements (trivial)	recycling schemes; language labelling
- conformity assessment	no	registration requirement in Spain	
- differences in enforcement	yes: different interpretation by NoBos	no	yes: hair loss issue; differing strictness
Do non-regulatory barriers remain even after removal of regulatory ones?	no	not significant	yes
- diff. standards or specs.	customer specs. – no barrier	no	no
- testing and certification	no	reimbursement procedures (e.g. TIPS in France)	special tests for Germany, but 'guidance', not regulations
Are costs of barriers significant?	no	no (but complaints about excessive tender requirements and translations)	no
What characteristics contribute to success?	few manufacturers; simple product – easy to standardize; few customers – keen to standardize	few, global manufacturers; high level of trade; strong trade association; high entry barriers – no threat	previous serious problems; desire for protection from cheap imports; high trade (low marg. cost)
What characteristics impede removal of technical barriers to trade?		public purchasers	local consumer requirements
Verdict	**successful**	**successful**	**mainly successful**

Table 18.2. (continued)   Effectiveness of approaches in the sample sectors

	Circular saws	Portable power tools	Gas cookers
Measures in force	MD (Annex IV); EMC; LVD	MD; EMC; LVD	Gas appliance directive
Are EN standards in place?	no	yes	partly, some prENs
Are there still regulatory barriers?	yes	yes	no
- technical regulations	no (but Health and Safety at workplace regs. may differ)	regulations on lock-on switches; user certification	no
- conformity assessment	no; but high CE-marking costs due to lack of standards; high cost for one-off machines	no	no
- differences in enforcement	yes; differing NoBo interpretation; extensive non-compliance reported	alleged non-compliance by some non-EU imports	some minor differences in interpretation of directives and ERs
Do non-regulatory barriers remain even after removal of regulatory ones?	no	yes	yes, but not significant
- diff. standards or specs.	no	voltage requirements; hire tool testing – needs higher specification	gas supply differences
- testing and certification	no	no	some national marks preferred by retailers
Are costs of barriers significant?	no, but significant compliance cost for CE-marking	no	no
What characteristics contribute to success?		a few dominant global firms	few EU multinational producers; little non-EU penetration
What characteristics impede removal of technical barriers to trade?	mainly SMEs; low barriers to entry – fear of freer trade	fear of low-cost non-EU competitors	
Verdict	**transition problems**	**mainly successful**	**successful**

Table 18.2. (continued)   Effectiveness of approaches in the sample sectors

	Cement	Electric cables	Pesticides
Measures in force	one Art. 30 case; [CPD in future]; public procurement also relevant	LVD (CE-marking from 1/1/97); HAR agreement	Agrochemicals Registration Dir. 91/414/EEC and Uniform Principles Dir. 94/43/EEC; GLP Agreement; Art. 30 cases
Are EN standards in place?	some for testing; ENV for categories and conformity procedures; awaiting mandates for CPD	yes, but LVD-style harmonization of different national standards; other national standards exist	no (proprietary products from common base chemicals)
Are there still regulatory barriers?	yes	yes, but weak	yes, very strong
- technical regulations	yes: composition, performance, grain size	building regulations, installation rules	banned ingredients, registration procedures; bans on parallel imports
- conformity assessment	yes	no	homologation and testing for registration
- differences in enforcement	(not applicable)	(not applicable)	(not applicable)
Do non-regulatory barriers remain even after removal of regulatory ones?	yes	weak	yes
- diff. standards or specs.	yes – applied by building regs., building codes, standards, professional qualifications, liability and insurance requirements	some national standards	climatic and dietary differences
- testing and certification	yes: technical approvals necessary	residence requirements of HAR agreement; some preference for national HAR marks	
Are costs of barriers significant?	generally no (testing is normal), but high for small, non-standard export orders	no (testing is cheap), but HAR is a testing and certification cartel	yes
What characteristics contribute to success?		several EU multinationals; quite significant trade; HAR is a protectionist scheme	
What characteristics impede removal of technical barriers to trade?	threat of dumping; cartelized industry until recently; high cost risks in use; high level of public procurement	fear of non-EU imports (low barriers to entry)	differentiated products; importance of R&D and patents; many SMEs in formulated (end-use) products
Verdict	**MRP not successful, but industry is harmonizing, CPD will assist**	**MRP is successsfully embodied in ENs and MRA (HAR agt.); but HAR is closed shop**	**MRP does not work**

Table 18.2. (continued)   Effectiveness of approaches in the sample sectors

	Structural steel	Carpets	Fortified food and drink
Measures in force	[CPD in future]	[partly by CPD in future]	numerous detailed harmonization directives (but not for vitamins); several Art. 30 cases
Are EN standards in place?	ECISS harmonization (by MR of national standards); draft Eurocode for steelwork construction	no; EN on fire safety being developed; work on other aspects has begun	no
Are there still regulatory barriers?	(no regulations existed previously)	yes	yes
- technical regulations	no	fire safety	notification rules; maximum content rules; banned ingredients; claims rules; also labelling, packaging, recycling regulations
- conformity assessment	no	different test standards; national test requirements	extensive testing required
- differences in enforcement	(not applicable)	(not applicable)	(not applicable)
Do non-regulatory barriers remain even after removal of regulatory ones?	yes	yes	not apparently – national differences are protected by regulation
- diff. standards or specs.	national standards; building codes; national registration systems for steelwork contractors	several distinct use classification schemes; different national standards.	
- testing and certification	related to building regulations and codes; insurance and liability: Ü-mark in Germany	testing for classification schemes; GÜT environmental scheme; embryonic MRAs for AFNOR and GÜT	(only for retailers' and customers' requirements)
Are costs of barriers significant?	no (testing cheap, and product variants are normal)	yes	yes – very costly homologation procedures
What characteristics contribute to success?	steel industry now becoming less nationalized; fairly high trade		
What characteristics impede removal of technical barriers to trade?	different construction codes, regulations and liability	dominance by Belgian industry; many SMEs; wide range of styles and variants	scientific uncertainty about the risks and benefits; dominance of SMEs in food processing.
Verdict	**MRP not invoked; voluntary harmonization; but other barriers remain**	**MRP not working; except with embryonic MRAs**	**MRP not working generally; but some notable successes**

Source: W.S. Atkins.

18.2.3. Overview

From this analysis it appears that both New Approach directives and MRP work best for sectors in which the level of intra-EU trade is already high, where there are a small number of dominant manufacturers, and where there are economies of scale which make it advantageous for manufacturers to acquire a significant share of the whole EU market. They are then prepared to work together to agree common standards or common testing procedures. Examples are air reservoirs, pacemakers, gas cookers, power tools (which had strict national regulations and needed harmonization); and steel and cables (which had divergent standards but weak regulation, so MRP works with voluntary common standards).

In sectors like cement, however, where again there are few suppliers but the economies of scale can be achieved within national markets, and where other factors (such as high transport costs, and the threat of dumping) make firms wary of increasing trade in this sector, firms are unwilling to initiate or cooperate with harmonization programmes or mutual recognition of testing, or to challenge regulatory barriers.

Sectors with many SMEs and little existing trade (which often may be because of long established technical barriers to trade) are less easy to tackle, because there is no concerted industry support and more vested interests in keeping markets apart (such as in the sectors of circular saws and carpets, and to some extent in the sector of toys).

Sectors where the hazards are less easy to measure (such as pesticides and fortified foods) tend to have divergent approaches to testing and to the relevant parameters for control and regulation. They are, therefore, difficult to tackle by either MRP or New Approach directives. Sectors where product innovation is important (such as fortified foods) are also difficult, except where the imperative for economies of scale is very strong (such as telecommunications and IT).

The study did not closely examine sectors where New Approach directives have not yet been implemented, except for cement and carpets under the CPD. Pressure equipment, pleasure craft and lifts, for example, which are products with proposed New Approach directives, are sectors where there are many SMEs, long histories of regulation in Member States, and no significant economies of scale, and so will be more difficult to implement.

Table 18.2 may give a somewhat biased impression that the New Approach directives are generally successful and the MRP generally unsuccessful. Such conclusions from this limited sample of products need to be qualified, however, for a variety of reasons:

(a)   The MRP products include Art. 30 cases, which are invoked where governments are positively erecting barriers, and there is generally no consensus on the need for harmonization. The New Approach directives, on the other hand, are implemented in response to a positive need for harmonization by industry.

(b)   MRP, and Art. 30 procedures, have undoubtedly been successful in preventing new barriers, but it is more difficult to show success in the removal of entrenched barriers. The successful cases also have specific application (a specific regulation in a specific Member State) rather than a generic one, so there are a large number of cases under MRP (each of which has narrow scope), but only a few measures (of generic application) under New Approach directives.

(c)   Some of the successful applications of MRP have had a profound effect by removing a total ban on a product, whereas the New Approach directives have generally simplified trade which existed previously, but which involved multiple testing or product variants. The case of Austrian energy drinks described in the section on fortified foods and drinks is a specific example of many cases of foodstuffs which can now circulate freely in most (but not all) Member States, despite the existence of national regulations which would prevent local manufacturers from marketing the product in some of them.

(d)   The New Approach directives which are successfully in force cover a narrow range of products. The New Approach directives which cover wide ranges of products (such as machinery, pressure equipment, construction products) are proving much more difficult to implement.

(e)   A massive effort in resources and time, and a complex infrastructure of standardization, conformity testing and certification and enforcement is dedicated to each of the New Approach directive products[9] (but probably much lower than the cost of resources which would otherwise have continued to be dedicated to national standardization activities in the absence of harmonization actions). On the other hand the resources dedicated to enforcing the MRP are minimal, and the case load huge.

18.3.   Review of the Eurostat business survey

The following two subsections briefly review two complementary surveys of the effectiveness of EC approaches to technical barriers to trade, which have been drawn upon in the sectoral analysis which follows.

As part of the 1997 Single Market Review, Eurostat commissioned a survey of businesses in several industry sectors, in order to measure their views on the importance and effectiveness of the whole range of SMP measures. Appendix F summarizes the findings of the survey relating to technical barriers to trade.

In all sectors, elimination of customs documentation and delays at frontiers were rated by firms as the most important positive impacts on their business, but after that, the measures related to technical barriers to trade were consistently rated to be the next most important. In most sectors between 25 and 50% of firms thought the measures had had a positive impact, between 25 and 50% did not detect any impact, and less than 10% thought they had a negative impact.

The main exception is the machinery sector, where as many as 20% of firms thought that harmonization of technical regulations and standards had a negative effect (these issues are illustrated in the chapters on air reservoirs, circular saws and electric hand tools). Even in these sectors, however, 48% thought harmonization had a positive impact, 45% thought mutual recognition was positive (although we suspect on the basis of our own interviews that some respondents would not know what this means, and would interpret it in a broad sense to include laboratory accreditation or improved information about national standards), and 33% found conformity assessment procedures to have a positive impact. However, in this sector

---

[9]   For the Machinery Directive, for example, we estimate that there have been several thousand people involved at some time in standardization activities, totalling many man-years of work, and there are probably hundreds on a continuing basis involved in testing and certification and in enforcement.

few firms thought the measures had no impact: almost all respondents were conscious of the effect of EC measures, which is in itself an important indicator of the success of the measures. Despite a significant number of negative views, the number of positive views far outweighed them.

The survey also indicated that large firms consistently found that the measures to remove technical barriers to trade were positive (around 50% compared to around 30% of small firms), and vice versa: more small firms found a negative impact (10–15% compared to 8–10% of larger firms). This is undoubtedly because the larger firms are more likely to be involved in cross-border trade and thus see the benefits outweighing any initial costs.

18.4. Review of trade organizations' perceptions

In 1995 DRI, a consultancy company, carried out a survey of the trade associations' perception of the impact of the single market. The study involved interviews of the key representative of all trade associations representing industrial and service sectors at the EU level.[10] We have used this analysis to help identify the type and extent of trade barriers in each of the 120 three-digit NACE sectors, described in Chapter 19.

The DRI survey concludes that the measures to dismantle technical barriers to trade have overall had a positive impact on all but a few industries:

> For example, the chemical plant industry argued that the single market had a neutral effect. The textile machinery industry is trading mainly with third countries and therefore reported that it has not benefited from the EC measures. The bicycle industry association claimed that very little was achieved with respect to common standards and mutual recognition. Nevertheless, other sector representatives reported overall positive results. The packaging machinery industry, telecommunications, the electrical machinery and the transport sectors and to a lesser extent the electronics industry, and others, stressed the positive effects of technical harmonization.

In most cases, trade associations thought that the most relevant measure implemented by the Commission is the free movement of goods in the single market. Nevertheless, it was reported that more efforts need to be made in order to facilitate free movement for all industries and avoid the creation of new barriers to trade. Most respondents stated that whilst in most cases the mutual recognition principle and technical harmonization facilitated intra-EU trade, technical harmonization was not complete.

Other factors which were seen to hinder the implementation of the SMP measures include: industry's concern about misinterpretation of directives (cited by the handling and lifting equipment industry); concern about the disappearance of SMEs (association for the bearings and transmission equipment); and the costs of compliance to additional testing requirements

---

[10]   The results were also included in the 1995/96 edition of *Panorama of EU Industry* published by the European Commission (DG III).

which causes problems for manufacturers' competitiveness (electrical equipment for industrial use).

19. The economic importance of technical barriers to trade and of the approaches adopted

This chapter extrapolates the information available from this study and other sources to an estimate of the global extent of the problem of technical barriers to trade, and the effectiveness of the various measures in removing them or preventing potential barriers from arising. This analysis draws to a large extent on the experience and prior knowledge of the consultants on the sectors not covered by this or other surveys. It is of necessity a stochastic analysis: we do not expect our assessment of the likely existence of barriers and the impact of barriers to be always correct in the sectors for which we have no direct information, but on balance we believe this gives a true overall picture. The analysis could, of course, be refined with much further research.

19.1. The analysis of product sectors

A summary of the types of technical barriers applying in each industry sector, and the measures which have been taken to remove the technical barriers to trade in each sector, is in Appendices D and E.

This assessment has been carried out by reviewing in turn each of the sectors of tradable goods (i.e. excluding services and construction) at the three-digit NACE level, using the DRI survey of trade associations, *EU Panorama of Industry 1995/96*, consideration of the product characteristics and analogy with our sample sectors, and the Consultants' in-house knowledge of the sectors.

From this analysis we have determined for each product sector:

(a) what type of barriers exist, or would have existed in the absence of single market measures, using the typology of barriers set out in Chapter 3. These have been categorized into:
  (i) technical regulations (marked 'T' in Appendix D), which might be removed by MRP or New Approach directives;
  (ii) other non-regulatory technical barriers (marked 'O'), which can only be removed by mutual recognition arrangements in the commercial sector;
  (iii) both regulations and other technical barriers to trade (marked 'TO'), where removal of regulatory barriers will still leave other problems;
  (iv) no barriers (marked 'N'), where no measures are needed;
(b) what type of measures have been taken for each product category:
  (i) detailed harmonization of regulations through the old approach (marked 'HR' in Appendix E);
  (ii) detailed harmonization of some aspects, but with the remaining technical regulations covered by the mutual recognition principle (marked 'HR/MRP');
  (iii) harmonization through New Approach directives (marked 'NA');
  (iv) mutual recognition of regulations via Art. 30–36, with no harmonization (marked 'MRP');
  (v) specific sectoral mutual recognition arrangements (e.g. EOTC Agreement Groups) for testing and certification (marked 'MRA');
  (vi) no measures necessary because there are no significant barriers (marked 'none').

The results of this analysis are shown in Figures 19.1 and 19.2.

Figure 19.1.   Existing barriers as a share of intra-EU trade and manufacturing value added (EUR-12)

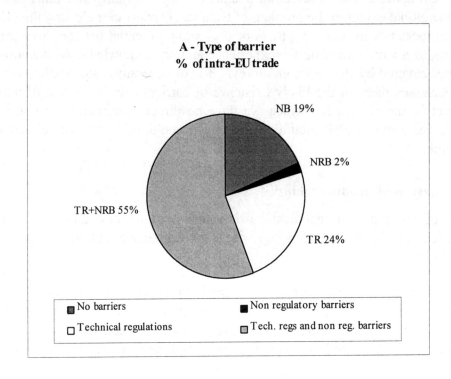

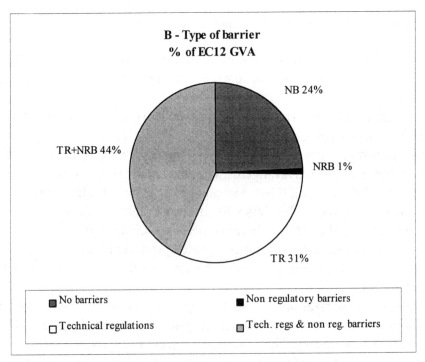

Figure 19.2. Application of approaches as a share of intra-EU trade and manufacturing value added (EUR-12)

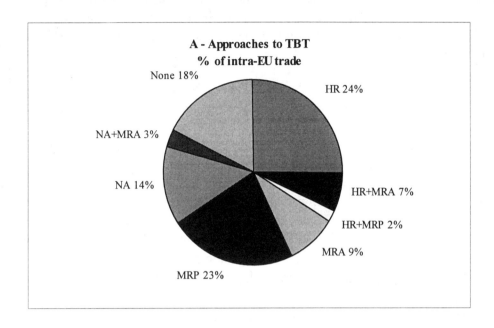

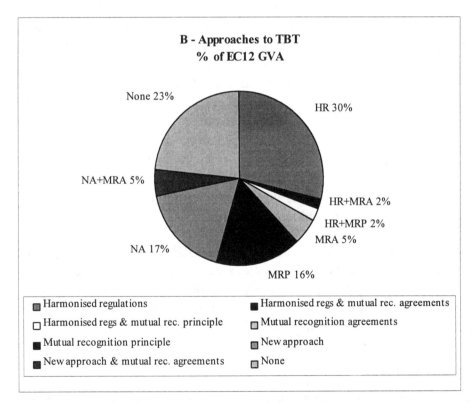

19.2. Existence of barriers

The sectors subject to each of the types of barrier, as shown in Appendix D, have been aggregated by their share of manufacturing value added (i.e. contribution to gross domestic product) and by their share of intra-EU trade (which are shown in Appendix E). From this analysis, Figure 19.1 shows the proportion of manufacturing GDP and intra-EU trade which is subject to the different types of barrier. It can be seen that:

(a) Three-quarters of intra-EU trade would be affected by technical barriers to trade (including those where barriers have already been eliminated). Since this trade would be much larger if these barriers did not exist, we can assume that much less than a quarter of potential trade is really free of any potential barriers. This shows the real importance of measures to remove technical barriers to trade in the completion of the single market.

(b) Of the trade potentially affected by technical barriers, about two-thirds (50% of all trade) would still be affected by other non-regulatory technical barriers to trade, even if national technical regulations were harmonized or mutually recognized.

(c) A mere 1% of trade is affected solely by non-regulatory barriers of the type which could be removed simply by voluntary arrangements, without the prior need to remove regulatory barriers. (It should be noted that in this analysis there is a judgement by the Consultants, in the cases where the potential barriers are related to pure customer preference for standards and testing without any impelling insurance, liability, or professional registration requirements, about whether the requirements are legitimate to the quality control requirements of the customer – and hence are not tied to national standards, and so not classed as barriers – and which are due to inherent national prejudices of customers about non-national products).

(d) As a share of gross value added in the manufacturing sectors, those with regulatory barriers take a larger share (29%) than they do in trade (21%). This is an indication that the regulatory barriers do inhibit trade. Conversely, the sectors with non-regulatory technical barriers as well as technical regulations have a smaller share of gross value added – which appears anomalous. The explanation must be that these are products which have a naturally high propensity to trade, and that is why the non-regulatory barriers (standards, customer testing requirements, insurance requirements etc.) have arisen as a protective (or protectionist) measure.

It should be noted that as a share of total EUR-12 GDP the volume of products subject to technical barriers to trade will be much smaller because some 60% of EU GDP is made up of services, most of which are not traded. On the other hand, barriers specific to service industries (banking registration rules, professional registration and qualifications etc.) may well be as important as those affecting manufactured goods.

19.3. Application of approaches

Figure 19.2 shows the extent of application of different approaches, in terms of the share of manufacturing value added and intra-EU trade. This shows that:

(a) 34% of trade is already harmonized by detailed harmonization (Old Approach) directives, and a further 17% is now or will soon be covered by New Approach directives, so that over half of all trade is already harmonized by EU approaches;

(b)   25% of trade is subject to national technical regulations without harmonization (or with detailed harmonization which only covers some aspects), and so is dependent upon mutual recognition of regulations (the MRP);

(c)   19% of trade is covered by mutual recognition arrangements for testing and certification bodies. Half of this (10% of trade) is made up of products which are harmonized under the New Approach directives or detailed Old Approach directives, but also have an existing arrangement between laboratories;

(d)   only 15% of trade is not aided by either harmonization or mutual recognition arrangements;

(e)   these data show the importance of technical barriers to trade, but also show how extensive the measures which have been taken are. While there is still a long way to go to make these measures completely successful in removing barriers, the programme of adoption of measures is virtually complete. They now have to be made to work perfectly.

19.4.   An assessment of the global effectiveness of approaches

This final section presents the Consultant's assessment of the overall impact of the various approaches taken to removing technical barriers to trade. The Consultant's appraisal by sector is set out in Appendix E. This has been based mainly on our knowledge of sectors close to the sample product sectors described in the case studies in Parts II and III of this report; knowledge of manifest problems of access to national markets from the cases being handled by the Art. 30 procedures, or reported by national bodies; and from consideration of the supply and distribution characteristics of the sectors.

The effectiveness of the various approaches taken for each three-digit NACE industry sector has been assessed on a five-point scale, as shown below:

*****   measures are successful and all significant barriers are removed;

****   measures are implemented and functioning well, but some barriers remain;

***   measures are adopted, but with implementation or transitional problems still to be overcome;

**   measures are proposed or implemented, but not effective or with operating problems;

*   no solution has been adopted;

Np   no significant technical barriers to trade, so no solution needed.

Figure 19.3 shows the assessment of the global effectiveness of measures, in relation to the volume of intra-EU trade. It can be seen from the figure that two-thirds of trade is now covered by measures which have either already completely or partially removed previous barriers, and a further 7% is covered by measures with implementation problems, and can be expected to remove them.

The case studies have shown, however, that even where the measures are successfully implemented, there often remain specific problems in one or two Member States, or in respect of specific characteristics of products, which may need to be dealt with. There is a judgement to be made about how much resources to devote to removing all potential barriers, however: often barriers exist which are an irritation to manufacturers and have a cost in terms of product adaptation or testing, but the cost or the diversion of trade is not large enough to warrant new measures. Such cases can often be dealt with by Art. 30 procedures or bilateral discussions between Member States if necessary.

A further 16% of trade is in sectors where measures are proposed or implemented, but are not yet effective – this includes the Construction Products Directive. A negligible 1% of trade is in sectors subject to barriers for which no solution has been adopted (this is in fact the hallmarking of precious metals and jewellery). It should be recalled, as discussed above, however, that some specific barriers still remain in sectors which have been harmonized or where MRP generally works well, but individual Member States present problems of non-compliance or special requirements.

Figure 19.3. Effectiveness of approaches as share of intra-EU trade and manufacturing value added (EUR-12)

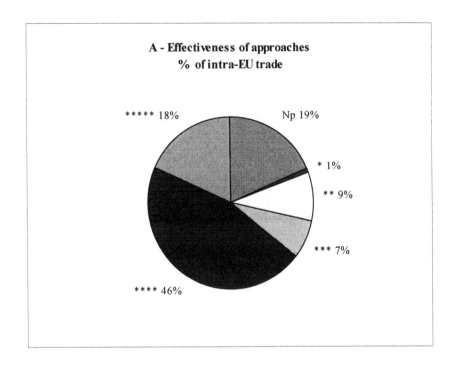

A - Effectiveness of approaches
% of intra-EU trade

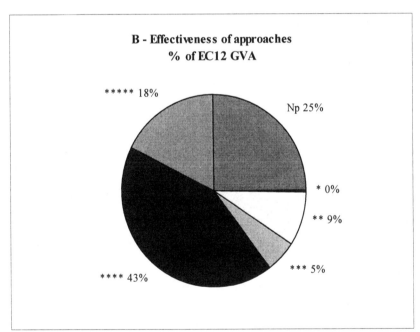

B - Effectiveness of approaches
% of EC12 GVA

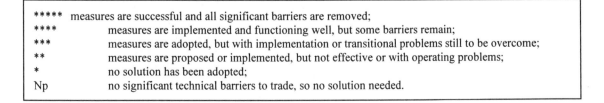

*****	measures are successful and all significant barriers are removed;
****	measures are implemented and functioning well, but some barriers remain;
***	measures are adopted, but with implementation or transitional problems still to be overcome;
**	measures are proposed or implemented, but not effective or with operating problems;
*	no solution has been adopted;
Np	no significant technical barriers to trade, so no solution needed.

20. Conclusions on EC policies and approaches

This final chapter summarizes the principal conclusions about the effectiveness of the approaches which have been drawn from the case studies, and from discussions with national authorities, standards bodies, industry and employers' organizations.

20.1. Review of the present position

Standards, testing and certification is probably the most important issue facing manufacturers who export in the increasingly global trading system. Every manufacturer in the EU's single market faces these issues. Even SMEs serving local markets compete with products from other EU Member States, made under different standards regimes (sometimes technically better, sometimes cheaper), and are having to adapt to the EU system of standards, testing and certification.

The EU's approaches have had a spectacular and widespread impact by setting up the structure for a new system of standards, mutual recognition of regulations and mutual recognition of testing and certification. The approaches are revolutionary and have never been tried in any trading group before. They will, when they are further operational, become a model for the future world trading system.

Industry, when it exports, complains about the costs and inconvenience of the old system of national technical regulations, standards and conformity requirements. But in the past it came to rely on this system of technical protectionism in its home markets. While welcoming the new system, industry is often unprepared for the changes, which entail significant transition costs for some firms, particularly those SMEs which are not involved in trade and have not previously been concerned about attestation nor had to adapt to new standards.

This revolution in the technical infrastructure has been achieved mainly in the short period from 1989 to 1995 (although the seeds were sown in the early 1980s). It includes the development of the New Approach directives, radical changes in the functioning of the European and national standards bodies, procedures for reporting and acting on new national regulations and standards, a global approach to testing and certification, development of accreditation systems based on ISO/EN45000, development of mutual recognition arrangements for testing and certification, the rapid adoption of certification systems for pre-qualification and for marketing purposes based on ISO 9000/EN29000, and the beginning of coordination of enforcement arrangements for the regulatory aspects of the system.

These approaches have overthrown systems of national standards built up over a century or more. The major national systems were, intentionally or otherwise, protectionist in nature. Many industry sectors and their trade associations are naturally trying to retain some of the old ways. Most industrialists see only the short-term impact on their own business, which entails transition costs, without understanding the whole system and the benefits of this to industry and customers. They complain about the difficulties of adapting and the uncertainties and lack of information. They also complain about the slow development of new standards, yet because individual firms have no protectionist interest in contributing to developing common standards, the old reliance on voluntary work by industry cannot cope with the huge volume of new standards required.

It will inevitably take about ten years for most of the new system of European standards to be put in place to support the directives and the conformity attestation system. The success of this might lead to the extension of the system to new products (including service sectors, in which CEN is beginning to become active). The new standards may also become *de facto* global standards (wherever ISO standards do not already exist). Because the EU is the world's largest single market, the world's exporting manufacturers will have to use European standards. The standards infrastructure is less well coordinated than the EU's; and Japan, by operating a largely closed market, has little influence on world standards. So Europe has to get it right, and that will need massive resources and enough time. Meanwhile, industry faces uncertainty and additional conformance costs.

In this phase of change, it is inevitable that some firms try to take advantage of the uncertainty to gain competitive advantage, by claiming their competitors do not meet the new standards, or pressing for new regulations; some evade the rules and some claim conformity falsely. This causes annoyance to manufacturers.

The coordination of enforcement (i.e. market surveillance by national enforcement authorities) which the EC is developing through the Common Approach, is now seen by many manufacturers as a priority. This would gain confidence in the new system and overcome resistance which could cause it to fail.

Because the change has been so rapid, policies and approaches have been developed as the legislation and infrastructure was being put in place. It has also been interpreted 'on the hoof' by national governments and by trade bodies. This leads to misunderstandings, lack of good information, changing interpretations, and on top of the natural complexity of the system, a body of legislation with sometimes inconsistent requirements. Simplification and consolidation of the legislation and development of good interpretative texts, information channels and training materials is now a priority.

The speed and breadth of the changes has also had the unfortunate side effect that attention and resources have been diverted from other important aspects. Principal among these are: the development of performance standards; mutual recognition arrangements in the non-regulated sector, and the development of efficient, non-discriminatory quality marking.

20.2. The New Approach directives

Those New Approach directives which have been in force for some time are evidently successful, and New Approach harmonization is generally welcomed by the case study industry sectors. Those enterprises in sectors where the system is in transition have many worries, however, and these centre around three main issues: the development of harmonized standards, CE-marking, and the coordination and enforcement of conformity procedures.

20.2.1. Transitional problems of European standardization

Industrialists, particularly those affected by the Machinery Directive (which requires a huge programme of standardization and covers a very wide range of distinct products) and those who will be affected by the Construction Products Directive (which has even greater problems of standardization), complain persistently about problems of standards, attestation and enforcement. Both these industry sectors have large numbers of SMEs, many of whom traditionally served only local markets. They feel threatened. Many of their complaints are justified, but are in reality transitional problems of adaptation to the new systems and procedures, and problems caused by the lack of standards or understanding of essential requirements in the period of development of the system.

The main problems related to standardization are listed below. These initial problems are likely to exist until the system is properly working, harmonized standards are prepared and well understood, the backlog of attestation needs is overcome, and the testing and certification capacity has adjusted to the long-run requirements.

Lack of standards

Over the last few years, the complaints from industry about the New Approach directives have been directed mainly at the slow preparation of mandates (particularly in the case of the CPD) and slow production of harmonized standards (particularly for the Machinery Directive). The lack of standards is still the main concern of manufacturers in the sectors which are in the process of adapting to the requirements of New Approach directives. Even though in theory most directives allow for attestation of conformity without manufacturing to standards, industrialists are especially concerned about the lack of standards precisely because the process of change in the regime creates uncertainty and worries about product liability.

Uncertainty and liability

The experience with the Machinery Directive indicates that the need for conformity with ERs without harmonized standards creates anew some of the costs that standardization is intended to remove, creates uncertainty and lays manufacturers open to liability claims – which is the problem businesses fear most.

Cost of testing

The cost of testing by NoBos or other third parties, when there are no standards to test against and no agreed test procedures, becomes prohibitive because test labs have to design test procedures from scratch for each new product they see, and will tend to over-design the tests and require long testing periods to insure themselves against liability claims. These costs should decrease as NoBos and manufacturers gain experience with attestation, and for many products (e.g. non-Annex IV machinery) the third party attestation costs will disappear when standards are available and manufacturers are able to follow the self-certification route.

Testing capacity

The capacity to deal with the huge increase in the volume and complexity of regulatory testing does not exist in some countries (e.g. the UK, which has a large testing and certification industry, but directed to process quality control and customer testing requirements, not mandatory approvals; and Greece and other smaller countries which have small testing industries without the breadth of capabilities needed). In this situation there are long delays in getting goods to market, test prices rise, companies have to take the risk of self-certification which they are unwilling to take, and testing bodies may be selective in the contracts they take so there is a risk of discrimination.

Diversion of resources

A number of interviewees commented that a consequence of the escalating workload of mandated standardization in support of New Approach directives or public procurement is the diversion of standardization effort away from quality/performance standards. Moreover, the industry volunteers who provide the resources for drafting and discussion of standards were supported by their companies in the past because they saw a direct benefit in terms of simplifying design and product development, avoiding being left behind in technical developments, and a possible protectionist effect of the standards. Some sectors of industry now see European harmonization as a cost and a threat to their previously protected position, and the volume of standardization work as a burden, so at the same time as the demand for voluntary work is increasing the incentive is removed. It is reported that both the quality and the speed of standardization work is consequently declining. This, in turn, has a knock-on effect on the resources available for voluntary standardization work for industry-led quality and performance standards.

20.2.2. Industry's reservations about CE-marking

The requirement for CE-marking has made the requirements of the New Approach directives very evident to manufacturers, and made clear their common European basis as distinct from the individual national laws or regulations which implement the directives, which would otherwise be the only visible sign of the directives to manufacturers.

The fact that the CE-marking is a visible sign to customers (as opposed to the enforcement authorities to whom the marking is properly addressed) is seen by some trade associations to create a problem, because they believe it will be assumed by customers to be a quality mark. At the same time, some manufacturers want to use the CE-marking to promote their products. Some NoBos have reported requests from manufacturers for CE-marking of goods which are not covered by any NA directive.

It is the convention that a product which carries a mark:

(a)   meets certain 'quality' standards which have been agreed by the consumer organizations and by the manufacturers and are in some sense superior to the specifications of other products legally on the market but not bearing the mark;

(b)   has been independently tested by a testing organization with facilities designed for the specific testing requirements of that product; and

(c)   provides some guarantee to consumers that in the event the product causes damage or is found to be defective or not to meet the standard, the manufacturer or certifying body will be liable.

There has been no publicity campaign to tell customers and consumers that the CE-marking means only that the product conforms with essential requirements laid down by the directives. This has several consequences. Firstly, proper competition between products on the basis of quality is undermined because products with low performance standards or at the margins of safety requirements are perceived to have a 'quality' mark. In particular, genuine quality marks are undermined. It is particularly unfortunate that the first visible appearances of the CE-marking were on low quality imported toys from South-East Asia where manufacturers deliberately used the marking prominently so that it would be confused with a quality mark. Secondly, some suppliers have lost faith in the New Approach because they see the CE-marking being applied falsely, or under differing interpretations of the requirements of the ERs, in this interim period when enforcement is not strictly applied or well coordinated.

The discussions with manufacturers in the machinery sectors (who are still in the process of adapting to the new requirements) reveal that there is still a lack of understanding and trust in the CE-marking. On the other hand, in those product groups where the directives have been in place longer manufacturers find it very helpful, although often they feel there is still some way to go to achieve consistent and efficient conformity assessment and enforcement.

20.2.3. Coordination of notified bodies and conformity assessment

It was mentioned by more than one interviewee that the quality of work by NoBos (as shown by the level of product performance against the ERs required to obtain attestation by different NoBos) varies widely. This suggests that:

(a) they may not be adequately co-ordinated and monitored; and
(b) they interpret ERs according to traditional national practices.

This discrepancy in the standard of attestation is almost inevitable in this transition period. Where there is a choice of self-certification or recourse to a NoBo, manufacturers will normally prefer self-certification only if there are clear standards available against which they can manufacture and be confident they are not at risk of liability claims. If there are no relevant standards, they will prefer third party attestation. But if there are no standards, the NoBos have to design their own test procedures and performance parameters. The establishment of coordination groups for NoBos is intended to enable them to do this, without creating unnecessary costs or developing divergent attestation criteria.

In those countries where liability law is stricter, or customers more litigious, NoBos and enforcement authorities will tend to impose stricter interpretation of the ERs and stricter testing. It is reported indeed that some NoBos will not carry out EC type-examination and conformity-to-type certification because they are worried about their own liability, and will only test against a harmonized standard. This defeats the purpose of NoBos if specific harmonized standards are not available or are not appropriate to the manufacturer's product.

On the other hand, there are reports of NoBos who will re-test and certify products which have already been failed by other NoBos.

Suppliers are already taking advantage of the differences in attestation criteria by shopping around for the NoBos which will provide fastest, cheapest and least strict attestation. This, unfortunately, is an example of competition driving out quality, because of poor enforcement.

One source also suggested that there is disagreement over whether NoBos should be generalists or specialists. One school of thought is that NoBos should be specialists in testing a limited number of products. The opposing view is that such a degree of specialization will generate monopolies or cartels, enabling NoBos to charge excessive fees.

The criteria for nomination of NoBos are also a cause for concern by industry. Notification is done by national administrations, not by expert accreditation bodies. The administrations are not necessarily competent to appraise testing and certification bodies. While some Member States rely on their independent accreditation bodies to carry out appraisals and surveillance, other Member States either do not have accreditation bodies who can do this, or they take a less technically rigorous approach, which may include notification of government departments' in-house laboratories without appraisal.

20.2.4. Market surveillance

Many manufacturers are concerned about weak enforcement of the requirements of the directives in some Member States, because they believe it allows products which are falsely CE marked to circulate. No firm evidence of this was presented for any of our sample products, however. It is clear, however, that the organizations, procedures and practice of enforcement differ between Member States.

20.3.   Mutual recognition

20.3.1. Comments on 83/189 and Art. 30 procedures

Discussions with Member States suggest that they now think twice before proposing new regulations. There are always pressures to introduce new regulations, so continuous vigilance to prevent new ones, and to remove unnecessary old ones, is required. The Molitor report (COM (95) 288) and the Delors White Paper (COM (93) 700) confirmed this need. The 83/189 procedures are the main force in this battle. The unpopularity of it with Member States is evidence of its effectiveness.

The key problem now, however, is whether enforcement authorities are knowledgeable and able to make proper decisions about legitimate products which should benefit from MRP but which may not meet the precise requirements of national standards and regulations, or where old rules and standards are still habitually referred to by industry and purchasers (see case studies on cables and cement).

20.3.2. Industry views

Attitudes of industry to MRP seem to be mixed. Many firms who have encountered problems in having their products accepted in one or other EU country are aware that they can invoke MRP. The case study of fortified drinks in Part II shows how manufacturers of energy drinks containing levels of caffeine and other ingredients banned in some Member States established themselves in Austria and obtained product approval in the UK in order to enter the German and Italian markets. A US manufacturer of engineered timber products spent several years (unsuccessfully) trying to obtain an *agrément* certificate in the UK in order to enter other EU markets where product approval procedures were seen to be more difficult, and was finally successful when Austria joined the EU because their products had already been widely used there by customers, without the need for statutory approvals.

In most cases, however, firms seem unaware of MRP. The cement case study showed that a major exporting firm actively decided not to market in France because of the need to have testing and product approvals to AFNOR standards since 1990, were unaware of the change in the French legislation introduced as a result of Art. 30 procedures, and when told about it did not believe that it would in practice make exporting any easier.

20.4. Testing and certification in the non-regulatory sphere

20.4.1. The role of EOTC

EOTC is criticized for failing to have much effect so far. It is a small organization with limited funds, and apart from initial EC funding and fees for consultancy work to the EC, it seems to have little support from industry. This is perhaps not surprising because of the conflicts and tensions which its establishment created. Its roles cut across many established interests.

It is required to restructure the foundations of the testing and certification industry which constitutes its own membership. Achievement of 'one-stop testing and certification' in Europe would remove a large proportion of its members' business. The industry has to be convinced that simplifying the system will lead to such growth in its own business, by extension of testing and certification to new sectors and customers, or through increased use by enforcement authorities, that they have a long-term interest. Without active promotion of mutual recognition arrangements and agreement groups from the industry, there can be no progress.

EOTC's action also conflicts with CEN/CENELEC's role. Development of agreement groups requires writing procedures for testing, and agreement on criteria and terminology. This would not be necessary if there were standards. Although disguised by different terminology, EOTC is expected to manage the development of a huge programme of standardization for testing and certification procedures without the resources to do so.

It also overlaps with the role of Notified Bodies. These are now trying to coordinate their activities. It could be seen as EOTC's role to do this, and it has tried to provide technical assistance to the NoBo co-ordination groups. The NoBos are a special subset of the testing and certification industry, which has been given a privileged and sometimes monopolistic position by the New Approach directives, with their own accreditation procedures, under the responsibility of national governments. The disparate nature of the NoBos themselves (private test labs, government and industry research organizations, local authorities) and of the notifying bodies will make it difficult to achieve a consistent accreditation procedure.

20.4.2. Quality marks

From the discussion in Sections 4.4.4 and 20.2, it is clear that many industry bodies, while welcoming the removal of barriers by the various approaches, are concerned about the potential effect on product performance and design quality of mutual recognition and harmonized standards related to minimum essential requirements. They are often concerned about CE-marking displacing industry-run quality schemes.

The objective of increasing competitiveness of EU industry leads to a policy conflict. Industry needs to raise performance standards and quality, develop quality labelling schemes, and promote testing and certification. Removing barriers may make this difficult, because it can divert the limited standardization resources away from performance standards. Industry also believes that setting harmonized minimum levels of protection for health, safety and the environment may bring standards of products down.

It is the opinion of the Consultant that quality marks in their various guises are essential to the functioning of markets. Competition on quality and increased competitiveness of EU products is an important objective of the single market. In international markets, the development of truly European marks would be a means to enable EU firms to compete not only on price but on quality, as long as quality marking schemes are open and non-discriminatory. Consumer organizations may have a role in supervision of the functioning of such quality marks. The quality marks should be open to any manufacturer or supplier, irrespective of their domicile or manufacturing location. The certification bodies should be subject to strict accreditation criteria (stricter than either EN 45000 or the NoBo criteria). There should be no market sharing between certification bodies awarding the marks. They should test against performance standards which set a high level of performance, and are clearly distinguishable from harmonized standards linked to the ERs of directives. The objective of European quality marks should be to mark out clearly European standards as superior to those of our trading partners.

APPENDIX A

Organizations interviewed

The following organizations were interviewed or submitted written information.

A.1.   National authorities

Délégation Interministérielle aux Normes, Sous-Direction de la Qualité pour l'Industrie et la
    Normalisation, France
Inspection du Travail et des Mines, Luxembourg
Ministère des Affaires Economiques, Département de la Qualité, Belgium
Ministerio de Industria y Energia, Spain
Bundesministerium für Arbeit und Sozialordnung, Germany
Bundesministerium für Wirtschaft, Germany
Bundesministerium für Wirtschaftliche Angelegenheiten, Austria
Danish Agency for the Development of Trade and Industry, Denmark
Ministere van Economische Zaken, Netherlands
Ministry of Trade and Industry, Greece
Ministry of Industry and Trade, Finland
Department of Employment and Enterprise, Ireland
Single Market Compliance Unit, Department of Trade and Industry, DTI, UK
National Forum for Conformity Assessment and Quality Policy, UK
Ministry of Industry and Commerce, Sweden
Ministry for Foreign Affairs, Sweden
National Board of Trade, Sweden
National Electrical Safety Board, Sweden
National Post and Telecom Agency, Sweden
National Board of Occupational Safety and Health, Sweden
National Board for Consumer Policies, Sweden
Ministerio dell'Industria, Italy

A.2.   Standards bodies

Association Française de Normalisation, France
Institut Belge de Normalisation, Belgium
Asociación Española de Normalisación, Spain
Instituto Portugues da Qualidade, Ministerio da Industria e Energia, Portugal
Deutsches Institut für Normung, DIN, Germany
Österreichisches Normungsintitut, Austria
Dansk Standards, DS, Denmark
Nederlands Normalisatie-Institut, Netherlands
Hellenic Organization for Standardization, ELOT, Greece
National Standards Authority of Ireland, NSAI, Ireland
British Standard Institute, UK
Swedish Standards Institution, Sweden
Swedish Electrical Commission, SEK, Sweden
Ente Nazionale Italiano di Unificazione, UNI, Italy

Comitato Elettrotecnico Italiano, CEI, Italy

A.3.   Other national organizations

Centre Français du Commerce Extérieur (CFCE), France
Chambre de Commerce du Grand-Duché du Luxembourg, Luxembourg
Euroguichet, Union Luxembourgeoise des Consommateurs, Luxembourg
Fédération des Entreprises Belges, Belgium
Confederación Española de Organizaciones Empresariales, Spain
Confederaçao da Industria Portuguesa, Portugal
Bundesanstalt für Materialforschung und Prüfung (BAM), Germany
Bundesverband der Deutschen Industrie e.V. (BDI), Germany
Deutscher Industrie- und Handelstag (DIHT), Germany
Wirtschaftskammer Österreich, Austria
Dansk Industri, Denmark
Federation of Greek Industry, Greece
Federation of Finnish Commerce and Trade, Finland
Chamber of Commerce, Finland
Irish Business and Employers' Federation, Ireland
SWEDAC, Swedish Accreditation Body, Sweden
Federation of Swedish Industries, Sweden
Federation of Swedish Commerce and Trade, Sweden
SINCERT, Italian Accreditation Body, Italy
CONFINDUSTRIA, Federation of Italian Industries, Italy
UK Accreditation Services (UKAS), UK
National Forum for Conformity Assessment and Quality Policy, UK

A.4.   European bodies

European Court of Justice, Luxembourg
CEN, European Standard Organization, Belgium
CENELEC, European Standard Organization, Belgium
European Commission, DG XV (Internal Market and Financial Services) (Directorates B1 and
     B2), Belgium
European Commission, DG III (Industry) (Directorates D1, D2, B1 and B4), Belgium
European Commission, DG XXIV (Consumer Policy and Consumer Health Protection),
     Belgium
CEPS, Belgium
ECOSOC, Economic and Social Council, Belgium
UNICE, Belgium
European Organization for Testing and Certification (EOTC), Belgium
European Co-operation for Accreditation of Laboratories (EAL), Belgium

A.5.   Simple pressure vessels

Z.I. Blanzat, Manufacturer, France
SMMT, Association, UK
Forster and Hales, Manufacturer, UK
Plant Safety, Notified Body, UK

Equal, Manufacturer, Spain
Wabco, Manufacturer, UK
Le Réservoir, Manufacturer, France
Iveco, Truck Manufacturer, Italy
Silitwerke, Manufacturer, Germany

A.6.   Implantable pacemakers

International Association of Prosthesis Manufacturers (IAPM), European Trade Association,
     Belgium
IAPM UK, Trade Association, UK
SNITEM France, Trade Association, France
Sorin Biomedica Spa, Manufacturer, Italy
ELA Medical, Manufacturer, France
Telectronics Ltd, Manufacturer, UK
Guidant, Manufacturer, Belgium
St. Jude Medical, Manufacturer, Belgium
InControl, Manufacturer, Belgium
Sorin Biomedica, Manufacturer, Netherlands
Medical Bionics Ltd, Distributor, UK
Assistance Publique des Hôpitaux de Paris, Customer, France
St Barts Hospital, Customer, UK

A.7.   Toys (dolls and similar)

Assogiocattoli, Association, Italy
Toy Traders of Europe, Association, Germany
British Toy and Hobby Association, Association, UK
Instituto Tecnologico del Juguete-AIJU, Notified body, Spain
Laboratoire National d'Essais (LNE), Notified body, France
Bluebird, Manufacturer, UK
Brio, Manufacturer, Sweden
Corolle, Manufacturer, France
Famosa, Manufacturer, Spain
Hasbro, Manufacturer, UK
Ideal Loisir, Manufacturer, France
Jesmar, Manufacturer, Spain
Zapf, Manufacturer, Germany
Mattel, Manufacturer, Netherlands
Tomy, Manufacturer, UK
Trudi, Manufacturer, Italy
European Association for the Coordination of Consumer Representation in Standardization
     (ANEC), Consumer association, Belgium
Robino, Importer, UK

A.8.   Circular woodworking saws

Department of Trade and Industry, UK
Woodworking Machinery Suppliers Association, Trade Association, UK

Demurger, Customer and manufacturer, France
Sedgwick & Co., Manufacturer, UK
Schuler, Manufacturer, Germany
Pedrazzoli, Manufacturer, Italy
Ortza S.Coop, Manufacturer, Spain
Browns Agricultural Machinery Co. Ltd, Manufacturer, UK
Holzma, Manufacturer, Germany
Mida, Manufacturer, Portugal
Penope Oy, Importer, Finland

A.9.   Electric handtools

Peugeot Outillage Electrique, Manufacturer, France
Black & Decker, Manufacturer, Italy
Bosch Elektrowerkzeuge Electric Power Tools, Manufacturer, Germany
Metabo, Manufacturer, Germany
Makita, Manufacturer, UK
Talleres Casals, Manufacturer and retailer, Spain
Hitachi, Manufacturer, Ireland

A.10.   Domestic gas cookers

Confédération Européenne des Fabricants d'Appareils de Chauffage (CEFACD), European
        Trade Association, Belgium
European Committee of Manufacturers of Electrical Domestic Equipment (CECED),
        European Trade Association, Italy
European Association for the Coordination of Consumer Representation in
        Standardization (ANEC), Consumer association, Belgium
Society of British Gas Industries (SBGI), Trade association, UK
GIFAM, Trade Association, France
Neff, Manufacturer, Germany
HKI, Manufacturer, Germany
Sippelfrickke, Manufacturer, Germany
Merloni, Manufacturer, Italy
Candy, Manufacturer, Italy
IAR, Manufacturer, Spain
Glynwed Domestic Appliances, Manufacturer, UK
British Gas, Retailer, UK

A.11.   Cement

CEMBUREAU, European Trade Association, Belgium
FEBELCEM, Trade Association, Belgium
Centre de Recherche Industriel du Ciment (CRIC), Belgium
Ministry of Communications and Infrastructure, Belgium
LOEMCO, Testing laboratory, Spain
Boverket, National Housing Board, Sweden
British Cement Association, UK
CIMPOR, Manufacturer, Portugal

Cementos Lemona, Manufacturer, Spain
Castle Cement, UK
Blue Circle Industries, UK
Ciments Français, France
Compagnie des Ciments Belges (CCB), Belgium
Finnsementii, Finland
Rugby Cement, UK
Cementa AB, Sweden
NORCEM, Norway
Sancem, Norway
Kerpen & Kerpen, Importers, Germany
Seament, Importers, UK
Cem-trade AB, Importers, Sweden
Silo Cement, Importers, Austria

A.12. Energy cables

Asociación Española de Fabricantes de Conductores Electricos Aislados, FACEL, Spain
Associaçao para o Estudo e Desarollamento Tecnológico de Cabos Eléctricos (APETCE),
    Association, Portugal
BASEC, Laboratory, UK
British Cable Makers Confederation, Association, UK
British Approved Service for Cables, Association, UK
Echeverria Cablerias del Norte, Manufacturer, Spain
BICC, Manufacturer, UK
Pirelli Cavi, Manufacturer, Italy
Nokia Cables, Manufacturer, Denmark
Plastic Insulated Cables, Manufacturer, UK
Siemens, Manufacturer, Germany
Eurelectric, Manufacturer, France
Concordia Electrical Wire and Cable Nottingham, Manufacturer, UK
Delta Energy Cables, Manufacturer, UK
Alcatel Cables, Manufacturer, France
Meritlink, Manufacturer, UK
Copper Cable Company, Manufacturer, UK

A.13. Pesticides

European Crop Protection Association (ECPA), European Trade Association, Belgium
Bureau Européen des Unions de Consommateurs (BEUC), European Consumers' Association,
    Belgium
Phytophar, Belgian Trade Association, Belgium
British Agrochemicals Association (BAA), UK
ANIPLA, Portuguese Trade Association, Portugal
ANFFE, Spanish Trade Association, Spain
Levington Horticulture, Manufacturer, UK
Bayer, Manufacturer, Germany
AgrEvo, Manufacturer, Germany
Rhône Poulenc Agro, Manufacturer, France

Bayer France, Manufacturer, France
Indalva, Manufacturer, Spain
Rhône Poulenc Agro, Manufacturer, Portugal

A.14. Structural steel

Department of the Environment, Governmental organization, UK
Steel Construction Institute, Association, UK
Syndicat National du Commerce des Produits Sidérurgiques, Association, France
British Iron and Steel Producers Association, Association, UK
Bundesverband des Deutschen Stahlhandels, Association, Germany
Österreichischer Stahlbauverband, Association, Austria
BISPA, Association, UK
European Convention for Constructional Steelwork, Association, Belgium
Steel Construction Institute, Association, UK
Assofermet, Association, Italy
Department of Trade and Industry, Governmental organization, UK
British Constructional Steelwork Association Ltd, Association, UK
Preussag, Mill, Germany
Arbed, Mill, Luxembourg
ENSIDESA, CSI Productos Largos, Mill, Spain
Watson Steel Ltd, Steelworks contractor, UK
Preussag Steel UK, Trading company, UK
Associated Steel Distributors, Distributor, UK
EIFFEL Construction Métallique, Contractor, France

A.15. Carpets and rugs

Union Française des Fabricants de Tapis, Association, France
Febeltex, Association, Belgium
Asociación de Fabricantes de Moquetas de España, Association, Spain
European Carpet Association, Association, Belgium
British Carpets Manufacturers Association, Association, UK
Berry Tuft, Manufacturer, France
Dura Tufting, Manufacturer, Germany
Alfombras Carpets, Manufacturer, Spain
Entreprises Balsan, Manufacturer, France
Louis De Porteere, Manufacturer, Belgium
Groupe Beaulieu, Manufacturer, Belgium
Lemogne Tapis Sarl, Importer-Retailer, Luxembourg
Tapis Saint Maclou, Distributor, France
Carpet Land, Retailer, Belgium
Centexbel, Testing Laboratory, Belgium
British Standard Institute, Standard Organization, UK

A.16 Fortified foods and drinks

Associazione Italiana Industrie Prodotti Alimentari, Association, Italy
FIAB, Trade Association, Spain

L'Alliance 7, Association, France
Fachverband der Nahrungs- und Genussmittelindustrie Österreich, Association, Austria
Unesda, Association, UK
Bundesverband der Deutschen Erfrischungsgetränke-Industrie e.V., Association, Germany
Bund für Lebensmittelrecht und Lebensmittelkunde e.V., Association, Germany
Finnish Federation of the Brewing and Soft Drinks Industry, Association, Finland
Dansk Laeskedrik Fabrikanter, Association, Denmark
Kelloggs, Manufacturer, France
Proctor & Gamble, Manufacturer, Germany
Müller, Manufacturer, Germany
Smithkline Beecham, Manufacturer, UK
AG Barr, Manufacturer, UK
Red Bull, Manufacturer, Austria
Power Horse, Distributor, Austria
Spitz, Manufacturer, Austria
Coca Cola, Manufacturer, Spain
Gazzoni, Manufacturer, Italy
Auchan, Retailer, France
Bilka Netto, Retailer, Denmark
Co-op, Retailer, Denmark
Dragofa, Retailer, Denmark
Enco Products, Distributor, UK

A.17. Water equipment: pipe couplings

Purac, Manufacturer, UK
Stantons, Manufacturer, UK
Biwater, Manufacturer, UK
Manib, Manufacturer, Germany
British Water, Association, UK
British Pump Manufacturers Association, Association, UK

APPENDIX B

Glossary of terms

Words normally have their common English meaning unless given a special meaning by the directives and other EC documents referred to. The principal special terms are set out below. Other terms are defined in the text of the report.

technical barriers to trade

technical specifications or other requirements which impose additional costs on the importers or suppliers of imported goods or services, which are not required of domestic suppliers, or which constitute a ban on imports by reason of their technical specification.

technical specification

a specification contained in a document which lays down the characteristics required of a product such as levels of quality, performance, safety or dimensions, including the requirements applicable to the product as regards the name under which the product is sold, terminology, symbols, testing and test methods, packaging, marking or labelling and conformity assessment procedures;
the term 'technical specification' also covers production methods and processes used in respect of agricultural products as referred to in Article 38(1) of the EC Treaty; products intended for human and animal consumption, and medicinal products as defined in Article 1 of Directive 65/65/EEC as well as production methods and processes related to other products, where these have an effect on their characteristics. (Dir. 94/10/EC)

other requirement

a requirement, other than a technical specification, imposed on a product for the purpose of protecting, in particular, consumers or the environment, and which affects its life cycle after it has been placed on the market, such as conditions of use, recycling, reuse or disposal, where such conditions can significantly influence the composition or nature of the product or its marketing. (Dir. 94/10/EC)

regulatory barriers

technical regulations or other requirements which impose additional costs on imported products or services, which are not imposed on domestic manufacturers (for example, by the need for product or packaging adaptation, testing and certification requirements, registration or similar compliance requirements).

non-regulatory barriers

technical specifications or other requirements, not being imposed by national *de jure* or *de facto* technical regulations, which impose additional costs on imported products or services.

technical regulation

technical specification and other requirements, including the relevant administrative provisions, the observance of which is compulsory, *de jure* or *de facto*, in the case of marketing or use in a Member State or a major part thereof, as well as laws, regulations or administrative provisions of Member States, [....] prohibiting the manufacture, importation, marketing or use of a product. (Dir. 94/10/EC)

de facto technical regulation

de facto technical regulations include:
– laws, regulations or administrative provisions of a Member State which refer either to technical specifications or other requirements or to professional codes or codes of practice which in turn refer to technical specifications or other requirements and compliance with which confers a presumption of conformity with the obligations imposed by the aforementioned laws, regulations or administrative provisions;
– voluntary agreements to which a public authority is a contracting party and which provide, in the public interest, for compliance with technical specifications or other requirements, excluding public procurement tender specifications;
– technical specifications or other requirements which are linked to fiscal or financial measures affecting the consumption of products by encouraging compliance with such technical specifications or other requirements; technical specifications or other requirements linked to national social security systems are not included. (Dir. 94/10/EC)

standard

a technical specification approved by a recognized standardization body for repeated or continuous application, with which compliance is not compulsory and which is one of the following:
– international standard: a standard adopted by an international standardization organization and made available to the public;
– European standard: a standard adopted by a European standardization body and made available to the public;
– national standards: a standard adopted by a national standardization body and made available to the

public. (Dir. 94/10/EC)

technical harmonization mandatory implementation of new technical specifications and other requirements at the EU (or other regional) level, with mandatory withdrawal of incompatible national requirements.

detailed harmonization technical harmonization which includes mandatory technical specifications for a product or service, for some or all of its regulatory aspects.

harmonized standards European standards developed by a European standardization body under a mandate from the European Commission, providing technical specifications compliance with which confers a presumption of conformity to the relevant New Approach directives.

European standards standards, voluntary or mandated, including pre-standards and harmonization documents, published by a European standardization body (e.g. CEN, CENELEC, ETSI and their associated bodies such as ECISS).

testing and certification all the activities of testing, inspection, certification of products, services and their suppliers.

testing testing of products to establish their conformity with standards or technical specifications of any kind, by in-house or third party bodies.

certification a process of inspection, testing and periodic surveillance of an enterprise to certify that it complies with a standard or procedure, particularly the EN29000 series of quality assurance standards for enterprises.

inspection inspection of equipment, other products or services in use to certify that they comply with regulations in force, e.g. health and safety in the workplace.

accreditation approval of laboratories, test-houses, inspection bodies and certification bodies by a recognized accreditation body against approved standards or criteria, e.g. the EN45000 series of QA standards for laboratories.

Mutual Recognition Principle the principle established by the ECJ and embodied in single market legislation, that products lawfully manufactured and placed on the market in one Member State must be allowed free entry into other Member States, unless there is a measure justifiable under Art. 36 (for reasons of public morality, public policy or public security, or the protection of people, animals, environment, national treasures, or commercial or industrial property) i.e. unless the Member State declines to recognize the equivalence of the objectives and levels of protection afforded by the exporting country's regulations.

Mutual Recognition Arrangement

an agreement between a group of testing and certification bodies which establishes the equivalence of their procedures, standards, test methods, criteria, calibration, facilities, QA systems, and establishing agreed formats for certificates and marks, for a given product or group of products.

conformity attestation

the testing and certification procedures necessary to establish conformity with harmonization directives, national technical regulations or standards.

type-testing

testing of a prototype of a product for attestation of conformity. EC type-examination is the type-testing specified by New Approach directives.

APPENDIX C

Characteristics of the sample products

Table C.1.   Sector characteristics: air reservoirs

Criteria	Characteristics
Importance of trade	High trade – few producers, sell worldwide – need harmonization
Number of firms (< 10, 10–100, 100–1,000, > 1,000)	< 10 – easy to get agreement
Size of firms, concentration	Mainly SMEs with some MNCs (motor manufacturers)
Ownership structure	Mainly private, independent firms, not part of conglomerates
Organization of the sector	Low/medium activity of national trade associations – vehicle sector highly organized and accustomed to harmonization
Degree of differentiation of products	Low
Customer type	Large industry – prone to set new standards
Health and safety hazards	High – therefore high regulation
Environmental and other hazards	Low – regulations limited to explosion risk – simple to harmonize
Technology of products	Mass production – want standards
Production technology change	Low – thus rigid standards are OK
Economies of scale/batch size	High – favours standards
Barriers to entry	High – few customers, established suppliers

Table C.2.   Sector characteristics: implantable pacemakers

Criteria	Characteristics
Importance of trade	High – important to remove TBTs
Number of firms (< 10, 10–100, 100–1,000, > 1,000)	< 10 – easy to agree on standards
Size of firms, concentration	MNCs – need harmonization because all sell EU-wide
Ownership structure	Mainly private, independent firms
Organization of the sector	Strong EU trade association: able to negotiate standards
Degree of differentiation of products	Low – thus easier to harmonize
Customer type	Public health authorities and private hospitals and clinics – prone to user standards, discrimination and public procurement rules
Health and safety hazards	Low to third parties – no strong resistance to harmonization
Environmental and other hazards	Low – no strong resistance to harmonization
Technology of products	High tech, low volume assembly – changing specifications, need flexible standards, need NA
Production technology change	Rapid
Economies of scale/batch size	For production low, high for development costs – need to reduce the number of variants, need harmonization
Barriers to entry	High – R&D and approval costs – want to keep approval but harmonized

Table C.3.   Sector characteristics: toys (dolls and similar)

Criteria	Characteristics
Importance of trade	High – high imports from third countries – need harmonization and seek EU standards for protection from low cost imports
Number of firms (< 10, 10–100, 100–1,000, > 1,000)	100–1,000
Size of firms, concentration	Mainly SMEs, few global – need to remove barriers
Ownership structure	Mainly private, some global quoted companies
Organization of the sector	Active EU and national trade associations help produce standards – active consumer associations – pressure for regulation
Degree of differentiation of products	High – no rigid standards, need good generic standards, NA
Customer type	Wholesalers/retailers to household consumers: fashion important
Health and safety hazards	High, because used by children – tendency to low costs, low quantities
Environmental and other hazards	Some – toxic substances
Technology of products	Mixed – from mass production to handicraft
Production technology change	Low – but rapid fashion change
Economies of scale/batch size	Potentially high – need large markets and harmonization
Barriers to entry	Medium – product approvals, advertising, large retail buyers – want generic standards

Table C.4.   Sector characteristics: circular woodworking saws

Criteria	Characteristics
Importance of trade	Medium/high – clustered manufacturing
Number of firms (< 10, 10–100, 100–1,000, > 1,000)	10–100
Size of firms, concentration	SMEs, not concentrated
Ownership structure	Private
Organization of the sector	Part of larger machinery industry/woodworking industries – low activity
Degree of differentiation of products	High
Customer type	Industry
Health and safety hazards	High
Environmental and other hazards	Low
Technology of products	Small batch assembly, high subcontractors
Production technology change	Low
Economies of scale/batch size	Low
Barriers to entry	Low, but static/declining competitive market

Table C.5.   Sector characteristics: electric hand tools

Criteria	Characteristics
Importance of trade	High
Number of firms (< 10, 10–100, 100–1,000, > 1,000)	10–100, with few dominant, global firms
Size of firms, concentration	A few large MNCs, some SMEs
Ownership structure	Global conglomerates
Organization of the sector	Strong and active EU and national trade associations
Degree of differentiation of products	Medium
Customer type	Retailers and builders merchants
Health and safety hazards	Medium
Environmental and other hazards	Low
Technology of products	Mass production – favours standards
Production technology change	Manufacturing developments (innovation in cordless equipment)
Economies of scale/batch size	Medium/high – favours standards
Barriers to entry	Advertising, brand loyalty

Table C.6.   Sector characteristics: domestic gas cookers

Criteria	Characteristics
Importance of trade	Medium (heavy product), differing national preferences and gas pressures
Number of firms (< 10, 10–100, 100–1,000, > 1,000)	10–100
Size of firms, concentration	Mainly MNCs, some SMEs in niches, quite concentrated
Ownership structure	Quoted companies, mainly part of large consumer appliance manufacturers
Organization of the sector	Two active EU and national trade associations
Degree of differentiation of products	Medium – few variants
Customer type	Retailers to household consumers
Health and safety hazards	High (gas)
Environmental and other hazards	Low
Technology of products	Mass production
Production technology change	low
Economies of scale/batch size	Quite high
Barriers to entry	High – brand loyalty

Table C.7. Sector characteristics: cement

Criteria	Characteristics
Importance of trade	Low
Number of firms (< 10, 10–100, 100–1,000, > 1,000)	Very low, < 10 major world firms – could negotiate common standards easily, but prefer separate national markets
Size of firms, concentration	Large MNCs
Ownership structure	Conglomerate, global
Organization of the sector	Strong EU trade association
Degree of differentiation of products	Very low
Customer type	Contractors and public procurement – existing technical standards
Health and safety hazards	Medium – dust, irritant, also risk of catastrophic failure in use in large structures – highly regulated
Environmental and other hazards	Low
Technology of products	Mass production – needs standards
Production technology change	Low – favours standards
Economies of scale/batch size	Very high – low marginal cost, tendency to dumping/aggressive competition, hence protectionist industry
Barriers to entry	High investment costs

Table C.8.   Sector characteristics: electric cables

Criteria	Characteristics
Importance of trade	Quite high
Number of firms (< 10, 10–100, 100–1,000, > 1,000)	100–1,000
Size of firms, concentration	Few dominant MNCs, many specialists
Ownership structure	Mainly conglomerates
Organization of the sector	Quite strong EU trade association
Degree of differentiation of products	Low, but a great number of variants
Customer type	Diverse – industrial companies and utilities
Health and safety hazards	High – related to insulation
Environmental and other hazards	Low/medium
Technology of products	Process technology
Production technology change	Automation – generally low change
Economies of scale/batch size	High but variable, small to very large batch size
Barriers to entry	Capital investment (medium)

Table C.9.   Sector characteristics: pesticides

Criteria	Characteristics
Importance of trade	High for active ingredients but low for formulated products
Number of firms (< 10, 10–100, 100–1,000, > 1,000)	Few, < 10 agrochemicals manufacturers and 100–1,000 manufacturers of formulated products
Size of firms, concentration	Concentrated for agrochemicals manufacturers, but some SMEs in formulated products
Ownership structure	Quoted companies and private companies
Organization of the sector	Active national trade associations, perhaps weaker at EU level
Degree of differentiation of products	High – no standards
Customer type	Wholesalers and cooperatives, then farmers
Health and safety hazards	Very high – highly regulated
Environmental and other hazards	Process industry – two tier (formulation and active ingredients)
Technology of products	High R&D, high innovation
Production technology change	High for active ingredients
Economies of scale/batch size	High – product approvals, R&D costs, patents – but low for formulated product
Barriers to entry	High – registration and approval procedures

Table C.10.   Sector characteristics: structural steel

Criteria	Characteristics
Importance of trade	Quite high
Number of firms (< 10, 10–100, 100–1,000, > 1,000)	10–100 (low 10's)
Size of firms, concentration	Large steel companies, national, diversified
Ownership structure	Mix of public and private
Organization of the sector	Strong trade association at EU level
Degree of differentiation of products	Low – many specifications but no difference between suppliers – standards easily comparable
Customer type	Stockists and traders
Health and safety hazards	Medium/high related to structural failure, but not highly regulated
Environmental and other hazards	Low
Technology of products	Process manufacturing, easy to switch between specifications
Production technology change	Low
Economies of scale/batch size	High economies of scale but low batch (large dimension/grade range)
Barriers to entry	High – scale of investment

Table C.11. Sector characteristics: carpets

Criteria	Characteristics
Importance of trade	High – concentration of manufacturing in Belgium
Number of firms (< 10, 10–100, 100–1,000, > 1,000)	100–1,000
Size of firms, concentration	SMEs – most have less than 300 employees
Ownership structure	Private
Organization of the sector	Active EU trade association and quite active national ones
Degree of differentiation of products	Standard techniques, huge variety of design – need flexible standards and classification
Customer type	Retailers, consumers and architects – need standards
Health and safety hazards	Medium/high – fire, chemicals – need regulations in some uses
Environmental and other hazards	High – dyes, glues, washing water – environmental labels
Technology of products	Mass production
Production technology change	Low
Economies of scale/batch size	Medium economies of scale – high volume, capital intensive – low batch size because of design variants
Barriers to entry	Low – but some investment and some testing – standards are not protective

Table C.12.   Sector characteristics: fortified foods and drinks

Criteria	Characteristics
Importance of trade	Medium – very diverse
Number of firms (< 10, 10–100, 100–1,000, > 1,000)	Over 1,000 – few dominants
Size of firms, concentration	SMEs, few global
Ownership structure	Private and some global
Organization of the sector	Many distinct trade associations (juices, drinks, yoghurts, etc.), quite active
Degree of differentiation of products	Quite high – branded goods, many formulations
Customer type	Wholesale and retail to household customer (especially children)
Health and safety hazards	Ingredients – diverse hazards, many unknown
Environmental and other hazards	Low, except for container recycling
Technology of products	Process technology, highly automated, integrated
Production technology change	More automation, but generally low
Economies of scale/batch size	High – need harmonization
Barriers to entry	High – advertising and product approval

Table C.13. Sector characteristics: water pipes and coupling

Criteria	Characteristics
Importance of trade	Medium
Number of firms (< 10, 10–100, 100–1,000, > 1,000)	10–100
Size of firms, concentration	Mainly large firms
Ownership structure	Public sector and private (steel/plastics)
Organization of the sector	Quite active national trade associations, weak at EU level
Degree of differentiation of products	Low, but different customer standards for dimension, material
Customer type	Large companies, large public sector – so regulation of products for consumer protection not necessary
Health and safety hazards	Medium – materials in contact with water
Environmental and other hazards	Low
Technology of products	Mass production
Production technology change	Some change in materials, generally low
Economies of scale/batch size	High
Barriers to entry	Quite high – experience

APPENDIX D
Analysis of barriers by NACE code

NACE	Activity sector	Type of barrier	Technical regulations on the product of the sector	Non-regulatory barriers	% GVA	% intra-EU trade
1100	Extraction of solid fuels	T	Environmental rules, e.g. S content	None (except purchasing policy of public utilities)	0.30	0.07
1200	Coke ovens	T	Environmental regs	None	0.02	0.03
1300	Extr. of petroleum & natural gas	T	Environmental rules; stockage rules	None (but intrinsic measurement and analysis requirements)	0.24	0.78
1400	Mineral oil refining	T	Health and safety and transport of dangerous substances	None (intrinsic analysis requirements)	6.44	1.60
1510	Extr. nuclear materials	TO	Health and safety; environmental regulations	Testing; code of practice, etc.	0.02	0.00
1520	Production of nuclear materials	TO	Health and safety; environmental regulations	Testing; code of practice, etc.	0.73	0.18
1600	Electr., gas, steam, hot water	N	None	None	8.52	0.63
1700	Water supply	N	None	None	0.80	0.00
2110	Extraction, prep. of iron ore	N	None	None	0.05	0.09
2120	Extraction, prep. of non-fer. met. ores	N	None	None	0.00	0.05
2210	Iron & steel industry (ECSC) 1 Construction uses	TO	Building regulations	National standards, being harmonized	0.67	1.13
2210	2 Other	N	None	None	0.67	1.13
2220	Manufacture of steel tubes	N	None	None	0.29	0.40
2230	Drawing, cold rolling of steel	N	None	None	0.37	0.52
2240	NF-metals (prod., prel. proc.) 1 Precious metals	T	Hallmarking	None	0.08	0.21
2240	2 Other	N	None	None	0.69	1.93
2310	Extract. of build. materials	TO	Construction sector; building regs.	Insurance, building control	0.44	0.19

Key: T = technical regulations   O = non-regulatory barriers
N = not significant   TO = technical regulations and non-regulatory barriers

NACE	Activity sector	Type of barrier	Technical regulations on the product of the sector	Non-regulatory barriers	% GVA	% intra-EU trade
2320	Salt, nat. phosph., peat	N	None	None	0.11	0.14
2410	Clay prod. for constr. purposes	TO	Building regs; insurance requirements (French decennial)	National standards, custom; public procurement specs	0.32	0.06
2420	Cement, lime, plaster	TO	Regulations on T&C, labelling, contents	National standards, building codes, etc.	0.62	0.11
2430	Struct. concrete, cement, plaster	TO	Building regulations	National standards, building codes, insurance/liability	1.08	0.10
2440	Manuf. of art. of asbestos	T	Environmental rules, health and safety regs	None	0.03	0.02
2450	Work. of stones & non-met. prod.	N	(environmental regulations on process not product)	None	0.34	0.16
2460	Grindstones, abrasive products	N	None	None	0.07	0.08
2470	Manuf. of glass & glassware 1 Construction	TO	Construction regulations	Insurance requirements for construction products	0.44	0.18
2470	2 Automotive	TO	Automotive regulations	Insurance requirements for construction automotive products	0.44	0.11
2470	3 Other	N	None	None	0.44	0.07
2480	Manuf. of ceramic goods	N	None	None	0.68	0.52
2510	Basic industr. chem., petrochem.	TO	Use restrictions on some products, packaging rules	National standards	3.15	6.98
2550	Paint, varnish, printing ink	T	Labelling; environmental rules; packaging, and waste	None	0.36	0.39
2560	Chemical products 1 Agrochemicals	TO	Use restrictions, approvals	Use guidance, etc.	0.29	1.84
2560	2 Hazardous chemicals	TO	Transport rules, labelling	Insurance requirements	0.29	1.84
2560	3 Other	T	Packaging, labelling	None	0.29	1.84
2570	Pharmaceutical products	TO	Use restrictions, approvals, parallel imports, and packaging rules	None	3.00	4.84

Key: T = technical regulations   O = non-regulatory barriers
N = not significant   TO = technical regulations and non-regulatory barriers

NACE	Activity sector	Type of barrier	Technical regulations on the product of the sector	Non-regulatory barriers	% GVA	% intra-EU trade
2580	Soap, detergents, perfume	T	Contents rules, packaging regs, use restrictions	None	1.12	0.82
2590	Manufacture of other chem. products 1 Hazardous	TO	Various	Insurance, etc.	0.21	0.46
2590	2 Other	N	None	None	0.21	0.46
2600	Man-made fibres industry	TO	Fire safety	User industry	0.21	0.63
3110	Foundries	N	None	None	0.77	0.20
3120	Forging, pressing, stamping	N	None	None	0.58	0.13
3130	Treatment of metal	N	None	None	1.14	0.26
3140	Structural metal products	TO	Building regs; insurance	Codes of practice; reg. of professions; national standards	1.03	0.31
3150	Boilers, reservoirs, tanks	TO	Insurance requirements	Codes of practice	0.77	0.18
3160	Tools & finished metal goods	N	None	None	2.69	1.74
3165	Domestic heating appliances	TO	Installation rules; pressure vessels regulations, building regulations	Insurance; codes of practice	0.99	0.94
3166	Manufacture of metal furniture	T	Health and safety at work	None	1.07	0.81
3210	Agricult. machinery & tractors	TO	Health and safety of machinery	T&C requirements; codes of practice	0.36	0.47
3220	Machine tools working metal	TO	Health and safety of machinery	T&C requirements; codes of practice	0.77	0.48
3230	Textile machin., sewing mach.	TO	Health and safety of machinery	T&C requirements; codes of practice	0.28	0.22
3240	Machines for food & chem. ind.	TO	Health and safety of machinery	T&C requirements; codes of practice	1.10	0.76
3250	Machines for iron & steel industry	TO	Health and safety of machinery	T&C requirements; codes of practice	1.34	1.00

Key: T   = technical regulations   O = non-regulatory barriers
N   = not significant   TO = technical regulations and non-regulatory barriers

NACE	Activity sector	Type of barrier	Technical regulations on the product of the sector	Non-regulatory barriers	% GVA	% intra-EU trade
3260	Transmission equipment	TO	Health and safety of machinery	T&C requirements; codes of practice	0.54	0.51
3270	Equipment for use in spec. branches	TO	Health and safety of machinery	T&C requirements; codes of practice	0.57	0.48
3280	Other machinery & equipment	TO	Health and safety of machinery	T&C requirements; codes of practice	2.98	2.79
3300	Office and DP machinery	TO	Public procurement	National standards and public procurement	1.47	3.84
3410	Insulated wires and cables	O	None	Codes of practice; national standards and installation rules	0.27	0.38
3420	Manuf. of electrical machinery	TO	Health and safety	Codes of practice	0.91	1.68
3430	Electr. apparatus for industrial use 1 Power and HT equipment	O	None	Public procurement, installation rules	0.18	0.48
3430	2 Other	O	None	Insurance	0.18	0.48
3440	Manuf. of telecoms equipment	TO	Telecoms and safety regulations	Network standards	3.64	1.35
3450	Manuf. of radios & TVs	TO	Broadcast and safety regulations	Network standards	1.41	2.99
3460	Domestic type electr. appl.	TO	Health and Safety rules	Installation rules	0.84	0.97
3470	Manuf. electr. lamps and others	TO	Safety regulations	Codes of practice; national standards	0.36	0.37
3510	Man. assembly motor vehicles	TO	Formerly extensive type approval	Insurance requirements	4.90	9.53
3520	Manuf. bodies for motor vehicles	N	None	None	0.37	0.23
3530	Manuf. of parts of motor vehic.	T	Formerly extensive type approval	None	1.99	2.12
3610	Shipbuilding 1 Naval	T	Public procurement	Defence standards	0.14	0.02
3610	2 Other	TO	Registration	Insurance requirements	0.28	0.04

Key: T = technical regulations O = non-regulatory barriers
N = not significant TO = technical regulations and non-regulatory barriers

NACE	Activity sector	Type of barrier	Technical regulations on the product of the sector	Non-regulatory barriers	% GVA	% intra-EU trade
3620	Manuf. of railway rol.-stock	TO	Public procurement	Network and national standards	0.23	0.37
3630	Manuf. of cycles, motor cycles 1 Cycles	T	Technical regulations for safety features	None	0.08	0.13
3630	2 Motorcycles	T	Road tax/licensing classes	None	0.08	0.13
3640	Aerospace equipment manuf.	T	Licensing, air worthiness, etc.	None	1.42	2.47
3650	Other transport equipment	T	Technical safety regulations	None	0.02	0.03
3710	Measuring and precision inst.	N	None	None	0.41	0.44
3720	Medical & surgical equipment	T	Public procurement; approved lists, etc.	None	0.43	0.26
3730	Optical instr., photo equipment	N	None	None	0.27	0.87
3740	Manuf. of clocks and watches	N	None	None	0.05	0.07
4110	Manufacture of oils and fats	T	Health & safety regs; packaging; purity	None	0.19	0.42
4120	Slaughtering, prep. of meat	TO	Health & safety regs; packaging; purity	Pure consumer preference	1.19	2.09
4130	Manufacture of dairy products	TO	Health & safety regs; packaging; purity	Pure consumer preference	0.92	1.55
4140	Proc. of fruit and vegetables	TO	Health & safety regs; packaging; purity	Pure consumer preference	0.38	0.82
4150	Proc. & preserving of fish	T	Health & safety regs; packaging; purity	None	0.18	0.32
4160	Grain milling	T	Health & safety regs; packaging; purity	None	0.13	0.08
4170	Manuf. of spaghetti, macaroni	T	Health & safety regs; packaging; purity	None	0.10	0.08
4180	Starch and starch products	T	Health & safety regs; packaging; purity	None	0.08	0.16

Key: T = technical regulations   O = non-regulatory barriers
N = not significant   TO = technical regulations and non-regulatory barriers

NACE	Activity sector	Type of barrier	Technical regulations on the product of the sector	Non-regulatory barriers	% GVA	% intra-EU trade
4190	Bread and flour confectionery	T	Health & safety regs; packaging; purity	None	1.06	0.32
4210	Cocoa and sugar confectionery	T	Health & safety regs; packaging; purity	None	0.73	0.61
4220	Animal and poultry foods	T	Health & safety regs; packaging; purity	None	0.39	0.34
4230	Manuf. of other food products	T	Health & safety regs; packaging; purity	None	1.13	0.82
4240	Ethyl alcohol, spirit dist.	T	Labelling, advertising regs; national monopolies; bottle recycling	None	0.51	0.31
4250	Wine of fresh grapes, cider	T	Labelling, advertising regs; national monopolies; bottle recycling	None	0.36	0.18
4270	Brewing and malting	T	Labelling, advertising regs; national monopolies; bottle recycling	None	1.56	0.18
4280	Soft drinks, nat. spa waters	T	Labelling, adv. regs; bottle recycling; drink additives, sweeteners, etc.	None	0.61	0.13
4290	Manuf. of tobacco products	T	State monopolies; advertising rules; labelling	None	2.89	0.45
4310	Wool industry	N	None	(Only customer requirements)	0.29	0.41
4320	Cotton industry	N	None	(Only customer requirements)	0.48	0.71
4330	Silk industry	N	None	(Only customer requirements)	0.24	0.27
4340	Prep. of flax, hemp, ramie	O	None	National marks	0.02	0.02
4350	Jute industry	N	None	(Only customer requirements)	0.01	0.02
4360	Knitting industry	T	Dyes, fire	(Only customer requirements)	0.58	1.28
4370	Textile finishing	T	Dyes, fire	(Only customer requirements)	0.32	0.44
4380	Carpets, linoleum, floor cover	TO	Fire regulations	National marks	0.24	0.37

Key: T   = technical regulations   O = non-regulatory barriers
      N   = not significant   TO = technical regulations and non-regulatory barriers

NACE	Activity sector	Type of barrier	Technical regulations on the product of the sector	Non-regulatory barriers	% GVA	% intra-EU trade
4390	Miscellaneous textile ind.	O	None	National marks	0.28	0.40
4410	Tanning, dressing of leather	N	None	None	0.13	0.23
4420	Leather products, substitutes	N	None	None	0.14	0.14
4510	Footwear	N	None	None	0.48	0.85
4530	Manuf. of clothing	T	Dyes, fire and other safety regulations for children's clothing	None	1.45	1.37
4550	Manuf. of household textiles	T	Fire resistance rules, labelling	None	0.15	0.19
4560	Manuf. of furs and fur goods	T	CITES	None	0.01	0.05
4610	Sawing and proces. of wood	N	None	None	0.19	0.12
4620	Semi-finished wood products	T	Construction products regs; agrement, etc.	None	0.26	0.21
4630	Carpentry & joinery components	TO	Construction products regs; agrement, etc.	Insurance; building codes	0.53	0.10
4640	Manuf. of wooden containers	N	None	None (note barrier to reuse of pallets, drum, etc.)	0.12	0.01
4650	Other wood manuf. (exc. furn.)	N	None	None	0.15	0.15
4660	Art. of cork and straw, brushes	N	None	None	0.07	0.10
4670	Manuf. of wooden furniture	T	Upholstery fire resistance; safety of office furniture	National standards but no real barriers to trade	1.46	0.64
4710	Manuf. of pulp paper board	TO	Recycling rules	T&C; national standards for packaging	0.74	1.10
4720	Proc. of paper and board	TO	Recycling rules	T&C; national standards	1.59	1.11
4730	Printing and allied industries	N	None	None	1.63	0.67

Key: T = technical regulations   O = non-regulatory barriers
N = not significant   TO = technical regulations and non-regulatory barriers

NACE	Activity sector	Type of barrier	Technical regulations on the product of the sector	Non-regulatory barriers	% GVA	% intra-EU trade
4740	Publishing	T	Copyright rules; obscene publications, etc.	None	0.50	0.75
4810	Manuf. of rubber products	N	None	National standards but not significant	0.69	1.10
4820	Retr., rep. of rubber tyres	N	None	National standards but not significant	0.02	0.02
4830	Processing of plastics 1 Packaging, etc.	T	Regs on contact with food, waste recycling	None	2.04	1.56
4830	2 Construction products	TO	Construction products	Insurance	1.02	0.78
4910	Manuf. articles of jewellery	T	Hallmarking	Codes of practice	0.26	0.64
4920	Manuf. of musical instruments	N	None	None	0.03	0.03
4930	Photograph. and cin. laborat.	N	None	None	0.13	0.02
4940	Toys and sports goods 1 Toys	T	National safety rules	None	0.11	0.21
4940	2 Sports	T	National safety rules	None	0.11	0.21
4950	Miscellaneous manuf. industries	N	None	None	0.15	3.69

Key: T = technical regulations   O = non-regulatory barriers
N = not significant   TO = technical regulations and non-regulatory barriers

APPENDIX E

Analysis of approaches by NACE code

NACE	Activity sector	Gross value added	% GVA	Intra-EU trade	% intra-EU trade	Measures	Measures	Likely status
1100	Extraction of solid fuels	3475.75	0.30	548.10	0.07	Not known	HR	4
1200	Coke ovens	185.25	0.02	253.40	0.03	None	MRP	4
1300	Extr. of petroleum & natural gas	2745.60	0.24	5775.10	0.78	None	MRP	3
1400	Mineral oil refining	74696.30	6.44	11909.30	1.60	Transport of dangerous substances	HR	5
1510	Extr. nuclear materials	237.60	0.02	0.10	0.00	Euratom + IAEA rules	HR	5
1520	Production of nuclear materials	8504.60	0.73	1352.40	0.18	Euratom + IAEA rules	HR	5
1600	Electr., gas, steam, hot water	98762.10	8.52	4720.30	0.63	None	None	0
1700	Water supply	9310.30	0.80	21.70	0.00	Water Quality Directives	HR	4
2110	Extraction, prep. of iron ore	523.20	0.05	636.50	0.09	None	None	0
2120	Extraction, prep. of non-fer met. ores	13.75	0.00	400.50	0.05	None	None	0
2210	Iron & steel industry (ECSC) 1 Construction uses	7781.15	0.67	8392.05	1.13	Construction Products Directive	NA	2
2210	2 Other	7781.15	0.67	8392.05	1.13	ECISS (non-harmonized) ENs, ECSC	MRP	4
2220	Manufacture of steel tubes	3384.70	0.29	3006.70	0.40	None	None	0
2230	Drawing, cold rolling of steel	4233.00	0.37	3869.30	0.52	None	None	0
2240	NF-metals (prod., prel. proc.) 1 Precious metals	884.25	0.08	1593.61	0.21	Precious Metals Directive	NA	1
2240	2 Other	7958.25	0.69	14342.49	1.93	None	None	0
2310	Extract. of build. materials	5055.90	0.44	1381.70	0.19	None	MRP	4

Key: HR = Harmonized regulations   NA = New Approach
MRP = Mutual recognition principle   MRA = Mutual recognition agreements

NACE	Activity sector	Gross value added	% GVA	Intra-EU trade	% intra-EU trade	Measures	Measures	Likely status
2320	Salt, nat. phosph., peat	1310.50	0.11	1017.50	0.14	None	None	0
2410	Clay prod. for constr. purposes	3681.10	0.32	478.50	0.06	CPD; PPD	NA	2
2420	Cement, lime, plaster	7201.80	0.62	786.50	0.11	CPD; PPD	NA	2
2430	Struct. concrete, cement, plaster	12497.70	1.08	749.50	0.10	CPD; PPD	NA	2
2440	Manuf. of art. of asbestos	400.30	0.03	184.20	0.02	Harmonized regulations	HR	4
2450	Work. of stones & non-met. prod.	3903.40	0.34	1200.50	0.16	None	None	0
2460	Grindstones, abrasive products	801.40	0.07	590.60	0.08	None	None	0
2470	Manuf. of glass & glassware 1 Construction	5151.95	0.44	1330.73	0.18	CPD	NA	2
2470	2 Automotive	5151.95	0.44	798.44	0.11	Automotive type approval	HR	5
2470	3 Other	5151.95	0.44	532.29	0.07	None	None	0
2480	Manuf. of ceramic goods	7916.00	0.68	3894.20	0.52	None	None	0
2510	Basic industr. chem., petrochem.	36510.70	3.15	51968.50	6.98	None	MRP	4
2550	Paint, varnish, printing ink	4178.10	0.36	2916.30	0.39	No specific measures	MRP	4
2560	Chemical products 1 Agrochemicals	3340.10	0.29	13701.00	1.84	GLP and detailed directives	HR+MRA	2
2560	2 Harzardous chemicals	3340.10	0.29	13701.00	1.84	GLP and detailed directives	HR+MRA	3
2560	3 Other	3340.10	0.29	13701.00	1.84	None	MRP	4
2570	Pharmaceutical products	34770.30	3.00	36094.20	4.84	GLP and detailed directives	MRA	2

Key: HR = Harmonized regulations   NA = New Approach
MRP = Mutual recognition principle   MRA = Mutual recognition agreements

NACE	Activity sector	Gross value added	% GVA	Intra-EU trade	% intra-EU trade	Measures	Measures	Likely status
2580	Soap, detergents, perfume	12996.00	1.12	6123.20	0.82	Harmonized regulations	HR	4
2590	Manufacture of other chem. products 1 Hazardous	2439.60	0.21	3439.80	0.46	GLP	MRP	4
2590	2 Other	2439.60	0.21	3439.80	0.46	None	None	0
2600	Man-made fibres industry	2468.30	0.21	4716.60	0.63	None	MRP	5
3110	Foundries	8905.70	0.77	1521.80	0.20	None	None	0
3120	Forging, pressing, stamping	6735.30	0.58	987.90	0.13	None	None	0
3130	Treatment of metal	13227.70	1.14	1942.00	0.26	None	None	0
3140	Structural metal products	11907.10	1.03	2284.50	0.31	CPD and public procurement	NA	2
3150	Boilers, reservoirs, tanks	8928.10	0.77	1330.40	0.18	Pressure Vessels	NA	2
3160	Tools & finished metal goods	31176.40	2.69	12985.00	1.74	None	None	0
3165	Domestic heating appliances	11465.30	0.99	6985.00	0.94	GAD and Hot water boilers	NA	3
3166	Manufacture of metal furniture	12376.20	1.07	6000.00	0.81	None	MRP	4
3210	Agricult. machinery & tractors	4139.30	0.36	3505.60	0.47	Machinery Directive	NA	4
3220	Machine tools working metal	8896.10	0.77	3600.00	0.48	Machinery Directive	NA	4
3230	Textile machin., sewing mach.	3278.60	0.28	1602.40	0.22	Machinery Directive	NA	4
3240	Machines for food & chem. ind.	12812.60	1.10	5691.40	0.76	Machinery Directive	NA	4
3250	Machines for iron & steel industry	15540.10	1.34	7461.60	1.00	Machinery Directive	NA	4

Key: HR = Harmonized regulations   NA = New Approach
MRP = Mutual recognition principle   MRA = Mutual recognition agreements

NACE	Activity sector	Gross value added	% GVA	Intra-EU trade	% intra-EU trade	Measures	Measures	Likely status
3260	Transmission equipment	6249.90	0.54	3773.10	0.51	Machinery Directive	NA	4
3270	Equipment for use in spec. branches	6579.40	0.57	3608.10	0.48	Machinery Directive	NA	4
3280	Other machinery & equipment	34602.20	2.98	20819.60	2.79	Machinery Directive	NA	4
3300	Office and DP machinery	17001.30	1.47	28575.00	3.84	CEN, CENELEC, ETSI; PPD; EOTC Agr. group	MRA	4
3410	Insulated wires and cables	3102.80	0.27	2842.20	0.38	HAR; LVD	MRA	4
3420	Manuf. of electrical machinery	10532.30	0.91	12482.50	1.68	LVD; EMC; MD	NA	4
3430	Electr. apparatus for industrial use 1 Power and HT equipment	2121.55	0.18	3590.50	0.48	Public procurement	MRP	4
3430	2 Other	2121.55	0.18	3590.50	0.48	LVD/EMC	MRP	4
3440	Manuf. of telecom equipment	42235.30	3.64	10092.80	1.35	TTE Directive; ETSI standards; public procurement; EMC	NA+MRA	4
3450	Manuf. of radios & TVs	16384.00	1.41	22291.10	2.99	TV broadcast standards; PP; EMC	HR+MRA	4
3460	Domestic type electr. appl.	9753.40	0.84	7262.00	0.97	LVD; LVAG + CCA	NA+MRA	5
3470	Manuf. electr. lamps and others	4154.60	0.36	2766.80	0.37	LVD; EMC; LUM agreement	NA+MRA	5
3510	Man. assembly motor vehicles	56808.20	4.90	71000.60	9.53	Harmonized regulations	HR	5
3520	Manuf. bodies for motor vehicles	4291.40	0.37	1720.80	0.23	None	None	0
3530	Manuf. of parts of motor vehic.	23064.30	1.99	15799.70	2.12	Harmonized regulations	HR	5
3610	Shipbuilding 1 Naval	1627.40	0.14	158.70	0.02	(Built to order)	MRP	4
3610	2 Other	3254.80	0.28	317.40	0.04	None	None	0

Key: HR = Harmonized regulations   NA = New Approach
MRP = Mutual recognition principle   MRA = Mutual recognition agreements

NACE	Activity sector	Gross value added	% GVA	Intra-EU trade	% intra-EU trade	Measures	Measures	Likely status
3620	Manuf. of railway rol.-stock	2696.10	0.23	2743.10	0.37	Public procurement	MRP	3
3630	Manuf. of cycles, motor cycles 1 Cycles	893.35	0.08	1000.70	0.13	None (Art. 30 cases)	MRP	4
3630	2 Motorcycles	893.35	0.08	1000.70	0.13	Vehicle type approval	HR	2
3640	Aerospace equipment manuf.	16506.60	1.42	18408.90	2.47	International standards	MRP	5
3650	Other transport equipment	211.20	0.02	232.70	0.03	None	MRP	2
3710	Measuring and precision inst.	4706.50	0.41	3308.40	0.44	(EMC)	None	0
3720	Medical & surgical equipment	4967.80	0.43	1972.10	0.26	Medical Devices Directives	NA	4
3730	Optical instr., photo equipment	3149.70	0.27	6518.30	0.87	None	None	0
3740	Manuf. of clocks and watches	563.00	0.05	540.40	0.07	None	None	0
4110	Manufacture of oils and fats	2251.50	0.19	3137.80	0.42	Harmonized food regulations	HR+MRP	4
4120	Slaughtering, prep. of meat	13775.30	1.19	15536.40	2.09	Harmonized food regulations	HR	4
4130	Manufacture of dairy products	10655.80	0.92	11572.80	1.55	Harmonized food regulations	HR	4
4140	Proc. of fruit and vegetables	4429.70	0.38	6097.70	0.82	Harmonized food regulations	HR	4
4150	Proc. & preserving of fish	2036.80	0.18	2358.20	0.32	Harmonized food regulations	HR	4
4160	Grain milling	1554.60	0.13	570.60	0.08	Harmonized food regulations	HR	4
4170	Manuf. of spaghetti, macaroni	1201.60	0.10	570.20	0.08	Harmonized food regulations	HR	4
4180	Starch and starch products	970.60	0.08	1177.70	0.16	Harmonized food regulations	HR	4

Key: HR = Harmonized regulations   NA= New Approach
MRP = Mutual recognition principle   MRA = Mutual recognition agreements

NACE	Activity sector	Gross value added	% GVA	Intra-EU trade	% intra-EU trade	Measures	Measures	Likely status
4190	Bread and flour confectionery	12299.60	1.06	2375.10	0.32	Harmonized food regulations	HR	4
4210	Cocoa and sugar confectionery	8512.80	0.73	4522.20	0.61	Harmonized food regulations	HR	4
4220	Animal and poultry foods	4511.20	0.39	2543.50	0.34	Harmonized food regulations	HR	4
4230	Manuf. of other food products	13100.40	1.13	6122.60	0.82	Harmonized food regulations	HR	4
4240	Ethyl alcohol, spirit dist.	5966.50	0.51	2301.90	0.31	Packaging, labelling but generally unharmonized	MRP	4
4250	Wine of fresh grapes, cider	4192.50	0.36	1367.00	0.18	Packaging, labelling but generally unharmonized	MRP	4
4270	Brewing and malting	18120.00	1.56	1361.10	0.18	Packaging, labelling but generally unharmonized	MRP	4
4280	Soft drinks, nat. spa waters	7126.60	0.61	993.40	0.13	Packaging, labelling but generally unharmonized	MRP	4
4290	Manuf. of tobacco products	33456.80	2.89	3367.60	0.45	None	HR	4
4310	Wool industry	3334.20	0.29	3020.20	0.41	None	None	0
4320	Cotton industry	5593.20	0.48	5307.90	0.71	None	None	0
4330	Silk industry	2793.60	0.24	2003.40	0.27	None	None	0
4340	Prep. of flax, hemp, ramie	195.50	0.02	178.50	0.02	None	MRP	5
4350	Jute industry	156.20	0.01	133.30	0.02	None	None	0
4360	Knitting industry	6769.50	0.58	9535.50	1.28	None	MRP	4
4370	Textile finishing	3743.40	0.32	3254.30	0.44	None	MRP	4
4380	Carpets, linoleum, floor cover	2818.50	0.24	2755.70	0.37	Some MRA; CPD	NA+MRA	4

Key: HR = Harmonized regulations   NA= New Approach
MRP = Mutual recognition principle   MRA = Mutual recognition agreements

NACE	Activity sector	Gross value added	% GVA	Intra-EU trade	% intra-EU trade	Measures	Measures	Likely status
4390	Miscellaneous textile ind.	3280.50	0.28	2969.80	0.40	None	MRP	0
4410	Tanning, dressing of leather	1486.40	0.13	1714.40	0.23	None	None	0
4420	Leather products, substitutes	1652.50	0.14	1015.60	0.14	None	None	0
4510	Footwear	5576.50	0.48	6332.80	0.85	None	None	0
4530	Manuf. of clothing	16779.40	1.45	10229.60	1.37	None	MRP	4
4550	Manuf. of household textiles	1750.20	0.15	1434.70	0.19	None	MRP	4
4560	Manuf. of furs and fur goods	140.80	0.01	380.40	0.05	None	MRP	5
4610	Sawing and proces. of wood	2190.80	0.19	890.30	0.12	None	None	0
4620	Semi-finished wood products	2970.20	0.26	1576.30	0.21	CPD (but no mandates, ENs)	NA	2
4630	Carpentry & joinery components	6187.50	0.53	726.60	0.10	CPD (but no mandates, ENs)	NA	2
4640	Manuf. of wooden containers	1335.40	0.12	80.60	0.01	None (note barrier on use of drums, pallets, etc.)	None	2
4650	Other wood manuf. (exc. furn.)	1795.40	0.15	1144.30	0.15	None	None	0
4660	Art. of cork and straw, brushes	841.70	0.07	737.50	0.10	None	None	0
4670	Manuf. of wooden furniture	16987.20	1.46	4773.60	0.64	None	MRP	0
4710	Manuf. of pulp paper board	8560.20	0.74	8222.10	1.10	Packaging and Waste Directive	HR	4
4720	Proc. of paper and board	18436.60	1.59	8277.10	1.11	Packaging and Waste Directive	HR	4
4730	Printing and allied industries	18938.30	1.63	5000.00	0.67	None	None	0

Key: HR = Harmonized regulations   NA = New Approach
MRP = Mutual recognition principle   MRA = Mutual recognition agreements

NACE	Activity sector	Gross value added	% GVA	Intra-EU trade	% intra-EU trade	Measures	Measures	Likely status
4740	Publishing	5759.10	0.50	5600.40	0.75	European copyright system	HR	3
4810	Manuf. of rubber products	8054.60	0.69	8209.60	1.10	None	None	0
4820	Retr., rep. of rubber tyres	220.10	0.02	160.70	0.02	None	None.	0
4830	Processing of plastics 1 Packaging, etc.	23687.40	2.04	11588.20	1.56	Waste Directive, food packaging rules	HR+MRP	3
4830	2 Construction products	11843.70	1.02	5794.10	0.78	CPD	NA	3
4910	Manuf. articles of jewellery	3072.10	0.26	4794.20	0.64	Hallmarking Directive	NA	1
4920	Manuf. of musical instruments	343.40	0.03	209.30	0.03	None	None	0
4930	Photograph. and cin. laborat.	1457.70	0.13	117.20	0.02	None	None	0
4940	Toys and sports goods 1 Toys	1323.80	0.11	1568.90	0.21	Toys Directive	NA	5
4940	2 Sports	1323.80	0.11	1568.90	0.21	None (Art. 30 cases)	MRP	4
4950	Miscellaneous manuf. industries	1684.40	0.15	27507.90	3.69	None	None	0
		1159630.40		745063.66				
		total GDP		total trade				

Key: HR = Harmonized regulations   NA= New Approach
MRP = Mutual recognition principle   MRA = Mutual recognition agreements

APPENDIX F

Analysis of Eurostat business survey

This appendix summarizes the results of the Eurostat business survey carried out in early 1995. Results are presented for questions directly relevant to this report for each industry sector covered by the survey, for EUR-12 Member States.

F.1. NACE code 15 data: manufacture of food products and beverages

Q.1 Please state whether the following single market measures have had an impact on your firm's activities

	Positive impact	No impact	Negative impact	Don't know
	(% of responding firms)			
Harmonization of technical regulations and/or standards	35.9	43.0	9.4	11.5
Mutual recognition of technical regulations and standards	29.8	46.7	8.3	15.1
Conformity assessment procedures	25.7	49.2	6.0	19.1
Simplified patenting procedures	12.7	64.2	1.6	21.4
The opening up of public procurement	11.0	69.8	2.6	16.7
The elimination of customs documentation	62.4	25.6	4.9	7.1
Deregulation of freight transport	44.5	42.6	2.6	10.3
The elimination of delays at frontiers	64.0	26.5	2.6	7.0
The change in VAT procedures for intra-EU sales	33.2	41.3	14.0	11.6
The liberalization of capital movements	21.9	61.4	3.7	13.0
Double taxation agreements	15.9	56.7	3.4	23.9

Note: figures may not always total 100 due to rounding.

After the elimination of delays at frontiers and customs documentation, the deregulation of freight transport and the change in VAT, harmonization, mutual recognition and conformity assessment procedures are the SM measure to have had a positive impact for the greatest number of firms. Up to 35.9% of companies said harmonization had a positive impact on their activities and 29.8% that mutual recognition had a positive impact. However, between 40% and 50% of respondents said these three measures had no impact.

Q.2   Please indicate, for each of the following possible areas, the importance of the SMP to the development of your company's strategy in recent years

	Very important	Quite important	Of little or no importance	Don't know/ not applicable
	(% of responding firms)			
Product standardization	14.7	20.1	38.3	26.9
Pan-European labelling and packaging	11.1	26.7	36.5	25.8

34.8% of firms thought European product standardization to be quite or very important. For 26.9% of them, the statement was not applicable or they did not know. For the remaining 38.3% it was of little or no importance. In comparison, pan-European labelling and packaging was considered important by slightly more firms (37.8%).

Q.3   What has been the effect of the SM on costs in the following areas?

	Increase	No change	Decrease	Don't know
	(% of responding firms)			
Testing and certification	8.3	11.2	40.3	40.4

40.3% of respondents said the cost of testing and certification had decreased as a result of the SM and another 40.4% of them did not know the answer to the question (it could be that it was not applicable).

Q.4   Please indicate whether you agree or disagree with the following statements regarding SM legislation as it affects your own firm or sector

	Agree	No opinion	Disagree
	(% of responding firms)		
The SMP has been a success for your firm	37.1	34.8	28.1
The SMP has been successful in eliminating obstacles to EU trade in your sector	48.8	32.2	19.0

37.1% of respondents agreed with the statement 'the SMP has been a success for your firm', and 48.8% said the SMP had been successful in eliminating obstacles to EU trade in their sector.

F.2. NACE code 16 data: manufacture of tobacco products

Q.1   Please state whether the following single market measures have had an impact on your firm's activities

	Positive impact	No impact	Negative impact	Don't know
	(% of responding firms)			
Harmonization of technical regulations and/or standards	27.4	62.8	1.3	8.6
Mutual recognition of technical regulations and standards	14.2	63.4		22.5
Conformity assessment procedures	16.9	22.7	2.2	58.2
Simplified patenting procedures	7.7	81.7	1.0	9.6
The opening up of public procurement	5.5	65.5		29.0
The elimination of customs documentation	46.6	42.8	2.1	8.6
Deregulation of freight transport	34.9	54.1		11.0
The elimination of delays at frontiers	26.6	61.2		12.2
The change in VAT procedures for intra-EU sales	13.7	7.5	56.4	22.5
The liberalization of capital movements	14.8	56.4		28.8
Double taxation agreements	19.6	55.7		24.7

Up to 27.4% of respondents said harmonization had had a positive impact on their activities and 14.2% that mutual recognition had had a positive impact. However, more than 60% of companies answered that harmonization and mutual recognition measures had had no impact. However, for conformity assessment procedures 58.2% said they did not know if conformity assessment procedures had had an impact or not on their activity. This is the only statement for which the percentage of 'don't know' is so high.

The number of companies in this industry which considered any of the SM measures to have had a negative impact is very low indeed (except for the change in VAT procedures which was declared to have had a negative impact by 56.4% of companies).

Q.2   Please indicate, for each of the following possible areas, the importance of the SM programme to the development of your company's strategy in recent years

	Very important	Quite important	Of little or no importance	Don't know/ not applicable
	(% of responding firms)			
Product standardization	8.7	27.6	61.3	2.4
Pan-European labelling and packaging	9.9	21.3	66.8	2.0

36.3% of respondents thought European product standardization to be quite or very important. For only 2.4% of them, the statement was not applicable or they did not know. For the remaining 61.3%, product standardization was of little or no importance to the development of their firm's strategy.

Q.3   What has been the effect of the SM on costs in the following areas?

	Increase	No change	Decrease	Don't know
		(% of responding firms)		
Testing and certification		38.1	23.6	38.2

More than one third of respondents did not know the answer to the question (or it was not applicable); 23.6% said the cost of testing and certification have increased as a result of the SM and 38.1% said the costs have not changed.

Q.4   Please indicate whether you agree or disagree with the following statements regarding SM legislation as it affects your own firm or sector

	Agree	No opinion	Disagree
	(% of responding firms)		
The SMP has been a success for your firm	15.9	24.0	60.1
The SMP has been successful in eliminating obstacles to EU trade in your sector	20.5	29.9	49.6

In the tobacco sector, the SMP is not considered a great success. As much as 60.1% of respondents disagreed with the statement 'the SMP has been a success for your firm' and 24.0% had no opinion. Slightly more companies (20.5%) agreed with 'the SMP has been successful in eliminating obstacles to EU trade in your sector'.

F.3. NACE code 17-18 data: manufacture of textiles and manufacture of wearing apparel; dressing and dyeing of fur

Q.1   Please state whether the following single market measures have had an impact on your firm's activities

	Positive impact	No impact	Negative impact	Don't know
	(% of responding firms)			
Harmonization of technical regulations and/or standards	15.0	68.4	7.2	9.5
Mutual recognition of technical regulations and standards	18.2	59.1	7.1	15.5
Conformity assessment procedures	14.5	69.7	2.5	13.3
Simplified patenting procedures	12.3	68.8	2.8	16.1
The opening up of public procurement	8.3	71.1	3.0	17.6
The elimination of customs documentation	62.2	25.5	6.6	5.8
Deregulation of freight transport	50.0	33.2	4.9	11.9
The elimination of delays at frontiers	65.4	23.8	2.5	4.0
The change in VAT procedures for intra-EU sales	37.0	33.4	17.4	12.1
The liberalization of capital movements	29.7	56.6	1.1	12.5
Double taxation agreements	21.5	56.8	2.7	19.0

In the textile manufacturing industry, harmonization and mutual recognition of technical regulations and standards together with the conformity assessment procedures are considered to have had a positive impact on the firms' activities by about 1/6 of respondents. 68.4% of respondents considered harmonization to have had no impact on their activities and as much as 69.7% of them said mutual recognition measures have had no impact on their activities.

Q.2   Please indicate, for each of the following possible areas, the importance of the SMP to the development of your company's strategy in recent years

	Very important	Quite important	Of little or no importance	Don't know/ not applicable
	(% of responding firms)			
Product standardization	5.9	22.5	50.6	21.0
Pan-European labelling and packaging	5.6	18.0	46.7	29.7

28.4% of firms thought European product standardization to be quite or very important. For 21.0% of them, the statement was not applicable (or they did not know). For the remaining 50.6%, it was of little or no importance. The answers to the question on pan-European labelling and packaging followed more or less the same pattern.

Q.3   What has been the effect of the SM on costs in the following areas?

	Increase	No change	Decrease	Don't know
	(% of responding firms)			
Testing and certification	3.5	8.0	48.8	39.7

Almost half (48.8%) of respondents considered that the cost of testing and certification had decreased as a result of the SM. Only 3.5 % thought the costs had increased and 8% thought that there had been no change.

Q.4   Please indicate whether you agree or disagree with the following statements regarding SM legislation as it affects your own firm or sector

	Agree	No opinion	Disagree
	(% of responding firms)		
The SMP has been a success for your firm	31.4	36.3	32.3
The SMP has been successful in eliminating obstacles to EU trade in your sector	44.2	31.2	24.5

The responses to the statement 'the SMP has been a success for your firm' spread almost evenly over the three possible answers. However, slightly more respondents (44.2%) said the SMP had been successful in eliminating obstacles to EU trade in their sector.

F.4. NACE code 24 data: manufacture of chemicals and chemical products

Q.1   Please state whether the following single market measures have had an impact on your firm's activities

	Positive impact	No impact	Negative impact	Don't know
	(% of responding firms)			
Harmonization of technical regulations and/or standards	38.3	40.7	9.4	11.6
Mutual recognition of technical regulations and standards	39.4	42.6	4.2	13.8
Conformity assessment procedures	31.1	43.2	6.6	19.0
Simplified patenting procedures	24.5	53.8	0.8	20.8
The opening up of public procurement	11.1	74.5	1.4	13.1
The elimination of customs documentation	72.7	21.1	4.2	2.0
Deregulation of freight transport	48.2	34.1	7.5	10.2
The elimination of delays at frontiers	67.2	26.3	2.5	4.0
The change in VAT procedures for intra-EU sales	38.4	30.0	25.9	5.7
The liberalization of capital movements	30.8	61.9	1.9	5.4
Double taxation agreements	33.5	52.4	2.3	11.8

More than a third of respondents in the chemicals sector said harmonization of technical regulations and conformity assessment procedures had had a positive impact on the activities of their firms.

Q.2   Please indicate, for each of the following possible areas, the importance of the SMP to the development of your company's strategy in recent years

	Very important	Quite important	Of little or no importance	Don't know/ not applicable
	(% of responding firms)			
Product standardization	10.5	28.5	35.0	26.0
Pan-European labelling & packaging	16.2	23.7	36.0	24.1

39.0% of firms thought European product standardization to be quite or very important. For 26.0% of them, the statement was not applicable or they did not know. For the remaining 35.0%, it was of little or no importance.

Q.3   What has been the effect of the SM on costs in the following areas?

	Increase	No change	Decrease	Don't know
	(% of responding firms)			
Testing and certification	8.6	19.9	32.9	38.6

About one-third of respondents said the cost of testing and certification had decreased as a result of the SM.

Q.4   Please indicate whether you agree or disagree with the following statements regarding SM legislation as it affects your own firm or sector

	Agree	No opinion	Disagree
	(% of responding firms)		
The SMP has been a success for your firm	35.2	40.0	24.8
The SMP has been successful in eliminating obstacles to EU trade in your sector	43.2	33.0	23.9

35.2% of respondents agreed with the statement 'the SMP has been a success for your firm', 24.8% disagreed, and 40.0% had no opinion. Slightly more respondents (43.2%) considered the SMP had been successful in eliminating obstables to EU trade in their sector and only 23.9% disagreed.

F.5. NACE code 28 data: manufacture of fabricated metal products, except machinery and equipment

Q.1 Please state whether the following single market measures have had an impact on your firm's activities

	Positive impact	No impact	Negative impact	Don't know
	(% of responding firms)			
Harmonization of technical regulations and/or standards	31.4	55.8	6.5	6.3
Mutual recognition of technical regulations and standards	31.8	54.7	5.2	8.3
Conformity assessment procedures	26.2	59.0	6.1	8.7
Simplified patenting procedures	11.2	66.4	1.5	21.0
The opening up of public procurement	11.1	72.1	5.6	16.4
The elimination of customs documentation	52.5	39.7	3.4	4.5
Deregulation of freight transport	40.1	46.9	2.0	11.1
The elimination of delays at frontiers	47.7	44.1	0.3	7.9
The change in VAT procedures for intra-EU sales	27.1	48.6	15.9	8.5
The liberalization of capital movements	20.9	64.1	1.4	13.6
Double taxation agreements	10.9	65.3	1.4	22.4

After the elimination of customs documentation, the elimination of delays at frontiers and the deregulation of freight transport, the harmonization and mutual recognition of technical regulations and standards are considered the SM measures to have had the most positive impact on the firms' activities. About a third of companies answered harmonization and mutual recognition have had a positive impact.

Q.2 Please indicate, for each of the following possible areas, the importance of the SMP to the development of your company's strategy in recent years

	Very important	Quite important	Of little or no importance	Don't know/ not applicable
	(% of responding firms)			
Product standardization	5.0	17.0	49.2	28.9
Pan-European labelling and packaging	4.2	13.4	45.2	37.1

Only 22.0% of respondents thought European product standardization to be quite or very important; this is low compared to other manufacturing industries. For 28.9% of them, the statement was not applicable (or they did not know). For the remaining 49.2%, it was of little or no importance.

Q.3   What has been the effect of the SM on costs in the following areas?

	Increase	No change	Decrease	Don't know
	(% of responding firms)			
Testing and certification	12.0	9.3	39.2	39.5

39.5% of the companies did not know the answer to the question (or not applicable) and another 39.2% said the cost of testing and certification had decreased as a result of the SM.

Q.4   Please indicate whether you agree or disagree with the following statements regarding SM legislation as it affects your own firm or sector

	Agree	No opinion	Disagree
	(% of responding firms)		
The SMP has been a success for your firm	31.1	39.1	29.7
The SMP has been successful in eliminating obstables to EU trade in your sector	37.5	44.3	18.2

31.1% of the companies agreed with the statement 'the SMP has been a success for your firm' and 37.5% said the SMP had been successful in eliminating obstables to EU trade in their sector. 18.2% considered there remained TBTs in the metal products sector.

F.6. NACE code 29 data: manufacture of machinery and equipment NEC

Q.1   Please state whether the following single market measures have had an impact on your firm's activities

	Positive impact	No impact	Negative impact	Don't know
	(% of responding firms)			
Harmonization of technical regulations and/or standards	47.7	26.4	20.7	5.2
Mutual recognition of technical regulations and standards	44.8	34.5	12.2	8.5
Conformity assessment procedures	32.9	47.8	8.0	11.3
Simplified patenting procedures	20.4	53.0	2.1	24.4
The opening up of public procurement	6.6	71.8	4.5	17.1
The elimination of customs documentation	77.5	15.4	2.9	4.2
Deregulation of freight transport	54.2	36.8	1.3	7.8
The elimination of delays at frontiers	68.1	26.4	0.3	5.2
The change in VAT procedures for intra-EU sales	40.0	40.0	13.0	7.0
The liberalization of capital movements	28.1	56.8	3.9	11.2
Double taxation agreements	18.4	54.3	3.1	24.2

The machinery and equipment sector is one of only two sectors where the greater number of firms considered the harmonization and mutual recognition of technical regulations and standards to have had a positive impact (47.7% and 44.8%). Up to 32.9% of the companies thought conformity assessment procedures had had a positive impact on their activities.

Q.2   Please indicate, for each of the following possible areas, the importance of the SMP to the development of your company's strategy in recent years

	Very important	Quite important	Of little or no importance	Don't know/ not applicable
	(% of responding firms)			
Product standardization	17.1	24.6	42.9	15.4
Pan-European labelling and packaging	5.6	19.2	52.0	23.2

In this sector more firms (41.7%) answered product standardization was very or quite important than in any other industry.

Q.3   What has been the effect of the SM on costs in the following areas?

	Increase	No change	Decrease	Don't know
	(% of responding firms)			
Testing and certification	12.3	15.0	28.0	44.7

More than 40% of the companies in the sector did not know the answer to the question; another 28.0% said the cost of testing and certification had decreased as a result of the SM whereas 12.3% thought they had increased.

Q.4   Please indicate whether you agree or disagree with the following statements regarding SM legislation as it affects your own firm or sector

	Agree	No opinion	Disagree
	(% of responding firms)		
The SMP has been a success for your firm	44.3	33.6	22.1
The SMP has been successful in eliminating obstacles to EU trade in your sector	45.2	32.6	22.2

44.3% of the companies agreed with the statement 'the SMP has been a success for your firm' and 45.2% said the SMP had been successful in eliminating obstables to EU trade in the machinery and equipment sector. However, 22.2% of respondents believe there remained obstacles to trade in their sector.

F.7. NACE code 30 data: manufacture of office machinery and computers

Q.1   Please state whether the following single market measures have had an impact on your firm's activities

	Positive impact	No impact	Negative impact	Don't know
	(% of responding firms)			
Harmonization of technical regulations and/or standards	44.9	44.3	10.1	0.7
Mutual recognition of technical regulations and standards	49.4	40.2	0.1	10.3
Conformity assessment procedures	51.3	37.0	2.2	9.5
Simplified patenting procedures	21.8	58.9		19.3
The opening up of public procurement	4.9	89.4	1.6	4.1
The elimination of customs documentation	66.4	22.6	11.0	
Deregulation of freight transport	44.3	36.7	7.9	11.1
The elimination of delays at frontiers	64.0	36.0		
The change in VAT procedures for intra-EU sales	48.9	36.0	14.6	0.6
The liberalization of capital movements	42.3	54.1		3.5
Double taxation agreements	16.7	47.8		35.6

A staggering 51.3% of respondents considered conformity assessment procedures to have had a positive impact. Generally speaking, this is the sector for which the SM measures have had the most positive impact (and the least negative impact).

Q.2   Please indicate, for each of the following possible areas, the importance of the SMP to the development of your company's strategy in recent years

	Very important	Quite important	Of little or no importance	Don't know/ not applicable
	(% of responding firms)			
Product standardization	5.5	24.4	56.9	13.2
Pan-European labelling and packaging	19.8	12.2	60.9	7.1

A total of 29.9% of firms thought European product standardization to be quite or very important. For 13.2% of them, the statement was not applicable or they did not know. For the remaining majority (56.9%), it was of little or no importance.

Q.3   What has been the effect of the SM on costs in the following areas?

	Increase	No change	Decrease	Don't know
	(% of responding firms)			
Testing and certification	21.8	8.8	40.7	28.7

Very unlike the other manufacturing sectors, 21.8% of the office machinery and computers industry said the SM measures had brought an increase in costs of testing and certification. This is rather more than what has been reported in other industries.

Q.4   Please indicate whether you agree or disagree with the following statements regarding SM legislation as it affects your own firm or sector

	Agree	No opinion	Disagree
	(% of responding firms)		
The SMP has been a success for your firm	51.7	34.2	14.0
The SMP has been successful in eliminating obstacles to EU trade in your sector	39.6	36.1	24.3

More than half the companies in this industry agreed with the statement 'the SMP has been a success for your firm'. 39.6% of respondents agreed with the statement 'the SMP has been sucessful in eliminating obstacles to trade in your sector'; however, 24.3% of respondents thought the SMP had not been successful in eliminating obstacles to EU trade.

F.8. NACE code 34 data: manufacture of motor vehicles, trailers and semi-trailers

Q.1 Please state whether the following single market measures have had an impact on your firm's activities

	Positive impact	No impact	Negative impact	Don't know
	(% of responding firms)			
Harmonization of technical regulations and/or standards	34.8	49.1	10.6	5.5
Mutual recognition of technical regulations and standards	48.1	43.1	3.3	5.5
Conformity assessment procedures	36.5	42.5	6.7	14.3
Simplified patenting procedures	9.3	71.7		19.0
The opening up of public procurement	14.2	74.4	2.5	8.9
The elimination of customs documentation	67.5	23.8	4.5	4.2
Deregulation of freight transport	41.3	44.2	0.5	14.0
The elimination of delays at frontiers	58.9	36.3		4.7
The change in VAT procedures for intra-EU sales	39.4	40.2	15.2	5.2
The liberalization of capital movements	21.4	58.1	0.4	20.0
Double taxation agreements	20.1	55.9		24.0

34.8% of respondents considered the harmonization of technical regulations and standards to have had a positive impact and 48.1% that mutual recognition had had a positive impact. Generally speaking, very few respondents thought the SM measures had had a negative impact.

Q.2 Please indicate, for each of the following possible areas, the importance of the SMP to the development of your company's strategy in recent years

	Very important	Quite important	Of little or no importance	Don't know/ not applicable
	(% of responding firms)			
Product standardization	12.8	19.1	44.2	24.0
Pan-European labelling and packaging	3.3	25.8	44.4	26.5

31.9% of firms thought European product standardization to be quite or very important. For 24.0% of respondents, the statement was not applicable or they did not know. For the remaining 44.2%, it was of little or no importance.

Q.3   What has been the effect of the SM on costs in the following areas?

	Increase	No change	Decrease	Don't know
	(% of responding firms)			
Testing and certification	5.5	17.9	30.4	46.2

Almost half of the respondents from the motor vehicle sector did not know the answer to the question and 30.4% thought the SM had had the effect of curbing the cost of testing and certification down.

Q.4   Please indicate whether you agree or disagree with the following statements regarding SM legislation as it affects your own firm or sector

	Agree	No opinion	Disagree
	(% of responding firms)		
The SMP has been a success for your firm	39.2	39.9	20.9
The SMP has been successful in eliminating obstacles to EU trade in your sector	41.9	43.3	14.9

39.2% of firms agreed with the statement 'the SMP has been a success for your firm', and 41.9% with the statement 'the SMP has been successful in eliminating obstacles to EU trade in your sector'.

F.9.   All industries by size of firm (number of employees)

Q.1   Please state whether the harmonization of technical regulations and/or standards has had an impact on your firm's activities

	Positive impact	No impact	Negative impact	Don't know
	(% of responding firms)			
20–49	30.4	50.2	11.1	8.3
50–199	35.5	45.7	10.9	8.0
200–499	37.6	46.3	8.1	8.0
500–999	33.2	52.8	5.9	8.2
≥1,000	49.4	39.0	4.5	7.2

The pattern of answers to this question seems to be as follows: the bigger the firm, the more the impact was felt to be positive and the less the measure was considered to have had no impact or a negative impact.

Q.2 Impact of mutual recognition on your firm's activities

	Positive impact	No impact	Negative impact	Don't know
	(% of responding firms)			
20-49	28.9	49.0	8.4	13.7
50-199	37.0	47.1	7.3	8.7
200-499	39.6	48.1	3.6	8.8
500-999	29.2	53.3	3.5	14.0
≥1,000	49.8	38.6	2.9	8.7

Half the firms from the smaller category 20–49 employees thought the measure had had no impact, whereas half the larger firms thought it had had a positive impact. Because bigger firms tend to be more export oriented than smaller ones, they felt more than others the impact of mutual recognition.

Q.3 Impact of conformity assessment procedures on your firm's activities

	Positive impact	No impact	Negative impact	Don't know
	(% of responding firms)			
20–49	25.1	55.5	5.2	14.2
50–199	25.8	54.1	7.4	12.7
200–499	30.5	53.2	3.3	13.0
500–999	29.0	56.3	3.6	11.1
≥1,000	35.3	50.6	1.9	12.2

For this particular question, the size does not seem to be very relevant. Bigger companies tended to think the impact slightly more positive, and less negative.

F.10.   All firms regardless of industry or size

Q.1: Please state whether the harmonization of technical regulations and/or standards has had an impact on your firm's activities.

Q.2: Please state whether the mutual recognition of technical regulations and/or standards has had an impact on your firm's activities.

Q.3: Please state whether the conformity assessment procedures have had an impact on your firm's activities.

	Positive impact	No impact	Negative impact	Don't know
	(% of responding firms)			
Q.1	32.8	48.4	10.6	8.2
Q.2	32.4	48.3	7.5	11.8
Q.3	25.9	54.9	5.7	13.6

Q.1: Most firms thought harmonization had had no impact (48.4%), one-third said that the measure had had a positive impact and only 10.6% considered it had had a negative impact on their activities.

Q.2: Very similar response as to Q1. Slightly more firms ticked 'don't know' for this question than for the previous one. Mutual recognition might be a concept slightly less well known than harmonization.

Q.3: More than half the firms thought harmonization had had no impact (54.9%), a quarter said the measure had had a positive impact and only 5.7% considered it had had a negative impact on their activities. Slightly more respondents answered 'don't know' to this question than to the previous two.

APPENDIX G

ECJ judgments involving free movement of goods and technical barriers to trade, 1991–94

Case number and name	Case reference	Object
C-306/88 *Rochdale B. C.* v *Anders*	[1992] I-6457	Sunday trading
C-369/88 *Delattre*	[1991] I-1487	Pharmacist's monopoly of the right to sell certain products
C-95/89 *Commission* v *Italy*	[1992] I-4545	Food additive, Articles 30 and 36 of the EEC Treaty – failure to fulfil obligations (addition of nitrates to cheese)
C-205/89 *Commission* v *Greece*	[1991] I-1363	Pasteurized butter – health certificate
C-235/89 *Commission* v *Italy*	[1992] I-777	Article 30 of the EEC Treaty, patents, compulsory licences
C-293/89 *Commission* v *Greece*	[1992] I-4577	Food additive – failure to fulfil obligations (addition of nitrates to cheese)
C-312/89 *Conforama*	[1991] I-997	Sunday trading – national legislation prohibiting the employment of workers in retail shops on Sundays
C-347/89 *Eurim-Pharm*	[1991] I-1747	Medicinal products imports
C-350/89 *Sheptonhurst*	[1991] I-2387	Sex articles – national legislation prohibiting the sale of sex articles from unlicensed sex establishments
C-369/89 *Piageme*	[1991] I-2971	Labelling and presentation of foodstuffs for sale to customer (label in language)
Joined Cases C-1/90 and C-176/90 *Aragonesa de Publicidad Exterior and Publivía*	[1991] I-4151	Advertising, national legislation on alcoholic beverages
C-30/90 *Commission* v *United Kingdom*	[1992] I-829	Article 30 of EEC Treaty, patents, compulsory licences
C-39/90 *Denkavit Futtermittel*	[1991] I-3069	Food – obligation to specify ingredients in food stuff
C-47/90 *Delhaize* v *Promalvin*	[1992] I-3669	Wine in bulk – prohibition of exports, designation of origin, Articles 34–36 of the EEC Treaty
C-62/90 *Commission* v *Germany*	[1992] I-2575	Importation of medicinal products by individuals – protection of public health ; limits for imports of medicinal products by individuals
C-290/90 *Commission* v *Germany*	[1992] I-3317	Interpretation of Articles 30 and 36 of the EEC Treaty, eye wash solutions – concept of medicinal/cosmetic product
C-344/90 *Commission* v *France*	[1992] I-4719	Food additive – failure to fulfil obligations (addition of nitrates to cheese)
C-375/90 *Commission* v *Greece*	[1993] I-2055	Food – frozen chickens – quantitative restrictions and protection of health
C-3/91 *Expotur*	[1992] I-5529	Designation of origin and indications of provenance
C-137/91 *Commission* v *Greece*	[1992] I-4023	Articles 5 and 30 of the EEC Treaty, obligation to provide information
C-207/91 *Eurim-Pharm* v *Bundesgesundheitsamt*	[1993] I-3723	Free trade agreement, parallel imports of medicinal products: quantitative restriction on imports
C-228/91 *Commission* v *Italy*	[1993] I-2701	Food – fish containing nematode larvae

Case number and name	Case reference	Cases
C-17/92 *Distribuidores Cinematográficos* v *Spanish State*	[1993] I-2239	National legislation intended to favour the distribution of national firms
C-37/92 *Vanacker and Lesage*	[1993] I-4947	Waste oil – obstacles to export, restriction on freedom to provide services
C-80/92 *Commission* v *Belgium*	[1994] I-1019	Radiocommunications, transmitters and receivers
C-93/92 *CMC Motorradcenter* v *Baskiciogullari*	[1993] I-5009	Obligation to give information
C-271/92 *LPO*	[1993] I-2899	Contact lenses – national legislation on the sales
C-292/92 *Hunermund and others* v *Landesapothekerkammer Baden-Württemberg*	[1993] I-6787	Goods sold in pharmacies – prohibition against advertising outside pharmacies
C-293/92 *Ludomira*	Removed from the register	Precious metals – compulsory hallmark
C-315/92 *Verband Sozialer Wettbewerb* v *Clinique Laboratoires and Estée Lauder*	[1994] I-317	Cosmetic – name liable to mislead the customers
C-317/92 *Commission* v *Germany*	[1994] I-2039	Medicinal products and instruments – national rules on the indication of expiry dates, failure to notify the Commission
C-373/92 *Commission* v *Belgium*	[1993] I-3107	Medicinal products – obligation in a Member State of importation to duplicate test certificates already carried out in the Member State of origin
C-391/92 *Commission* v *Greece*	[1995] I-1621	Food – baby milk – prohibition of sales outside pharmacies
C-17/93 *Van Der Veldt*	[1994] I-3537	Food and food labelling – prohibition of bread and other bakery products whose salt content is higher than 2%
C-55/93 *Van Schaik*	[1994] I-4837	Motor vehicles – national legislation facilitating roadworthiness testing in conjunction with periodic servicing of motor vehicles
Joined Cases C-69/93 and C-258/93 *Punto casa and PPV*	[1994] I-2355	Sunday trading prohibition
C-131/93 *Commission* v *Germany*	[1994] I-3303	Prohibition of importation of live freshwater crayfish
C-293/93 *Houtwipper*	[1994] I-4249	Precious metals, compulsory hallmarks
C-314/93 *Rouffeteau and Badia*	[1994] I-3257	Article 30 of the EEC Treaty, Directive 88/301/EEC, telecommunications terminals, prohibition on telephones which have not been approved, re-export
C-320/93 *Ortscheit*	[1994] I-5243	Medical products – imported products not authorized, prohibition of advertising
C-324/93 *Evans Medical and MacFarlan Smith*	[1995] I-563	Medical products – diamorphine imports
C-51/94 *Commission* v *Germany*	[1995] I-3599	Food labelling – substances included in products
C-134/94 *Esso Española* v *Comunidad autónoma de Canarias*	[1995] I-4223	Petrol products – obligation of stockages

Bibliography

Centre for European Policy Studies [1992], 'The European Community without technical barriers', *CEPS Standards Programme: Paper No 1*, 1992.

Centre for European Policy Studies [1992a], 'Cats and Mice: The politics of setting EC car emission standards', *CEPS Standards Programme: Paper No 2*, 1992.

Centre for European Policy Studies [1992b], 'Fixing European Standards: Moving beyond the Green Paper', *CEPS Standards Programme: Paper No 3*, 1992.

European Commission [1985], *Completing the Internal Market: White Paper from the Commission to the Council*, COM(85) 310 final, June 1985.

European Commission [1990], 'The Development of European Standardization: Action for faster technological integration in Europe', COM(90) 456 final, October 1990.

European Commission [1994], *A New Community Standards Policy*, Vol. 4, July, Luxembourg, Office for Official Publications of the European Communities, 1994.

European Commission [1994a], *Guide to the implementation of Community harmonization directives based on the new approach and the global approach*, first version, Luxembourg, Office for Official Publications of the European Communities, 1994.

European Commission [1995], *The Single Market in 1995*, Luxembourg, Office for Official Publications of the European Communities, 1995.

European Commission [1995a], 'Communication from the Commission to the Council and the European Parliament on the broader use of standardization in Community policy', COM(95) 412 final, October 1995.

European Commission [1995b], Information and Notices, *Official Journal of the European Communities*, C 280, 25 October 1995.

European Commission [1996], 'Report from the Commission on the Operations of Directive 83/189/EEC in 1992, 1993 and 1994', COM(96) 286 final, June 1996.

European Commission [1996a], *Panorama of EU Industry 1995–96*, Luxembourg, Office for Official Publications of the European Communities, 1996.

European Commission [1995], 'Organisation actuelle des groupes d'organismes notifiés dans le cadre des directives d'harmonisation communautaires basées sur la nouvelle approche et l'approche globale', CERTIF 95/4, July 1995.

European Commission [1996], 'National Regulations Affecting Products in the Internal Market - A Cause for Concern', February 1996.

European Committee for Electrotechnical Standardization [1996], 'Identifying the Trees in the Forest', Conference papers, Brussels, February 1996.

European Committee for Standardization [1994], *The New Approach*, Belgium, Delphi, 1994.

European Committee for Standardization [1995], *Standards for Access to the European Market, The Technical Programme 1995–1996*, No 2, Belgium, Delphi, 1995.

International Laboratory Accreditation Conference Committee 1 [1996], 'Draft Information Document: Role of Testing and Laboratory Accreditation in International Trade', Working Group 6, January 1996.

Machado Jorge, Henrique, CEPS [1994], 'Assured Performance, The Role of Conformity Assessment in Supporting the Internal Market', *CEPS Standards Programme: Paper No 60*, 1994.

Massini, Pierre, and Van Gheluwe, Jean-Pierre [1993], *Community legislation on machinery*, Luxembourg, Office for Official Publications of the European Communities, 1993.

Mattera, A. [1995], 'La procédure en manquement et la protection des droits des citoyens et des opérateurs lésés', *Revue du Marché Unique Européen*, 3/1995, 1995.

Nicolas, Florence [1995], *Common standards for enterprises*, Luxembourg, Office for Official Publications of the European Communities, 1995.

OECD, 'Consumer product safety standards and conformity assessment: their effect on international trade', Directorate for Financial, Fiscal and Enterprise Affairs, Committee on Consumer Policy, DAFFE/CP (95) 14.

Orgalime [1993], 'Orgalime Position — European Standardization and the New Approach to Technical Harmonization and Standards — An assessment of recent developments with recommendations for action', September 1993.

Strawbridge, Geoff [1993], 'The New Approach — from experiment to experience', *BSI News*, January 1993.